A CELEBRATION OF 50 YEARS OF MOTOWN

Copyright Alex MacKenzie ©2009
First Published in Great Britain 2009 by:
Together Publications LLP
Orchard Lea
Winkfield Lane
Windsor, Berkshire
SL4 4RU England

British Library Catalogue in Publication Data:
MacKenzie Alex, The Life and Times of The Motown Stars

Book design, layout and typesetting:

Particular Design & Print Limited
9 Ryefield Court, Ryefield Way
Silsden
West Yorkshire
BD20 0DL
England

40twenty Design
York Eco Business Centre
Amy Johnson Way
Clifton Moor
York YO30 4AG
England

Printed in Great Britain by:
Blue Ribbon Press
Unit 12 The Business Village
Wexham Road
Slough
Berkshire
SL2 5HF

Marketed and Promoted by:
Right Recordings Ltd
177 High Street
Harlesden
London NW10 4TE

Catalogue Number: RIGHT068
ISBN No: 9781842260142   £17.99

Dedicated to:

Lynne, Charlotte and James
for letting me focus on this project.

Thanks to:

Without whose support this book would not have been possible:

Billy Wilson thanks for the help and support and some great pictures.

Jill Stemp for her patience and support with this project.

Allan Bate my business partner and great friend, by creating our company NVQUK, and making it successful, this gave me the opportunity to take time out to complete this project.

To Sharon White, Pat Moody, Sam Sawyer and Diane Robson and all the staff at NVQUK, thank you for developing NVQUK into the successful company it is today, and so creating the space for me to undertake this book.

Hilary (Hils) Thornton and Stephen Collier and the team at Particular Design & Print Limited and 40twenty Design for the great work producing the design, layout and typesetting.

John Kaufman for his skills in bringing the book to life.

Special thanks to David Landau, Harriet Lester and John Speer at Right Recordings.

Claire and her team at Hudson PR.

Toby Walker at www.soulwalking.co.uk for his help with Chapter Four.

Lars "LG" Nilsson at Seabear Studios for his contribution to Chapter Five.

Jaybee at www.california-ballroom.info for letting me tap into her network and the introduction to various artist and associates.

Malcolm Cook Tour Manager of the 1965 Tamla Motown UK tour for the use of those rare images from that tour, and providing the background to the profile on the Tamla Motown Label.

Ralph Terrana at www.soulfuldetroit.com for some great images.

Jeanne Sorensen from Waterford Michigan of J Reed Entertainment for her help with The Miracles entry.

Joan for her continued support and guidance.

Cindy Nicole at Blue Ribbon Press.

Editors Note

The list of individuals in this book is not intended as an exhaustive list of those associated with Motown; in particular the Detroit Years 1959 to 1972, indeed the publisher would like to encourage any of the following categories of people to contact them so, as and when a second edition is considered, their information is to hand.

1. If your profile is in this book and you would like to amend, add to, or enhance the factual information contained in this book.

2. The publisher would be grateful for information on Pam Sawyer, Taylor Cox, Shelly Berger, Gloria Jones, Al Cleveland, Kelly Ernest, Hal Davis, Willie Hutch, Jeffery Bowen, Mike McLean, Michael Masser, Weldon A McDougal III, Lloyd Price, Ed Townsend, Ernest Kelly, Ralph Seltzer and from the UK Motown office Gordon Frewin, who through either time constraints or lack of up to date information, we were unable to place in this publication. Gordy family members who have fallen into this category are, Iris Bristol Gordy, George Gordy and Fuller Gordy.

3. If you were employed or associated with Motown (in particular in Detroit between 1959 and 1972) and would like the editor to consider an entry in this publication.

Contact can be made via email: alex.mackenzie@togetherpublications.com

Or write to:
Together Publications Ltd
C/O Alex MacKenzie
Orchard Lea
Winkfield Lane
Windsor
Berkshire
SL4 4RU
England

All chart listing's are based on US charts i.e. billboard, if not the country of origin will be stated i.e. UK No1.

Abbreviations Used

H-D-H	Holland-Dozier-Holland
UK	United Kingdom
R&B	Rhythm and Blues
LP	Long Player (Vinyl)
CD	Compact Disc
Motown	Motown Record Company
J 5	Jackson 5
UA	United Artists
HOB	House of Beauty
L.A	Los Angeles
CEO	Chief Executive Officer
Blvd	Boulevard
Inc	Incorporated
ARMADA	American Record Manufacturing and Distribution Association
NAACP	National Association for the Advancement of Coloured People
NOW	National Organisation for Women
SCLC	Southern Christian Leadership Conference
MAA	Motown Alumni Association
GM	General Motors
HAL	Heroes and Legend Awards
AKA	Also Know As
JOBETE	Jobete Music Co. Inc
PLC	Public Limited Company
USA or US	United States of America
A&R	Artist and Repertoire
PBS	Public Broadcasting Service (USA)

foreword by Bobby Rogers
Founder member of The Miracles

Hard to believe that Motown is celebrating 50 years; it seems like yesterday I was singing on street corners and at parties with my group The Orchids before my time with The Miracles.

I remember being in school with Ronnie White and Pete Moore studying to work in the automotive and airplane industry – this was going to be my future but the music won! Ronnie and Pete were singing with Smokey (Robinson) and Claudette's brother Emerson Rogers. The Orchids split up, Emerson left for the army and I became one of The Matadors rehearsing in Claudette's basement.

The classic Miracles line-up. Left to Right: (back row) Pete Moore, Ronnie White, (front row) Bobby Rogers, Claudette Robinson and Smokey Robinson.

The Miracles had a shaky beginning; no real musical charts but we performed at the Apollo Theatre in New York anyway. Our show was a flop but thanks to Ray Charles (on the show with us) and his sax player we were able to get real charts and eventually made it down to the honoured first floor dressing room. Our portrait is hanging in the theater now.

The Miracles performed all over the world. One of my best memories was meeting Paul McCartney, Ringo Starr and John Lennon while we were in England and thanks to Dusty Springfield, Motown artists were singing to fans in the UK. I don't think any of us thought about the history we were making - we were making music and having fun.

The artists listed in this book are my Motown family and although we don't see each other as much as we once did; I love them all. I'd like to give a big thank you to Alex MacKenzie for putting this "family tree" together and to the Motown fans for bringing our family into their lives.

Bobby Rogers

Introduction

Originally incorporated on 12th January 1959 by Berry Gordy as the Motown Recording Company with Tamla Records issuing the first singles. The name Tamla derived from the Debbie Reynolds hit "Tammy", Berry Gordy had wanted to use "Tammy" as the name for the label, unbelievably the name had gone, so after a slight change it became "Tamla". The Four Major US labels used were Motown, Tamla, Gordy and Soul, with the Tamla Motown name used for the UK/European market Motown has, over the course of its history, owned or distributed more than 45 labels in varying genres, including the above labels, but also Mel-o-dy, Miracle, Rare Earth, and Mo-west. Motown left Detroit for Los Angeles, California in 1972, and remained an independent company until 1988, when Gordy sold the company to MCA.

Many labels have left their mark on the R&B and Soul Music Scene. The record labels Sun, Atlantic, Chess, Stax/Volt, and lots of others left a permanent mark on this genre of music by honing distinctive styles and attitudes. Only one label, however, is immediately identified as a genre of its own (and not just by scholars and record collectors). Motown, to anyone who's listened to popular music since the 1960's is not just a label, but a sound that ranks among the most distinctive in music history.

The Motown Empire, eventually grew into the biggest Black-Owned business in America. This was a success story as unlikely as those of Elvis or the Beatles. Berry Gordy was a former boxer and jazz record-store owner, (this enterprise would fail) a bit player on the fringes of music. Berry Gordy was struggling on the edges of the R&B music business in the late 1950's, writing some hits for Jackie Wilson, which became hits, but not earning Berry Gordy any money as such. Berry Gordy did however write the hit "Lonely Teardrops" which allowed Berry to concentrate on his song writing skills and leave his job at the car factory.

On the strength of this success, in 1959 he borrowed money from his family (the famous loan scheme operated by the Gordy family) to start an independent production company. After leasing hits by Marv Johnson and Barrett Strong to other labels, Berry Gordy formed his own labels. The releases would appear both on Motown and other labels like Tamla, Gordy, and Soul.

Motown quickly established itself in the early 1960's with hits by The Miracles, The Marvelettes and Mary Wells. It was Berry Gordy's increasingly refined and systematic production techniques, however, that would ensure that the label continued to succeed and grow. The Motown sound has often been compared to an assembly line, drawing upon the influence of Detroit's automobile plants (where Berry Gordy worked for a short time), with performers, songwriters, producers and musicians using a basic tried and tested blueprint.

In its heyday, Motown was home to the most commercially successful production of Soul, R&B and Pop Music ever produced. Motown developed many superstars, but performers were only part of the story. Equally important were the songwriters, including such masters as Smokey Robinson and the Holland-Dozier-Holland team; producers (who often doubled as songwriters); The Funk Brothers (unaccredited on the actual record label until the 1970's) as the backing musicians, (including the remarkable bassist James Jamerson and drummer Benny Benjamin) who gave the music its rock-solid foundation following the vision of owner Berry Gordy to produce music for the masses.

The reason often stated for the non-credits for the musician was to "keep the secret" from other labels. Berry Gordy well understood the contribution The Funk Brothers made to the music, and I can see why this argument is used, but at that time the majority of The Funk Brothers were salaried musicians and their role was as such. It is only with hindsight we can really appreciate their contribution.

You can almost always spot a Motown Record: memorable melodies, great bass lines, punchy tambourines and handclaps, horns and strings (normally courtesy of the Detroit Symphony Orchestra), and vocals that have a gospel flavour with the call-and-response lines between the lead and backup singers. For me they split into the ballads and dance groove, the love song and the original drum and bass approach.

If it were indeed true that Motown's formula was nothing more than an assembly line, it most likely would have "run out of steam" quickly. Berry Gordy's genius was that it was able to spin almost infinite variations (ballard, dance, soulful tunes) while still retaining an instantly recognisable sound, endearing itself to millions through these innovations and familiarity.

Motown releases might have shared many general similarities, but in time its superstars would develop strong identities of their own. The Miracles, led by Smokey Robinson (who wrote many of Motown's best songs, both for The Miracles and other artists), handled both romantic ballads and up-tempo dance tunes.

The Temptations were the most polished soul group of their day, as against The Four Tops gritty and emotional output. Mary Wells and The Marvelettes recorded the most "soulful" singles around. Stevie Wonder would develop into a gifted songwriter and instrumentalist and would become Motown's longest serving artist. Martha Reeves and The Vandellas were Motown at its most feverish and gospel-influenced, The Supremes were, (aside from the Beatles) the most successful pop group of the 1960's. Marvin Gaye (along with Stevie Wonder) would prove to be the most eclectic and innovative singer/songwriter on the Motown roster, not even reaching his musical maturity as an artist (like Stevie Wonder) until the 1970's. On top of this roster of stars was Junior Walker who cut the label's earthiest, most party-oriented R&B.

These were the superstars; there were other fine performers who recorded a notable body of work for Motown in the 1960's, including Gladys Knight, Brenda Holloway, Edwin Starr, Kim Weston, Tammi Terrell and The Contours. The label's roster was so deep, in fact, that some illustrious artists were neglected; the Detroit Spinners didn't have a "big hit" until they left Motown in the early 1970's, The Isley Brothers had only one major hit with "This Old Heart of Mine (Is Weak For You)" and several minor hits during their several years there and early 1960's, soul star Chuck Jackson had only minimal success after moving to Motown.

Even the stars sometimes expressed dissatisfaction about how they were promoted and directed by Motown, but they most likely knew that their success was at least equally attributable to the label, as to their own talents. A good example was Mary Wells' surprise decision to leave Motown in 1964 just after her number one hit, "My Guy". Promises of a big record contract and a movie career took her away from Motown. Mary Wells never had another big hit; without the Motown team of writers and producers Mary Wells became just another soul singer.

The loss of Mary Wells was covered by the burgeoning careers of other Motown stars, but Berry Gordy faced a much more serious problem in late 1967, when the song writing and production team of Brian Holland, Lamont Dozier and Eddie Holland demanded an accounting of their royalties. After initiating a suit against Motown, the trio left the label to establish a company of their own. Invictus and Hot Wax for a brief moment, looked like it would created another "Motown" with acts Chairman of the Board, Freda Payne etc but it was not to be. For a few years, Motown's fortunes were unaffected; they launched The Jackson 5 as superstars, and producers such as Norman Whitfield infused Motown with contemporary funk, psychedelia, and social commentary on tracks like The Temptations' "Cloud Nine", "Psychedelic Shack" and "Ball of Confusion".

Motown's golden age formally ended, in 1971/72, when the company moved from Detroit to Los Angeles. This may not be truly reflected by "record sales" as Motown had many successes in the 1970's and 1980's, however, around this time, the careers of some of Motown's mainstays, such as Martha Reeves and The Marvelettes had petered out and lost record sales.

Diana Ross had already left The Supremes, Marvin Gaye and Stevie Wonder recorded some truly great albums in the 1970's, including my all time favourite, the ground breaking "What's Going On" by Marvin Gaye, these two artists in particular showed their true gifts as songwriters and performers for the first time, as well as expanding their lyrical concerns beyond the romantic themes that Motown had largely stuck to. Motown honed a distinctive sound, they were simply a Soul/R&B/Pop record label, albeit the largest and most successful one.

When people talk about the Motown sound, they are normally referring to those 1960's and early 1970's recordings. The most successful label of its day and the most successful independent label of all time, one which I can't see being repeated. It was the most influential factor in establishing African-American music as an integral part of mainstream US culture and world record buying people.

In a recent interview Warren "Pete" Moore of The Miracles explained his theory on why Motown will never happen again. It's simple, in the 1960's there was more "love" around, fewer egos and more of an attitude to help each other.

Now headquartered in Detroit and New York City, Motown was merged with Universal Records to create the Universal Motown Records Group, an umbrella division of Universal Music which oversees the releases and catalogues for Motown, Universal, Blackground, Republic, Cash Money, Casablanca and other labels.

Yesterday was the birthplace of today. Today is twenty-five years of climbing and building, and of opening doors and breaking old rules.

Today is also love songs, and guys and girls songs, wounds left unattended for far too long, songs to march to, fly to, to make love to.

Its music pure and simple and soulful, and if you insist, full of promise and determination, unity and humanity: today is the birthplace of forever.

Marvin Gaye, at the Motown 25 Yesterday, Today Forever. Concert on the 25th March 1983.

Marvin Gaye.

CHAPTER ONE

HOW MOTOWN GOT IT TOGETHER

Chapter One: How Motown Got It Together

Motown would establish itself as the largest independent record company in the world (and the largest business of any kind owned by an African American). A unique assembly line song production process that was as inventive as it was successful. The initial hits by Barrett Strong, The Marvelettes and The Miracles at the beginning of the decade and the explosion of The Jackson 5 in the early 1970's were simply bookends to an unprecedented run of commercial and artistic achievements. In the mid-1960's Motown was especially dominant, and the company, more than any other label, defined the 1960's.

The numbers are astounding, between 1960 and 1970 the average chart hits produced was 67% to the number of singles Motown released (the industry standard "chart hit" to issued singles ratio was around 10%). Of the records issued 56% of those songs were No1 on either the pop or R&B charts, and 21% topped both charts. In 1964, when The Beatles began setting some records of their own, Motown released sixty singles, 70% of which hit the charts and nineteen made it to No1. The Supremes alone racked up five consecutive No1 pop hits starting with "Where Did Our Love Go" in 1964. In 1966 Motown's chart hits ratio topped 75% which shows the dominance of the label by the mid-1960's. There is a famous example of a memo sent by Berry Gordy (of which a copy is held at Hitsville) that stated; only records that would reach the Top 10 were to be released, for The Supremes it stated, only number one records would be released.

2646 West Grand Boulevard, now the museum entrance.

As the 1960's progressed, Motown continued to expand, absorbing rival record labels, and resuscitating the careers of acts (like The Four Tops) who had languished with other record companies before hooking up with Motown's crack song writing and production team. By 1966 the company had one hundred performing acts under contract, its chart dominance continued, spearheaded by the songs of Smokey Robinson and the Holland-Dozier-Holland trio, performed by The Supremes, The Four Tops and The Temptations. Motown had realised its self-declared title as "The Sound of Young America".

Over the years Motown had taken over six other houses surrounding the original office on West Grand Boulevard. However, Motown was to relocate a large amount of its administration function to downtown Detroit (Donovan Building) in 1968.

The twin heavyweights of the British invasion, The Beatles and The Rolling Stones, both recorded (and performed) Motown songs throughout their careers "Please Mr. Postman", "Ain't Too Proud to Beg" "Just My Imagination (Running Away with Me)" among others. Barrett Strong's "Money" is the only song by an outside artist that both groups recorded in their entire careers. Very few covers by any group, however, managed to match up to the Motown originals.

In the beginning, Motown always seemed to be a step ahead of the competition. But browsing through the Motown releases of the period, one notices a subtle change in both the compositions and their themes. Raw R&B songs (like The Contours' dance party smash "Do You Love Me?") and early rock vocal harmony style (such as The Marvelettes' girl group innocent number "Please Mr. Postman") eventually gave way to the polished craftsmanship of the mid-sixties.

More experimental songs (especially lyrical) began to crop up towards the end of the decade Marvin Gaye's "What's Going On" being the best example. Motown came into being during a turbulent period in American history with the "Civil Rights" movement. In the late sixties and early seventies especially, Motown began to reflect (perhaps somewhat belatedly) on the social and political flavour of the times.

Songs like Marvin Gaye's "What's Going On" The Temptations' "Ball of Confusion" and "Papa Was a Rolling Stone" Edwin Starr's "War" and even "Love Child" by The Supremes were indications that Motown was as much a product of the times as they were an influence upon them.

Everyone becomes strongly attached to some of the music in his or her lives, and it is sometimes difficult to give an objective account of particular songs when they are wrapped in the warm fuzziness of nostalgia and sentiment. Having said that, is there something tangible or concrete about this music that explains the strong hold it continues to have on our collective psyche?

That Sound

Most Motown singles of the era used a common verse chorus (or verse bridge chorus) pop song structure, with the occasional short instrumental break or key change after the second chorus that catapulted the tune into its final verse. The songs often began with a quick introduction of the dominant instrumental hook or vocal refrain; the bass and guitar licks kicking off The Temptations' "My Girl" for example, or the whispery chorus opening The Supremes "Baby Love". What distinguished Motown's songs was the traditional gospel, R&B and Blues elements that were welded together to make the song 'Soulful' yet with a 'Pop' song feel to it. It was a marriage made in heaven. As Thomas 'Beans' Bowles said it was rhyme up front, not buried in the song.

2648 West Grand Boulevard housing the famous "Motown Studio A".

Motown's 'secret weapon' was the relationship between the bass guitar player and the drummer, James Jamerson and Benny Benjamin. In the early stages of Motown, and into the early 1970's (when Motown ceased production at Hitsville Studio A), bassist James Jamerson played on over 90% of Motown's recording and 99% of Motown's chart topping songs. Benny Benjamin elevated the rhythm with a traditional blues shuffle, using a snare brush in one hand, and a drumstick in the other. Then add the rest of The Funk Brothers, and all the elements came together producing a beautiful Motown song.

Songs were spun out in innumerable variations, some more a product of Gordy's policy of following up a hit with a quick sound alike whenever possible (the common practice of the era), while others were inventive rearrangements of specific song structures and harmonies. Martha and The Vandellas' "Quicksand" and "Livewire" were obvious attempts to trade on the success of their original hit "Heatwave". On the other hand, The Supremes "Where Did Our Love Go" and The Four Tops "I Can't Help Myself" are totally distinct songs with identical underlying harmonic structures and similar melodies.

The Motown Factory

The organisation that created these songs was about as close to a musical "hit factory" as popular music has produced. Motown (which of course took its name from the Motor City), in fact, liked to brag that the Detroit auto industry wasn't the only successful assembly line in town. Ford, GM, and Chrysler may have produced

Recording Studio A was at the back of the "Hitsville" building on the lower ground floor, also the residence of Berry and Raynoma Gordy in upstairs rooms.

the classic cars, but Motown produced the classic songs.

The company was certainly unusual, especially considering the racial issue of the time. It's truly amazing that a wholly black owned, independent music company was flourishing in an overwhelmingly white, corporate industry (and based light years away from the entertainment capitols of New York and Los Angeles), it had a highly structured, formula driven business that produced songs that had the highest chance of charting against any other music label.

Berry Gordy's Motown didn't so much break the rules as create new ones. It drew strength from its uniqueness, and was able to turn all the characteristics that set it apart and which might have been seen as "barriers" into advantages. As an independent company with total control over everything from production to publishing, Motown was free from outside artistic or financial influence. By being in Detroit (rather than New York or Los Angeles), gave Motown unlimited access to talent without (for many years) the large music corporation knowing the talent was there. Its somewhat isolated Detroit location helped Berry Gordy keep his talented songwriters and artists out of the reach of competition, which might want to spirit them away.

Eventually location made no difference when it came to competitors wanting to take the artist from Motown. From 1964 word had 'got out', and local and major record companies started trying to grab Motown artists. The prime example was the case of Mary Wells. She was at her prime with Motown, when a major record company 'stole' her from Motown.

However, one of Berry Gordy's greatest problems was getting his money from the distributors, he had to send the records on consignment, and finances were so tight that if they didn't get a hit on the following record, they stood the chance of losing the company; even during their 'hay day' the problem still occurred.

The assembly line depiction of Motown is not just a fanciful analogy. Company employees even punched a time clock at the start of the monthly meetings; everyone had to sing the company's official song, a kind of musical pledge written by none other than Smokey Robinson. Berry Gordy pitched his songwriters and producers against each other on a regular basic, Berry Gordy's tactics apparently worked. Motown feeding off each other's talent, establishing partnerships and finding success that had eluded them outside the offices and studios at Hitsville.

Hit making at Motown had become a regimented and streamlined process by the mid-1960's, everybody knew their role. The process would start with (for example) Brian Holland, Lamont Dozier and Eddie Holland would work up the lyrics and basic tune. When this was finished they'd take it to the Motown house band, known as The Funk Brothers. The backing track would be 'laid down' ready for the artist to provide vocals (normally at a later stage).

In the first few years of "Hitsville Studio A" the musician, artist etc were all in the studio recording, but as the volume of tracks increased, this became impossible, so the system of The Funk Brothers laying down the tracks became the norm.

Motown was now a 'twenty four' hour enterprise with "Studio A" never to close until the fateful day in 1972 when a notice was pinned to the recording studio door saying session to re-scheduled (it never was). The studio worked on through the Detroit Riots, all the civil unrest, until its move to California.

Every producer was assigned to an artist, there was competition between the producers, and the writers to see who wrote and produced the best songs. It was an unwritten rule that the producer with the last hit on an artist had first option on their next release. Berry Gordy always said "competition breeds champions".

When the artists were performing together on a live stage, they would compete for positioning in the shows. They where always aiming for the final slot on the show, the rule was whoever had the biggest applause moved to the end of the show.

Berry Gordy featured in a publicity handout from the artist re-produced in the Detroit Free Press.

There were situations where an artist or group wasn't around Hitsville when production was scheduled, the person cutting the demo sang the song so well, that the company recorded the demo as the final cut. If the song had been earmarked for a particular artist (e.g. The Supremes) from the start, then the producers arranged for that artist to do that song. What's amazing is that it was all done in Motown's less than acoustically perfect studio (although the studio was acoustically reinforced and sound proofed by Berry Gordy's father).

Although Motown had several high performing songwriter/producers, (including Berry Gordy), these included Smokey Robinson and Holland-Dozier-Holland these individuals accounted for the largest number of the chart hits for Motown. Smokey Robinson wrote for The Miracles and for acts like Mary Wells and The Temptations, while Holland-Dozier-Holland wrote many of the hits for Martha and The Vandellas, The Supremes and The Four Tops, among others.

All the Motown employees were marvellously versatile. Eddie Holland wasn't just part of a song writing team, he was a former singer who scored a hit of his own with Motown in 1962 "Jamie". Smokey Robinson didn't just sing chart toppers with The Miracles. He wrote and produced hits for others. Barrett Strong, singer of one of the first Motown hits, "Money" was also a writer, responsible for records like The Temptations' "Ball of Confusion (That's What The World Is Today)" with partner Norman Whitfield.

Tamla Motown UK tour newspaper cuttings.

It is the combination of Holland-Dozier-Holland which remains Motown's most legendary song writing and production team. With H-D-H, the Motown "Hit Factory" reached its pinnacle. Lamont Dozier and Brian Holland initially worked together with only modest success in the early 1960's. Eddie Holland joined after abandoning his performing career. Beginning with the ebullient "Heatwave" by Martha and The Vandellas in 1963, Holland-Dozier-Holland reeled off twenty eight more top 20 songs over the next three years; including some of the best known Motown hits (the trio is responsible for more number one songs than any other non performing song writing team in music history).

What might have become a routine process, song writing by numbers in the hands of lesser talent, was an always evolving and inventive game for the trio, who shared lyrical, melodic and harmonic responsibilities, then cut demos for the musicians and artists to study. They repeatedly dipped into their bag of musical tricks to come up with songs that were unmistakably Motown.

The Motown house musicians "The Funk Brothers" were probably the least recognised link in the Motown

The Funk Brothers.

production chain, but the success of the music is almost inconceivable without them. As salaried musicians, they were relatively obscure employees behind the scenes at Motown, often playing in their own time to small audiences at local clubs. With the songwriters they laid down the track, gave the track the full Motown Sound affect (and in many cases adapted the track) playing with energy and professionalism. This success has never been repeated and I guess it never will? They played on thousands and thousands of classic Motown records, recorded day after day in the Hitsville Studio A the "Snake Pit".

Composed mostly of older musicians with jazz backgrounds, with years of intense collaboration, this made the band impeccably tight and endlessly inventive. With the pulsating drumming of Benny Benjamin and the melodic bass lines of James Jamerson, this put an unmistakable label on the Motown recordings of the era. These musicians also had an incalculable influence on many of Motown's top performers. Stevie Wonder, for one, honed his keyboard and drumming skills under the guidance of Earl Van Dyke and Benny Benjamin while hanging out in the studio.

Motown's grip on the artists extended far beyond the recording studio, the company owned its own publishing, management and booking (run by Esther Gordy Edwards) it even had its own "finishing school". Maxine Powell instructed performers how to walk, talk, and dress in a manner that promoted the company's sleek image. In house music coaches (run by Maurice King) and choreographers (Cholly Atkins) put performers through endless rehearsals (closely monitored by the ever-vigilant Berry Gordy), sometimes for months, before an act was unveiled to the public or a record finally released. Nothing was left to chance.

"Motortown Revues", as they were called in those early days, were touring performances by various line-ups of the Motown roster representing another "face" of the Motown marketing strategy. Performances were staged to help promote the company as a whole, as much as its individual artists. The tours also provided an "education" for performers, when they found they were up against the racial barriers of the times, (especially in the south) with segregated dressing rooms and separate performances for black and white audiences and less than enthusiastic receptions from local officials.

2657 West Grand Boulevard; Artist Development was located directly across from 2648 West Grand Blvd "Hitsville".

While Motown actively cultivated a cross-racial audience, it was also aware of its position at the forefront of black enterprise and culture. Although it's not well known, Berry Gordy released Martin Luther King Jnr "I Have A Dream" speech as a single in 1963, and produced three of the speeches by the civil rights leader. When Martin Luther King Jnr was assassinated, Berry Gordy gave Corretta Scott King (Martin's wife) the master tapes of those recordings and the rights to any royalties.

Motown's Legacy

Motown's explosive growth in the sixties could not continue indefinitely, even though to many at the time it must have seemed like it would. With the "family" environment, the majority of the stars being from Detroit and the rigid production system Berry Gordy had constructed, it had to eventually change. The company simply outgrew itself and stars and employees began to seek more control over their work (or greater compensation for it). The best example of this was Holland-Dozier-Holland (who left the company in 1968) in dispute over their role at Motown.

Then the unthinkable happened; Motown relocated to Los Angeles in 1971, "Studio A's" final recording session was in 1972, the Hitsville Building was left as a shell, being used primarily as a base for the "forgotten" employees. Some say Detroit has never really recovered from this exodus. Many employees and performers did not make the move. Berry Gordy later conceded that, as far as producing music was concerned, the company would have been better off had it stayed in Detroit.

The Jackson 5 explosion in 1970/71 with their first single, "I Want You Back" (recorded in December 1969) being the last successes of the traditional, original Motown assembly line, where Motown managed the writing, production etc. Berry Gordy wanted to branch out into other areas of the entertainment industry, most notably movies, and Los Angeles was the place to be.

Although the West Coast move effectively marked the end of an era at "Motown of Detroit", the company hardly disappeared from the charts. The Motown stars continued to score huge successes in the 1970's. Stevie Wonder became one of the biggest acts in the music business, and The Jackson 5 and Michael Jackson continued to score major hits. The Commodores (Motown's all time biggest seller) and Lionel Richie both had huge success in the 1970's and 1980's, while Diana Ross became a successful solo artist. Motown stalwart Smokey Robinson, continued to write and record hits into the 1980's. When Berry Gordy sold Motown in 1988, (the company was sold for $61 million) Rick James, DeBarge, and Boyz 11 Men went on to be international artists under the "new" Motown label, the artist list continues to grow to this day.

The music from the seminal period in the 1960's and 1970's, however, remains the core of the Motown catalogue, and is as popular and vibrant today as it was when it was first released. Turn on the radio or TV, go to the movie, chances are you'll soon run into some of that legendary Motown sound.

Featuring the originals line-up; Jackie Jackson, Tito Jackson, Jermaine Jackson, Marlon Jackson, Michael Jackson.

CHAPTER TWO

MOTOWN HISTORY

Chapter Two: Motown History

By the late 1950's, Detroit was perhaps the largest city in the United States that did not have a strong independent record company. With the establishment of Motown, the local talent had an outlet, and they starting showing up at the Motown offices. With a rich history in jazz and blues, Detroit had a large number of clubs on which Motown would eventually draw. The Motown Record Company issued the largest number of 45s records ever released by a record company.

Berry Gordy, who was born in Detroit, Michigan in 1929, was the seventh of eight children of Berry Gordy Snr and Bertha Gordy. His parents moved to Detroit from Milledgeville, Georgia in 1922. His father ran a plastering contracting business and his mother sold insurance and real estate, they also ran a grocery store and print shop.

In 1953

Berry Gordy dropped out of school after his junior year to become a professional boxer, before going into the army. Berry Gordy then leaves the army after service in Korea and opens a jazz record store called the 3-D Record Mart that was financed by Berry Gordy's family.

In 1955

The jazz record store failed, and Berry Gordy starts working on the Ford automobile assembly line in Detroit. While working on the assembly line, Berry Gordy is constantly writing songs in his head to relieve the boredom, and then submitting them to magazines, contests and singers.

In 1957

His first success as a songwriter comes when Jackie Wilson (also from Detroit) records "Reet Petite", a song Berry Gordy, his sister Gwen Gordy and Billy Davis (under the pseudonym of Tyran Carlo) had written. "Reet Petite" became a modest hit and earned Berry Gordy $1000 for the song. However, with this income he leaves the Ford assembly line to concentrate on developing his song writing. Over the next two years he co-wrote four more hits for Jackie Wilson, "To Be Loved", "Lonely Teardrops", "That's Why" and "I'll Be Satisfied". Berry Gordy later chose the title "To Be Loved" for his autobiography.

With success as a songwriter, Berry Gordy decided to produce his songs himself. His first production was titled "Ooh Shucks" by the Five Stars, which was released on George Goldner's "Mark X" label. In this year, Berry Gordy is introduced to Smokey Robinson, while The Matadors (as The Miracles were then known) auditioned for the manager of Jackie Wilson, Nat Tarnapol. He turned the group down because he felt their sound and four-man-one-woman line up were too similar to The Platters, this was the start of a lifelong friendship and business relationship between Smokey Robinson and Berry Gordy.

In 1958

Berry Gordy produced a record by Eddie Holland titled "You", which was leased to Mercury records. Also that year, Kudo Records issued four more of Berry Gordy's productions, the first Marv Johnson release, "My Baby O", and Brian Holland (of the future Holland-Dozier-Holland team) single "Shock". With Smokey Robinson and the Holland brothers, Berry Gordy, had by accident discovered three incredible songwriters and producers, which would later transform Berry Gordy's Motown in to the hit making factory Berry Gordy had envisaged.

Also in that year, two young teenagers auditioned for Berry Gordy, called Raynoma Liles and Alice Mayberry, Berry was not impressed with the two teenagers, but thought Raynoma Liles could help him with song writing duties and preparing cord sheets (Raynoma unusually had perfect pitch). Berry Gordy and Raynoma Liles then moved onto developing the "Rayber Music Writing Company" a combination of Ray's and Berry Gordy's first name, the business idea was to charge budding artists who wanted to make a record, using their facilities.

Berry Gordy then produced a record by Herman Griffin titled "I Need You" on the H.O.B (which stood for House of Beauty) label, it was the first song to be published by Berry Gordy's publishing company, Jobete (pronounced "Jo-bet"), and the publishing company was named after his three children, Hazel Joy (Jo), Berry IV (Be) and Terry (Te). "I Need You" was also the first record to credit the Rayber Voices, background singers, formed from their "Rayber Music Writing Company".

After this success, but disappointed at the amount of royalties received from these records, Smokey Robinson suggests to Berry Gordy that he start his own record label.

Berry Gordy did create another label before the Motown Recording Company was established, called the Rayber label. It was developed two months before Motown, there was only one artist on that label called Wade Jones with the single "I Can't Concentrate" the only known recording.

In 1959

On January 12, 1959 Berry Gordy starts his own record label, called Tamla. An "umbrella" organisation would be created called the "Motown Recording Company" the original Tamla label would become a subsidiary of the "Motown Recording Company". Berry Gordy had originally wanted to call his label "Tammy", after a Debbie Reynolds film, but that title was already taken. Tamla Records was located at 1719 Gladstone Street in Detroit (pre-West Grand Boulevard).

Hitsville USA.

Purchased 2nd August 1959, Berry Gordy moves into the 2648 West Grand Boulevard (also the residence of Berry Gordy and Raynoma Gordy in upstairs rooms) and called the building "Hitsville USA" with the famous sign above the window "Sound of Young America". The first hit recording to come out of that studio was a song that cultivated a party atmosphere, the recording was Barrett Strong hit song "Money (That's What I Want)".

The first release was Marv Johnson's "Come to Me" leased to United Artists who would distribute the single and it became a moderate hit. Marv Johnson's next release "You Got What It Takes" became Berry Gordy's first production to break into the pop Top 10.

Tamla Records label.

Berry Gordy and Thelma Gordy (nee Coleman) divorce, they have three children, Berry Gordy Jnr IV, Hazel Joy and Terry. After the divorce, Berry Gordy marries Raynoma Liles, they have one son called Kerry and Smokey Robinson and Claudette Rogers also marry.

Key personnel start to arrive at "Hitsville", Berry Gordy's first hired musician is Joe Hunter pianist, original member and band leader of the in house band, which would evolve into The Funk Brothers, the next key member of the in house band arrives, the bass player James Jamerson to work in "Studio A". Mable John is the first female signed by Berry Gordy to Motown's Tamla label, The Satintones are the first group to be signed to the

Motown label and Al Abrams becomes the first person of non-African American descent to work at Motown.

In 1960

The Motown label is established in early 1960, although "Bad Girl" by The Miracles is pressed in September 1959, on the Motown label as test pressing only. "Shop Around" released later in the year on Tamla, went onto become a No2 chart hit, helping to establish The Miracles, and also to Motown itself, it became Motown's first million seller.

Also during this year, a local girl singing group named The Primettes auditioned for Berry Gordy. He was impressed with the group, but asked them to finish school and then come back. The Primettes came back to Motown after graduating, and were signed in January 1961. The group's name was changed to The Supremes, and they had their first release on Tamla in April of 1961. There were four members of The Primettes: Diane Ross, Mary Wilson, Florence Ballard and Betty McGlown. Betty McGlown would leave shortly afterwards to leave the three original members to become The Supremes.

Also in 1960, Berry Gordy acquired the contract of a young Washington DC based singer named Marvin Gay (Marvin would change his name to Gaye shortly afterwards). Harvey Fuqua (who became Berry Gordy's brother-in-law) was the leader of The Moonglows, and Marvin Gaye was a member.

Mary Wells approached Berry Gordy at a talent show; Berry Gordy signed her immediately and released a song she had written called "Bye Bye Baby" in December of that year. Mary Wells would prove to be the first international star for Motown, and be called the "First Lady of Motown".

Berry Gordy also discovered that year, another singing group called the Otis Williams and The Distants; eventually the group merged with another group The Primes (after being called The Elgins for a short time), and changed their name to The Temptations, releasing their first record on a new subsidiary label called Miracle in 1961. Their success was not to be as immediate as Mary Wells, but it would eventually eclipse Mary's career and be far more successful.

In 1961

January sees the signing of Jimmy Ruffin to Motown, he is placed on the short lived

"Miracles" label, only Jimmy Ruffin and The Temptation issue singles on this label.

Robert Bateman discovers The Marvelettes at a talent show at Inkster High School. In August, Bateman and Brian Holland co-produced The Marvelettes' first record, "Please Mr. Postman" and it became the first Motown record to reach the pop charts' No1 position. Interestingly, this single is Motown's only top ten hit of that year. Marvin Gaye's first recording "Let Your Conscience Be Your Guide" is released; it goes on to be a modest chart hit.

The classic line-up of Wanda Young, Gladys Gorton and Katherine Anderson.

Also in 1961, a young blues singer named Martha LaVaille meets William "Mickey" Stevenson, Head of the Motown A&R Department at a local club. William "Mickey" Stevenson asks her to audition for him, but she came on the wrong audition day. Leaving his office for a while, he asks her to answer the phones while he was away, she did such a good job that he hired her on the spot.

When Mary Wells misses a recording session, Martha Reeves (using her stage name Martha LaVaille) called a local girl group she was a member of (The Del-Phis), to do the recording session. They recorded "There He Is (At My Door)", which was released on the Melody subsidiary. The record was a flop, but the group continued to be used for background vocal work.

On the 18th April Motown purchase 2644/46 West Grand Boulevard as headquarters for the Jobete Publishing Company (now the museum entrance).

The Supremes have their first release on the Tamla label in April, the single is not a success, recording five more unsuccessful singles, and they earned the nickname "The No Hit Supremes". At one of the famous "Friday Staff Meetings" Smokey Robinson is named Vice President of Motown Records a position he will hold until 1988. Eddie Holland returns to Motown after his contract with United Artists comes to an end.

In 1962

April sees the establishment of Motown's third major label, Gordy. Two further labels are added to the company, Mel-o-dy and VIP.

With a new name, Martha and The Vandellas back Marvin Gaye on his hit "Stubborn Kind of Fellow" (they performed live on stage as "Marvin and The Vandellas"). The Top Ten hit "You've Really Got a Hold on Me" by The Miracles establishes them as the number one group at Motown. Marvin Gaye records his first hit with "Stubborn Kind of Fellow". The song writing and production team Holland-Dozier-Holland are formed, this team will eventually transform Motown, often called a "hit making factory within a hit making factory".

Workshop Records label.

Berry Gordy forms a jazz subsidiary label called "Workshop Jazz"; the label is established in order to convince the most talented jazz musicians in Detroit, to play on his pop music sessions. Berry Gordy enticed them with promises of album releases on the label. Berry Gordy knew that even the most successful jazz album sales would be minuscule compared to the numbers he could generate in popular music. Berry Gordy kept his promise to the musicians, and the 11 albums released on the label are some of the rarest albums on any Motown label.

Berry Gordy moved into his own office space with the purchase of 2650 West Grand Boulevard on the 23rd January, the offices are used by Berry Gordy, Esther Gordy Edwards and Ralph Seltzer. If you visit or see photographs of "Hitsville" it is the vacant ground, to the left of "Hitsville", which burned to the ground in 1971. Also added to the "Motown Empire" is 2652/54 West Grand Boulevard as the Motown Administration block on the 23rd January 1962.

Berry Gordy and Raynoma Gordy divorce, however, Raynoma continues to work at Motown, in November and December the first "Motor Town Revues" start at The Apollo Theatre in New York and Kim Weston signs to Motown under the name "Wright Specials". Another key member of the in house band Earl Van Dyke joins Motown, quickly becoming leader of the band after the departure of Joe Hunter, it was during his time that the band eventually becomes known as The Funk Brothers.

Motown starts to make inroads in to the pop charts (as opposed to the R&B charts) with four Motown singles reaching the Top 10.

In 1963

The Holland-Dozier-Holland team's production of "Come and Get These Memories" released in early 1963 by Martha and The Vandellas on the Gordy label (a subsidiary of Motown) is often credited as being the beginning of "The Motown Sound".

Berry Gordy meets a group that had released their first single in 1954 when they were called the "Four Aims". By 1956, when they released a single on Chess, the group had changed its name to The Four Tops. When The Four Tops are first approached by Berry Gordy, they didn't accept his contract. They thought the company was still too small for them to join. So they took the contract with them, and Berry Gordy didn't see them for two years, before they finally signed.

Ronnie White, a member of The Miracles, arranged for an audition for an eleven year old, blind singer named Stephen Hardaway Judkin, (although some articles have used the name Steveland Morris). Berry Gordy was impressed with his talent, and said the boy was a "wonder". Signed to a Motown and renamed "Little Stevie Wonder", his live recording from the Regal theatre in Chicago called "Fingertips, Part 2" reached the No1 spot on the pop charts.

The Supremes were unsuccessful with their first six singles, which were produced by either Berry Gordy or Smokey Robinson. In late 1963, the group were assigned Holland-Dozier-Holland, and they produced their seventh single, "When the Lovelight Starts Shining Through His Eyes" which reached a respectable No23, their follow-up song "Run Run Run" does not chart.

The first singles released in the UK start to appear on the Oriole label through a distribution deal arranged by Motown. Harvey Fuqua joins Motown as an in house producer, bringing with him stars from his own label including, Junior Walker and The All Stars, The Spinners (aka Motown and Detroit Spinners) and Shorty Long and Marvin Gaye marries Anna Gordy, they have no children.

The Velvelettes are the first group from outside the city of Detroit to sign with Motown and Norman Whitfield joins Motown's Quality Control Department. Six singles would reach the top ten in the US and Motown's finance starts to generate significant funds, the company would make sales of $4.5 million.

In 1964

In July, The Supremes start a run of five consecutive No1 hits, "Where Did Our Love Go", "Baby Love", "Come See About Me", "Stop! In the Name of Love" and

"Back In My Arms Again" all produced by Holland-Dozier-Holland. "Baby Love" by The Supremes, becomes their first UK No1 hit.

Based on record sales, The Supremes went on to become the third largest selling artists in recording history, behind The Beatles and Elvis Presley.

The Supremes appear on UK television for the first time (with The Dave Clark Five) as guests of Dusty Springfield and make their first appearance on "The Ed Sullivan Show". Dave Godin launches the Tamla Motown Appreciation Society in the UK. Smokey Robinson produced "My Guy" for Mary Wells, which also went to No1 pop hit, and Motown's third. Motown reached the No2 spot with the Holland-Dozier-Holland produced "Dancing in the Street" by Martha and The Vandellas. The label was certainly living up to the sign painted on the front of their headquarters at 2648 West Grand Blvd., "Hitsville U.S.A." and "The Sound of Young America".

George Clinton and The Parliaments sign to Motown, but none of their recordings are released, however, Motown owned the rights to the group's name, so George Clinton had to change the name to Funkadelic when they left in 1967.

Tamla Motown tour advertising.

Marvin Gaye makes his first appearance on UK television in November and a major singing star for the year is Brenda Holloway. The "First Lady of Motown" Mary Wells leaves for 20th Century Fox. Maxine Powell joins the label to help form the "Artist Development Department". Motown have five top ten hits, with four of them reaching No1.

In 1965

The "hits just kept on coming", with five No1 hits, they are the Smokey Robinson produced "My Girl" by The Temptations. Holland-Dozier-Holland produce "Stop! In the Name of Love", "Back in My Arms Again" and "I Hear a Symphony" by The Supremes and "I Can't Help Myself" by The Four Tops, Motown also has six other releases that reach the Top 10. Times are good for Berry Gordy with his purchase of "Gordy Mansion" an old Car Magnate's residence in Detroit. However, there is sad news for Berry Gordy, Loucye Gordy Wakefield, his sister, dies on the 29th July 1965 in Detroit, and she was Vice President of Motown and a Director of Jobete.

Junior Walker and The All Stars had the first hit on the new Soul label, the Top 10 instrumental "Shotgun". The Supremes become the first act to open at the Copa in New York, Brenda Holloway tours with The Beatles on their US tour and Brian Holland is promoted to Vice President of Motown.

The Tamla Motown label is launched in the UK, with the EMI label undertaking distribution for Motown, the first issue on Tamla Motown is The Supremes' recording

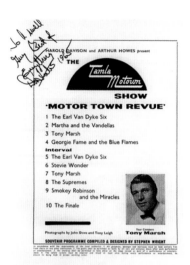

Tamla Motown Show Running Order.

of "Stop! In The Name Of Love". The Motown stars appear on a special "Ready Steady Go" production in the UK, this is followed by "The Motor Town Revue" in the UK, with mixed revues and some half empty venues; the tour was to help launch the Tamla Motown label.

In 1966

Motown signed Gladys Knight and The Pips to the Soul label (a subsidiary of Motown); they are assigned to a young producer named Norman Whitfield. He had previously recorded Marvin Gaye on a song that Norman Whitfield and Barrett Strong had written called "I Heard It Through the Grapevine". When Berry Gordy refused to release the Marvin Gaye version of the song, Norman Whitfield recorded it with Gladys Knight and The Pips, and the song went to No2.

When the Marvin Gaye version of "I Heard It Through The Grapevine" was finally released on an album in 1968, the song became a No1 pop hit, and today is remembered as the definitive version of a classic song and at the time became the biggest Motown single ever released.

Berry Gordy signed The Isley Brothers in 1965 to Tamla label, their biggest hit for Motown would be the Holland-Dozier-Holland produced "This Old Heart (Is

Weak for You)" released in this year. Ashford and Simpson are signed to Motown as song writers on the back of their hit for Ray Charles called "Let's Go Get Stoned".

Norman Whitfield takes over the production of The Temptations from Smokey Robinson; his first production for The Temptations is "Ain't Too Proud to Beg", which he co-wrote with Eddie Holland. Norman Whitfield teams up with Roger Penzabene for The Temptations next hit, "I Wish It Would Rain". Norman Whitfield's next collaborator is Barrett Strong, they go onto to write for The Temptations, the result was a new sound for Motown called "Psychedelic Soul". This made The Temptations the biggest selling male group of the 1960's.

2657 West Grand Boulevard Artist Development, which was located directly across West Grand Blvd was purchased 12th January 1966. Berry Gordy was so impressed by the quality of the output from Golden World and Ric-Tic labels he purchases them from Ed Wingate and Joanne Bratton in September. Some of the recordings feature The Funk Brothers moonlighting on the records, the premises then became "Motown Studio B". With the purchase of Golden World and Ric-Tic, Edwin Starr, J J Barnes and other artists transfer to Motown.

Motown's dominance of the charts, in particular the R&B charts is confirmed by the award of all top three categories, achieving 1-2-3 spots for male and female groups, top male group went to The Four Tops, the top female group was The Supremes, the top record was "I Can't Help Myself" by The Four Tops and best instrumental group was Junior Walker and The All Stars.

At the annual BMI awards dinner, Holland-Dozier-Holland receive eight awards, Jobete twelve, with Lennon and McCartney only receiving five. Motown announces establishment of a West Coast office in Los Angeles, with the intention of moving into film production and Ron Miller joins Motown as an in house writer.

Motown produced 14 songs that reached the Top 10 and three that reached No1 spot.

In 1967

Motown had outgrown West Grand Boulevard by 1967 in regards to administration of the company; Berry Gordy decides to move to Woodward Avenue in Detroit. The ten-storey building was only one hundred yards north of the Fox Theatre and on the same side of the street, however, the

The Gordy Mansion.

studios stay at West Grand Boulevard. Berry Gordy moves to Los Angeles, but keeps the Gordy mansion for his trips back to Detroit.

In the summer of this year, Tammi Terrell (while on stage with Marvin Gaye) collapses into Marvin Gaye's arms, she is diagnosed with a brain tumour, and sadly dies in March 1970 aged only 24. William "Mickey" Stevenson becomes the first high profile writer producer to leave Motown for MGM records; Kim Weston (his wife) leaves with him and also signs for MGM. Florence Ballard is asked to leave The Supremes and is replaced by Jean Terrell.

Early promotional photo of Chuck Jackson.

Chuck Jackson signs to Motown, but fails to establish himself as a major artist at Motown. Ewart Abner joins Motown from Vee Jay records as director of International Talent Management, beginning a long association with Motown and in particular, Berry Gordy.

Roger Penzabene Roger commits suicide on New Eve 1967 in Detroit, Michigan Roger had found out that his wife was having an affair, but could not bring himself to leave her, he wrote "I Wish It Would Rain" based on this situation.

Thirteen Motown singles reached the Top 10 charts; "Love is Here and Now You're Gone" and "The Happening" by The Supremes reached No1. Motown had five major labels active: Motown, Tamla, Gordy, Soul and V.I.P.

In 1968

Dennis Edwards replaces David Ruffin as the lead singer for The Temptations. Motown Los Angeles branch offices are expanded with new artists from this area signed.

Arguably the most successful writers and producers in music history, Holland-Dozier-Holland leave Motown. The Holland-Dozier-Holland team are forced into inactivity from 1968 to 1970 due to lawsuits concerning their departure from Motown. Holland-Dozier-Holland establishes two labels in 1970, Hot Wax and Invictus, and had major success with acts such as Chairmen of the Board, Flaming Ember, Freda Payne and others.

The Jackson 5 win an amateur talent show at the Apollo Theatre in New York. Marvin Gaye releases "I Heard It Through The Grapevine" it reaches the No1 spot in the US and stays there for nearly two months, also a No1 hit in the UK.

Motown's first television special, produced by the company is shown. TCB "Taking Care of Business" is released, featuring The Temptations and Diana Ross and The Supremes and a soundtrack from the show is also released. Berry Gordy and Diana Ross become constant companions.

For the week ending December 28, Motown had five records out of the Top 10 chart hits in the US:

1	Marvin Gaye, "I Heard It Through the Grapevine"
2	Stevie Wonder, "For Once In My Life"
3	Diana Ross and The Supremes, "Love Child"
7	Diana Ross and The Supremes and The Temptations, "I'm Gonna Make You Love Me"
10	The Temptations, "Cloud Nine"

Motown had 12 singles in the Top 10, and three No1, including The Jackson 5's first release "I Want You Back".

In 1969

In its tenth year of operation, Motown continued to have large numbers of hit records. The loss of Holland-Dozier-Holland had not affected record sales as had been predicted, indeed many of the record buying public haven't noticed their departure.

William "Benny" Benjamin (Nickname: Papa Zita) the drummer with The Funk Brothers dies on the 20th April in Detroit Michigan. Jean Terrell signs as a solo artist with Motown, although her career at Motown would be as replacement for Diana Ross in The Supremes.

Gladys Knight introduces a new group from Gary, Indiana, next Bobby Taylor contacted Susanne de Passe, and she pestered Berry Gordy until he finally agreed to come and listen to the group. The Jackson 5 are signed to Motown and four of their first six singles, released between late 1969 and mid 1971, went to No1 on the pop charts, with the two that missed the No1 spot reaching No2. Berry Gordy credits the writing and production on Jackson 5 records to "The Corporation", which was a team consisting of Berry Gordy, Freddie Perren, Deke Richards and Fonzie Mizell.

Motown established the Rare Earth label to issue white psychedelic rock music and other alternatives to R&B. The label was handled by the West Coast offices of Motown, Rare Earth also was the name the first group signed to the label; their first album contained a twenty-minute version of The Temptations' hit, "Get Ready" that was also produced by Norman Whitfield. The Rare Earth label was also used for material leased from EMI in England, including the Pretty Things and Love Sculpture.

Motown acquired the distribution rights to the Chisa Label, which was founded by Hugh Masekela and Stewart Levine. Shorty Long, the solo artist, dies in a boating accident on the Detroit River.

Motown had 12 singles in the Top 10, with "I Can't Get Next to You" by The Temptations, "Someday We'll Be Together" by Diana Ross and The Supremes and "I Want You Back" by The Jackson 5 reaching No1.

In 1970

Kiki Dee becomes the first white UK artist to be signed by Motown. The final

Kiki Dee.

performance of Diana Ross and The Supremes occurred at the Frontier Hotel in Las Vegas, which was recorded and issued as an album. Jean Terrell replaced Diana Ross as lead singer of Diana Ross and The Supremes.

Motown became more conscious of its roots by establishing a new subsidiary label called Black Forum in 1970, releasing spoken word records by Dr. Martin Luther King, Jnr., Stokely Carmichael and black poets Langston Hughes and Margaret Danner. The management of Chisa, VIP, and Rare Earth labels are transferred to Motown's West Coast office.

Tammi Terrell loses her battle against a brain tumour and dies in March. Berry Gordy and Sammy Davis Jnr form the Ecology label, and Stevie Wonder and Syreeta Wright marry in Detroit.

Six of the 14 Motown singles that reached the Top 10 went to No1, including for the first time (for Motown), "War" by Edwin Starr, one of their more politically motivated songs.

In 1971

The Spinners leave Motown for Atlantic Records; however G C Cameron stays at Motown, Motown increases TV production, producing "Diana!" a television special with Diana Ross, and "Going' Back to Indiana", a Jackson 5 special cartoon series and Diana Ross marries Robert Silberstein in Las Vegas. The "New" Supremes with Jean Terrell on lead vocals perform for the first time on the "The David Frost Show".

The Loucye Gordy Wakefield Memorial Fund is established after a "The Sterling Ball" held at the Gordy Mansion in Detroit. A new subsidiary was established called Mowest and the first release was "What the World Needs Now Is Love b/side Abraham, Martin, and John" The Mowest label was controlled by the West Coast office of Motown and was used for talent developed by that office.

Berry Gordy with Martin Luther King in a publicity handout re-produced in the Detroit Free Press.

Michael Jackson's first solo release "Got To Be There" is issued, Marvin Gaye is given creative control of his recordings, and the first fruits is the "What's Going On" album, for which he wrote, produced, sang and played most of the instruments. "What's Going On" is acknowledged as one of the greatest albums ever made.

Stevie Wonder reaches twenty one and he renegotiated his contract to give him complete creative control of his music, with total artistic control of his albums, as well as the rights to his own songs. Stevie Wonder releases two albums under this arrangement, "Where I'm Coming From" and "Music of My Mind". Stevie's next two albums, "Talking Book" and "Innervisions", would add to his musical innovations. Rev Martin Luther King's speech "Why I Oppose The War In Vietnam" issues on the Black Forum label wins a Grammy Award for best spoken work recording.

Motown has 11 singles reach the Top 10 with just one No1 "Just My Imagination (Running Away with Me)" by The Temptations.

In 1972

As the Los Angeles offices continued to grow and the Detroit headquarters are become smaller, a company newsletter in March 1972, stated, "There are no plans at present to phase out the Detroit operations, as many rumours suggest". However, in June Motown announced that it was closing its Detroit offices and moving its headquarters to Los Angeles. Berry Gordy agrees to Esther Gordy Edwards staying in Detroit to manage the "Hitsville" building. Many Motown fans believe the company's heart and soul was lost when it abandoned Detroit, they believe its most creative days were the 13 years from 1959 to 1972.

The last Motown group or solo artist to record in "Hitsville Studio A" are The Commodores, with the album "Machine Gun", although not issued until 1974, this remains the last commercial recording undertaken there.

Suzanne de Passe becomes Corporate Director of the new Creative Production Division, The Commodores are signed to Motown, primarily as an opening act for The Jackson 5, The Four Tops leave Motown for Dunhill records and Smokey Robinson introduces Billy Griffin as his replacement while on The Miracles farewell tour.

The film "Lady Sings The Blues" staring Diana Ross, premiers, it receives an Academy Award nomination for her portrayal of Billie Holiday. Somewhat of a "down" year for Motown with only 4 singles reaching the pop Top 10, however, two of them did go to No1: "Papa Was a Rollin' Stone" by The Temptations and "Ben" by Michael Jackson.

In 1973

Berry Gordy resigned as President of Motown Records to become Chairman of the Board of Motown Industries, which included the record, motion picture, television and publishing divisions and Ewart Abner II, a Motown Vice President becomes President of Motown Records. Motown is now the number one black owned business in the US.

"Papa Was A Rollin' Stone" wins three Grammy Awards; these are recognised as Motown's first Grammy awards. Paul Williams from The Temptations is found not far from "Hitsville" after committing suicide and Jermaine Jackson marries Hazel Gordy in Beverley Hills. Stevie Wonder's new album, called "Innervisions", is released and wins five Grammy awards.

Motown had five No1 pop singles in the year, including, "Let's Get It On" by Marvin Gaye, "Keep on Trucking" by Eddie Kendricks, "Touch Me In the Morning" by Diana Ross and "You Are the Sunshine of My Life" and "Superstition" by Stevie Wonder.

In 1974

Stevie Wonder's new album titled "Fulfillingness' First Finale", became the No1 album within three weeks of its release and also won five Grammy's.

Motown formed a country subsidiary label called Melodyland and signed TG Sheppard, Pat Boone, Dorsey Burnette and Ronnie Dove among others. A legal dispute over the label name Melodyland arose in 1976 and the name was changed to Hitsville.

The Commodores had their first album released, titled "Machine Gun". The album was the last commercial recording from "Hitsville Studio A" It went on to become a gold record in five countries. The Commodores went on to become Motown's best selling act during the 1970's, for the period of 1974 to 1980, they averaged two million album sales per year.

Marvin Gaye undertakes a US tour, the first since Tammi Terrell had collapsed in his arms seven years previously. Only four Motown singles reached the Top 10 and only Stevie Wonder's "You Haven't Done Nothing" reached the No1 spot.

In 1975

Stevie Wonder receives the five Grammy Awards for the album "Fulfillingness First Finale",

The Commodores.

Smokey Robinson comes out of a two year period of retirement to perform in Los Angeles and "The Jackson 5" leave Motown for Epic having to sign as "The Jacksons" as Motown held the rights to the name. Jermaine Jackson, (who had married Berry Gordy's daughter), stayed with Motown as a solo artist, Randy Jackson replaces him.

Ewart Abner resigned as President of Motown Records and Berry Gordy temporarily replaces him. Barney Ales, a former Vice President of the company (who had stayed in Detroit), rejoined Motown, with the purchase of the Prodigal Label. During the year, Diana Ross starred in her second movie, "Mahogany" which was not as well received as "Lady Sings the Blues".

A low point in Motown history, as only one Motown release "Boogie on Reggae Woman" by Stevie Wonder made the Top 10.

In 1976

Stevie Wonder releases the "Songs In the Key of Life" album, which enters the pop charts at No1 and the album wins four more Grammy Awards. Berry Gordy and Mike Curb formed a new country label named MC, which inherited many of the same artists that were on Melodyland/Hitsville, and Florence Ballard, one of the original members of The Supremes, dies in Detroit from cardiac arrest aged only thirty two.

The fortunes of the company rebounded with six Motown releases reaching the Top 10, including two hits by The Commodores. Three of the company's releases reached No1, including "Love Hangover" and "Do You Know Where You're Going To?" by Diana Ross and "Love Machine (Part 1)" by The Miracles.

Between 1977 to 1979

Motown had three No1 pop hits, "Sir Duke" and "I Wish" by Stevie Wonder, and "Got to Give It Up (Part 1)" by Marvin Gaye, two singles by The Commodores make the Top 10. Marvin Gaye and Anna Gordy Gaye are divorced and The Temptations leave Motown for Atlantic records, Louis Price replaces Dennis Edwards as lead singer.

Diana Ross and Rob Silberstein are divorced and Motown starts production on the remake of the film "The Wizard Of Oz" to be called "The Wiz", staring Diana Ross and Michael Jackson. The Supremes officially dis-banded following a farewell tour, Suzanne de Passe becomes Vice-President of Motown Industries, and Berry Gordy IV becomes Vice-President of the Creative Division.

In 1978, Smokey Robinson produces the film "Big Time" along with a sound track to the film, Berry Gordy Snr dies in November 1978, and the major stars at Motown record a tribute single "Pops We Love You".

The only No1 hit in 1979 was The Commodores' recording of "Still", with "Three Times a Lady" and "Sail On", the group had the most Top 10 singles successes for the label, with only "Send One Your Love" by Stevie Wonder reaching the Top 10 in that year. Berry Gordy Snr's autobiography "Movin' Up" is published and Rick James is signed to the Gordy label and his first album "Come and Get It" eventually went on to sell 2 million copies.

In the 1980's

Stevie Wonder begins his campaign to have Martin Luther King's birthday declared a holiday in 1980, and in that year Jay Lasker becomes President of Motown Records. In 1981, Marvin Gaye starts a two year exile in Europe, staying, firstly in London, before settling in Ostend, Belgium. Georgeanna Tillman passes away from Sickle Cell Anaemia in the same year. Rick James issues his breakthrough album in 1981 "Street Songs", which sold over three million copies.

Hubert Johnson, a former member of The Contours, commits suicide in 1981, followed by one of the biggest shocks at Motown, Diana Ross leaves and signs with RCA records. The No1 hits for that same year include, "Endless Love" a duet by Diana Ross and Lionel Richie, "Being With You" by Smokey Robinson and "Oh No" by The Commodores.

In 1982, another big name leaves Motown with Columbia Records signing Marvin Gaye and Lionel Richie starts his solo career at Motown, by formally leaving The Commodores. The No1 hit for Motown is "Truly" by Lionel Richie.

In 1982, Motown went to a consolidated numbering system for all albums released on the three remaining active labels, Motown, Gordy and Tamla, starting with Motown 6000ML by Bettye Lavette. In addition to the 3 major labels, Motown also released albums in the 6000 series on the Latino label, which was Motown's attempt at a Hispanic label.

By 1983, Lionel Richie had become Motown's biggest star with the No1 singles, "All Night Long" and "You Are" and Motown purchase the back catalogue of Hi

records, its most well known artist is Al Green. Motown sign the Mary Jane Girls for the Gordy label, most of their material is produced by Rick James. In May, the NBC TV broadcast the concert to celebrate 25 years of Motown called "Motown 25: Yesterday, Today and Forever" and Motown launches the Morocco label, shortened from Motown Rock Company.

Motown continued to sell massive numbers of albums, culminating with Lionel Richie's 1984 "Can't Slow Down", which became the largest selling album in the company's history when it sold 10 million copies worldwide.

Lionel Richie.

In 1984, Motown have only two No1 hits, "I Just Called To Say I Love You" by

Stevie Wonder and "Hello" by Lionel Richie and Rockwell is signed to Motown in 1984, he releases "Somebody's Watching Me", Rockwell is Berry Gordy's son Kennedy.

In April 1984, Marvin Gaye dies from a gunshot wound; the gun had been fired by his father. Over the next few years, Motown struggles with cash flow problems, and apart from Lionel Richie and Stevie Wonder to a lesser extent, the hits have started to "dry up". Even though *Motown record label.*
Motown sold millions more albums during the 1970's and 1980's then it had in the 1960's. By 1986, Motown had failed to adapt to the latest trends in black music, such as rap and hip-hop. About the same time, MCA was turning into a black music powerhouse, and many in the industry thought that Motown was a spent force.

In June 1988, Berry Gordy sold Motown for $61 million to a partnership between MCA and Boston Ventures, with Berry Gordy retaining the ownership of the Jobete Publishing catalogue. Berry Gordy was always the consummate businessman. As good as he was as a judge of talent and hit songs; he was most of all an entrepreneur who transformed an $800 loan into the largest black owned business in United States history. In 1976, he pretty much summed it up when he said: "I earned 367 million dollars in 16 years. I must be doing something right!" Jheryl Busby, a music executive, was identified as the person to lead the revival of Motown by MCA records.

Fortunately for Jheryl Busby, Smokey Robinson's "One Heartbeat" album, released towards the end of Berry Gordy's reign, became one of Motown's most successful records of the 1980's, which gave MCA a bit of momentum after the purchase of the label. It also helped that one of the first releases, by the group "Boys 11 Men", was also a major hit.

In 1987, "Hitsville Studio A" was converted into the "Motown Historical Museum" with Esther Gordy Edwards as its first president. The building looks unremarkable except for a sign above the porch identifying it as "Hitsville USA" and a showcase in the front window, but this is where it all started.

Motown founder Berry Gordy lived in an upstairs room in the back of the house, while downstairs, in a small room (that started life as a garage) is the recording studio christened the "Snake Pit" by the musicians who recorded there. It served as the foundation to what would eventually become the Motown Record Company;

it will always be remembered for the music, musicians and artists it created during the 1960's. Never in history has one company produced so many top ten hits as Motown did during that marvellous decade. Today's commercials and movies are testimony to the great Motown songs of the 1960's, which are heard more than ever before.

CHAPTER THREE

NEW MOTOWN

Chapter Three: New Motown

In 1988, the unthinkable was being considered, Motown founder Berry Gordy was interested in selling the company he founded in 1959 in Detroit and had turned into one of the world's most successful music labels, a brand name whose old songs are more popular than ever.

One of Berry Gordy's last acts at Motown In 1988, was to bring Jheryl Busby in as the company's President and Chief Executive. Shortly after his appointment Berry Gordy sold the company for $61 million to a partnership between MCA Records and Boston Ventures. While at MCA, Jheryl Busby had helped discover and promote such groups as New Edition, and The Jets, and solo artists, Bobby Brown and Jody Watley. Jheryl Busby was credited with turning the company's black music division at MCA into the industry's black music sales leader. Jheryl Busby was confirmed by the new owners as Motown's President and Chief Executive, gaining a 10% ownership of Motown in the process, after a few years MCA sold to Polygram, and Motown was eventually bought by Universal.

Using the established stars, Lionel Richie, Smokey Robinson and Stevie Wonder, to "kick start the company". Jheryl Busby was also able to bring back Diana Ross to the label as both artist and executive He was now responsible for signing and developing new acts, including Boyz II Men, Queen Latifah, Another Bad Creation and Johnny Gill.

In mid 1988, Motown had success with The Temptations, whose album "Special" was on the charts for almost five months. The label signed an act with a formidable track record, the Pointer Sisters and if you include the DeBarge family and Berry Gordy's son Kenneth, who performed under the name Rockwell, Motown, did bring a few new acts that made a breakthrough in the 1980's.

Motown's Los Angeles Building.

Motown then had four No1 hits on the black music charts, double the number it had during the two previous years. The best news was that they didn't come from Motown's heavy hitters Smokey Robinson, Stevie Wonder or Diana Ross, but from new acts. Two were by the Boys 11 Men, a teenage quartet comparable to the Jackson 5, and New Edition, whose debut album sold a million copies; another was by the New York quartet "Today". The fourth marked a resurgence in the career of veteran Stacy Lattisaw, while Smokey Robinson's new single, "Everything You Touch", entered the Billboard Black Top 10.

By 1990, Motown had "turned the corner" with five songs reaching No1 on the R&B charts, and sales of the company's albums rising from the previous years No10 spot to No. 4 on the R&B album charts, Motown had twenty seven singles and eleven albums on the charts. Several albums, including those by Smokey Robinson and Johnny Gill, had advance orders of more than 300,000 copies, sales figures that were more solid than Motown had had in years.

The label was changing into a contemporary R&B label, hiring producers such as Teddy Riley and the team of L.A. and Babyface, and by recording rappers such as Wrecks-N-Effect. Sound tracks for the films "Do the Right Thing" and "House Party", which showcase rap acts such as Public Enemy, Force M.D.'s and L.L. Cool J, also have updated Motown's image.

As part of the 30th anniversary celebration, the company signed a deal with the makers of Pepsi-Cola to sponsor a new version of its once-popular Motor Town Revue, which sent a rotating package of new acts on the road.

In 1993, MCA sold the company to PolyGram. When Motown President Jheryl Busby's contract expired in late 1995, Andre Harrell got a call.

Andre Harrell to Motown

Andre Harrell was recruited to lead Motown Records with a remit to bring back the glory days and return to its musical roots. Andre also knew that somewhere, somehow, Motown's hit making machine had slipped away, leaving a faceless shell where the country's proudest record label once sat in "Hitsville Detroit". Here, in this studio-turned-museum, lies the rich legacy bequeathed to him when he was named Motown president.

This young business wizard, who led Motown into its fifth decade, thought he could bring the magic back. His bosses thought he could too, paying him a reported $20 million a year to do so. Detroit was justifiably elated when Harrell publicised plans to open a Motown office in Detroit. Motown's Main Headquarters did move to New York from Los Angeles. Andre Harrell made no apologies for tearing pages from the old Motown book. Andre did try to reinstate Berry Gordy's system.

Andre Harrell hired a slew of talent scouts, moving the emphasis from "Motown Cafes" back to records. He was looking to revise the Berry Gordy assembly-line system, with in-house choreographers, artist development specialists, and vocal coaches, even a charm school. Andre Harrell tried to blast his way into the hearts of black fans, but none scored the sort of crossover success that made Motown an international name.

"We're just going to make music that's a little more upbeat in spirit, not as dark, with images that are a little friendlier across the board", he stated. "Music that's African-American based, but very pop, without selling out the music, basically what Berry Gordy did".

However, it did not work out; Andre Harrell was replaced by George Jackson, the flamboyant young executive who led Motown for two rocky years.

George Jackson became the next President for Motown

The next President and CEO for Motown was George Jackson, with a new roster of exciting stars and one of the richest catalogues in popular music. George Jackson was a film and TV executive that helped produce such projects as the "House Party" series. "I have always been inspired by the entrepreneurial brilliance of Berry Gordy, the legacy of Motown and the classic foundation it was built upon".

The music business was still sceptical. Motown has struggled to find acts to support Boyz II Men on the charts. George Jackson did try to guide Motown Records into the 21st century, hoping to establish it once again as a leader in today's competitive environment. Sadly, George died of a heart attack in February 2000 aged 42.

Kedar Massenburg follows George Jackson

In January 1999 the appointment of rising R&B executive Kedar Massenburg to president was announced. Kedar Massenburg and his vice President KoJo Bentil, Kedar Massenburg brought to Motown what is now referred to as "Neo-Soul".

This style of music takes you back to the days of rhythm and blues, and acoustic instrumentation. The Temptations jumped back on the hit scene by selling over a million copies, and receiving a Grammy for the "Phoenix Rising" album. Kedar Massenburg brought in artists such as Brian McKnight, Erycka Badu, and newcomer India Arie (who has also recorded with John Cougar Mellencamp). Kedar Massenburg was part of the new generation at Motown looking at the "new territory" in the music scene, and seemed to be successful at getting back to the basics of Motown music.

Kedar Massenburg was replaced by Sylvia Rhone

In 2005, Kedar Massenburg was replaced by Sylvia Rhone, former CEO of Elektra Records. Motown's current roster still include R&B singers India Arie, Erykah Badu, plus new artists, Mya, Kem, Yummy Bingham, pop singer Lindsay Lohan, reggae singers Damian and Stephen Marley, and rappers Trick Trick and Nick Cannon.

Universal/Motown: 1999 - present

By 1998, Motown had added stars such as 702, Brian McKnight, and Erykah Badu to its roster. In December of 1998, PolyGram was acquired by Seagram, and Motown was folded into the Universal Music Group. Ironically, Seagram had purchased Motown's former parent MCA in 1995, as such Motown was in effect reunited with many of its MCA corporate siblings (Seagram had in fact, hoped to build a media empire around Universal, and started by purchasing PolyGram). Universal briefly considered shutting the floundering label, but instead decided to restructure it.

Diana Ross, Smokey Robinson, Stevie Wonder and The Temptations had remained with the label since its early days (although both Diana Ross and The Temptations each recorded for other labels for several years). Diana Ross left Motown from 1981 to 1988 but returned in 1989 and stayed until 1999, Smokey Robinson left the label briefly in 1999, and The Temptations in 2004. Stevie Wonder is today the only artist from Motown's "classic" period still on the label. Modern Motown releases feature a new stylized "M" logo for the label; reissues of classic Motown material continue to use the mod "M" logo first introduced in 1965.

Future Developments

The G M Renaissance Centre in downtown Detroit has now been opened for approximately two years, incorporating restaurants, car museum, entertainment complex and riverside walks etc. The references to the historical link to music and cars in Detroit are there for all to see.

The historical museum "Hitsville USA" on West Grand Blvd still draws up to 100,000 visitors a year and is a major tourist attraction.

Motown stars to make it big in Advertising

Motown has agreed to an advertising deal between a dozen of its artists and such companies as Gap Inc., Sears, Heineken, Hanes, Verizon, AT&T and Haagen-Dazs. You will see Bryan McKnight showing off jeans, The Temptations slurping down ice cream and Erykah Badu slugging back Heinekens.

Financially, the company is in the black for the first time in more than a decade. Motown is again receiving Grammy nominations for its work.

The Influence of Motown on Today's Music

Motown is not just about music. It's about style and showmanship as well as good music with catchy lyrics. Back in the 1960's, when Motown was at the pinnacle of its success, some of these artists were part of that special "Motown Sound" groups like The Temptations, The Four Tops, and The Supremes. There were solo artists like the musical genius Stevie Wonder, Smokey Robinson and the late Marvin Gaye. These artists defined a generation (or two) with the sound, style, dancing etc; this influence can still be heard in much of the music produced today. How many times on radio, television or in the cinema do you hear references to the "Motown Sound"? All of these artists, as well as others from the Motown family, have influenced the way music and the styles of the groups are presented to us today.

Boyz II Men

This group is the best illustration of artists from the 1990's that were influenced by the Motown group of the 1960's. Boyz II Men take their lead from The Temptations and The Four Tops, they lined up together next to each other so that they could all do their dances and sing their harmonies together. They also dress the same as each other on stage, by doing this, no one member stands out from the other person on stage. Their dress is also very neat and clean-cut. They have all had major success singing slow songs, whether its "Baby I Need Your Loving" by The Four Tops or "My Girl" by The Temptations, or "End of the Road" by the Boyz 11 Men, the slow song has made the biggest impression for them in the music industry.

Boyz II Men recorded "End of the Road" for the soundtrack to the film "Boomerang". This song was written by Babyface, it topped the US charts for 13 weeks, beating the old record of 11 weeks set by Elvis Presley's "Don't be Cruel" and "Hound Dog" in 1956 for the longest-running No1 of the rock era.

Babyface

Many believe that he is the best song-writer/producer of all time (I'm not so sure). My vote would always go to Smokey Robinson; Smokey Robinson was musically the most influential artist in regards to establishing the "Motown Sound".

Babyface has written for just about every artist around today. Smokey Robinson's ability to write for another artist and make it sound like it was their song is something Babyface does as well. They both have had greater success writing and producing for other artists than themselves. I agree Babyface is an excellent writer and producer, but Babyface wasn't the first and "Smokey" to my mind, led the way for the singer/songwriter model.

En Vogue

They bring the influence of the "Motown Sound" to their music and their stage act as well. They of course don't take their lead from The Four Tops or The Temptations, but instead they follow the lead of The Supremes. En Vogue's decade was the 1990's with love songs like "Don't Let Go" and "I'll Never Get Over You (Getting Over Me)". These songs are not just love songs, they sing about women's feelings, emotions etc, and these were all started by the songs of The Supremes.

The lyrics of En Vogue are obviously a little bit "stronger" from a woman's point of view because the times have changed since the 1960's. Their styles are also very similar in their act. The Supremes were always known as a group that was glamorous and sexy with their long glittered dresses and their hair always perfectly set. En Vogue brings that look of sex appeal up to date in their act. They are all very attractive women who wear very flattering outfits when they perform on stage or in their music videos.

Sampling

We often find ourselves turning on the radio and hearing a song that maybe we never heard before but yet we somehow recognise the tune or the beat or even the chorus that is played in the background. This happens because we have heard that part of the song played in a song that was released in another time by another artist.

Motown continues its strong influence in today's music because many of the biggest songs on the radio are being taken from older Motown songs. A good example of this is in the summer of 1997 a song by the late Notorious B.I.G. "Mo' Money, Mo'

Problems" uses a sample from a Diana Ross song "I'm coming out". Even more recently, Puff Daddy wanted to pay tribute to Motown by re-doing The Jackson 5's "I want you back" with a more hip-hop beat of course, for the 40th Anniversary of Motown.

Another example was the Coolio song for the movie Dangerous Minds, "Gangsta's Paradise" he sampled the Stevie Wonder song "Past time Paradise" in order to inform the people of all the hardships which the people living in poverty were facing everyday.

New Edition

When they first came onto the music scene in the early 1980's, they were the Jackson 5 recreated. They were young boys who could dance and sing songs. They even admitted to wanting to be like The Jackson 5 when they first started. If you listen to the songs "Candy Girl" or "Popcorn Love", you could very easily mistake Ralph Tresvant's voice for a young Michael Jackson.

Motown Forever

Motown is influencing the music that you are listening to today. Put on an old Temptations' CD then go ahead and listen, because you never know if you're going to hear that song come up again on a "Puff Daddy" or a "Blackstreet Boy's" album.

Whether you listen to this music or not, you have definitely heard these Motown songs before, they are timeless classics. They are after all, the forefathers of R&B music. There probably isn't one R&B artist today that wasn't influenced by Motown and the "Motown Sound".

CHAPTER FOUR

MOTOWN STARS ""THE LIFE AND TIMES""

Chapter Four: Motown Stars "The Life and Times"

The list of individuals in this book is not intended as an exhaustive list of those associated with Motown; in particular the Detroit Years 1959 to 1972, indeed the publisher would like to encourage you write to with any suggestion for extra entries. Therefore, the list of stars and Motown employees contained within this book is not the ultimate list of those responsible for "The Motown Sound".

I hope this book revives your memories of Motown, gets you up to date on your favourite stars (mine being Marvin Gaye), surprising for a label that had prided itself on being in style, there's plenty of sex, drugs and rock and roll. There's the odd bizarre death, and some interesting starts and finishes to some of the star's careers.

I now realised that this book was started only few years after Berry Gordy started Motown in January 1959. In 1964 I started listening to this music from America that was super cool, with the kids I hung around with. I really fancied myself as a "Mod", with Scooter (complete with all the accessories), Parker, a regular visitor to the pubs and clubs which played "Soul Music" in the North of England. I may have listened to other labels and artists, Stax, Atlantic, Aretha Franklin and Otis Redding. I have also been turned onto the Philly sound of Nile Rogers and Bernard Edwards. I even like some of the current R&B stuff as well.

I started to put pen to paper about seven or eight years ago, but the roots of this book are nights at the "Blackpool Mecca Northern Soul Night", The Spinning Wheel in Manchester, Wigan Casino, Hole in the Wall and Mecca in Bradford. I then, started to keep lots of information of this "new music" (underground as it was then, it sounds so "twee" now) this then formed my opinion on the Motown, Soul Music etc in general and eventually led to this book.

My first actual visit to Detroit was not until June 2008 when I visited the Motown Historical "Studio A" and first met Billy Wilson (although over the years we had many telephone calls and emails). Incredibly, I ended up at the funeral of Ben Crosby a famous son of Detroit and realised what special people Detroiters are, the warmth just shone through and I personally thank Kiley for her invitation to the funeral.

This book couldn't have happened without the support of all the individuals who contributed to this book. My visits to Detroit have left a lasting memory of wonderful people always ready and willing to help. Who would have thought when I was sixteen that I would be standing in "Hitsville Studio A" on this "hallowed ground" where my music was made?

To those individuals who provided the essential ingredients of checking that information was correct and where appropriate, supplying stories and photos, big thanks to you all. You are all too numerous to mention, but you know who you are.

This chapter concentrates on the contribution these individuals make to the "Motown Story", with a brief description of their lives, before and after Motown if relevant, we ask questions like, what happened to Berry Gordy, The Temptations, Martha Reeves? Are Holland-Dozier-Holland still around, is Stevie Wonder still making music? If you are interested in this book, I bet you have, like me a great love for this label, with the memories the music brings, yes, it only seems like yesterday since we were dancing and singing to this music, I hope this book takes you back to good days, when a particular piece of Motown music is played and life was good and uncomplicated, as Ewart Abner said when being interviewed in the 1990's as to why Motown has a place in so many hearts, "We started school with this music, we had our first girlfriends or boyfriends, we had our first jobs, we became engaged, we married, we had children, in some case, we divorced, we started again, and all the time the soundtrack was Motown music, this music is engrained into two generations of people, and still being listen to by the next generation".

As a reflection of the enduring appeal and perceived relevance that Motown stars still have, what better example could there be than the invited appearance of Stevie Wonder, celebrating on the eve of Barack Obama's inauguration ceremony. Many people believe that one of the many reasons why Barack Obama captured the hearts and minds of America was his wholehearted embrace of black music culture. It was he who chose Stevie Wonder to join Bruce Springstein in the "The We Are One" concert held on the eve of the Presidential Inauguration. Like us he had grown up listening and being moved by Stevie Wonder's incomparable talent. (Apparently Stevie Wonder's rendering of "Signed Sealed Delivered I'm Yours" was Obama's unofficial anthem) this represents how far the black artist has travelled in the last fifty years.

Regarding the changing fortunes of another "Child of Motown" have we seen the end of Michael Jackson's career? Whether this is the case, or a revival of fortune will occur based on his performances booked in London for the summer of 2009, remains to be seen. What is certain is that black musicians remain at the forefront of the music industry.

With fifty individuals in this book I have suggested tracks that I associate with the individuals concerned, I have gone for the best track (in my opinion), not necessarily the greatest hits of the individual concerned. Listen to these tracks while reading the book, and don't just listen to the song, look out for the James Jamerson's bass line, the strings of the Detroit Symphony Orchestra, the wonderful lyrics telling the story of love, pain, happiness and sorrow, the stunning arrangements, production techniques that were way ahead of their time, but most of all listen to some of the best music ever produced.

Ewart Abner

Known as Ab Born 11th May 1923 in Chicago, Illinois - Died 27th December 1997 in Los Angeles, California

Motown Connection: Executive Assistant to Motown Records Founder Berry Gordy-Executive-Vice-President of Jobete Music Company Incorporated and Stone Diamond Music Corporation-Vice-Chairman of the Motown Historical Museum in Detroit Michigan-Vice-President of International Management (Motown Artist Management Organisation)-Personal and Business Manager of Stevie Wonder.

Ewart G Abner Jnr was an influential music industry executive, who released the first Beatles records (in the United States), negotiated the landmark sale of the Jobete music catalogue to EMI Music. Ab, as his friends and colleagues

Ad centre with Art Sheridan and Jimmy Bracken.

know him, began his career in the record industry in Chicago in 1948 pressing the "old style" 78 rpm. In 1950 (along with Art Sheridan) Ab started Chance Records; featuring his two newly discovered groups The Flamingos and The Moonglows.

In 1954, he joined Vee-Jay Records as General Manager, eventually becoming President and a Partner at Vee-Jay. At Vee Jay, Abner was credited with developing such major artists as The Staple Singers, the Four Seasons, The Dells, Gene Chandler, Jerry Butler, The Impressions, John Lee Hooker, and Jimmy Reed. The label was a staple of the "Northern Soul" scene and many of the label's records became highly collectable.

Ab founded and headed ARMADA (American Record Manufacturing and Distributing Association), one of the record industry's first professional organisations. After hearing him speak at a music industry convention Berry Gordy brought Ab to Motown in May 1967. In his memoir, "To Be Loved", Berry Gordy writes expansively about "Ab", whom he describes as a man whose speaking skills "electrified the audience with passion, conviction and guts. I knew that I would always respect that man".

From 1967 to 1975, Ab served at Motown in a variety of positions. Ab's first position was Vice President of International Management, where he was instrumental in directing the careers of Marvin Gaye, Diana Ross and The Supremes, The

Temptations, Smokey Robinson and The Miracles, The Four Tops, Stevie Wonder, The Jackson 5 and many other Motown Stars. In 1971, he became Vice President of Marketing, and in 1973 he became President of Motown Records.

After leaving Motown in 1975, for 10 years Ab became the Personal and Business Manager of Stevie Wonder. He organised Stevie Wonder sponsored marches, one notable march was the one to Washington, D.C in support of legislation, to establish a national holiday, in honour of Dr. Martin Luther King Jnr. After his work with Stevie Wonder he re-joined Berry Gordy as his Executive Assistant at the Gordy Company in Los Angeles.

Abner was active in a variety of civil rights and human rights organisations and campaigns, including Black Music Association, Braille Institute, Hands Across America, NAACP, NARAS, NOW, Operation Push, SCLC, Urban League, and We Are the World.

Numerous awards and honours, including an ACE Award, a NAACP Image Award, and his induction into America's Music and Entertainment Hall of Fame have acknowledged his contributions.

Ab was married to Olivia Watson Abner for 32 years; his children with Olivia were called Tony and Allison, his children from earlier marriages were called Billie "Nitchka" Piantino, Ewart G. Abner III, Diane Patterson, Casey Abner and Chemin Ware.

Born in Detroit, Michigan

Motown Connection: First National Promotional Director of Tamla Records, Motown Records, all of it's affiliated labels, and Jobete Publishing Company - First person of non-African American descent to work at Motown.

Al was raised in a Jewish sect of a polish community in Hamtramck, Michigan a suburb of Detroit. Al was a brilliant youngster, and graduated at the age of 15 from high school. He worked a number of jobs throughout his teen years, though he had to lie about his age to get employment in the neighbourhood; he eventually went to work for Handlemans Distribution (record distributor), and the McCann-Erickson advertising firm.

Al was a fan of Black Music and had already written articles in the Detroit Tribune (a local Black newspaper in Detroit). The newspaper allowed him to create his own community and music stories and he called his articles "The Central Chatterbox."

In 1959, Al went for an interview (along with a friend) to 1719 Gladstone, the home of Berry Gordy and Raynoma Lyles (who would later become Berry Gordy's second wife), the friend was being interviewed for a $15 per hour chauffeur's position. The company was the "The Rayber Music Writing Company", where Berry Gordy and Raynoma Lyles were making a living by charging people to record their songs in their studio. The "Rayber Music Writing Company", was a pre Motown venture before their move to West Grand Boulevard to open "Hitsville Studio A". Although Al's friend was not hired, he

Al Abrams.

persuaded Berry Gordy (although Berry Gordy was hesitant at first), to offer Al a position with the company, Berry Gordy gave him a record from one of his lesser know labels Zelman Records (if you had $100 anyone could record on this label). The artist on the label was a Yugoslavian immigrant living in Windsor, Canada that used the name Mike Powers. The name of the song was entitled "Teenage Sweetheart." Berry Gordy told Al that if he could get that record played on the radio he would hire him.

Al took the record to one of two recognized Black music radio stations WCHB (the other being WJLB) and offered the record to DJ Larry Dixon. Al convinced the station to play the record, while during that time Berry Gordy just happened to be driving in his car and listening to the station! Berry Gordy staying "true to his word" offered him a position at Motown, making him the first non-African-American of Jewish descent to work at what would become The Motown Record Corporation.

Al left Motown in 1966. He eventually ended up working with Stax Records, with Florence Ballard (after she left the Supremes) and Holland-Dozier-Holland on their newly formed Invictus Records, after they left Motown to start their own label.

Born in Detroit, Michigan

Motown Connection: Head of Marketing and Promotion - Vice President and General Manager of Motown - President of Motown - Motown Songwriter - Motown Producer.

Barney was a key person who helped Motown to break the "colour" barrier in the 1960's. Barney helped Motown to cover the white record market, without compromising the company's music style. Barney started as the head of sales for Motown, and for a period of time had an all white marketing staff to help promote Motown music, which did cause some concern with other Motown employees.

Barney started in the music business in 1955 for Capitol Records as a stockman, eventually becoming a systems branch manager, then promotion manager. Barney then moved to Warner Brothers as branch manager in Detroit in 1958. Barney met Berry Gordy while distributing records for his sister's label Del-Phi (Owned by Gwen Gordy and Harvey Fuqua) in Detroit. Before meeting Berry Gordy Barney had known Harvey Fuqua (who was dating and would eventually marry Gwen) for many years. After this meeting Berry Gordy asked Barney to hang on to talk to him, the offer was to distribute a "Tamla Record" by Smokey Robinson. The next offer was to come to the studio and both Berry Gordy and Barney "hit it off" instantly. After about five months Berry asked Barney to join Motown and as they say "The Rest Is History" this was now 1960.

Barney was instrumental in the purchase of Ric Tic and Golden World records by Motown. The record label "Prodigal" was owned by Barney using Motown as its distributor, eventually "Prodigal" would become part of Motown. Other record labels such as "Rare Earth" were managed by Barney, but owned by Motown. Barney was known for his stern approach in asking distributors to pay on time for Motown, and was therefore instrumental in securing Motown's survival

L to R: Marvin Gaye and Barney Ales.

Barney was also a good friend of Mickey Most, the UK record producer who was one of a very rare breed who recorded in "Studio A" while not employed by Motown.

In the sixties it was rumoured that Barney had connections to the "Mafia", although the FBI was called into check these rumours out, no evidence was ever found to confirm the rumours. Likewise, a rumour that Barney actually owned Motown was just that, a rumour.

However, Barney (along with other Motown's top executives), kept their artists and musicians contractually tied to the Motown, to such a degree, that the artist and musicians were always looking over their shoulders to make sure "Motown spies" weren't lurking. Barney participated in this "spying" to safeguard Motown's unique "formula" from being copied by other record labels by using only Motown's artist and musicians. Motown executives didn't want the "formula" to be interrupted through "bootleg sessions" being undertaken by their artists or musicians.

Eventually Barney moved on to be Vice-President and General Manager of Motown. When Motown left Detroit in 1972, Barney had no intention of moving to California with Berry Gordy; although, the separation was amicable and Berry Gordy asked him to stay on in Detroit, Barney eventually left Motown only to come back in the mid 1970's and continued as President of the company, until Jay Lasker replaced him in 1979. Barney now lives in the Florida area.

Born Richard Allen on the 12th August 1932 in Memphis, Tennessee - Died 30th June 2002 in Detroit, Michigan

Motown Connection: Drummer/member of The Funk Brothers (Motown In House Band).

Richard provided the relentless beat on The Vandellas' "Heatwave", The Supremes' No1 single "Baby Love", (a hit in both the USA and the UK) and also played on Marvin Gaye's "How Sweet It Is To Be Loved By You", The Four Tops' "I Can't Help Myself", The Temptations' "The Way You Do The Things You Do" and "Get Ready", Stevie Wonder's "Signed, Sealed, Delivered, I'm Yours" and hundreds of other tracks.

Richard moved to Michigan in the mid-Fifties. Richard worked at the factory of the motor components' manufacturers AC Delco in Flint before relocating to Detroit a couple of years later. Richard played drums in various rhythm and blues and jazz bands that performed in night-clubs around Detroit, places like the Flame Showbar, the Bluebird and Watts Mozambique, where he caught the eye of Benny Benjamin, Motown's original drummer.

From 1961, Richard became Benjamin's understudy and his eventual replacement after Benjamin's death in 1969. Throughout the 1960's, the tiny Studio A at 2648 West Grand Boulevard (affectionately known as "The Snake pit") saw round the clock recording. With three drummers (Uriel Jones completed the trio) taking it in shifts to lay down the backing tracks for the Motown producers and arrangers. The assembly-line approach to recording favoured by Motown's founder Berry Gordy paid huge dividends for Motown, but meant House Band "The Funk Brothers" never got credited for their work, either on the record sleeve or to the record buying public. A documentary entitled "Standing in the Shadows of Motown" released in 2002, directed by Allan Slutsky, reunited session men like Richard and the guitarists Eddie Willis and Joe Messina to tell their story through archive footage and interviews.

Richard Allen acquired the nickname "Pistol" because of the way he hammered the snare drum to emphasize the "four on the floor" rhythm, which was such an integral part of the "Motown Sound". Like most of the session players, Richard only received flat fees of about $10 an hour.

The extent of each musician's involvement (and therefore Richard's involvement) and their exact contribution to each track is still emerging as Motown researchers check details from the original recording logs. The researchers are now including session details on The Temptations and Marvin Gaye anthologies, unfortunately, many of the musicians involved have since died, and the survivors can't receive royalties on these performances.

A sad twist for the majority of The Funk Brothers (including Richard), was when Berry Gordy relocated the Motown Company to Los Angeles in 1972, only James Jamerson's presence was deemed necessary. California had plenty of session musicians and none of The Funk Brothers got any redundancy or severance pay, just a note on the studio door saying: "Session Cancelled" and "Will Reschedule".

Motown never did reschedule and Richard started to play jazz sessions around Detroit well into his sixties. In 1972 he contributed to "Scorpio", the much-sampled Top 10 solo hit released by another Motown veteran Dennis Coffey.

The documentary film 'Standing in the Shadows of Motown', was released with a "Funk Brothers" soundtrack album which won two Grammy's in 2003.

Signature sound: would be the relentless beat on the Martha and The Vandellas hit "Heatwave".

Richard died after a long battle with cancer aged 69. Richard is survived by his wife Barbara and ten children.

Formed In Detroit, Michigan in 1959 Group Members: Louvain Demps, Jackie Hicks, Marlene Barrows, Anne Bogan and Pat Lewis

Motown Connection: Members of either the Rayber Singers or The Andantes (Motown Studio A Background/Session Singers).

Along with The Funk Brothers, a vital element of the "Motown Sound" unrecognised or credited by Motown until many years later. Their main contribution was made in the "Studio A", providing a consistency to the recording (similar to The Funk Brothers) for the artists at the time.

Like any new business, cash flow problems plagued Motown, Raynoma Liles, (a.k.a. Miss Ray) developed the Rayber Music Writing Company with Berry Gordy) as a remedy. Rayber, a combination of Ray's and Berry Gordy's first name (Raynoma would eventually become Berry Gordy's second wife), charged artists who wanted to make a record. They advertised on a local radio station and caught the ear of their first client, Louvain Demps.

Louvain would eventually sing as part of the Rayber background singers (which included Brian Holland, Sonny Sanders, Raynoma, and occasionally Gwendolyn Murray). Eventually, Jackie Hicks and Marlene Barrow (who had worked with Louvain on occasions), joined Motown and in early 1962 they were put with Louvain and Anne to form The Andantes .One of their first recordings was back up to Marvin Gaye on "Mr. Sandman". The Andantes also cut their own unreleased 45 record in 1964 on VIP (a division of Motown) "(Like a) Nightmare" b/side "If You Were Mine".

They were used extensively throughout the Motown sessions taking place in "Studio A" from The Marvelettes to soften their "roughness", to the Four Tops (from "Baby, I Need Your Loving" through to "Still Waters") to "give depth to the tracks". They also sang with Martha Reeves and the Vandellas on several records including "My Baby Loves Me" (interestingly The Four Tops were in the background singers on that record), and "I Should Be Proud".

The Andantes became the number one studio back up singers, in fact, the Andantes were so versatile in their singing structure, that The Andantes replaced the

Marvelettes on their last album "The Return Of The Marvelettes"; the only Marvelettes to sing on the recording was Wanda Rogers on lead vocals. Like the Funk Brothers, Motown's House Band, they "moonlighted" on other labels in Detroit and other cities while still at Motown.

As background singers Motown expected them to create a feel to a record, which The Andantes did on many records including, Mary Well's "My Guy", Stevie Wonder's "For Once In My Life". They were also expected to fill in on records, when members may have not been needed or wanted. They backed Diana Ross on "Love Child", and Martha Reeves on every Martha and The Vandellas' recording after Annette Beard left. Holland-Dozier-Holland used The Andantes to smooth The Marvelettes' infectious, but shaky harmony, they also used them on The Four Tops for the high end of a song, (a technique Thom Bell employed with The Detroit Spinners and his other groups in the 1970's).

Their smooth, quality, gospel/chorale sound was so valuable that Motown never gave them a chance to record on their own, (apart from the single "Like A Nightmare", which was never released). Motown didn't want the Andantes out promoting a record when Motown's studios operated around the clock.

UK producer Ian Levine recorded the Andantes under his Motorcity label in the early 1990's. The tracks include a remake of "Two Sides To Love", as well as The Fascinations' "Girls Are Out To Get You", "Hurricane", "Lightening Never Strikes Twice", and a new version of their ultra rare Motown single "Like A Nightmare". Levine Demps also recorded as a solo artist.

Motown had approximately 15,000 recordings in their Jobete catalogue from the Detroit era; it is suggested that The Andantes were on over 75% of the Motown recordings, either individually or as a group.

Anne Bogan sang lead on the Tamla single, "I'm Gonna Hold On Long As I Can" in 1968. In 1969 Anne also sang lead on The Marvelettes, "Everybody Knows (But You)" from the LP, "In Full Bloom".

Pat Lewis - Replaced Anne in 1965, but left a year later for a solo career at Solid Hit and Golden World Records. Pat was also a member of Isaac Hayes' Hot Buttered Soul group. Pat returned in 1975 until 1996 when Thelma Hopkins (of Tony Orlando and Dawn) replaced her.

Nicholas "Nick" Ashford Born 4th May 1943 in Fairfield, South Carolina (raised in Willow Run, Michigan) - Valerie Simpson Born 26th August 1948 Bronx, New York

Motown Connection: Part of In House Song Writing Team - In House Producer and Arranger - Background Vocalists for Motown.

Nick and Valerie met in New York, where they were members of a gospel group at the White Rock Baptist Church in Harlem. They began song writing together and joined the staff of Scepter/Wand Records, writing rhythm and blues hits for Chuck Jackson and Maxine Brown. In 1964, as Valerie and Nick, they recorded "I'll Find You" on Glover Records. Success came when they wrote a song called "Let's Go Get Stoned" recorded by Ray Charles in 1966. Immediately afterward's, Motown signed them as a staff song writing and production team.

Nicholas Ashford and Valerie Simpson's songs are better known as "Ashford and Simpson". The husband and wife song writing team has been responsible for an impressive string of chart-topping pop/soul and R&B hits, including "Reach Out and Touch Somebody's Hand" and "Ain't No Mountain High Enough", recorded by Diana Ross (but recorded by many other artists). Their fans will also know them as recording artists in their own right. Recording up to 12 albums already, including, "Stay Free", "Is It Still Good To You", "Street Opera", and their biggest hit, "Solid". Like the title of one of their biggest hits, their long-time professional and personal relationship is still a "solid one".

Employed at Motown starting around 1967 as a song writing and production team. Their first recording was with Marvin Gaye and Tammi Terrell, later they recorded their songs with Diana Ross. Ashford & Simpson acted as producers on the Diana Ross version of "Ain't No Mountain High Enough", while the Marvin Gaye and Tammi Terrell version was produced by Johnny Bristol and Harvey Fuqua.

Valerie recorded lead vocals on most of the 1969 Marvin Gaye and Tammie Terrell album "Easy", when Tammie was recovering from a malignant brain tumour. Valerie voice was so similar to Tammie's, that for decades nobody knew of the vocal replacement until the release of the 1985 David Ritz biography "Divided Soul: The Life and Times of Marvin Gaye", although Valerie Simpson is quoted as denying this in a book written by Tammi's sister Ludie Montgomery.

In 1973, they began recording together for Warner Brothers while continuing as songwriters for Motown. Nick and Valerie married in 1974 after working together for ten years professionally. As songwriters and producers, Nick and Valerie always longed to record their own songs. Motown didn't share that longing, so the couple left for Warner Bros., recording a string of hit singles and several albums, including three gold LPs, and in 1982 went to Capitol Records.

Their ability to produce and work successfully with other artists has kept the duo in demand as producers, leaving them very little time for their own projects. In between tours, the duo worked on a book and then a score of a Broadway musical. A major part of the couple's success is their ability to write songs that other artists adapt as their own.

Album Track: "You're All I Need To Get By", Marvin Gaye and Tammi Terrell.

Born 1934 in Philadelphia, Pennsylvania

Motown Connection: Percussionist/member of The Funk Brothers (Motown In House Band).

The son of a Domestic worker and father who was a labourer. His mother and father separated when Jack was at a young age, and was therefore raised by his mother with two other sisters and five brothers. Jack attended the same school as John Coltrane, the Grenoff School of Music, and was drafted into the Army in 1958.

Jack's first introduction to Motown was through Marvin Gaye, who in 1963 asked Jack (as part of The Charles Harris Trio) to join him on his US tour. After the tour Jack was invited back to "Hitsville" by Marvin and subsequently, to join the blossoming house band which would evolve into the "Funk Brothers".

Widely known as the percussionist for Motown Records' in-house Funk Brother's band during the 1960's and early 1970's. Jack is most famous for playing the tambourine on hundreds of Motown recordings. His definitive performance is on "War" by Edwin Starr; other notable songs Ashford played tambourine on include "Nowhere to Run" by Martha and The Vandellas, "You Can't Hurry Love" by The Supremes, "I Heard It Through the Grapevine" by Marvin Gaye, "Don't Leave Me This Way" by Thelma Houston, and many more. He also played vibes, shakers, and the marimba on the label's recordings, such as The Miracles' "Ooh Baby Baby".

After Motown Jack then recorded on Whitfield Records (Norman Whitfield left Motown to form his own label), playing on most of the recording. Jack was also employed in the publishing arm of Whitfield records. Times were hard in the 1980's with little session work available. However, recognition came in the shape of Allan Slutsky's documentary "Standing In The Shadows Of Motown" which re-established The Funk Brothers, and started the group touring again. Sadly Jack is one of the last remaining original Funk Brother's with us, Jack married Peggy White in 1954.

Signature sound: Marvin Gaye's "What's Going On" also listen to him using woodblock, vibes, and the oldest (and largest) tambourine in the world on many of the Motown hits.

Born in 1925 in Austin, Texas

Motown Connection: Musical Director - Music Arranger - Composer and Producer - Motown Artist/ Musician - Academy Award for his work on the 1972 film "Lady Sings The Blues" (A Motown Products Film).

Gil has worked as composer, producer and musical director for performers like Diana Ross and The Supremes, The Four Tops, The Temptations, Stevie Wonder, Marvin Gaye, The Jackson 5, Gladys Knight and many, many more, including non Motown artists Curtis Mayfield, Liza Minelli. Dizzy Gillespie, Miles Davis, Duke Ellington, Count Basie.

Leaving school at fifteen, Gil received a scholarship for a medical course (run by the Army), did two years of university always planning on finishing his medical scholarship and becoming a doctor, However, Gil dropped out university before he qualified. Gil then had numerous jobs including a waiter and busboy. However,

horn playing started to dominate Gil's life and became his career. Gil left Austin Texas when he was still 17 years old to pursue his musical career. Through his horn playing Gil did get to meet Harry James, and Louis Armstrong. Gil's next contact was Gene Krupa who recommended Gil to Lionel Hampton, which eventually led to Gil playing with Benny Goodman.

With his work at Motown, Gil became a highly influential figure and was in great demand being called the "24 hour man" because of the demand for his services. It was as musical director to the "Super Stars" at Motown that earned Gil a place in Motown History.

Eventually Gil got tired of the hectic music world in the USA, and settled in Australia in the early 1980's, (although he hadn't played trumpet professionally for 23 years), Gil started playing again on the Melbourne jazz scene.

Gil now lives quietly with his wife and two children near Mornington Peninsula in the outer suburbs of Melbourne, Australia.

Cholly Atkins

Born Charles Atkins aka as Pops or Cholly on the 13th September 1913 in Alabama. Died 19th April 2003 in Las Vegas, California

Motown Connection: Master Dancer - Head Choreographer for Motown – Teacher - Theatrical Director.

Most of Motown's acts had to attend the label's "artist development" program. Motown's talented choreographer Cholly gave each Motown act its own distinctive, polished, and synchronised on-stage moves. Working closely with Maxine Powell, (who taught the artists the finer arts of poise, manners, and social grace), Cholly created the "look" that many Motown Artists would take with them through out their careers.

Cholly was known as the "man with the moves". He began his professional career in 1929 as a singing waiter near Buffalo, New York. He met William Porter, another singing waiter and they formed a vaudeville-style song-and-dance act known as the Rhythm Pals. When the team folded in the late 1930's, Atkins' skills landed him a job dancing and choreographing acts for the renowned Cotton Club Boys, who were appearing with Bill Robinson in "The Hot Mikado" at the World's Fair.

In the early 1940's, Atkins teamed with singer and dancer Dottie Saulters and toured with the Mills Brothers, the Earl Hines Band, the Louis Armstrong Band and the Cab Calloway Review. In 1946, Atkins teamed with Charles "Honi" Coles and formed the "tap dancing" act of Atkins and Coles, which toured with the Count Basie, Cab Calloway, Lionel Hampton, Charlie Barnell and Billie Eckstine.

They worked solidly through the 1950's, but by the decade's end "tap dancing" became out of favour and took a sharp decline. However, in 1962, Cholly's dancing and coaching skills came to the attention of the Shaw and William Morris agencies of New York, which eventually led to the offer of becoming the staff choreographer for Motown, Cholly stayed with Motown from 1965 to 1971. Between 1953 and 1994 (before and after Motown) Cholly directed, staged, and choreographed acts for countless artists, including Smokey Robinson and The Miracles, Marvin Gaye, The Temptations, Supremes and Aretha Franklin. Cholly worked, mentored and knew Gladys Knight and The Pips even before they arrived at Motown, and remained firm friends.

Atkins and Coles.

He taught the artists to perform with rhythmic dance steps, turns and gestures drawn from the rich bedrock of American vernacular dance and, in doing so, created a new form of expression "vocal choreography" just watch The Temptations at the height of their popularity and you are watching Cholly's contribution to Motown and the wider entertainment world.

He has won numerous gold records for his choreography and in 1989 won a Tony for his choreography in "Black and Blue". In 1993, recognising his vast contributions to American culture, the National Endowment for the Arts awarded him its highest honour, a three year choreographer's fellowship to record his memoirs and to tour colleges and universities teaching vocal choreography as a dance genre. Master dancer, choreographer, teacher, and director, Cholly Atkins was the quintessential American dance artist.

Without doubt Cholly's contribution to American Culture has been extraordinarily significant. Cholly died in Las Vegas at the age of 89.

Bob Babbitt

Born Robert Kreinar in Pittsburgh, Pennsylvania

Motown Connection: Bassist/member of The Funk Brothers (Motown In House Band).

Bob is most famous for his work as a member of Motown Records' studio band, The Funk Brothers, from 1967 to 1972. Bob did simultaneous sessions with original Motown bassist James Jamerson (both together and at separate sessions). Over the course of his Motown career it is suggested that Bob played on over 200 Billboard Hot 100 Top 40 hits, for Motown and other related labels.

Bob was raised in Pittsburgh (a town renowned more for its steel-making than music), by Hungarian parents, Bob received classical training on upright bass, but at 15, inspired by early rhythm & blues hits like Bill Doggett's "Honky Tonk" and Red Prysock's "Hand Clappin", he began performing in local nightclubs. Two years later, after hearing his first electric bass in a local club, Bob traded his upright for a 1960's Jazz Bass.

Bob moved to Detroit in 1961, after he had turned down a music scholarship, worked on construction sites during the day and played clubs at night. Within a year he had joined a local band, The Royaltones, this group recorded several singles; including a Top 10 hit called "Flamingo Express". The group caught the attention of singer/guitarist Del Shannon, and they became his touring and recording band through 1965. Bob also played on the Jimi Hendrix album "Crash Landing".

While in Detroit Bob worked for local R&B producer Ed Wingate, who owned Golden World Records/Studio. It was during this period that Bob first came into contact with some of Motown's (moonlighting) musicians, including keyboardists Joe Hunter, Johnny Griffith, guitarist Eddie Willis, drummer Benny Benjamin, and bassist James Jamerson. "Edwin Starr's" Agent Double 0 Soul was Bob's first contact with James Jamerson, doing a two-bass session at Golden World (moonlighting with the other Funk Brothers),

By 1967, in addition to steady work at Golden World, he was busy at United Sound, Bob's work included classic R&B records of the period, "I Just Wanna Testify" by The Parliaments, "Love Makes the World Go Round" by Dion Jackson, and "Cool Jerk" by The Capitols. Later other non-Motown hits include "With This Ring" and "I Love You 1000 Times" by The Platters.

Joining Motown when Berry Gordy bought Golden World, (Bob had tried to join Motown in 1965), by auditioning for The Supremes' road band, but was talked out of it by Ed Wingate. Bob's first position at Motown was playing live dates with Stevie Wonder, and Bob's first recording was the song "We Can Work It Out". Then followed "Touch Me in the Morning", "Signed, Sealed, Delivered", "Smiling Faces", "War" and "Tears of a Clown" to name a few.

One interesting project around this time was Jeff Beck and drummer Cozy Powell (from the UK) working at "Hitsville" with Bob and some of the other musicians, but nothing ever came of those sessions. Jeff Beck did offer Bob work in London (as part of his band) but was blocked by Motown, because he was under contract. A solo record never came to anything or an album project with a group called "Scorpion". To supplement his income, Bob became a professional wrestler for six months-but he wisely chose to retire before Killer Kowalski had a chance to bite off his ear. In the early 1970's, Bob got the opportunity to be involved with Marvin Gaye's "What's Going On" project which became Motown's all-time biggest selling album at the time.

When Motown left for Los Angeles and the sessions at Hitsville stopped, Bob decided to move to New York in 1973, and his first dates included Mardin projects for Bette Midler and Barry Manilow. Bob and drummer Andrew Smith (another ex-Motown musician) became one of the hottest new rhythm sections in town recording with Stephanie Mills, Jim Croce, and Bonnie Raitt to Engelbert Humperdinck and Frank Sinatra. Working with the Philadelphia International Records legendary producer Thorn Bell on such Spinners' classics as "Then Came You", "Games People Play" and "Rubber Band Man".

Having worked briefly in 1976 on a Tracy Nelson session Bob moved to Nashville in the 1980's working with Louise Mandrell, Carlene Carter, and many other country artists. Bob also worked with Robert Palmer in the 1980's on the record "Don't Explain"

Next came, playing bass for Gladys Knight and The Pips on Buddah Records. The result was a double-platinum, Grammy-winning No1 international hit "Midnight Train to Georgia". In the summer of 1993 Bob returned to the Philadelphia's Sigma Sound Studios to record in that famous studio. Still involved in session work and as Bob says "they're still calling me, so I figure I must have been doing something right for the past 30 years". Bob has been a participant in the annual Rockin Christmas Fund charity fundraiser event held each year to help needy kids.

Signature songs: include the most notable bass performances are "Signed, Sealed, Delivered (I'm Yours)" by Stevie Wonder, "War" by Edwin Starr, "The Tears of a Clown" by Smokey Robinson and The Miracles, "Mercy Mercy Me (The Ecology)" by Marvin Gaye and "Ball of Confusion (That's What the World Is Today)" by The Temptations.

Born Florence Glenda Ballard aka "Flo" or "Blondie" on the 30th June 1943 in Detroit, Michigan - Died 22nd February 1976 in Detroit, Michigan

Motown Connection: Background singer - Member of The Supremes - Occasional Lead Vocals - Solo Artist.

Born and raised in Detroit (However, some references quote Rosetta Mississippi as her birth place) to Jessie Ballard and his wife Lurlee. Jessie Ballard had been born Jessie Lambert, but had been adopted by a family named Ballard and taken their name. Florence known as "Flo", was the eighth of fifteen children. While at school Florence undertook music classes and had already started singing solo at churches and other functions in addition to taking music classes in school. At school Florence earned the nicknamed "Blondie" because of the soft auburn hair and fair complexion. At the age of fourteen, Florence along with a group of friends formed the group The Primettes as a "sister group" to local Detroit group The Primes and started to perform at gigs in Detroit. Florence was the lead in forming the group with Mary Wilson, (who had lived in the same neighbourhood), and had performed at the same talent show, with Betty McGlown and Diana Ross.

The Primettes did release a one record "Tears of Sorrow" b/side "Pretty Baby" for Lupine Records in 1960, they also sang backing vocals for other singers on that label, before unsuccessfully auditioning for Berry Gordy at Motown. Berry Gordy gave the reason that they should first finish school before trying for a musical career, however after hanging around "Hitsville" for many months, they eventually signed to Motown in 1960.

By 1961 they had changed their name to The Supremes (with prompting from Berry Gordy) to reflect a more "up beat" name, at this time Barbara Martin (who had replaced Betty McGlown) then left, and the group continued with the same line up until Florence left in 1967. Florence sang lead vocals on the group's second release, "Buttered Popcorn" following the trend at the time to share lead vocals among the three members. Florence never again sang lead vocals on a single release, but did on future Supremes' albums, most notably "It Makes No Difference Now" from The Supremes "Sing Country, Western and Pop", and "Ain't That Good News" from "We Remember Sam Cooke" album, Florence also recorded lead vocals for two tracks on a Christmas album, "Silent Night" and "O'Holy Night".

Between 1961 and 1963, The Supremes released eight singles, none of which charted, becoming known as the "no-hit Supremes" in this period the group provided background vocals, hand claps etc for the established artists at Motown including Marvin Gaye, The Temptations (whom they had known and worked with when they were called The Primes). During these years, all three took turns singing lead vocals, but with Florence Ballard looked on as the "lead vocalist" of the group. Most of their early material was written and produced by Berry Gordy and or Smokey Robinson. Then in December 1963, Berry Gordy decided to try The Supremes with his production team of Holland-Dozier-Holland on a single called "When the Lovelight Starts Shining Through His Eyes" this recording became their first chart entry, reaching No23 on the charts.

With this success, Berry Gordy allocated Holland-Dozier-Holland to produce their next recordings; this resulted in almost five years of unparalleled success. By early 1964, The Supremes had recorded and released the single "Where Did Our Love Go" (Diana Ross was now confirmed by Berry Gordy as the lead vocalist) interestingly the song had been originally intended to be recorded by The Marvelettes. In August 1964, while The Supremes were appearing on Dick Clark's "Caravan of Stars", the single "Where Did Our Love Go" went to No1 on the US pop charts; it was also their first recording to chart in the UK, where it reached No3. Followed by four consecutive US No1's "Baby Love" (which was also their first No1 hit in the UK), "Come See About Me", and "Stop! In the Name of Love" and "Back in My Arms Again". "Baby Love" was nominated for the 1965 Grammy Award for Best Rhythm & Blues Recording, and "You Keep Me Hangin' On" was awarded the 1966 Grammy for Best Pop single. They would go onto have twelve No1 hits in the US, with all these singles being international hits around the world (in particular the UK, Europe and Japan).

Everything changed for Florence in 1967, Motown had decided to change the line up of The Supremes, giving the reason for her departure that the strain of touring had become too great for her. However, it is widely reported that Berry Gordy thought Florence's behaviour, drinking heavily, late for recordings etc, was deemed increasingly to be unprofessional behaviour by her. The removal from the group only pushed Florence further into a chronic depression and alcoholism. These were taken into consideration, and again it is widely reported that these factors weighed heavily on Berry Gordy as he took the decision to dismiss Florence from the group in July 1967. Florence was replaced by Cindy Birdsong (from Patti LaBelle and the Bluebells). Florence's final performance with the group was their first appearance at the Flamingo Hotel in Las Vegas.

In 1968, Florence married Tom Chapman who had been Berry Gordy's chauffeur, and when Florence left The Supremes and Motown, Tom Chapman followed. Tom

Chapman then became her manager, and in July 1968 negotiated for Florence her new solo recording contract with ABC. Released that year the singles produced by George Kerr, "It Doesn't Matter How I Say It (It's What I Say That Matters)" with the b/side "Goin' Out Of My Head" and "Love Ain't Love" by Robert Bateman on ABC Records with the b/side "Forever Faithful" were not a commercial success.

Over the next couple of years, Florence continued to try and develop her solo career, including in 1968 a performance with Bill Cosby at the Auditorium Theatre in Chicago, in 1969 performing at one of Richard Nixon's inaugural balls in Washington DC.

Between 1970 and 1971, Florence unsuccessfully sued Motown for additional royalty payments she believed were due. Despite receiving a payment of $160.000 from Motown, she filed an unsuccessful $8.5 million lawsuit against Motown. Florence would name Cindy Birdsong, Jean Terrell, Diana Ross, and Mary Wilson, along with Motown Records and International Management Corp in the lawsuit claiming "conspiracy" to oust her from the Supremes as the basis of the claim. After the unsuccessful action against Motown, Florence would eventually also sue her lawyer for not presenting her claim correctly and for mis-management of the funds she had received.

Around this time Florence lost her home and had to move into the public housing and welfare system, the final part to the decline came after the birth of another daughter in 1972, Tom Chapman left Florence, her finances were depleted and Florence became depressive which fuelled her addiction to alcohol and pills. For the next few years Florence was to keep out of the public eye, while she struggled to make ends meet.

In 1975, it look like Florence could be "turning the corner" Florence had received a settlement from an accident in which she had broken her leg after slipping on a patch of ice in Detroit. With the accident settlement money, purchasing a small house in Detroit she made a decision to return to singing, and also reconciled with her estranged husband. With the female rock group "The Deadly Nightshade", Florence performed at a concert held at Detroit's in June 1975. Following the success of this performance, Florence received requests for newspaper and television interviews, including an appearance on the local Detroit talk show "The David Diles Show".

Sadly, Florence died on 22nd February 1976, of coronary thrombosis, Florence was thirty-two years old. It was suggested at the time that the years of addictions to chemicals and alcohol, had weakened her system, causing the fatal cardiac arrest.

Married Tom Chapman in 1968, and had three daughters, of which two Michelle and Nicole were twins, her third child was Lisa.

Born Jimmy Jay Barnes on 30th November 1943 in Detroit, Michigan

Motown Connection: Solo Artist/Singer - Songwriter.

J.J. began his solo recording career in 1960 with a single release on Kable Record Label of Detroit, the arrangement and song is now deemed to be "way ahead of its time", the recording was called "Won't You Let Me Know".

In 1963 he released four singles for Fred Brown's "Mickay's Label". "Mickays Records" were based on 14th Street Detroit, and was just south of the 20 Grand Club, and was a large operation for Detroit at the time. The legendary "Poor Unfortunate Me" single followed on "Ring Records" before he made the move to a well known suburban area in Detroit called West Davison.

A move to Ric-Tic by J.J. produced his first record for them, another superb song, "Please Let Me In" b/side "I Think I Found A Love". Co-arranged by Richard Parker and Don Davis, it unfortunately failed to chart. The follow-up "Real Humdinger" b/side "I Ain't Gonna Do It" was equally impressive and helped J.J overcome his earlier disappointment by achieving No80, R&B No18. A cover of the Beatles hit, "Day Tripper" came next before J.J.'s final recording in August 1966, and the excellent "Say It". During this time, J.J. would join a little known group called the Delphis. The group consisted of Annette Sterling, Rosalind Beard, Martha Reeves, and Gloria Williamson; the group would later evolve into the legendary Motown group Martha and The Vandellas.

When Motown bought out Golden World a month later, it was the start of a "nightmare" period for Barnes. Although he recorded many tracks with the studio, nothing was released, because it was felt that he sounded too much like Marvin Gaye.

Once his contract had run its course with Motown, J.J. then joined the Groovesville Label in 1967 where "Baby Please Come Back Home" reached No61, R&B No9. J.J follow this record with, "Now That I've Got You Back", which also did reasonably well, a R&B No44. The next move was to "Revilot Records" in the following year, which resulted in another four singles including the classic "Our Love Is In The Pocket".

In the late 1960's and early 1970's, J.J.'s recordings (like Edwin Starr), would gain a new lease of life via England's developing Northern Soul Scene. This led to some new material on John Abbey's Contempo label, which was based in London.

Barnes currently lives in Detroit, Michigan and is still performing in the UK.

Born in Detroit, Michigan

Motown Connection: Motown In House Producer - Talent Scout - The First Motown Audio Engineer - Singer (The Satintones and Rayber Singer) - Motown Songwriter.

Robert played a key part in the early success of Motown Records having been an In House Producer, a talent scout, and engineer with the label in the early 1960's. Robert started with Motown as a vocalist, singing background with the Rayber singers (Brian Holland, Raynoma Liles-Gordy, Sonny Sanders, Louvaine Demps, Bateman, and on occasion Gwendolyn Murray and Berry Gordy). He became the first engineer  during the early years of Motown, and was the architect of the Motown sound in those early years. When the Motown Record Company was created in January of 1960, his group the Satintones (Chico Leverett, Sonny Sanders, James Ellis, and Robert) was the first all male group on the label.

Robert also co-wrote the million-selling "Please Mr. Postman", Motown's first number one pop record. Robert also co-wrote the classic ballad "If You Need Me" with Wilson Pickett and Sonny Sanders. Solomon Burke's version peaked at number two R&B charts for five weeks and "Right Now and Not Later" was later recorded by the Shangri-Las. He produced one of the few solo singles by The Supremes, using Florence Ballard as lead on the record "Love Ain't Love" on ABC Records.

Bateman was the uncle of singer/songwriter/producer Jeffree Perry whose credits include the Steppers' classic "Love's Gonna Last", "100 Proof Aged in Soul", Diana Ross' "One Love in My Lifetime" and Jackie Wilson's "Beautiful Day". He co-produced several Motown acts with Brian Holland under their condensed pseudonym of Brianbert.

A friend of Marvelettes member Georgia Dobbins was offered a blues song called "Please Mr. Postman". Georgina Dobbins rewrote the song, (retaining only the title) collaborating with the rest of the group on how the song should be presented. The group took the song to producers Bateman and Holland. However, Georgina Dobbins who was the writer and lead singer of the group at the time of the audition, was stopped by her father, from signing the contract for her to continue with the group. She therefore had to leave the group; Wanda Young replaced her in the group but with Gladys Horton thrust into the limelight to take over in Georgina Dobbins' place as lead vocalist.

The group rehearsed for two weeks before recording "Please Mr. Postman" with a 22-year-old drummer named Marvin Gaye. The Marvelettes' "Please Mr. Postman" b/side "So Long Baby" went gold, reaching the No1 on R&B charts (it was number one for seven weeks), it then went to number one on the pop chart late 1961.

The original members of The Satintones: L to R: Chico Leverett, Sonny Sanders, James Ellis and Robert Bateman.

Robert also co-wrote its follow-ups, "Twistin' Postman" and the number four R&B hit "Playboy". Flushed with the success of "Please Mr. Postman", Robert turned to New York to explore bigger opportunities, nothing major developed and Robert came back to Detroit.

"Please Mr. Postman" was covered by the Carpenters on their Horizon album. Released as a single, it went to number one in the pop charts in early 1975. The Beatles' version can be found on "The Complete BBC Sessions".

Born William Benjamin (Nickname Papa Zita) on the 25th July 1925 Birmingham, Alabama - Died 20th April 1969 in Detroit, Michigan 1969

Motown Connection: Drummer/member of The Funk Brothers (Motown In House Band).

Benny is credited with helping create the "Motown Sound" via his unique drumbeat and was loved by all the musicians at "Hitsville USA". Benny was the first drummer to work in "Studio A", employed by Berry Gordy from 1958 to his early death in 1969. Berry Gordy identified that Benny's drum beats were much harder than any of the other R&B and Blues drummers residing in Detroit at the time, and his timing was impeccable, which was the main reason why Berry Gordy employed Benny.

Benny has been identified by most Motown observers as one of the most influential musicians in developing the "Motown sound", (along with bassist James Jamerson). Benny provided the backbeat, while James Jamerson introduced the characteristic bass introductions to records like The Supremes. "My World Is Empty Without You". Not known for his  timekeeping, Benny's excuses were legendary for being late to Hitsville's recording sessions (including one where he claimed to have been sitting on his mother's step with his ex-old lady's boyfriend when someone pulled up in a car and shot him).

Benny was known for his explosive drum fills and pickups, (just listen to "This Old Heart Of Mine" by The Isley Brothers) Benny could play any type of groove, whether, deft brushwork, latin-influenced, or pounding beat, Benny's signature drum style defiantly defined the "Motown Sound".

The basic Funk Brothers line-up - built around the core of Benny, James Jamerson, and pianist Earl Van Dyke was in place by 1964, recording virtually around the clock in "Studio A" (aka the Snake pit) at Motown's "Hitsville USA" on West Grand Street in Detroit.

Some of the producers would not do a session unless at least two of the Funk Brothers were present namely, Benny Benjamin and James Jamerson. Berry Gordy stated in his autobiography "To Be Loved", "He was so good on the drums and had a feel no one could match; he had a distinctive knack for executing various rhythms all at the same time. He had a pulse, a steadiness that kept the tempo better than a metronome. Benny was my man". Benny's main musical Influences were Buddy

Rich, Tito Puentes Instruments Played: A studio drum set comprised of Ludwig, Slingerland, Rogers and Gretsch components.

Although a lifelong heroin user and alcoholic, Benny never let these addictions stop his prowess on the drums, towards the end of his days in "Studio A" Benny's addictions did eventually catch up with him and Benny's music did suffer. In 1969 the ravages of his addictions caught up with him and caused his death from a stroke in Detroit. It is suggested that as Benny started to wane it took two drummers to replace him, the two being Uriel Jones and Richard "Pistol" Allen, these two still (in my opinion) figured significantly in developing the "Motown Sound" and their contribution should not be underestimated.

On the 10th March 2003 Benny was inducted into the Rock and Roll Hall of Fame. Thought by many to be long overdue, this award followed the documentary "Standing In The Shadows Of Motown" which paid tribute to the collective musicians know as "The Funk Brothers"

Signature sound: would be in my opinion either "This Old Heart Of Mine" The Isley Brothers or "Behind A Painted Smile" again by The Isley Brothers.

Born Sondra Williams on the 21st May 1944 in Stockton, California

Motown Connection: Motown Solo Singer - Motown Background Vocalist - Songwriter.

Sondra was raised in Los Angeles the daughter of a pastor, and had been active in church choirs since the age of six. Sondra recorded for Vee-Jay Records distributed by Atlantic "He's Got The Whole World In His Hands" b/side Heartaches, "Spiritual Oldies" and "He's Got The Whole World In His Hands" b/side "Heartaches" in 1964. A single recording for Simpson Records "It's A Blessing" b/side "Since I Found Him" was issued in the same year.

Blinky with her husband Robert Powell.

Sondra went to Detroit to meet Shelly Berger, The Temptations Manager "looking for all the world like a church girl, in my little white gloves and hat". Shelly Berger, who became Sondra's manager, signed her to Motown and Sondra would go on to be a show-stopping show opener for The Temptations.

Shelly Berger chose the song she debuted on Motown "I Wouldn't Change the Man He Is", in 1968, although the original was released in 1964 by Brenda Holloway on Tamla. This record would become the most famous to come out of her days at Motown. The song was written by Ashford & Simpson, (although it is also suggested that the song was written about Lovin' Spoonful studio bass player James Killingsworth) in 1968. Ashford & Simpson at the time were "riding high" at Motown with the Marvin Gaye and Tammi Terrell duets and Sondra was so excited at the thought of them producing her. "The only problem Sondra remembers" is they took so long in the studio, "I fell asleep and they had to send someone looking for me". After this record she was being talked about as one of the label's future stars.

Sondra also worked with Edwin Starr for the Gordy release "Oh How Happy" b/side "Ooh Baby Baby" in 1969 (interestingly some copies were issued on red vinyl) the song was originally released in 1965 by The Miracles on Tamla. While with Motown Sondra recorded on not just Motown, but also the Soul and Mowest Labels. Sondra's last single was on Motown "You Get A Tangle In Your Lifeline" b/side "This Man Of Mine" in 1973.

By 1974 Sondra had signed to Reprise, recording "Walk With Me Jesus" b/side

"When Love Calls Your Name" The next part of her career was forming Blinky Williams and The Hollywood Choir with members Blinky Williams (piano), occasional members Brenda Holloway (vocals) and Starletta DuPois (vocals). Sondra then debuted as one of the original COGIC singers, (group name stands for Church Of God In Christ), with Andre Crouch, Sandra Crouch, Billy Preston, Edna Wright, Frankie Karl, and Gloria Jones. Sondra's recent appearance was backing country superstar Garth Brooks on a Donny and Marie Osmond Christmas special.

One interesting footnote to Blinky's career at Motown was during the "Lady Sings the Blues", film, it was her voice the young Billie hears when she keeps playing the song, "Ain't Nobody's Business" on the ancient gramophone.

Sondra married Robert Powell and resides in Los Angeles, California.

Album Track: "I Wouldn't Change The Man He Is", Blinky.

Born Thomas Bowles in 1927 in South Bend, Indiana - Died 31st January 2000 in Detroit, Michigan

Motown Connection: Played with The Funk Brothers - Part of Motown's Artist Management Division - Motown Artist.

Nicknamed "String Bean", later shortened to "Beans", because of his lanky, 6ft 5in frame was a great saxophonist, Beans was an unsung hero behind the scenes during the early days of Motown. Beans was a great musician, part of The Funk Brothers who's work in "Hitsville USA Studio A" helped establish and create "The Motown Sound", Beans also undertook a management role at Motown, was also the spiritual "father" and "gentle giant" of Motown and the Detroit's jazz scene.

Beans started to play the clarinet at about the age of 9 and was working professionally as a saxophonist at age 16. He came to Detroit in 1944 to attend Wayne State University. He later toured with such musicians as Illinois Jacquet, Bill Doggett and Lloyd Price.

It was Beans who originated the idea of the "Motortown Revue", which took Motown's young talent on the road, helping to increase record sales and jump-start many Motown artists' careers. Beans was road manager for the early "Motortown Revues, Beans also had the first "Black Band" to record on the Tamla label, called "The Swingin' Tigers".

Beans wasn't a household name in the early days of Motown, (such as Stevie Wonder and Marvin Gaye) along with the many other Motown stars whose records he graced with his saxophone and flute work. Beans wrote the melody for the smash hit that launched Stevie Wonder's career, the record "Fingertips Pt. 2". Bean's smooth flute and baritone sax added his personality to Marvin Gaye's "What's Going On" The Supremes' "Baby Love" and Martha and The Vandellas' "Heat Wave". To name just a few.

In the 1960's, Beans led a Detroit band called the Swinging Dashikis, which often backed up Motown acts. He also served as Chairman of the Graystone Jazz Museum in Detroit. Berry Gordy brought Bowles into his fledgling company firstly, into the artist management division, where he mentored many of the label's young stars, Stevie Wonder, The Supremes, Martha Reeves, The Temptations, The Marvelettes and Gladys Knight and The Pips. Beans would chaperone the stars on their tours; teach the stars "the ropes" in regards to how show business worked and how to behave on the road.

Beans died at age 73 after a long battle with cancer in Detroit.

Born in the State of Missouri

Motown Connection: Receptionist – Songwriter - Director of Writers Relations at Motown.

An original Motowner Janie started as the receptionist at "Hitsville USA" co-wrote with Berry Gordy, "Money (That's What I Want)". She was only sixteen at the time, influenced by Berry Gordy. Janie was known for her creativity, ingenuity and perseverance in the early pioneering days of the "Motown Sound". Janie was influenced early in life by diverse musical styles including both country music and gospel. Janie beginning her professional song-writing career as a teenager.

Janie's first two songs (which she co-wrote with Berry Gordy) were included on Jackie Wilson's album, "Lonely Teardrops". Then came her most famous collaboration (again co-written with Berry Gordy), the international hit "Money (That's What I Want)", this song has been covered more than 200 times by artists including The Beatles, The Rolling Stones, Barrett Strong (the original!), Muddy Waters, The Supremes, The Flying Lizzards, and Waylon Jennings.

Other famous recordings include, "Too Busy Thinking About My Baby" by Marvin Gaye, "Your Old Stand By" by Mary Wells, "All the Love I've Got" by The Marvelettes, "Time Changes Things" by The Supremes, and "Contract on Love" by Stevie Wonder.

Janie's involvement with Motown continued to grow and she was soon named Director of Writer's Relations for the company. In all, Janie worked for Motown for twenty years before starting a business of her own.

While working for Motown in California, Janie saw at first hand the challenges that young entertainers faced when attempting to break into the entertainment industry. In a conversation between her and good friend, music producer and songwriter Eric Wheelwright, she explained that it broke her heart to see young peoples' dreams crushed after meeting with the label in hopes of landing a record deal.

The part that bothered her most was the fact that if the record executive did not like the product that was being presented to them they would not offer an explanation to the young people regarding the reason they were not interested or what they could do to improve themselves. Her concern was that if no one offered the young people any guidance or advice, how would they ever learn? This led Janie to found the Heroes and Legends awards (H.A.L.) which is hosted in Beverly Hills, California each year. The Heroes And Legends Award (HAL) is noted as one of the largest Motown related events in the world, second only to the fund raising dinner given by the Motown Historical Museum in Detroit every year.

The award show is a scholarship fund-raiser to assist youths involved in the arts and to further their education. It also connects them with industry executives in the fields of television and film as well as music.

Berry Gordy is among one of the many contributors and event attendees each year. Past guests and performers have included Janet Jackson, Boys II Men, Eric Wheelwright and Stevie Wonder to name only a few.

Although she still writes, (within the confines of her Beverly Hills Offices), Janie also manages her own publishing company, Mountain Goat Music, and publishes Entertainment Connection Magazine.

Janie has been honoured by BMI with a Certificate of Achievement for "Money" and "Too Busy Thinking About My Baby". The late "Jack the Rapper" presented Janie with the "Vivian Carter" Award in recognition of her contributions and longevity in Black Radio. As recently as December of 2003 she was recognised by the City of Los Angeles during "LA Music Week" for her extraordinary musical talent and contribution.

Album Track: "Too Busy Thinking About My Baby", Marvin Gaye.

Born Johnny William Bristol on the 3rd February 1939 Morgantown, North Carolina - Died on 2nd March 2004 Brighton, Michigan

Motown Connections: In House Staff Writer - In House Producer and Arranger - Married Berry Gordy's niece Iris Gordy - Singer with Gwen Gordy's Tri-Phi label.

Though born in Morgantown, North Carolina, Johnny began his career in Detroit when he teamed with Jacky Beavers doing duets for Gwen Gordy's Tri-Phi label in Detroit during the early 1960's. Johnny met Jackie Beavers during a period of National Service in the US Air Force. They cut the original version of "Someday We'll Be Together", a major hit for Diana Ross and The Supremes in 1969 Johnny was the session's producer, and also the male voice doing harmony.

With Harvey Fuqua (his production partner for several years), Johnny discovered a band that was originally known as the Nix "Stick" and the Rhythm Rockers. Billy Nix was the lead of the group which consisted of Billy Nix (drums), Autry Dewalt (sax), and Fred Patton (piano/ lead vocals) and later Willie Woods (guitar). When Nix went to the army, the sax player took the band to Battle Creek and changed their name to the "All Star Band", later the band changed the name again to Junior Walker and The All Stars. Johnny and Harvey Fuqua co-produced Junior Walker and The All-Stars' remake of "How Sweet It Is" in 1966, then co-wrote and produced "What Does It Take?". Johnny wrote and or produced songs for Diana Ross, Marvin Gaye and Tammi Terrell, Smokey Robinson, David Ruffin, Edwin Starr, Michael Jackson, Gladys Knight and The Pips, Martha Reeves, Jimmy Ruffin, The Spinners, The Four Tops, and Stevie Wonder. "Ain't No Mountain High Enough", "25 Miles", "Help Me Make It Through The Night", "I Don't Want To Do Wrong" and "Yester-Me, Yester-You, Yesterday" were some of the songs featuring Johnny's input. Johnny was professionally and personally part of Motown, and was an influential figure at Motown from 1961 to 1973 through his marriage to Iris Gordy, and he was held in high regard by Berry Gordy.

Though Johnny was the original person to sing the Diana Ross and The Supremes hit "Someday We'll Be Together", he shelved the song until one day he decided to perform the song again. Therefore, he recorded the song with an orchestra, and the Jones Girls as background vocalists, with the intention of him getting an opportunity to have a release under the Motown banner. But, Berry Gordy had other plans for the song, after hearing the nearly finished tune. Berry Gordy suggested that instead of Johnny singing the song he should let Diana Ross try it. Johnny agreed, and during the session, Johnny coached Diana Ross through the recording. Berry Gordy liked the song so well, that he decided to leave the recording as it was with Johnny's coaching track included, and the rest is history. The irony is that The Supremes didn't know that they weren't singing background on the recording until decades later.

He left Motown in 1973 and signed with MGM as a solo artist in 1974. His first single, "Hang On In Their Baby", was his biggest hit; it was number two R&B and number eight pop that year. Johnny enjoyed two more sizeable hits for MGM, "You And I" and "Leave My World" in 1974 and 1975.

He moved to Atlantic in 1976, and scored his last hit with "Do It To My Mind", a number five R&B record. The Osmonds also had a number one record in England with Johnnys "Love Me for A Reason". The remade "Hang On In There Baby" as a duet with Alton McClain for Polydor in 1980 was a hit, and Johnny then did another duet with Ami Stewart titled "My Guy/My Girl" for Handshake Records. Johnny also recorded for Motorcity label, and scored a British hit with "Man Up in The Sky" in 1989.

Johnny's most recent entry into the charts was "Come To Me" for Whichway in 1991. Johnny was also productive as a writer and producer in the 1970's and 1980's; Tarvaras, Buddy Miles, Tamiko Jones, Real Thing, O.C. Smith. Margie Joseph recorded his compositions in the 1970's, and Johnny produced a Four Tops remake of "I'm Ready For Love" In 1985, Johnny briefly returned to Motown but with little success. Johnny has his own recording studio in Brighton, Michigan and a record label called "Bushka Records".

During his illustrious career, Johnny wrote over 300 songs that have been recorded, published and released by artists such as Johnny Mathis, Tom Jones, Buddy Miles, Jerry Butler, Boz Scaggs, Taveras and Marlena Shaw.

At the time of his death, Johnny was 65, he was finalising plans to tour the UK and finishing up a gospel album. Berry Gordy's niece Iris Gordy was Bristol's second wife; they divorced in the early 1970's. Karla Gordy Bristol is their only child. Johnny has two children from his first marriage son Johnny Bristol Jnr, Shanna. Johnny also married Maude Bristol Perry; Maude was Battle Creek, Michigan's first woman mayor. Johnny died of a heart attack in Brighton, Michigan.

Album Track: "Someday We'll Be Together", Diana Ross and The Supremes.

Born Edward Brown on the 13th September 1932 in Clarksdale, Mississippi (but raised in Memphis, Tennessee) - Died 28th December 1984 in Los Angeles, California

Motown Connection: Marvin Gaye's valet - Percussionist /member of The Funk Brothers (Motown In House Band).

Brown was raised in Memphis, learning to play virtually every hand-held percussion instrument but particularly excelling on the bongos and congas. After relocating to Detroit, he worked the local nightclub circuit before joining Motown in 1962; Eddie had been Marvin Gaye's valet which proved his introduction to Motown. Eddie's gift was infusing the percussion into the "Motown Sound" using elements of Latin and jazz grooves. The Funk Brothers bandleader Earl Van Dyke once estimated Brown played on "at least 97 percent of all the music that came out of Motown".

Eddie was (along with Jack Ashford) the primary studio percussionist, Eddie played congas, bongos, the gourd and claves. During the heyday of Motown Records in Detroit, Eddie served as a crucial element in producing some of the best soul/pop music ever produced. Among Eddie's best-known performances on Motown include "(I Know) I'm Losing You" by The Temptations, "I Second That Emotion" by Smokey Robinson and The Miracles, and "If I Were Your Woman" by Gladys Knight and The Pips.

Eddie had one other great role (apart from his musical ability) to play for The Funk Brother's. In the "pressure cooker" atmosphere of the "Hitsville Studio A", they desperately needed a comedian to keep things from "boiling over" and Eddie was the comedian. A master at stopping a session as players doubled over in laughter while Bongo wailed on about James Jamerson's mother (his favourite target) or some other unsuspecting victim.

Remarkably, he couldn't even read music, in The Funk Brothers' documentary "Standing in the Shadows of Motown", keyboardist Joe Hunter claimed that during sessions, Eddie simply replaced his sheet music with nudie magazines. As Motown's focus shifted from in house producer recordings to more artist driven recordings based on LPs, rather than singles Eddie started to work with Marvin Gaye on his concept album "What's Going On". Eddie left his mark on classic recordings including, Marvin Gaye's "Let's Get It On" album and single and Stevie Wonder's "Songs in the Key of Life". However, it was Eddie's work with Marvin

Gaye on the concept album "What's Going On" (with a remarkable performance captured on a DVD issued in 2007 by Motown) that left a permanent on his career.

When Motown relocated the label from Detroit to Los Angeles, Eddie followed (like some of the other Funk Brothers), to the West Coast in the mid 1970's Eddie had hoped to still do session work/record for Motown while picking up recording sessions for other labels. Similar to the other Funk Brothers that moved Eddie never really settled and found it impossible to regain the magic that he had been a part of Detroit and "Hitsville" in particular. In subsequent years Eddie did tour with Marvin Gaye and Liza Minnelli.

Eddie died from a heart ailment at the age of just 52 leaving a wife Geraldine and five children.

Signature songs: Would be "Cloud Nine" and "Beauty Is Only Skin Deep" by The Temptations, "What's Going On" by Marvin Gaye. The "What's Going On" is by far and away one of my all time favourites.

Born in July 1946 in Houston, Texas

Motown Connection: In House Writer - Assisted Fuqua in Artist Development - Recording various Motown artists' shows for Artist Development - Musician: Organ, Guitar, Celeste, Electric Piano, Vibraphone, Clavinet - Producer.

Vernons family moved to the east side of Detroit, Michigan from Houston in 1946 the year Vernon was born. The fourth of six siblings, he attended Southeastern High School, where he was an honours student and earned a letter in music in 1962. Vernon graduated at 16 and joined the Air Force, where he received the 95 Award of Excellence in 1964.

Livin' Proof record cover.
L to R: Vernon Bullock, Stephen Rice and Sterling Rice.

Vernon's first job was at the age of ten as an organist for the Episcopal Church pastored by the late Father John Thomas Walker. Vernon then formed the jazz quartet the "Minor Four" because they were all 16 at the time. Vernon also had a half-hour gospel music show on TV, guests included Mahalia Jackson and the Le Chantels, a choir that his sister, Sadie, belonged to. Venon's father was a major influence on his music ambitions. Vernon's father sang tenor in a gospel group called the True Tones with two of his brothers and a cousin. Vernon's father also worked with Blues singer John Lee Hooker, the two families lived together during his early childhood and Vernon's parents are godparents to John Lee Hooker's two oldest daughters, Diane and Vera.

Vernon's most successful compositions were "What Does It Take to Win Your Love", an international hit for Junior Walker and The All Stars and "If I Can Build My Whole World Around You", another international hit for Marvin Gaye and Tammi Terrell. Vernon followed this with "Yesterday Dreams" by The Four Tops; next came "Hold On (To Your Dreams)", a minor hit for William "Wee Gee" Howard (who sang "In the Rain" as a member of the Dramatics). "Hold On (To Your Dreams)" has also been recorded by The Staple Singers, Living Proof, Public Announcement, and The Chilites.

Iris Gordy (Berry Gordy's sister) set up an audition on behalf of Motown, in which Vernon accompanied Sadie (his sister) too. Iris was dating Vernon's older brother,

K.D at the time, (both were classmates at Cass Tech High). The audition was not successful so Motown did not offer anything to Sadie. However, Vernon started hanging out at "Hitsville" in Detroit, trying to get into the recording sessions. Luckily the persistence paid off, one day Vernon played a couple of songs he had written, and was signed to an exclusive three-year contract with Motown. He stayed with Motown from 1965 to late 1970.

Vernon was one of the youngest employees at Motown, where Tammi Terrell adopted Vernon as her little brother. Vernon co-wrote and worked with Mickey Stevenson, Kim Weston, Sylvia Moy, Ivy Hunter, Johnny Bristol, and Harvey Fuqua and Gwen Gordy-Fuqua while at Motown. Vernon considered Harvey Fuqua to be his mentor, writing his most popular songs with him. Apart from his song writing duties, Vernon assisted Harvey Fuqua in Artist Development, working closely with Maurice King (band director) and Cholly Atkins (choreographer). Part of his responsibilities while in the Artist Development, was to travel around the country recording various Motown artists' shows for the purpose of reviewing and refining their acts. Vernon (like many of the other Motown Artists) moonlighted at various Detroit nightclubs, including the Twenty Grand, Vertigo West, and the Moon Supper Club, as a lighting director. Vernon worked with Florence Ballard when she was released by Motown in 1967. Vernon left Motown to continue working with Harvey Fuqua when he moved to Louisville Kentucky.

The "New Birth" venture was created by Vernon who introduced it to Harvey Fuqua in 1970 with the idea of establishing several acts separately who would perform as a self-contained show. The act that got the first hit record would get top billing, and the others would be supporting acts. Vernon co-wrote many songs on early albums' by The Nite-Liters, and Love, Peace and Happiness for the "New Birth" concept.

Vernon later produced the "Young Hearts" two LPs on 20th Century Fox Records, and also did work for The Dells, Little Richard, Johnny Taylor, Booker T and The MG's, and many others.

In 1977 Bullock created a funk-soul group on the Ju-Par label calling themselves "Livin' Proof" with Stephen and Sterling Rice. In 1978 they released their first recording with the self-entitled album "Livin' Proof".

Vernon once lived in Englewood, CO; had they stayed, their daughter would have attended Columbine Senior High. From June 1995 to March of 1997 Vernon put together a multi-artist recording, "A Dream for the Children", for the benefit of the Columbine students. Tragically, five of Vernons daughter's classmates were killed 8th April 1999. Vernon also worked with Ver-Bul Enterprises/Mafundi Music Group in Beverly Hills, California.

Jheryl Busby

Born on the 5th May 1949 in Los Angeles, California – Died 9th November 2008 in Malibu, California

Motown Connection: President and Chief Executive of the Motown from 1988 to 1995 – First President of the Motown After Sale To MCA/Boston Ventures.

Jheryl grew up in South Central Los Angeles and attended John C. Fremont High School next he attended Long Beach State College, but did not complete his studies, instead leaving after only two years, his first work was as an inventory clerk at Mattel Toys, before leaving he had been promoted to new-toy coordinator.

Jheryl's start in the music business came through doing promotional work for Stax Records in the early 1970's, the work entailed visiting music stores, trying to educate and sell the latest releases from Stax to the music store owner and trying to get merchandise space in their music store. He became the head of West Coast promotion and marketing at Stax. Jheryl proved so successful in this role that he came to the interest of the major labels and moved on to promotional and artist-development roles at Casablanca, Atlantic, CBS and A&M Records.

After working with these labels, Jheryl moved to MCA Records and rose to become President of the company's black music division by 1984. His skill was to make a priority of signing established performers such as Patti LaBelle and Gladys Knight, who had lost their record company deals in the post-disco era.

While at MCA, he also helped discover and promote such groups as New Edition, and The Jets, and solo artists, Bobby Brown and Jody Watley, helping them "cross over" from the R&B roots to the more mainstream top-40 chart hits. Jheryl is credited with turning the company's black music division at MCA into the industry's black music sales leader.

In 1988, one of Berry Gordy's last act's at Motown was to bring Jheryl in as the company's President and Chief Executive for the label, shortly after his appointment Berry Gordy sold the company in 1988 for $61 million to a partnership of MCA Records, who had become the distributor of Motown's recording a few years earlier, and Boston Ventures, an investment group. Jheryl was confirmed by the new owners as Motown's President and Chief Executive, gaining a 10% ownership of Motown in the process.

Using the established stars, Lionel Richie, Smokey Robinson and Stevie Wonder, to "kick start the company". Jheryl was even able to bring back Diana Ross to the label as both artist and executive. Responsible for signing and developing new acts, including Boyz II Men, Queen Latifah, Another Bad Creation and Johnny Gill.

By 1990, Motown had "turned the corner" with five songs reaching the No1 on the R&B charts, and sales of the company's album's rising from the previous years No10 spot to No4 on the R&B album charts.

Jheryl also got the backing of some of the early Motown stars on the direction he was taking Motown, Smokey Robinson is quoted as saying "I had tremendous respect for the way he continued the Motown legacy", When Polygram Records bought Motown for $301 million in 1993, Jheryl was retained as President, however, Jheryl was forced out of the company in 1995 after a legal dispute with MCA.

In 1998, Jheryl became a majority shareholder along with Janet Jackson and Magic Johnson in Founders National Bank, the first black owned and operated commercial bank in California, he remained a shareholder after several mergers with other black owned banks. At the time of his death, he was Vice Chairman of the Board of Directors of OneUnited Bank.

Jheryl's next major role in the music industry was as head of the urban music division at "DreamWorks Records" in 1998. Leaving "DreamWorks" in 2001, later in 2001 he was named President of Def Soul Classics. His next venture was "Umbrella Recordings", which he created with producer Mike City, which released the Carl Thomas album "So Much Better" in 2007 and Patti LaBelle's "The Gospel According to Patti LaBelle", her first gospel album.

Sadly, Jheryl was found dead in a hot tub at his home in Malibu California, either of natural causes or a possible accident. He was aged 58 years old.

Walter "Choker" Campbell

Aka "Choker" Born on the 21st March 1916 in Shelby, Mississippi - Died 20th July 1993 in Detroit, Michigan

Motown Connection: Musician - Band Director - Artist on the label - Campbell was also a recording artist in the fifties.

Choker played tenor sax and was the leader of the road band used in the "Motown Revues". Also band leader when recording sessions were undertaken at the Graystone Ballroom in Detroit (the ballroom was owned by Motown). Choker was a recording artist in the fifties, recording for several labels including Atlantic Records, where he shared billing on a few singles with blues icon, Joe Turner.

Big Joe Turner with the Choker Campbell Orchestra in the background.

Walter "Choker" Campbell was a saxophone player who had a wealth of experience as an artist and a bandleader even before he went to Motown in the early 1960's. Although Campbell and his group did some studio recording for Motown, both as a solo act and as backing musicians, the Choker Campbell Orchestra's main contribution to Motown was as the house band for the "Motortown Revues".

Choker Campbell.

When Choker joined Motown his main focus was the 'Motortown Special'. Eventually the tours were renamed and billed as the 'Motortown Revue'; the final name was the 'Motown Revue' and bandleader Walter "Choker" Campbell was the band leader for all of the variations.

By the mid-1960's, Choker and his band had moved on to other labels and artists including the Leah Dawson. Choker later recording had a "Motown Sound" feel, particularly in "My Mechanical Man" (which also manages to take a swipe at the Marvelettes' "Don't Mess With Bill" and Edwin Starr's "Agent Double-O-Soul"). The record "Strange Things Happen" was a nice change of direction (a great bluesy ballad) that finds the artist Leah Dawson lamenting her man's shabby treatment after she had built him up. Campbell's band provide fine background accompaniment to the song.

In 1969, he established the Tri-City Recording Co. in Saginaw Michigan, including its own recording studio. Choker lived in Detroit until his death in 1993.

Chris Clark

Born on the 1st February 1946 in Santa Cruz, California

Motown Connection: Singer - In House Writer - Dated Berry Gordy - Screenwriter for "Lady Sings the Blues" - Video Editor for Motown's Video Center - Vice-President for Motown Productions - Vice President of Creative Development for Motown Films.

Clark became famous in England as the "white Negress" (a nickname meant as a compliment), since the six-foot platinum blonde, blue-eyed soul songstress toured with fellow Motown artists. Better known in Europe than in the States, particularly in Britain, by Northern Soul fans.

The United States' answer to Dusty Springfield, Chris began her career with Motown during the 1960's. She was signed a "tall, tan, blue-eyed, bluesy-sounding" recording artist, who soon moved on to writing and co-writing music for herself and other Motown acts. Chris only managed to have one hit it was on the R&B singles chart. "Love's Gone Bad" in 1966, produced by Holland-Dozier-Holland's, "Love's Gone Bad", was a song based on the aftermath of a break-up. Berry Gordy (who Chris dated for a while) wrote the song "Do Right Baby Do Right" for her, this was her first single on Motown. In 1968 her debut album "Soul Sounds" was a sophisticated take on vintage Motown, alternately breezy and bluesy with little to suggest that the recordings were by then three years old.

CHRIS CLARK
Motown Recording Artist

Early Motown publicity photograph.

In 1972, Berry Gordy, then asked Chris to become the screenwriter for Motown's multi-Academy Award nominated film, "Lady Sings the Blues", from which she received a nomination. Chris's next role was to overseeing Motown's Video Centre, and working as a video editor. Chris then served as Vice President of Creative Development for Motown Films, later Chris became Vice-President for Motown Productions (motion pictures and television) in Los Angeles. Chris did make really some good singles while at Motown, but sadly they weren't hits, recording songs like "I Want to Go Back There Again", "Whisper You Love Me Boy" and Smokey Robinson's "From Head to Toe" while with Motown.

Chris also photographed many of the Motown artists over the years and now uses these images to create art pictures/posters. Chris developed a process, which transforms her photographs into fine works of art. The procedure begins with selected images and graphics being placed on top of one another Chris then adds her own creative and artistic enhancements, and places her finished pieces on canvas.

In 1982 she married Academy Award-winning screenwriter and novelist Ernest Tidyman. Sadly, after only two years of marriage he died of a perforated ulcer in 1984. In the coming years, after several attempts to get different projects launched in Hollywood, Chris decided to move to Arizona, and returned to her areas of expertise, photography. In 1990, Chris took a journey to Africa, where she spent more than six weeks photographing and experiencing the culture, people, landscape and wildlife so dear to her heart.

In the early 1990's, Chris recorded with Ian Levine for the Motorcity label. Motown's UK 2-CD "Anthology" was released in 2005 and made the No1 spot on the Northern Soul Charts, staying there for an unprecedented three months.

During this time, Chris travelled overseas to open for the Temptations and The Four Tops for the fourteen UK dates in their European tour. She later headlined two tours of her own. Since then, Chris has been actively involved in the creation and promotion of her Motown Artists 50th artwork, resulting in a recent exhibition of her work at the Pelican Art Gallery in Petaluma, CA.

Most recently she has been working with Reel Music on the April 2009 re-release of her classic "Soul Sounds" album on CD. Berry Gordy summed it up best when he declared: "I think Chris Clark is one of the greatest white authentic blues singers of all time. I was fascinated by her phrasing, her subtlety, her wit and her unadulterated soul. I hope this re-release will bring her the recognition and audience she deserves".

Album Track: "Loves Gone Bad", Chris Clark.

Formed in 1967 at Tuskegee Institute in Alabama

Original Members: Lionel B. Richie Jnr Born 20th June 1949 in Tuskegee, Alabama (Left The Group in 1982) - Thomas McClary born 6th October 1949 in Eustis, Florida (Left The Group in 1982) - Milan Williams Born 28th March 1948 Okolona, Mississippi - Died 9th July 2006 in Houston, Texas (Left The Group in 1987) - William "Clyde" King Born 30th January 1949 Tuskegee, Alabama - Ronald La Pread Born 4th September 1946 Tuskegee, Alabama (Left The Group in 1986) - Walter Orange Born 10th December 1946 Florida.

Later Additions: J.D. Nicholas - James Dean - Sheldon Reynolds (left the group in 1987).

Motown Connection: Group - The last Motown Group or Solo Artist to Record in "Hitsville Studio A" in 1972.

The Commodores.

The Commodores' place in Motown History is assured by being the group to record the last commercial recording in "Hitsville Studio A", producing the album "Machine Gun".

The group was formed in 1967 at Tuskegee Institute in Alabama, where all of the members were students, they came together as a result of two groups "The Mystics" and "The Jays", performing for one year as the "The Mystics" in 1968, then changing the name to The Commodores in 1969, between then and 1972, they started performing from their regional base, which included Tuskegee, Montgomery and Birmingham, before moving onto the New York funk scene. The place at which they became most well known was at "Small's Paradise" in Harlem. There is one pre-Motown album on Atlantic, "Keep On Dancing" the result of a one off deal. They changed the name to The Commodores, when Walter "Clyde" Orange gave King a dictionary and told him to pick a name, the name he picked was the Commodores, the original line-up consisted of William "Clyde" King, Thomas McClary, Ronald LaPread, Walter "Clyde" Orange, Lionel Richie and Milan Williams. Interestingly, Lionel Richie was the group's saxophonist in the group's early days, not the group's lead vocalist.

Bennie Ashburn their manager (who died 1982), introduced them to Motown executive Suzanne de Passé in 1972, their signing to Motown in that year came after the group was told to be in New York City for an audition, the group did not know the audition was for The Jackson 5 tour, and two weeks later they were informed that they had been selected for the tour. They opened for The Jackson 5 for two and a half years. The group's first release on Motown was the instrumental dance recording taken from the album of the same name called "Machine Gun", written by Milan Williams, the recording became their first top ten hit. This was the last commercial recording undertaken at "Hitsville Studio A". This recording is now used at many of the biggest American sporting events, and was featured in many films, including "Boogie Nights" and "Looking for Mr. Goodbar".

Their second No1 R&B hit single and No7 chart hit was "Fancy Dancer" followed by one of their best known chart hits "Easy". It reached No1 on the pop charts, however, their soul/funk style of recording was more evident on their next release and would become the group's anthem, "Brick house". The arrangement and vocals are by Clyde Orange. Two consecutive No1 one singles would follow, the dance recording "Too Hot Ta Trot" and the Ballard "Three Times a Lady." Next was the recording of "Still", which would become the last No1 hit for the group with Lionel Richie before his departure.

In 1976, they played a forty-two-city tour with the O'Jays, followed in early 1977, with a successful Australian tour and a world tour in 1977 and 1978. Also in 1978, they toured the US, and performed with the Rolling Stones and Earth, Wind, and Fire. In 1977, they played themselves in the movie, "Thank God It's Friday", which was released by Columbia in 1978; Motown co-produced the film with Casablanca Records. In 1978, The Commodores were named the No1 R&B group by Rolling Stone magazine. Three albums were released in between 1975 and 1976, "Caught in the Act", "Movin' On" and "Hot On The Tracks" and are considered the height of their funk style music period.

While still a member of the group, Lionel Richie recorded "Endless Love" with Diana Ross the single reached No1 on the charts. The success of the single then prompted Lionel Richie to leave the group to follow a solo career. Before Lionel Richie's departure, the group had a string of hits, which included "Old Fashion Love", "Lady (You Bring Me Up)" and "Oh No" which was used in the film "The Last American Virgin", the single reached No4 on the US charts. The Commodores also recorded many songs that were not releases and never charted, the most famous being "Zoom", later covered and made into a chart hit by the group, Fat Larry's Band.

By 1982, Lionel Richie left the group and their first album without Lionel Richie was "Commodores 13" released in 1983. Their next album, "Nightshift" (a tribute to Marvin Gaye and Jackie Wilson) came out in 1985 and produced the hit single of the same name, (it also won the group its only Grammy Award for Best R&B Performance by a Duo or Group With Vocals), another change to the group came when Thomas McClary left in 1982, to pursue a solo career and to develop a gospel music company, and was replaced by Sheldon Reynolds, and by J. D. Nicholas (ex-member of the group Heatwave) in 1984. With this success The Commodores became one of Motown's most successful groups of the 1970's and 1980's, they had seven No1 songs and many other top ten hits on the pop charts.

The Commodores left Motown in 1985; they had perceived that Motown gave a commitment to releasing the group's album prior to Lionel Richie's solo release. However, the label did not honour the commitment and proceeded to release Lionel Richie's solo project first. Consequently, the group left the label and signed with Polydor in the same year and recorded the top ten hit "Going' to the Bank".

Ronald LaPread left in 1986 and moved to New Zealand, and Sheldon Reynolds left to join the group Earth, Wind and Fire in 1987. Milan Williams left the group in 1989, and sadly died in 2006. Today, The Commodores consist of Walter "Clyde" Orange, James Dean, J.D. Nicholas and William "Clyde" King, performing around the world and they are managing their own label, Commodore Records. William "Clyde" King married songwriter Shirley Hanna-King (who co-wrote "Brick House" in 1976); they have four children, Adam, Ryan Hanna, Leah Hanna and Noah. Since the late 1990's, Walter "Clyde" Orange has also been working with singer/songwriter Craig Deanto.

Formed in Detroit, Michigan in 1958 as The Blenders changing the name to The Contours in 1960

Original Members: Joe Billingslea - Billy Hogg - Billy Gordon - Hubert Johnson committed suicide in 1981 - Leroy Fair (not shown) - replaced Billy Rollin (not shown) - Huey Davis Born in Columbus Mississippi - Died 23rd February 2002 in Detroit.

Secondary members: (People that later joined the group while at Motown) Benny Reeves (Brother of Martha Reeves) - Sylvester Potts - (Took the place of Leroy Fair) - Joe Stubbs died in 1998 (Brother of Levi Stubbs of the Four Tops) - Dennis Edwards (Later joined the Temptations as their lead singer).

Motown Connection: Motown Group - Background Singers.

The Contours was the first act signed on the Gordy Label, "Do You Love Me?" released in 1960 established the group's trademark wild vocals, heavy backbeat and fancy dance steps. The Contours went through many personnel changes over the years, recorded other "party" singles (notably "First I Look at the Purse"), but felt that they were "playing second fiddle" to Motown's other vocal groups and therefore never really established themselves as an "A List" group with Motown. All the Motown money (they felt) was behind The Four Tops and The Temptations. They knew they could make it, but they believe that they weren't pushed like the others

In 1958 Billy Gordon, Billy Hoggs, Joe Billingslea and Billy Rollins formed a quartet named "The Blenders". After a short period of playing together, the group decided to replace Billy Rollins with Leroy Fair. In 1960, the late Hubert Johnson, a cousin of the late Jackie Wilson, joined the group, making it a quintet. After a visit to a recording studio called "Flick and Contour Records", the group "borrowed" part of the name and changed its name to The Contours.

In late 1960 (with some encouragement from Jackie Wilson) Berry Gordy signed The Contours to a recording contract with Motown. Their first release in January 1960 was "Whole Lotta Woman" b/side "Come On And Be Mine". The record did not have much success. Shortly afterward, Leroy Fair was asked to leave saying Leroy couldn't handle the required choreography (despite his great voice). The group replaced him twice before eventually finding Sylvester Potts as a permanent replacement for Leroy Fair. This group then recorded their second single for Motown "The Stretch" b/side "Funny" which again was not a success.

In 1962, Berry Gordy created a new label for Motown Records called the "Gordy" and signed The Contours as its first group on the label. In the summer of 1962, the group recorded the Berry Gordy record, "Do You Love Me?" resulting in the group's (and label's) first hit. Within two weeks of its release, the song roared to No2 on the Billboard Hot 100, taking the No1 spot on the R&B charts and No3 on the pop charts. It remained on the charts for five months. The record was the "Gordy" label's first million-seller, and it still holds the record as Motown's fastest rising hit of all time.

In 1963, the group charted with another hit, "Shake Sherry" and in 1964, they again charted with "Can You Do It?" and that year they recorded a ballad entitled "The Day When She Needed Me". However, by the time this song was released, the group would undergo major changes to the line up.

Citing irreconcilable creative differences with Motown and the group, in 1964 at a meeting with Berry Gordy, Billy Hoggs, Joe Billingslea and Sylvester Potts announced they were quitting. A week later Hubert Johnson also resigned, leaving Billy Gordon as the only original member of the group. Motown reconstructed the group as a quartet, adding Council Gay, Jerry Green and Alvin English. The reconstituted group recorded and released "Can You Jerk Like Me?" b/side "The Day When She Needed Me" by the earlier members of The Contours. Both songs charted in 1965. The reconstituted group also charted "First I Look At the Purse" in the same year.

After less than a year, in early 1965 Sylvester Potts returned to the group replacing Alvin English. However, almost immediately afterwards, the only remaining original member, Billy Gordon, resigned and was replaced by Joe Stubbs (former lead singer of the Falcons and brother of The Four Tops' Levi Stubbs). This "new" set of personnel charted "Just a Little Misunderstanding" in 1966. Joe Stubbs would soon resign and was replaced by Dennis Edwards (who would later replace David Ruffin in The Temptations). With Denis Edwards as lead The Contours charted "It's So Hard Being a Loser" in 1967. After their contract with Motown expired, The Contours disbanded.

About 1971 original member Joe Billingslea revived the group, playing a few dates around the country. By 1981, the group consisted of Joe Billingslea, Council Gay, Arthur Hinson, Martin 'Beanie' Upshire and C. Autry 'Breeze' Hatcher. In 1984, Arthur Hinson left the group and was replaced by current member R. Charles Davis. A week later, Council Gay left and Sylvester Potts returned to the group. In 1987, Hatcher left the group and Arthur Hinson returned.

In the 1980's and 1990's the group had to undertake "day jobs" while waiting for their second big break. "Our lead vocalist, Martin 'Beanie' Upshire, and Charles Davis are painting contractors, C. Autry Hatcher works at the Ford Rouge plant, Sylvester Potts started his own version of the group", said Billingslea, and he was a state corrections officer in addition to being a Contour.

In July 1988 "Do You Love Me?" was included in the movie, "Dirty Dancing", starring Patrick Swayze and Jennifer Grey. This revived the song and it returned to the pop charts for eight weeks. The movie soundtrack spawned a "Dirty Dancing Concert Tour", which featured The Contours and other artists including Bill Medley, Eric Carmen, Ronnie Spector, Merry Clayton and a set of dancers from the movie. A week before the tour was due to start; Beanie Upshire was replaced by Darrel Nunlee. This version of The Contours played the ten-month "Dirty Dancing Tour", entertaining over two million fans in eight countries.

On July 20, 1989, The Contours were inducted into the Rock and Roll Walk of Fame outside Royal Oak's Metropolitan Musicafe in Royal Oak, Michigan. They also received the Smokey Robinson Heroes And Legends Award in 2000 and have been nominated for The Rock and Roll Hall of Fame. They continue to perform in the US and abroad.

In 1990 they recorded "Album Running in Circles" for UK producer Ian Levine's Motorcity label, also in that year Arthur Hinson left the group and The Contours continued as a quartet until 1993 when Darell Nunlee left and Gary Grier and Al Chisholm were added taking the group back to a five-man form. This configuration existed until early 2004, when Sylvester Potts quit and was replaced by Dupree Sims. Sims then left and in 2006, Odell Jones was added to bring the group to its current configuration.

In July 1999, yet another Dirty Dancing CD, "Dirty Dancing: More Dirty Dancing [Original Recording Re-Mastered]" which included "Do You Love Me?" was released. In all, re-released version's contributed to ten million new copies of the song.

Joe Billingslea and The Contours are among the acts featured in a DVD released by Motown in January 2007 called "Motown: The Early Years", featuring their appearances on the Public Broadcasting System specials.

Album Track: "Its So Hard Being A Loser", The Contours.

Formed in 1968 in Los Angeles, California Members; Berry Gordy - Freddie Perren - Deke Richard - Alfonso "Fonzie" Mizell

Motown Connection: Writing and Production Team for Motown.

The line up of The Corporation. L to R: Deke Richards, Berry Gordy, Freddie Perrin and Fonzie Mizell (Jackson 5 at the front).

In 1968 Motown created the writing production team The Clan consisting of Deke Richards Frank Wilson, R. Dean Taylor and Pam Sawyer, this would set the template for the creation of The Corporation (The Corporation not to be confused with the 1969 Capitol Records Artists) was based on similar lines, with Deke Richards transferring to this new group employees. The Clan had produced The Supremes' "Love Child", which was a No1 hit in late 1968. Both The Clan and The Corporation were formed after the departure of Holland-Dozier-Holland. Berry Gordy was looking for individuals who would not be easily recognised by the public (as H-D-H had been), but would fill the gap left by Holland-Dozier-Holland.

Shortly after moving to California, Washington, DC schoolmate's pianist Freddie Perren and bassist Fonzie Mizell teamed up with guitarist Deke Richards, (Berry Gordy joined later) While working on song ideas, the trio came up with "I Wanna Be Free". They thought about giving the song to Motown acts Gladys Knight and The Pips or Diana Ross. When Berry Gordy joined the group Berry Gordy suggested that the song with (some revisions) would be good for a group he'd just signed. Berry Gordy thought the sound of the Jackson 5 would be an updated version of Frankie Lynon and the Teenagers ("Why Do Fools Fall In Love"). The song evolved into "I Want You Back". The Corporation were behind the early Motown hits of the Jackson 5 including their three consecutive No1 Pop hits "1 Want You Back", "A B C" and "The Love You Save".

The Corporation wasn't responsible for the Jackson 5's fourth consecutive number one single, "I'll Be There" (Berry Gordy co-wrote the song with Willie Hutch, Bob West and producer Hal Davis), but they had a strong presence on the group's LP, "Third Album" in late 1970.

The Corporation's next contribution was "Mama's Pearl", No2 R&B in early 1971. "Goin' Back To Indiana" was never released as a single, but it received an amazing amount of radio play, (very unusual in those days) and was the title of The Jackson 5's 1971 ABC TV special (with guests Bill Cosby and Tom Smothers) and the soundtrack album was a hit in late 1971.

The next single, the glistening ballad, "Maybe Tomorrow" was a major R&B hit, and made the lower parts of the pop charts in 1971. The Corporation written and produced LP track, "It's Great To Be Here" was sampled by the Motown hip hop trio 702 for their hit single, "All I Want" from their 1996 album "No Doubt". The Corporation also produced a hit for, Martha Reeves and The Vandellas, including "Bless You" in late 1971. Freddie Perren Fonzie Mizell and Deke Richards planned to release albums as The Corporation, but that never happened.

Album Track: "Love You Save", The Jackson 5.

Born Henry R Cosby aka "Hank" Born on the 12th May 1928 in Detroit, Michigan - Died 22nd January 2002 Detroit, Michigan

L to R: Paul Riser, Herbie Williams, Robert White, Hank Cosby and James Jamerson.

Motown Connection: In House Songwriter - In House Producer - In House Arranger.

Hank's important contribution as a songwriter and record producer for Motown may not be as recognised as some of the more "famous" personnel at Motown, but Hank was involved with many "landmark" recordings at Motown.

Born and raised in Detroit, Hank became a musician and learnt the tenor saxophone, while serving in Korea, Hank played in a military band. By the late 1950's, Hank was playing in the Joe Hunter band, which included the early core of "The Funk Brothers" Joe Hunter, James Jamerson and Benny Benjamin. They were part of the backing band that accompanied Jackie Wilson and this brought them into contact with Jackie Wilson's manager, a certain Berry Gordy.

At Motown one of Hank's first positions was to mentor the 12 year old Stevie Wonder. In 1963 a song co-written by Hank was captured live and recorded at the Fox Theatre Detroit. The song "Fingertips" was part of an album which demonstrated Stevie Wonder's enormous talent. "Fingertips" also highlighted Stevie Wonder's exceptional harmonica playing, later the single would top the US charts. Hank also wrote Stevie Wonder's follow-up, "Workout Stevie Workout". A modest man, Hank always stressed that Stevie Wonder took the credit for the songs that they wrote together.

Normally Stevie Wonder would come up with a melody, Sylvia Moy would write the lyric and Hank the arrangement. All three shared the song writing credit and the hits included "Uptight (Everything's Alright)" "I Was Made To Love Her" "Shoo-Bee-Doo-Bee-Doo-Da-Day" and "My Cherie Amour".

In 1968 Stevie Wonder and Hank wrote an instrumental track and stuck for words, they asked Smokey Robinson for a lyric. The resulting song, "Tears of a Clown", was included on the Miracles' LP "Make It Happen". The song was spotted by an employee in Motown subsidiary label Tamla-Motown's UK office; it was issued as a single in 1970, becoming a UK No1 and was then released in the US repeating its success. As late as 1970, (when Stevie Wonder had started writing his own songs), they collaborated on "Never Had a Dream Come True" single.

Hank wrote and produced hits for many other artists including Jnr Walker and The All Stars, Martha Reeves and The Vandellas. Notable singles included "No Matter What Sign You Are" in 1969 for Diana Ross and The Supremes. He was also part of the team who wrote and produced the 1968 single "Love Child" and 1969 "I'm Livin' in Shame", both for Diana Ross and The Supremes, and the anti-Vietnam song "I Should Be Proud" in 1970 for Martha Reeves and The Vandellas. With Mickey Stevenson, Hank wrote and produced "That's the Way it Goes" for Marvin Gaye in 1965 and the classic Marvin Gaye and Kim Weston duet "It Takes Two" in 1967. In 1970 Cosby advised Marvin Gaye against continuing with his self-indulgent album "What's Going On", like many at Motown Hank had not appreciated that Gaye was radically changing soul music.

Hank thought that Berry Gordy was making a mistake by shifting Motown's operations to Los Angeles although Hank knew that Motown had to change, with reluctance, Hank did move to Los Angeles, California.

Outside Motown, Hank produced "Mirror Image" in 1974 for Blood, Sweat and Tears and in 1978 "We Meet Again" a solo album for Martha Reeves. Hank also discovered the solo singer Colonel Abrams and recorded him for Polydor.

By the 1980's Cosby had retired from the business and his later years were marred by ill health.

Stevie Wonder played "My Cherie Amour" at Hanks funeral, Hank was married with three sons, of whom one son pre-deceased him.

Album Track: "My Cherie Amour", Stevie Wonder.

Carolyn Crawford

Born in Detroit, Michigan

Motown Connection: Singer - Background vocals.

It is suggested that Carolyn was only thirteen years old when she signed to Motown in 1963 after attending a talent contest organised by the radio station WCHB in Detroit, the prize being a recording contract with the Motown. Carolyn was placed on the Tamla label (a subsidiary of Motown) firstly acting as backup vocalist for other Motown artists at "Hitsville Studio A". While on Tamla label, Carolyn recorded three singles, her debut single, "Forget About Me", which proved unsuccessful, Carolyn's next release was a minor US hit in 1964, written and produced by Smokey Robinson's called, "My Smile Is Just A Frown (Turned Upside Down)". Carolyn third release called, "When Someone's Good To You", was not successful in the US, but became a massive northern soul hit in the UK.

Other recordings at Motown include, "I'll Come Running" in 1964, "My Heart", "Devil In His Heart", "Too Young, Too Long", and "Until You Came Along".

Carolyn left Motown after these recordings, and also left the music industry until the 1970's, returning briefly as a background vocalist and occasional producer of minor disco hits, before joining the Detroit Soul Group Chapter 8, in 1975. Carolyn left the group a year later (to be replaced by Anita Baker), and joined the vocal trio Hodges, James and Smith.

Signing with Mercury records in 1978, Carolyn re-launched her solo career with her first album for the label called "My Name Is Caroline", in 1979, Carolyn had a minor hit called "Coming On Strong", followed by the album "Nice And Soulful" also in 1979.

In the 1990's Carolyn recorded for Ian Levine's Motorcity label, releasing the record "Heartaches". Today, Carolyn's singles and unreleased session material from her Motown days are popular on many Motown compilations albums, including the "Cellar Full Of Motown" series recordings.

Billy Davis

Aka Roquel Billy Davis and Tyran Carlo Born on the 11th July 1932 in Detroit, Michigan - Died 2nd September 2004 in New Rochelle, New York, New York State

Motown Connection: Billy co-wrote hits for the Brunswick Records star Jackie Wilson along with Motown founder Berry Gordy and his sister Gwen Gordy - A cousin of Lawrence Payton (The Four Tops) - With Gwen and Anna Gordy, Billy Davis set up Anna Records in Detroit - Writer and Producer (with Berry Gordy) in the early days of Motown.

Only the most ardent Motown fans would know Billy, but this Detroiter played a key role in Motown's early days. Billy attended the Northern High School (whose ex-pupils included James Jamerson, one of the legendary Motown 'Funk Brothers') the Wayne State University, and the Maurice King School of Music (the musical director of artist development at Motown Records for ten years). Billy was a singer, a songwriter, and a producer of distinction.

His career started when a friend Joe Battle, encouraged him to write songs and send them to record labels. Joe Battle sent these compositions to a California Record Company, several months later Billy received a check for $356 for a song called "Lessie Mae."

An original member of "The Four Aims" which later evolved into "The Four Tops" For the first three years Billy was a "de-facto" member (the introduction coming from Lawrence Payton his cousin.) Their demo was enough to get them signed to Chess Records in Chicago. However, they had no hits during their time with Chess, but Billy's talent for producing songs was recognised. These records being passed on to other Chess Artists (like The Flamingos and The Moonglows).

While Billy was dating Gwen Gordy, she introduced Billy to her brother Berry Gordy. They began writing songs together including "Reet Petite" credited to Berry Gordy and "Tyran Carlo," (one of Billy a.k.a); it reached the lower parts of the charts for Jackie Wilson in 1957. One historic footnote regarding "Reet Petite" was it took a record 29 years 42 days to reach the top spot in the UK. First released in the UK on the 15th November 1957, when the re-release reached No1 on 29th November 1986. With Gwen Gordy also credited, they also wrote the next Jackie Wilson record (his biggest hit up to that point), "Lonely Teardrops," which made it into the Top 10 in early 1959.

After parting company with Nat Tarnopol of Brunswick (Jackie Wilson's Record Company), Billy, with Gwen and Anna Gordy, established their own record label Anna Records in Detroit. Their first hit in 1960 was with "Money" the record was sung by Barrett Strong, (Barret Strong would later team up as Norman Whitfield as a writing partner in the late Sixties). "Money" written by Berry Gordy and Janie Bradford was released using Anna Records as the distributors, but was a Motown Record.

Billy, through his relationship with Berry Gordy, was instrumental in helping establish Motown (from around 1959 to 1961) towards the end of his involvement, Harvey Fuqua (of The Moonglows) arrived to help Berry Gordy start the national push for recognition of the Motown and Tamla labels. Harvey would eventually marry Gwen Gordy, and eventually Billy found himself being squeezed out, not just by Harvey but by the rapid rise in Motown's fortunes.

Billy went back to Chicago, and took over A&R at Chess Records, Billy changed the direction of the label from "blues label" to a more soul/pop sound, and Billy worked with Etta James, re-signed "The Dells", and introduced new acts, like Fontella Bass. Another song co-written by Billy and Chess staff pianist and producer Leonard Caston, 'I Had a Talk With Man', went to No3 on the R&B charts for Mitty Collier, in the autumn of 1964.

When "Rescue Me" by Fontella Bass was released in 1965 and became an international hit, because of this success for the next three years Ad Agency McCann-Erickson (a New York-Based Advertising Agency) kept approaching Billy to join them. In 1968 Billy finally became their Senior Vice-President, and Music Director. Billy wrote "I'd Like to Teach the World to Sing," (co-written with Roger Cook and Roger Greenaway), which became a worldwide hit, 1971-72; it became a platinum record for the New Seekers. Billy also wrote "Have a Coke and a Smile", and "I was Raised on Country Sunshine", another hit jingle. Davis moved on to other accounts like Nescafe, before producing the tune responsible for convincing millions that the time to relax is "Miller Time".

Billy also worked with or wrote songs for Little Milton, Aretha Franklin, Marvin Gaye, James Brown, The Supremes and Gladys Knight. Shortly before his death in 2004, he produced an album for Australian Kate Cerberano.

Huey Davis

Born Huey Marvin Davis in 1939 Columbus, Mississippi - Died 23rd February 2002 Detroit, Michigan

Motown Connection: Guitarist for The Contours.

Huey moved to Detroit with his father in the Fifties, after leaving Columbus in Mississippi to pursue a career in music. In 1958 Billy Gordon, Billy Hoggs, Joe Billingslea and Billy Rollins formed a quartet named "The Blenders". After a short period of playing together, the group decided to replace Billy Rollins with Leroy Fair. In 1960, the late Hubert Johnson, a cousin of the late Jackie Wilson, joined the group, making it a quintet. After a visit to a recording studio called "Flick and Contour Records", the group "borrowed" part of the name and changed its name to The Contours.

In late 1960 (with some encouragement from Jackie Wilson) Berry Gordy signed The Contours to a recording contract with Motown. Their first release in January 1960 was "Whole Lotta Woman" b/side "Come On And Be Mine". This group then recorded their second single for Motown "The Stretch" b/side "Funny" which again was not a success. In the summer of 1962, the group recorded the Berry Gordy record, "Do You Love Me?" resulting in the group's (and label's) first hit. Huey was the guitarist on that record and it remained the high spot of his recording career.

After their contract with Motown expired, The Contours disbanded in the late Sixties, Huey then went to work in the construction industry and as a security guard (a career that he adopted up until his death). In July 1988 "Do You Love Me" was included in the movie, "Dirty Dancing", starring Patrick Swayze and Jennifer Grey. This revived the song and it returned to the pop charts for eight weeks. The movie soundtrack spawned a "Dirty Dancing Concert Tour", which featured The Contours and other artists including Bill Medley, Eric Carmen, Ronnie Spector, Merry Clayton and a set of dancers from the movie.

Huey was 63 when he died at his home in Detroit, Huey was survived by five children, several grandchildren and his brother.

Born 1948 in New York City, New York

Motown Connection: Creative assistant to Berry Gordon - President of Motown Productions - Co-writer the screenplay, "Lady Sings the Blues" - Executive producer of "Motown 25: Yesterday, Today, Forever" and "Motown Returns to the Apollo" plus many other Motown Projects.

After dropping out of college in 1967, Suzanne became the talent co-ordinator at the Cheetah Club on Manhattan's East Side, New York. Then Suzanne was introduced to Berry Gordy (by future Supremes member Cindy Birdsong) who hired Suzanne as his creative assistant.

Suzanne was given the accolade of introducing The Jackson 5 to Motown, but it was Gladys Knight who used her influence to bring the Jackson 5 to the company, Gladys Knight wrote to Berry Gordy suggesting that he check out the group, however, credit for the group's discovery is sometimes mistakenly given to Diana Ross. This apart, it is without doubt, Suzanne's influence that helped shape the group's development at Motown. Suzanne was responsible for signing, coaching, and developing Motown's most popular act of the 1970's.

In 1973 Suzanne helped to produce television specials such as TCB and G.I.T. on Broadway, both starring Diana Ross and The Supremes and The Temptations. Involved in virtually every aspect of the company, producing the screenplay for the Oscar-nominated "Lady Sings the Blues" in 1972 which starred Diana Ross as Billie Holliday, Suzanne (and Lonne Elder III) became the first African-Americans to be nominated for an Academy Award for writing. Suzanne co-wrote "Lady Sings the Blues" with Terence McCloy and Chris Clark (former Motown Recording Artist).

In 1981, Berry Gordy appointed her as President of Motown Productions, when the company began its big push into TV production. Its first success was the stunning Emmy-winning variety special "Motown 25: Yesterday, Today, Forever" on NBC in 1983, which included Michael Jackson's first showing of his ability to "moonwalk". Also in 1983 Suzanne expanded Motown beyond its musical boundaries with a series of dramatic specials including the 1983 CBS drama "Happy Endings" which teamed John Schneider and Catherine Hicks.

For much of the remainder of the decade, Suzanne and Motown looked to its rich history for a series of TV specials, featuring the "Motown Revue" by NBC in 1985, (hosted by Smokey Robinson) to the Emmy-winning "Motown Returns to the Apollo" again by NBC in 1985, to the long-running "Motown on Showtime" from 1986 to 1990. Suzanne was also developing Lionel Richie's solo career (after he left the Commodores), launching Rick James and the funk era.

After Berry Gordy sold Motown, Suzanne entered into a producing partnership with Berry Gordy and among their first projects in 1989 was the Emmy-nominated CBS project Western "Lonesome Dove". Adapted from the novel by Larry McMurtry, the programme proved a surprising success, leading to several sequels (i.e. "Return to Lonesome Dove" CBS 1993; "Larry McMurtry's Street of Laredo" CBS 1995) and a syndicated series ("Lonesome Dove: The Outlaw Years/Lonesome Dove: The Early Years" 1994-96).

Now firmly entrenched as one of the media's most successful female producers, Suzanne oversaw such diverse shows as the roller derby update "Rollergames" (1989) and the documentary "Small Sacrifices" by ABC in 1989, starring Farrah Fawcett as a woman who attempted to kill her own children.

In 1991, Berry Gordy withdrew from production and allowed Suzanne to create her own de Passe Entertainment, (with Suzanne Costin as number two). In 1992 came "Liberators", a PBS project about the African American troops who liberated concentration camps during World War II, as well as the Emmy-nominated ABC biopic "The Jackson's: An American Dream". Working from McMurtry's novels, she as executive produced both "Buffalo Girls" by CBS in 1995 and "Larry McMurtry's Dead Man's Walk" by ABC in 1996.

de Passe Entertainment then launched the weekly sitcom "Sister, Sister" by ABC between 1994 and 1995 and The WB between 1995 1999, which starred Tia and Tamara Mowry as twins literally separated at birth. The sitcom "On Our Own" (ABC, 1994-95) starred the Smolletts, a family of six performing siblings who bore more than a passing resemblance to the Jackson's while "Smart Guy" (The WB, 1997-99) starred the Mowrey's younger brother Tahj as a boy genius.

Suzanne served as executive producer of the Emmy-nominated NBC "The Temptations" in 1998 and her company also developed similarly-themed projects on singers Jackie Wilson and Marvin Gaye, as well as one on the life of Elaine Brown, the leading Black Panther who was also a Motown recording artist in the early 1970's.

Suzanne is still the CEO of television production company de Passé Entertainment and perhaps, second only to Oprah Winfrey, ranks as one of the most prominent and important African-American women working in television. Suzanne is an honorary member of Alpha Kappa Alpha Sorority, Inc.

Album Track: "I Want You Back", The Jackson 5.

Born Reba Jeanette Smith on the 1st February 1928 - Died 17th February 2001 in Ojai, California

Motown Connection: Recording Artist - First White Artist Signed to Motown - Debbie and Deke Richards collaborated on Writing and Producing for Motown.

Debbie Dean had a long and varied career, but with a limited amount of success, Debbie recorded under many names such as, Penny Smith, Debra Dion and as Debbie Stevens for ABC Paramount and Roulette Records.

In 1960, Berry Gordy made Debbie the first white artist signed to any of his labels. The blond-reddish-haired singer debuted as Debbie Dean with "Itty Bitty Pity Love" b/side "But I'm Afraid" in August 1961, but it was never promoted as Motown decided to "pull" the record in favour of an "answer record" to The Miracles' "Shop Around" entitled "Don't Let Him Shop Around" a month after the record hit the charts (in September 1961). The song by Berry Gordy, and his sister Loucye Wakefield never troubled the charts. Debbie's third single, "Everybody's Talking About Me" b/side "I Cried All Night" released in March 1962 did no better. It was rumoured that Motown founder Berry Gordy was trying to change Motown's image to reflect the sign above the door at West Grand Blvd the "Sound of Young America", and that Debbie (who was 34 at the time) may not have fitted this image.

After Motown, Debbie migrated to California where she attempted to get her career back on track, this included Debbie working in night-clubs around California, Debbie also entered many talent shows and showcases and was offered a few low key acting roles. Nobody in California knew she was an ex-Motown artist and assumed she was just a singer who was try-ing to break into show business. Debbie did get a one-off deal with Sue Records, (as Debra Dion) she released "Don't Bug Me Baby" b/side  "I Want to Know If Your Love Is Real" in 1964, but It failed to chart. Debbie didn't have another release until 1966, (as Debra Dion again), but this time for Treva Records; unfortunately, the single "Take My Hand" failed again.

While working at a California club, Debbie was introduced to and became a friend of Deke Richards (employed by Motown at the time, but would become part of the in house writing and producing team The Corporation). Deke was there with his band Deke and The Deacons and often opened for Ike and Tina Turner. After seeing her performance, the two struck up a conversation and Debbie spoke of her earlier career at Motown. The revelation stunned Deke, with Deke's help, Debbie renewed her ties with Motown and the two collaborated on many songs, the most notable "I Can't Dance to That Music You're Playing" (Martha and The Vandellas), "Honey Bee" (The Supremes), and "Why Did You Leave Me" The Temptations. Betty Boo would later record "I Can't Dance to That Music You're Playing" the hit single (using a combination this and "Hey DJ") was a minor hit for Betty Boo.

Reverting to the name Debbie Dean, she recorded some new material (produced by Deke), but only one single came out, "Stay My Love" b/side "Why Am I Loving You" on VIP (a Motown Subsidiary Label), but no success again for this single made Motown pull the second single, "You Asked Me,". Debbie became a life-long California resident and Debbie did stay on the fringes of music for the rest of her career, but without any major success.

Born Pauline Matthews on the 6th March 1947 in Little Horton, Bradford, West Yorkshire, England

Kiki Dee on a Tamla Motown tour.

Motown Connection: First White British Artist To Be Signed by Motown - Solo Artist.

Kiki and I share the same birthday place, Bradford, West Yorkshire; in its time the city was the centre of the textile industry in the UK, the classic Northern city with its mills and factories. Both her father and brother worked in the mills as weaving overlookers all their working lives (as did my own family). Her father worked at one point at Salts Mill in Saltaire, Bradford, now world famous for its David Hockney's exhibition of his work. Although my research has not linked Kiki to the "Northern Soul Scene", apart from a single release which was played at Northern Soul venues, she must have been aware of its existence and the music coming out of the movement. Kiki had a typical English upbringing which included with her brother and sister a trip to the seaside every year with her parents. The designation would be the Yorkshire seaside resorts of Scarborough, Whitby or Blackpool.

Kiki's first performances at the start of her career were around the clubs of northern England with a local band from Bradford in the early 1960's. Her first recordings were as a session singer, singing backing vocals for Dusty Springfield, among others, and was well regarded by other singers of the time, who could not understand how she had become a major solo artist in her own right. Mitch Murray who came up with her stage name Kiki Dee, and also wrote her first single, "Early Night". She did record a single in 1965, released in that year that was called "Why Don't I Run Away From You" which was a big hit on Radios London and Caroline in 1965. The 1968 recording, "On a Magic Carpet Ride", which was originally a b/side, never charted, but remained popular on the Northern Soul Scene.

In the US Kiki's soulful voice brought her to the attention of Barney Ales, who at the time was Motown's Head of Marketing and Promotion, Barney Ales invited her to Detroit and was so impressed with her style and vocals that he offered and Kiki accepted, a recording contract with Motown, becoming the first white British artist to be signed by the label. Interestingly, when Kiki arrived none of the creative people knew who she was or why she was in Detroit. Kiki released her first Motown single in 1970, followed by her first album "Great Expectations", "Great Expectations'" had no real commercial success when issued by Motown, however, Kiki was proud of the work she produced while in Detroit. Kiki stayed for twelve weeks while recording the album, and she has always expressed that the experience was priceless.

In the days before BBC Radio 1, Kiki was a regular performer of other cover hits on the BBC Light programme; she also starred with a group of session singers in the BBC Two TV programme "One More Time". Kiki also appeared in an early episode of The Benny Hill Show in January 1971, performing the Blood, Sweat and Tears hit, "You've Made Me So Very Happy". Kiki next signed with Elton John's record label Rocket Records, her first major solo hits were "Amoureuse" written by French performer and songwriter, Véronique Sanson in 1973, and "I've Got the Music in

Me" written by Tobias Stephen Boshell in 1974. Her most famous song was a duet with Elton John, entitled "Don't Go Breaking My Heart", which was released in 1976 and went to No1 in both in the US and UK chart. This recording gave her the international recognition which she thought would have come from her Motown contract.

Kiki also recorded for other labels after leaving Rocket Records, including the 1980 album "Kiki Dee's Greatest Hits" for Warwick Records and for the Ariola label the 1981 album "Perfect Timing"

Top right: Ken East (EMI), centre: Martha Reeves, bottom right: John Reid (UK Motown Label Manager), bottom left: (one of The Vandellas), the other two unknown.

and the hit single "Star" which between 1987 and 1990 became the theme music to the BBC One TV programme "Opportunity Knocks". Also in 1981, Kiki did another duet with Elton John, recording a cover of the Four Tops' song "Loving You Is Sweeter Than Ever". In 1982, Kiki supplied backing vocals to Elton John's album "Too Low for Zero". Kiki also performed at 1985 "Live Aid", reprising "Don't Go Breaking My Heart" with Elton John, and performing backing vocals on the other songs in his set.

In 1987 now signed to EMI Records Kiki had a minor album hit with "Angel Eyes" and also appeared in musical theatre, notably in the lead role in Willy Russell's West

End musical "Blood Brothers", at the West End opening (after touring for six months) where she took on the role (originally played by Barbara Dickson for the 1981 production), this production is still running today, and Kiki received an Olivier Award nomination in 1989 for her acting skills. In 1990, she contributed to the last recording studio collaboration between Alan Parsons and Eric Woolfson, on the album "Freudiana", performing "You're On Your Own". There followed in 1991 the greatest hits package "Spotlight on Kiki Dee Greatest Hits" on Rocket Records and did further collaboration with Elton John in 1993 with another duet for his Duets album, a cover version of Cole Porter's "True Love", which reached No2 in the UK charts.

The next album release was the 1994 "The Very Best of Kiki Dee" on the Polygram label which was a modest No62 UK chart hit, followed by the 1995 "Almost Naked" and "Where Rivers Meet" the first two albums Kiki recorded with Carmelo Luggeri, both on the Tickety-boo label. In 2005 Motown finally released an album covering her stay at the label called "Love Makes The World Go Round: The Motown Years" issued by Universal Records/Motown records and also in that year the album "The Walk of Faith" Kiki's third album with Carmelo Luggeri, on Spellbound Records was released. The next album was the 1975 recorded album "Cage The Songbird" which was finally released by EMI (along with Kiki other EMI recordings) in 2008, interestingly, Kiki holds the rights to the entire back catalogue of her Rocket recording, kindly given to Kiki by Elton John, which are leased to EMI.

Kiki is still touring with her music partner, Carmelo Luggeri and performs semi acoustically in concert all around the UK and Europe occasionally making TV appearances to enhance her music career, Kiki also has her own web site at www.kikiandcarmelo.com. Kiki when approached about this publication is quoted as saying "I still love to sing live and communicate with an audience and as long as I feel I have my voice and my song writing, I will keep going", Kiki lives and records from home in Hertfordshire.

Born on the 16th June 1941 in Detroit, Michigan

Motown Connection: Musician - Background Singer - Singer - Writer - Producer - Arranger - Part of Holland-Dozier-Holland Team - Record Label Owner (Hot Wax and Invictus).

Born and raised in Detroit, Michigan, Lamont grew up listening to his father's record collection of seasoned pop/jazz singers. Lamont sang in the Baptist gospel choir and to the classical music his aunt played on the family piano. By age 10, he started collecting his own records (from Johnny Mathis to Frankie Lymon), wrote his first lyrics at 11, added music at 12 and by the age of 13, knew he wanted to be a singer. Lamont was a part of Detroit's late 1950's vibrant jazz/vocal scene, singing with the Romeos and The Voice Masters. Lamont's first record was "Lets Talk It Over" written and produced by Berry Gordy released in 1960 on Berry Gordy's sister's label, Anna Records, and was credited to Lamont Anthony (Lamont's stage name).

Singer/songwriter/producer Lamont Dozier was part of the legendary Motown production team of Holland-Dozier-Holland. Lamont's part of the team was the creation of the melodies. A major force in the 1960's early 1970's pop and R&B chart, firstly with Motown, then the team later formed Invictus and Hot Wax Records, and enjoyed success with the Chairman of the Board, Freda Payne, 100 Proof Aged in Soul, the Honey Cone and 8th Day. It seemed for a short while after their departure from Motown to form their own labels, that history would repeat itself, but by the late 1970's their run of success with Invictus and Hot Wax came to an end.

By 1962, Eddie Holland replaced Freddy Gorman, who at the time was working with Brian Holland (Eddie's brother) and Lamont and the team made their debut with the Marvelettes' "Locking Up My Heart." As they say the rest is history, going on to become one of the most successful record producing teams in the history of the music industry. Lamont also worked with Berry Gordy on Motown singles for Marv Johnson.

In 1963 it all came together for Holland Dozier Holland, beginning with The Supremes' No1 international hit "Where Did Our Love Go?" Lamont along with his writing/arranging/production team of Holland-Dozier-Holland enjoyed a phenomenal five-year run at the top of the R&B and pop charts, selling millions of records for Motown. As the team has stated many times, they became a "hit factory" within a hit factory. Many other Motown acts benefited from their input including, The Four Tops, who recorded many HDH songs, achieving international No1 hits "I Can't Help Myself (Sugar Pie, Honey Bunch)" and "Reach out I'll be There".

In 1967 Holland-Dozier-Holland, wanting a share of Motown's success and bitter over their lack of creative control, left Motown with the intention of creating their own record label. However the team quickly became entangled in legal disputes with Motown (at Berry Gordy's instigation) and as a result they were barred from writing and producing any material for the next few years.

However, by 1970, they were able to form their own labels, "Invictus" and "Hot Wax" where they wrote and produced hits for the Chairmen of the Board and Freda Payne.

In 1973 the first splits began to appear in the Holland-Dozier-Holland team, Lamont signed with ABC Records as a solo artist. His debut ABC album, "Out Here On My Own", yielded the hit ballad, "Trying to Hold on to My Woman" and the upbeat "Fish Ain't Bitin'" with its President Nixon reference ("tricky dick trying to be slick").

Lamont's next album, "Black Bach", included the singles "Let Me Start Tonight", "All Cried Out", "Put Out the Fire", "Rose" and "Thank You for the Dream." Also around this time, Lamont produced and wrote most of the songs for the self-titled debut album of actor Lawrence Hilton-Jacobs (best known as Boom Boom Washington of the sitcom Welcome Back Kotter). Despite becoming a collector's item in the years to come (because of the quality of the production), the album wasn't a sales success.

Moving to Warner Brothers Records in 1976, Lamont's next album was "Right There". The album was full of smooth ballads including, "Groovin' on a Natural High", "With a Little Bit of Mending (We Could Be as Good as New)", "Joy", "Ain't Never Loved Nobody (Like I Love You)", "Wild Frame of Mind" and "Good Eye". The album briefly charted when it was released, but again was not a major success. Lamont's next Warner Brothers album was in 1977, called "Peddlin' Music on the Side", and again only charted briefly. The 12" version of "Going Back to My Roots" by Lamont has become collector's items, and was later turned into an international hit when covered by Odyssey for their 1981 disco hit.

The 1979 dance-oriented album "Bittersweet" was produced by former colleague at Motown Frank Wilson, but Lamont was not getting the breakthrough or chart success he required. Lamont did have a hit single in 1980 producing for the group Zingara a record titled "Love's Calling" (with James Ingram on lead vocal).

By 1981 Lamont had signed to the ARC label (American Recording Company). The album "Working on You" was issued early in that year. The high tempo "Cool Me Out" was the first single issued becoming a favourite song on the UK Northern Soul Scene. The albums had smooth ballads and was a very much pop oriented including, "Nobody Told Me", the title track and "Too Little Too Long" and "Why (Ain't My Love Enough)". Lamont's next move was to the independent label M&M, created by former Motown executives Mike Roshkind and Mike Lushka. One single, the jubilant "Shout It Out", did hit the lower reaches of the charts in early 1982.

Lamont next moved to Europe (particularly England) for two very productive years, asked by "Pete Waterman (of British production trio Stock, Aitken & Waterman) to meet Alison Moyet, Simply Red, Boy George and Eric Clapton, from this visit came the major international hit "Two Hearts". The song was a collaboration between Lamont and Phil Collins and came from the soundtrack of the film "Buster"; the recording earned the duo a Grammy, a Brit award, a Golden Globe, and an Oscar nomination.

This attention led to one last major piece of work for Atlantic Records, Lamont's 1991 album "Inside Seduction". Lamont and his wife, Barbara Ullman Dozier, then started their own company, sharing the day-to-day business responsibilities. Lamont's first album, "Lamont Dozier...An American Original", earned Lamont Grammy nomination for "Best Traditional R&B Vocal Album". However, because it was only available over the Internet, few people ever knew it existed.

Lamont Dozier issued a CD in 2004 called "Reflections of ..." This album finds Lamont re-interpreting 12 international No1 hits singing all of the lead and background vocals including, "I Hear A Symphony", "Baby Love". Lamont's personal favourites are the first single, "I Hear a Symphony" and "My World Is Empty Without You".

Lamont still remains active in the music industry and was inducted in 1990, as part of the Holland-Dozier-Holland team into the Rock and Roll Hall of Fame. Regularly featured in radio and television documentaries, and winning the prestigious Ivor Novello award in 2004 in London, England, with everyone from dance music star Mya to alternative rock band Linkin Park, sampling his songs, the music still lives on. Completing his Broadway musical "Roll Over Beethoven," and launching new artists on Jam Right, he is married with three children.

Aka "Chunk of Funk," Born on the 8th July 1930 in Detroit, Michigan - Died 18th September 1992 In Detroit, Michigan

Motown Connection: Pianists/Bandleader of The Funk Brothers (Motown In House Band) - Arranger.

Earl was born in Detroit and was undertaking music lessons by age 5, doing his first paying performances as a musician at age 14. Trained as a classical pianist Earl took lessons at the Detroit Conservatory of Music. Eventually playing professionally as a teenager with Barry Harris, Yusef Lateef, Tommy Flanagan, Roland Hanna, Kenny Burrell, and Hank Jones. In between factory work, part-time playing jobs, and two stints in the Armed Services, Earl caught tuberculosis and spent two and a half years in a veteran's administration hospital.

In 1956, jazz guitarist Emmett Sleigh hired Earl to play in his band, Emmett Sleigh and the Sleighriders. Next Earl was hired to replace departing organist Jimmy Smith in Chris Columbo's band. While later touring with Lloyd Price (a future colleague at Motown) Earl met fellow Detroiter James

Jamerson in Rockville, New York in 1959. Working with Jackie Wilson on "Reet Petite", "To Be Loved", "Lonely Teardrops", and "That's Why I Love You So" brought Earl into contact with James Jamerson who had been recording with Motown Records. Berry Gordy had written or co-written all of Jackie Wilson's hits to that point. And James Jamerson encouraged Earl to move back to Detroit and consider working for Motown. Earl had moved to New York to play with rhythm and blues bands.

Returning to Detroit in 1961, turning down the first offer to join Motown as a session player, Earl joined Motown in 1962. With the offer of regular work, he quickly became part of the studio-recording band (eventually becoming The Funk Brothers). Considered one of Motown's outstanding studio musicians, however, Earl wasn't the only piano player, Motown's first pianists were Joe Hunter and pianist Johnny Griffith. When Hunter left Motown in 1963, Mickey Stevenson (Motown's A&R man) named Earl as the bandleader for The Funk Brothers.

As bandleader to bassist James Jamerson, and drummer Benny Benjamin, other key members were guitarists Robert White, Eddie Willis, and Joe Messina; percussionist Eddie "Bongo" Brown; vibes/percussionist Jack Ashford; and later, "replacement" drummers Uriel Jones and Richard "Pistol" Allen. Earl and the rest of the band were on call 24 hours a day, every day of the week. Earl started a musician's strike during a 1965 European tour when the band was asked to play backing tracks for Motown acts appearing on a British television show. Originally, they had been told that the acts were all going to lip-sync. After that incident, Earl was looked on as a "father" figure by the rest of his fellow Motown Funk Brothers.

Motown wasn't too keen about Earl, and the rest of The Funk Brothers recording for other labels. Several music entrepreneurs, local and otherwise, took advantage of the situation offering the band more money, leading to The Funk Brothers being heard on a lot of "backdoor sessions" for the local Golden World and Ric Tic label owned by Ed Wingate. The band can be heard on "Agent Double 0 Soul by Edwin Starr in 1965 and "Stop Her On Sight" in 1966, on Ollie McLaughlin's Karen label, "Cool Jerk" by The Capitols in July 1966. Making the trips to nearby Chicago, The Funk Brothers played session on several records for producer Carl Davies including "I Just Wanna Testify" by the Parliaments in 1967.

Also in 1967 The Funk Brothers did background sessions for "Just Be Sincere" and "(Your Love Keeps Lifting Me) Higher and Higher" which set the stage for Jackie Wilson's mid 1960's comeback and was his second No1 R&B in October 1967, followed by "Since You Showed Me How to Be Happy" a hit in November 1967, "I Get The Sweetest Feeling" in June 1968, "Can Feel Those Vibrations" and "This Love Is Real" in November 1970. The Funk Brothers also travelled south to record in Muscle Shoals and Atlanta among other cities. During the 1960's, it was rumoured that Dionne Warwick's song writing/producing, duo Burt Bacharach and Hal David would have clandestine meetings with The Funk Brothers to discuss various projects.

Motown made it known, if not by words, but certainly by action, that they wanted Earl (and The Funk Brothers) to remain in the recording studio, laying tracks for Motown's Artists. However, the Funk Brothers wanted to release an album of their own and reluctantly Motown issued, "Earl Van Dyke Plays the Motown Sound" and The Earl of Funk in September 1970, both released on Motown's subsidiary label Soul. Neither release was what they really wanted, which was a jazz album. On the album Earl Van Dyke "Plays the Motown Sound", Van Dyke played organ over existing Motown tracks. Motown objected to the word "funk," so both releases carried the moniker Earl Van Dyke and the Soul Brothers.

After years of chronic health problems and a heroin addiction, Benny Benjamin died and James Jamerson's alcoholism began to take its toll which Earl took very badly. The Funk Brothers began to bicker with the label about their pay scale and their lack of name recognition (the musicians were never listed on the back of the album sleeves). Motown Records relocated to Los Angeles, partly based on Berry Gordy's desire to become involved in the motion picture business and the era of The Funk Brothers (based on Hitsville Studio A) came to an end.

During the early 1970's, Earl began to accompany mainstream acts when they would appear in the Detroit area and began working with Freda Payne as her musical director. Earl joined the in-house band at the Hyatt Regency in Dearborn, Michigan, the backing singers included Sammy Davis Jnr, Vic Damone, Mel Tormé. Earl was still performing locally in Detroit in the 1980's and did advertising jingle recording sessions, the occasional session work, including The Four Tops on "Catfish" for ABC Records, in October 1976, and "The Show Must Go" again for ABC Records in October 1977. Earl also undertook local festivals, worked with the Jimmy Wilkins band, and his own group of musicians.

For a couple of years later in the mid-1980's, Earl lived in California, before moving back to Detroit after not being able to adjust to the California lifestyle. Earl was successful in gaining a job at the Detroit Board of Education at Osborne High School.

He retired in 1991, but continued to play the piano and organ. Earl was then diagnosed with the debilitating carpal tunnel syndrome. The following year in September of 1992, at the age of 62, Earl died of prostate cancer at Harper Hospital in Detroit.

Signature songs: The introduction to "Stop Her On Sight" in 1966 by Edwin Starr, at first not a Motown song, but this moonlighting session became part of the Motown catalogue on the purchase of Golden World.

Dennis Edwards

Born on the 3rd Feb 1943 in Birmingham, Alabama

Motown Connection: Background Singer - Vocalist with The Contours - Member of The Temptations.

Ruffin, Edwards and Kendrick.

Dennis was the son of the Reverend Dennis Edwards Snr, he began singing at two years old, in his fathers' church, but his family moved to Detroit when he was seven. As a high school student, Dennis sang with "The Crowns of Joy" gospel group, and then formed a soul-jazz band called "Dennis Edwards and the Firebirds" in 1961, inspired by organist Richard "Groove" Holmes, followed by a single for an obscure Detroit label called International Soulville Records. The recording called "I Didn't Have To (But I Did)" b/side "Johnnie On The Spot", the record has become a very rare recording on the Northern Soul scene in the UK.

While performing in Detroit clubs, Dennis and the group were heard by Motown bass player James Jamerson and he suggested that Dennis come to Motown for an audition. After the audition Dennis joined the Contours in 1967 as their lead singer, the group were already signed to Motown, and one of his most memorable recordings was "It's So Hard Being A Loser," but Dennis was soon to replace David Ruffin as lead singer of The Temptations in 1968, when David Ruffin was asked to leave the group. Dennis's first appearance as a Temptation was in July 1968, however, David Ruffin continued to show up at Temptation's performances uninvited and would join them on stage. Eventually security guards had to be used to keep him David Ruffin away.

Dennis then spent the next nine years in that role, taking lead vocals on such songs as "Cloud Nine", "I Can't Get Next to You", "Ball of Confusion" and "Psychedelic Shack" as well as the groundbreaking singles "Papa Was a Rolling Stone" and "Masterpiece". With Dennis as lead vocalist on "Cloud Nine" and "Papa Was a Rollin' Stone", both won Grammy Awards, interestingly, when the recording of "Papa Was a Rollin' Stone" was first presented to the group, Dennis allegedly refused to sing the first verse, because his father had actually died on "the third of September", just like the father portrayed in the song. It is suggested that Dennis was offended by this coincidence and accused songwriters Norman Whitfield and Barrett Strong of deliberately assigning him the verse; they denied that the lyric assignment was intentional.

Dennis remained in The Temptations until being asked to leave by Otis Williams in 1977, just before the group's departure from Motown to Atlantic Records. Staying at Motown he started his solo career which proved unsuccessful; however, Dennis did rejoin The Temptations in 1980, when they returned to Motown. In 1982, Dennis recorded with David Ruffin and Eddie Kendricks as part of the "Reunion" album and subsequent tour.

Dennis was again replaced in 1984 by Ali-Ollie Woodson, Motown re-launched Dennis's solo career, with the 1984 single "Don't Look Any Further", a duet with Siedah Garrett. It didn't make it to the top of the R&B charts; its melody was later incorporated by rappers Eric B and Rakim, the follow-up, "(You're My) Aphrodisiac" was a Top 20 R&B single. "Coolin' Out" was Dennis's final hit, reaching No23 on the pop charts, Dennis returned to The Temptations in 1987, briefly teaming up with ex-Temptations David Ruffin and Eddie Kendrick's in the trio Ruffin/Kendrick's/Edwards, but nothing was ever released. After the deaths of both David Ruffin and Eddie Kendricks, the project obviously came to an end.

During the 1990's, Dennis began touring under the name "Dennis Edwards and The Temptations", prompting a legal battle between himself and Otis Williams. It was decided that Dennis's group would be called "The Temptations Review featuring Dennis Edwards", the name that Edwards tours under to this day. The current group includes Paul Williams Jnr., David Sea, Mike Patillo and Chris Arnold.

When problems arose between Dennis's replacement Ali-Ollie Woodson and The Temptations in 1987, Dennis was brought back once again to replace him, but the relationship again soured when asked to leave by Otis Williams in 1989, for the third and final time by Otis Williams.

I last met Dennis in 2008 at Ben Crosby's funeral in Detroit; Ben Crosby had been Dennis's manager.

Esther Gordy Edwards

Born on the 25th April 1920 in Oconee, Georgia

Motown Connection: Sister of Motown Records founder Berry Gordy - First to do Company Accounting - Director of the Artists Personal Management Division - Manager of Motown Records overseas activities - Vice president and Chief Executive Officer - Worked for Gordy Foundation, (which provides scholarships for Detroit's youth) - Founded the Motown Historical Museum in Detroit.

The sister of Motown Records' founder Berry Gordy, Esther held various titles within the Motown organisation during her career. In the label's early years, she was fond of saying; she was Berry Gordy's "gal Friday", a versatile musician who kept the label running smoothly in many capacities. Later she was the director of the Artists Personal Management Division, helping to develop the careers of Diana Ross, Stevie Wonder, and Marvin Gaye. Esther also applied her financial expertise to the management of the growing corporation, assuming the titles of Vice President and Chief Executive Officer of Motown Records, Esther was a vital ingredient to the success of Motown.

Edwards was named after her paternal grandmother, Esther Johnson, a Georgia slave. Esther was the eldest female among the eight children born to Berry Gordy Sr. (whose father was also named Berry Gordy) and his wife Bertha. Esther moved to Detroit with her family as a child, after Berry Gordy Snr made a large profit on a lumber deal and fearing violence from local whites, moved north. After the family moved to Detroit, Esther attended Howard University Washington DC and Wayne State University, Detroit.

Most of the Berry Gordy Snr children, shared their father's business sense. After the Second World War, Esther opened a print shop, called the Gordy Printing Company, with two of her brothers, (not including Berry Gordy, who seemed uninterested in business). However a hint of things to come was apparent when a radio commercial jingle he composed for the print shop boosted the business substantially.

In the 1950's Esther established a family loan fund called the "Ber-Berry Co-Op" (named for her parents); the idea was that each family member would contribute ten dollars a month, and the resulting pool would finance new business projects. One of the first loan applicants was Berry Gordy, who in 1959 asked for $800 to start what eventually became the Tamla and then the Motown record label. The one dissenting voice was Esther who gave Berry Gordy the toughest questions, "I just wanted to know how he intended to pay it back; he didn't have a job".

After Berry Gordy established Motown, Esther was to become part of the new business. One of her first jobs was to assist in booking and managing the national and international tours that did much to put Motown on the map. As Motown grew, Esther became more and more involved with Motown's financial operations, and became Vice President and CEO in the Motown.

When Motown moved to Los Angeles California Esther decided to stay in Detroit. When the label departed, Esther established her Detroit offices in the label's former "Hitsville USA" headquarters, a house on West Grand Boulevard. Never interested in pursuing a life in show business or earning massive salaries, Esther decided that the ties she had cultivated over the years in Detroit were most important to her, so Esther continued to manage Motown's affairs in Detroit, which included several scholarship and foundation operations.

Esther left her mark on the city of Detroit in other ways, serving on the boards of directors of the Detroit Bank of the Commonwealth and the Greater Detroit Chamber of Commerce. In the 1970's, Esther was the main organiser behind many of her husband's political campaigns, and became involved with numerous not for profit organisations. Esther was also instrumental in launching the city's annual Sterling Ball fundraiser for inner-city children's organisations.

One of Esther's greatest achievements must be the work Esther did for Motown and how Esther helped secure its position in musical history. Esther carefully maintained the house on West Grand Boulevard (the site of the original Motown studios "Hitsville USA Studio A") in their original condition and worked toward turning the site into a museum. The Motown Historical Museum opened in the 1980's and soon began to attract visitors from around the country and from all over the world. Esther was the director of the museum.

Esther Gordy Edwards married twice. She had one son, Robert Berry Bullock, by her first husband, and in 1951 she married politician George H. Edwards, later one of the first African-American members of the Michigan State Legislature.

The Elgins

Formed Detroit 1962, Disbanded 1967 Members; Sandra Mallett (a.k.a. Sandra Edwards) - Johnny Dawson - Cleo "Duke" Miller - Robert Fleming

Motown Connection: Motown Group - Background Singers - Sandra Mallett (a.k.a. Sandra Edwards) was a solo artist at Motown.

Over the years there have been quite a few groups calling themselves The Elgins, but this entry is entirely dedicated to the Motown Group who achieved two R&B/pop hits in 1966 with their debut for Motown "Darling Baby" and "Heaven Must Have Sent You". Both songs were written and produced by Holland-Dozier-Holland, and "Heaven Must Have Sent You" was a particular favourite of the UK Northern Soul Scene.

There was a Los Angeles "doo wop" group, another group of Elgins who recorded for Congress Records, and Ritha Mae, while managing future The Temptations (of later Motown fame) even used the name for a while. The Temptations when signed to Motown used the name The Elgins when introduced to Berry Gordy.

A publicity handout from the artists.

Before the group was formed in 1962, Sandra Mallett had recorded "It's Going to Be Hard Times" b/side "Camel Walk" for Tamla as Sandra Mallett and The Vandellas. The group (which later became The Elgins) was formed in 1962 as a vocal trio called The Downbeats, (with Johnny Dawson, Cleo Miller and Sandra Mallett a.k.a. Sandra Edwards) with Robert Fleming joining later in 1966. Robert Fleming had occasionally accompanied Marv Johnson including background work with The Elgins (unaccredited) on "Once Upon a Time" prior to Johnson's hits for United Artists Records. As The Downbeats they recorded for the Lupine label before signing for Motown (assigned to the Tamla label). Their releases for the Motown label were relatively unsuccessful.

Motown had intended to issue the group's debut record "Darling Baby" on the VIP label, (a subsidiary of Motown Records) using the name The Downbeats. However, before Motown shipped the "Darling Baby" record Berry Gordy insisted on the name change, the record was issued with the group's new name The Elgins. It was reported that Berry Gordy had insisted on the name change for the group, when The Temptations stopped using The Elgins name for their group. The song had been adapted from Lamont Dozier's solo release, "Dearest One" (Melody Records in

June 1962) by Holland-Dozier-Holland. VIP label failed to promote their records outside the greater Detroit area, which ultimately affected their sales. The group did a follow up album, "Darling Baby", and another record, "I Understand My Man," but chart success eluded them and they disbanded shortly afterwards in 1967. Motown did re-release "Heaven Must Have Sent You" in 1971, "Put Yourself in My Place" again in 1971. Both songs made the Top 20 in the UK but were only a minor hit in the US. The Elgins did tour the UK in the 1970's with Yvonne Vernee-Allen replacing Sandra Mallett.

In the late 1980's early 1990's, Ian Levine (under his Motorcity label) worked with a "new group" under The Elgins name including, Johnny Dawson who was the only original Elgin in the line-up, Yvonne Vernee-Allen who had replaced Sandra Mallett (now using the name Sandra Edwards), this new "line-up" recorded a remake of "Heaven Must Have Sent You", for the Motorcity label. They did the two albums "Take the Train" and "Sensational". Bonnie Pointer had a major hit with "Heaven Must Have Sent You" in September, 1979. Ian Levine also recorded a solo effort by Sandra Edwards again under the Motorcity label.

The original recordings and some unreleased recordings up to 1968 of the group time at Motown (including the album, "Darling Baby"), can be found on The Motown Anthology released in 2007.

Album Track: "Stay In My Lonely Arms", The Elgins.

Formed in Detroit in 1953

Members: Levi Stubbs (Born Levi Stubbles) 6th June 1936 in the North End District of Detroit - Died 17th October 2008 in Detroit Michigan - Renaldo "Obie" Benson Born 14th June 1947 in Detroit - Died June 1st July 2005 in Detroit Michigan - Lawrence Payton, Born 2rn Mach 1938 in Detroit Michigan - Died in 20th June 1997 in Detroit Michigan - Abdul "Duke" Fakir, Born 26th December 1935 in Detroit, Michigan.

Motown Connection: Group - Background Singers.

Founded in Detroit Michigan as The Four Aims, lead singer Levi Stubbs (a cousin of Jackie Wilson and brother of The Falcons' Joe Stubbs), and Abdul "Duke" Fakir, Renaldo "Obie" Benson and Lawrence Payton they remained together for over four decades.

L to R: Levi Stubbs, Abdul "Duke" Fakir, Renaldo "Obie" Benson and Lawrence Payton.

With the help of Payton's songwriter cousin Billy Davis (aka Roquel Davis), The Four Aims signed to Chess Records in 1956, changing their name to The Four Tops to avoid confusion with The Ames Brothers. Over the next seven years, The Four Tops endured unsuccessful tenures at Chess, Red Top, Riverside Records and Columbia Records. Without any hit records to their name, The Four Tops toured frequently, developing a polished stage presence and an experienced supper club act. In 1963, Berry Gordy who had worked with Billy Davis as a songwriter in the late-1950's, convinced The Four Tops to join the roster of his growing Motown Record Company.

The Four Tops are the most stable, consistent, and dependable of the successful R&B/pop vocal acts to emerge from Motown Records in the 1960's. Abdul "Duke" Fakir is now the only original servicing member. Unlike other Motown groups including The Temptations, The Supremes and the Miracles they have had no personnel changes, until the death of Lawrence Payton their lead singer (Levi Stubbs) never felt the need to become a solo artist. The Four Tops had everything that Berry Gordy wanted from his "Motown Stars", (apart from, it is suggested, their dance routines) they still had the gospel feel to their delivery added to an R&B style, but with enough pop appeal for Motown "crossover" audiences.

Initially, Berry Gordy was going to record them on his Workshop Jazz subsidiary, and an album was prepared for that label. This album has been the subject of much speculation over the years. Titled "Breaking Though with The Four Tops", it is pictured on an early Motown inner sleeve. Whether the album was ever released is subject to debate. My research suggests the album was never released (over the years plans for it to be released had surfaced, but nothing yet) If an album released in 1963 was ever found it would certainly be one of the most valuable Motown LP's in existence.

In addition, they filled in time by singing backup on Motown singles such as The Supremes' "Run, Run, Run" and "When the Lovelight Starts Shining Through His Eyes". Their first substantial hit "Baby, I Need Your Loving" in July 1964, was written and produced by the team of Holland-Dozier-Holland, setting the pattern for a series of songs showcasing Levi Stubbs's emotive wail set against the Benson-Payton-Fakir harmony line.

The first follow-up single, "Without the One You Love (Life's Not Worth While)", missed both the pop and R&B, "Ask the Lonely", released early in 1965, was a Top 30 pop hit and a Top 10 R&B hit, and from there, The Four Tops' fortunes began to improve. Need and longing would be the hallmarks of Stubbs's singing on such songs as "Ask the Lonely", which launched a string of R&B Top 10/pop Top 40 hits over the next two years.

Its follow-up, "I Can't Help Myself" in April 1965, hit No1 and was followed by "It's the Same Old Song" in July, "Something About You" in October, more hits followed in February 1966 with "Shake Me, Wake Me (When It's Over)", "Loving You Is Sweeter than Ever" in May 1966. A second No1 record, "Reach Out, I'll Be There" was released in August 1966 and brought The Four Tops' their biggest hit, and one of the most popular Motown songs ever, a No1 on the US and UK pop charts it soon became The Four Tops' signature song. The follow up was "Standing in the Shadows of Love" in November 1966, with three more releases in 1967 "Bernadette" in February 1967, "7 Rooms of Gloom" in May 1967, and "You Keep Running Away" in August 1967.

By now, The Four Tops were the most successful male Motown act in the United Kingdom (in the United States, they were second only to The Temptations), and began experimenting with more mainstream pop hits. They scored hits with their versions of Tim Hardin's "If I Were A Carpenter" in late 1967 (mid-1968 in the US) and the Left Banke's "Walk Away Renée" in early 1968. These singles and the original "I'm In a Different World" were their last hits produced by Holland-Dozier-Holland, before they left Motown after disputes with Berry Gordy over royalties.

Without Holland-Dozier-Holland the quality of The Four Tops' output began to decline, and the hits became less frequent. The group worked with a wide range of other Motown producers, including Ivy Jo Hunter, Ashford & Simpson, Norman Whitfield and Johnny Bristol, but without any real significant chart success.

Their first major hit in a long time came in the form of 1970's "It's All in the Game", produced by Frank Wilson. Frank Wilson and The Four Tops began working on a number of innovative tracks and albums together, echoing Norman Whitfield's psychedelic soul work with The Temptations. Their 1970 album "Still Waters Run Deep" was an early attempt at a "concept" album. It also served as an inspiration for Marvin Gaye's 1971 classic album "What's Going On", the title track of which was co-written by The Four Tops' Obie Benson.

In addition to their own albums, The Four Tops were paired with The Supremes, (who had just replaced lead singer Diana Ross with Jean Terrell), for a series of albums billed under the joint title "The Magnificent Seven". "The Magnificent Seven" was released in 1970, and "The Return of the Magnificent Seven" and "Dynamite!" was issued in 1971. While the albums themselves did not do well on the charts, "The Magnificent Seven" album track featured a Top 20 version of Ike and Tina Turner's "River Deep Mountain High", produced by Ashford & Simpson. The 1971 single "A Simple Game" featured backing vocals from members of the UK group "The Moody Blues". The song did not do well on the US charts, but reached No3 on the UK charts, they scored one more R&B Top Ten with Motown, with "(It's the Way) Nature Planned It".

When Motown relocated to Los Angeles, California in 1972, acts such as Martha Reeves and The Vandellas and The Marvelettes been had slowly sidelined to focus on newer acts such the Jackson 5, and now solo Diana Ross. Berry Gordy was moving into film and television production. Many of the Motown artists from the start of Motown, opted to stay in Detroit, including The Four Tops.

The Four Tops moved from Motown to ABC-Dunhill, where they worked with songwriter/producers Dennis Lambert and Brian Potter, with The Four Tops' Lawrence Payton helping as a producer and arranger. "Keeper of the Castle" was their first pop Top 10 hit since "Bernadette" in 1967; follow-ups such as "Ain't No Woman (Like the One I've Got)" (another top 10 pop hit), the Top 20 "Are You Man Enough?" (from the movie "Shaft In Africa"), "Sweet Understanding Love", "Midnight Flower", and "One Chain Don't Make No Prison" all hit the R&B Top 10 between 1972 and 1974. By the release of "Catfish" in 1976, The Four Tops hits had gone into decline, and the group concentrated on live performances. By securing a deal with Casablanca Records in 1980, The Four Tops made a comeback in 1981 with the No1 R&B hit "When She Was My Girl", which just missed the Billboard Pop Top 10, peaking at No11.

The Four Tops returned to Motown for a short time in 1983 and were featured on the company's television special Motown 25: Yesterday, Today, Forever. One of the highlights of the show was a battle of the bands between The Four Tops and The Temptations, styled on similar competitions Berry Gordy had staged during the 1960's. Levi Stubbs and Temptation Otis Williams decided the Temptations/Tops battle would be a good one to take on the road, and both groups began a semi-regular joint tour.

L to R, (top row): Abdul "Duke" Fakir, Lawrence Payton. (front row): Renaldo "Obie" Benson, Levi Stubbs.

The first of The Four Tops' albums under their new Motown contract was "Back Where I Belong", produced by Holland-Dozier-Holland, including the R&B Top 40 single "I Just Can't Walk Away". Only two more Four Tops albums would be released by Motown, the 1985's "Magic" and the 1986's "Hot Nights" In 1987, the Four Tops decided to leave Motown again, this time for Arista Records, buying back the masters they had recorded, the result was 1988's "Indestructible", the title track of which was the group's final Top 40 hit. It was also featured in the 1988 Sci-Fi cop film, Alien Nation.

The Arista record contract provided a unique opportunity to pair the group's popular lead singer Levi Stubbs with fellow Arista artist, Aretha Franklin, who was at the height of her own 1980's comeback. This resulting duet was the song "If Ever A Love There Was", which became a popular R&B hit, as well as being featured on the soundtrack of the motion picture "I'm Gonna Get You Sucka".

In addition to their own recordings, The Four Tops also worked in the fields of television and films. The group as a whole performed a song for the 1982 film Grease 2, and Levi Stubbs performed the vocals for the man-eating plant Audrey II in the 1986 musical film "Little Shop of Horrors" and the voice of the evil Mother Brain on the Nintendo-based NBC Saturday morning cartoon Captain N: The Game Master from 1989 to 1991.

Since the late-1980's, the Four Tops have focused on touring and live performances, only recording one album, 1995's "Christmas Here With You", released on Motown in June 1997. In July 1997 Lawrence Payton died as a result of liver cancer. At first, Levi Stubbs, Obie Benson and Duke Fakir toured as a trio called The Tops. In 1998 they recruited former Temptation, Theo Peoples, to join the act to restore the group to a quartet.

By 2000, Levi Stubbs had become ill with cancer and Ronnie McNair was recruited to fill in the Lawrence Payton position, while Theo Peoples took over as lead singer (replacing Levi Stubbs). In 2005 Obie Benson passed away from lung cancer, with Levi Stubbs dying in 2008 after a long illness. Lawrence Payton's son Roquel (real name Lawrence Payton, Jnr.) replaced Benson as the new bass singer.

The Four Tops featured in several television specials, including Motown 45, and several by PBS, including a 50th anniversary concert dedicated to the group, The concert turned out to be bittersweet; it featured a brief appearance of the wheelchair-bound Levi Stubbs, and a memorial to Lawrence Payton, announced by Obie Benson. Obie Benson appeared on one more PBS special, before his death, the PBS special, titled "Motown: The Early Years", featured a message of Obie Benson's passing following the credits.

When I last saw Levi Stubbs interviewed he was in poor health, but had one last wish to have another No1 hit, sadly Levi died on the Died 17th October 2008 in Detroit Michigan without achieving this.

Obie Benson made his last appearance with the group in April 2005 on "The Late Show with David Letterman" Soon after this appearance he was taken ill. He suffered a leg amputation because of circulation problems, and then had a heart attack and lung cancer was diagnosed. Duke is now the last remaining original member of The Four Tops.

The group was inducted into the Rock and Roll Hall of Fame in 1990, and into the Vocal Group Hall of Fame in 1999. In 2004, Rolling Stone Magazine ranked them No79 on their list of the 100 Greatest Artists of All Time. After similar releases in the Motown "Definitive DVD" series on The Miracles, The Temptations, The Supremes, and Marvin Gaye, The Four Tops' Motown Definitive DVD, "Reach Out", is planned for release in November 2008.

Album Track: "I'll Turn To Stone", The Four Tops.

Melvin Franklin

Born David Melvin English aka "Blue" Born on the 12th October 1942 in Montgomery, Alabama - Died 23rd February 1995 in Los Angeles, California

Motown Connection: Background Singer - Member of The Temptations - Melvin's nephew was Rick James a future Motown Artist - Melvin had a fondness for the colour blue, and so he was nicknamed "Blue".

Melvin Franklin was the first child of six, his father was a preacher and autoworker named Willard, his mother was Rose. Melvin moved with his family to Detroit at the age of nine, taking on his mother's surname of Franklin for his stage name, Melvin's career began at Wingert Elementary School in Detroit, playing Scrooge in a Christmas play. Melvin transferred to Northern High School, where he joined the school choir. He briefly attended college in Texas and at Wayne State University.

Melvin then started performing with local groups around Detroit including, The Voice Masters which included future Motown producer Lamont Dozier and David Ruffin (a distant cousin of Franklin), and frequently performed with his cousin Richard Street. In 1960, Melvin started to use his mother's basement as a rehearsal room for a new group which combined the group he had formed with Otis Williams called The Distants, with The Primes, including Paul Williams, Eddie Kendrick and Eldridge Bryant, the new group took the name The Elgins, (not to be confused with the future Motown group of the same name). Gaining an audition, with Berry Gordy at his first studio on St. Antoine in Detroit as The Elgins they signed to Motown, before changing the name to The Temptations and being signed to Motown subsidiary label Miracle. Also at this time Eldridge "Al" Bryant was replaced by David Ruffin.

The Temptations began singing background for many of the Motown artists already signed to Motown, including early Mary Well's recordings. The group's break through hit "The Way You Do the Things You Do" was their first US Top 20 hit, followed by "I'll Be in Trouble", "Girl (Why You Wanna Make Me Blue)", "Get Ready", "Just My Imagination", and "Please Return Your Love to Me". Without doubt the most successful Temptation's recording from this time was the Smokey Robinson (who wrote and produced the No1 hit) "My Girl".

The first phase of The Temptation's career was guided by Smokey Robinson, who usually wrote and produced their material, next came the collaboration with Norman Whitfield and Barrett Strong who wrote and produced the psychedelic soul recordings where all five Temptations undertook lead vocals, with such recordings as the Grammy winner "Cloud Nine" and "I Can't Get Next to You".

Melvin and Otis Williams were the only two Temptations never to leave the group, resulting in Melvin becoming one of the most famous bass singers in soul music. Melvin did take lead vocals on recordings mainly on album tracks including, "I Truly, Truly Believe" from the album "Wish It Would Rain" in 1968, his signature tune (a live performance) of Paul Robeson's "Ol' Man River", next came "The Prophet" from the album "A Song for You" in 1975. Melvin's skills were usually called upon to deliver ad-libs, harmony vocals, by the time of The Temptations psychedelic soul era, Melvin was taking on sections of the main verses. Melvin's line from The Temptations' 1970 No3 hit "Ball of Confusion (That's What the World Is Today)", signing "and the band played on", became another Melvin signature vocal.

In the late-1960's, Melvin was diagnosed with rheumatoid arthritis, the symptoms of which he combated with cortisone so that he could continue performing. The constant use of cortisone left his immune system open to other infections and health problems; as a result Melvin developed diabetes in the early 1980's and later contracted necrotising fasciitis.

In 1978 Melvin was shot in the hand and the leg when trying to stop a man from stealing his car. After this incident Otis Williams insisted that Melvin take time out from recording and performing to help with his recovery, but Melvin continued to record and tour with the group despite these medical issues. During a tour of England in 1994, Melvin had to use an oxygen tank backstage, and had to be taken to and from the stage in a wheelchair. Melvin's last performance with The Temptations was in July of 1994.

On 17th February 1995, after a series of seizures in his sleep, Melvin became unconscious and was taken to hospital, where he would remain, never regaining consciousness, for six days until his death from heart failure aged 52.

Melvin was survived by his wife, Kimberly English, and his four children David, Jnr, Davette, Felicia and Niquos.

The Funk Brothers

Formed in 1959 in Detroit as Session Musicians Members Listed Below

Motown Connection: The Funk Brothers (Motown In House Band).

No story about Motown would be complete without talking about The Funk Brothers. They were the core of backing/session musicians that played on almost every Motown recording that came out of "Hitsville Studio A" in Detroit and by doing so helped create the "Motown Sound". The recording studio was also known by its nickname "The Snake Pit" because of the steps you went down into it, and its small size.

Berry Gordy knew and was part of the 1950's Detroit's jazz community, from this community Berry Gordy found the core of the musicians (and also future artists) that would form the backbone to Berry Gordy's new label Motown. "The Motown Story" may focus on Berry Gordy and the stars he created, and rightly too. However, without The Funk Brothers, there would not have been a "Motown Sound".

If Motown had recorded and promoted them, for example as "Earl Van Dyke and The Funk Brothers" they would have been as successful as Booker T and the MG's, who became better known for their own work than for backing the likes of Otis Redding and Sam and Dave. If musicians had been routinely listed on album covers (as they are now), names like Benny Benjamin, James Jamerson, Beans Bowles, Earl Van Dyke would have been identified earlier as the musicians who created the "Motown Sound", instead only Motown insiders and "hardcore" fans knew them.

It is widely accepted that The Funk Brothers revolved around the bass player James Jamerson, drummer Benny Benjamin, (although Benny Benjamin was not an original Funk Brother). In the original core group of musicians with Benny Benjamin and James Jameson was guitarist Robert White, Eddie "Chank" Willis and Joe Messina. An additional bassist Bob Babbitt was added later, the keyboard player and bandleader was originally Joe Hunter followed by Earl Van Dyke, drummers along with Benny Benjamin was Richard "Pistol" Allen, Uriel Jones, on percussionist and vibes where Jack Ashford and Eddie "Bongo" Brown playing Saxophones was Henry "Hank" Cosby, Andrew "Mike" Terry and Thomas "Beans" Bowles.

The full list of Detroit musicians involved:

Keyboards: Joe Hunter band leader 1959-1964 - Earl Van Dyke band leader 1964-1972 - Richard "Popcorn" Wylie 1959-1962 - Johnny Griffith 1963-1972 Johnny Gittens 1963-1967 - Ted Sheely 1963-1967.

Guitarists: Robert White 1959-1972 - Eddie "Chank" Willis 1959-1972 - Joe Messina 1959-1972 - Larry Veeder 1959-1962 - Dave Hamilton 1959-1962 - Marvin Tarplin 1961-1972 (Smokey Robinson and The Miracles' road and studio guitarist) - Cornelius Grant 1963-1972 (The Temptations' road guitarist/band leader) - Dennis Coffey 1967-1972 - Melvin "Wah Wah Watson" Ragin 1968-1972 - Ray Parker (occasionally) - Ray Monette(occasionally).

Bassists: James Jamerson 1959-1972 - Clarence Isabell 1959-1962 - Tony Newton 1963-1967 - Bob Babbitt 1967-1972 - Eddie Watkins 1968-1972 - Tweed Beard (occasionally) - Joe Williams (occasionally) - Michael Henderson (occasionally) - Joe James (occasionally).

Drums: William "Benny" Benjamin 1959-1969 - Richard "Pistol" Allen 1959-1972 - George McGregor 1959-1962 - Clifford Mack 1959-1962) - Marvin Gaye 1959-1962 - Uriel Jones 1963-1972 - Frederick Waites 1963-1967 - Andrew Smith 1968-1972.

Percussion and Vibes: Jack Ashford 1959-1972 tambourine - Eddie "Bongo" Brown 1959-1972 congas, bongos, the gourd and claves - Dave Hamilton 1959-1962 - James Gittens 1959-1962 - Jack Brokensha 1963-1972.

Trumpets: Herbie Williams - John "Little John" Wilson - Marcus Belgrave - Russell Conway - Johnny Trudell - Floyd Jones - Maurice Davis - Billy Horner - Don Slaughter - Eddie Jones all on a session basis.

Saxophones: Henry "Hank" Cosby - Andrew "Mike" Terry - Norris Patterson - Thomas "Beans" Bowles - Teddy Buckner - Ronnie Wakefield - "Lefty" Edwards - Eli Fontaine - Ernie Rodgers - Kasuka Malia - Eugene "BeeBee" Moore - William "Wild Bill" Moore - Angelo Carlisi - Dan Turner Bernie Peacock - Larry Nozero - Lanny Austin all on a session basis.

Trombones: Bob Cousar - George Bohanon - Paul Riser - George Bohanon - Jimmy Wilkens - Don White - Carl Raetz - Patrick Lanier - Bill Johnson - Ed Gooch all on a session basis.

Flute: Dayna Hartwick on a session basis.

Strings: Gordon Staples and the Detroit Symphony Orchestra Strings Section between 1959-1972.

Joe Hunter was the original band leader between 1959-1964, while Motown recruited Van Dyke around 1961 after work with several jazz bands and Aretha Franklin. When Joe left in 1964 Earl was given the role of band leader by william "Mickey" Stevenson. The group was originally called the Earl Van Dyke Quartet; later they renamed the group to Earl Van Dyke and The Funk Brothers. The group got its name "Funk Brothers" from a local radio DJ by the name of Martha Jean the Queen, who was broadcasting live at the Chit Chat Lounge and the "Funk Brothers" name was not based on a musical connotation but on a sexual innuendo about a lady the band spotted.

In the studio, Earl Van Dyke always made the point that at recording sessions the musicians did more than just play "what they were told". The producer would come in with some words, humming some tune. Earl Van Dyke put the chords down and we'd have Willy Shorter or Paul Riser write it out. You can figure out how much we contributed." According to Uriel Jones, it was an unusual occasion when a producer came in with a tune worked out entirely.

The consensus appears to be that many of the Motown artists didn't record with the Musicians. That's not to say that the Motown musician's weren't there when the vocalists recorded their tracks; in some cases (particularly in the early days) the vocalists, and musicians recorded simultaneously, due to the fact that Motown started with only 2-track recording.

As the years went on, the number of tracks multiplied, and it was no longer necessary to have the vocalist and the musician's record together. The producers would call in the musician's, record the music, a demo lead vocal and background vocals, and the singers would come in at another time to record the vocal for the track. In essence, the musicians and artists barely ever saw each other.

Motown wasn't too keen about The Funk Brothers recording for other labels. Several music entrepreneurs, local and otherwise, took advantage of the situation offering the band more money, leading to The Funk Brothers being heard on a lot of "backdoor sessions" for the local Golden World and Ric Tic label owned by Ed Wingate. The band can be heard on "Agent Double 0 Soul" by Edwin Starr in 1965 and "Stop Her On Sight" in 1966, on Ollie McLaughlin's Karen label, "Cool Jerk" by The Capitols in July 1966. Making the trips to nearby Chicago, The Funk Brothers played session on several records for producer Carl Davies including "I Just Wanna Testify" by The Parliaments in 1967.

Also in 1967 The Funk Brothers did background session for "Just Be Sincere" and "(Your Love Keeps Lifting Me) Higher and Higher" which set the stage for Jackie Wilson's mid 1960's comeback and was his second No1 R&B in October 1967. "I Get The Sweetest Feeling" in June 1968. The Funk Brothers also travelled south to record in Muscle Shoals and Atlanta among other cities. During the sixties, it was rumoured Dionne Warwick's song writing/producing, duo Burt Bacharach and Hal David would have clandestine meetings with The Funk Brothers to discuss various projects.

While working with Golden World Record the majority of the Funk Brothers used the name "San Remo Golden Strings" The name San Remo came about as a result of a vacation taken by Ed and JoAnne Wingate of Golden World Label to the town of the same name. The first recording by the San Remo Golden Strings was "Hungry for Love" b/side "All Turned On" which was released in August 1965 The arranger on the album was Gil Askey, himself to be a future Motown employee.

It would be six months before another release, "Festival Time" b/side "Joy Road", "Festival Time" is a great up tempo number and was ably turned into a vocal by the great Laura Lee on Ric-Tic. "To Win Your Heart" has a big following in the UK and was interestingly released around the same time as "Festival Time". The flip "Joy Road" was a celebration of the road, which runs for 40 odd miles from the heart of Detroit to the west and Ann Arbor.

The final San Remo release came in August 1966. "Quanto Sei Bella" b/side "International Love Theme" was written by JoAnne and arranged by Mike Terry and Bert Keyes, a legendary New York arranger who worked briefly with Golden World in 1962.

Motown made it known, if not by words, but certainly by action, that they wanted The Funk Brothers to remain in the recording studio, laying tracks for Motown's Artists. However, The Funk Brothers wanted to release an album of their own and reluctantly Motown issued, "Earl Van Dyke Plays the Motown Sound" and "The Earl of Funk" in September 1970, both released on Motown's subsidiary label Soul. Neither release was what they really wanted, which was a jazz album. Motown objected to the word "funk," so both releases carried the moniker Earl Van Dyke and the Soul Brothers.

The total number of Detroit musicians who had contact with the Motown studio was enormous. In fact, it seems most of the musicians in the over-30 generation spent at least some time in "Hitsville" studios. Younger pop artists and session musicians like Ray Parker Jnr., Sylvester Rivers and Gregg Phillinganes worked and developed their skills in the Motown studios.

Motown Records relocated to Los Angeles, partly based on Berry Gordy's desire to become involved in the motion picture business and the era of The Funk Brothers (based on Hitsville Studio A) was coming to an end As the company began shifting its focus out to California, eventually things changed. Some of the Detroit musicians followed Motown to California, including James Jamerson and Earl Van Dyke who reluctantly went to California to work for the Motown West Coast operation, but found it too alien to his Detroit perspective, while other "Funk Brothers" continued to record in Detroit (but not at the level of the 1960's). It all ended with a note on "Studio A's" door: "session cancelled will reschedule". "I'm still waiting for them to reschedule" said Jack Ashford in his biography, "No severance, no nothing".

Eventually, Motown stopped all production in Detroit and the use of "Hitsville Studio A" ceased. The remaining Funk Brothers and Detroit musicians associated with Motown Detroit operation came to an end.

Never recognised by Motown for their contribution, the accolades and recognition came in the shape of the Allan Slutsky documentary "Standing In The Shadows Of Motown" which re-established The Funk Brothers, and started the group touring again. Although too late for many of the group this film and soundtrack won many awards and finally brought to attention their contribution to creating the "Motown Sound". They generated sales of over 300 million records.

Signature sounds: Listen to any of the massive number of international hits, but "Heaven Must Have Sent You by" The Elgins gives a good impression of how "together" these guys were.

Album Track: "Heaven Must Have Sent You", The Elgins.

144

Gwendolyn Gordy-Fuqua

Born Gwendolyn Gordy in Detroit - Died 8th November 1999 in San Diego, California

Motown Connection: Songwriter - Producer - Owner Anna Records with her sister Anna (Who Distributed Early Motown Records) - Artist Development.

Born and raised in Detroit, Michigan to Berry Gordy Snr and Bertha Gordy, both from Georgia, from a family of ten children, which included sisters Esther and Anna who would help their brother Berry Gordy establish Motown along with Brother Robert Gordy.

Gwen and Anna landed the photo/cigarette concession at the Flame Show Lounge in Detroit and met all the stars who performed there, including Billie Holiday, Sam Cooke, and Jackie Wilson. It was a lucrative business and helped show their entrepreneurial skills coupled with their good looks to this audience.

Gwen then started writing songs with her then boyfriend Billy Davis (aka Roquel Davis) who often used the name Tyran Carlo for these writing credits. Next with Gwen's brother Berry Gordy and Billy Davis the three became a formidable team, writing for the Five Stars, Jackie Wilson, Marv Johnson, and many others. The team wrote five hit singles in a row for Jackie  Wilson starting with "Reet Petite", followed by "Lonely Teardrops", "That's Why I Love You So", "To Be Loved" and "I'll Be Satisfied". The team then disbanded due to a disagreement with Nat Tarnapool, Jackie Wilson's manager bringing an end to the relationship and any further writing opportunities for the team.

Gwen, Anna and Billy Davis (later joined by Harvey Fuqua) formed Anna Records, although Billy Davis would drop out later from this venture. Anna Records (named after Anna Gordy), included artists Joe Tex, The Voice Masters, Johnny Bristol and Jackey Beavers, Lamont Anthony, Herman Griffin and David Ruffin. They agreed a distribution deal with Chess records, part of the deal was to send Harvey Fuqua to Detroit to work with Anna Records. Although problems between Gwen Gordy and Billy Davis started before Harvey Fuqua arrived in Detroit, within a short space of time Gwen was dating Harvey Fuqua which prompted Billy Davis to leave and form Checkmate Records, (which Chess distributed), taking David Ruffin and releasing "Mr. Bus Driver," and "Action Speaks Louder Than Words," on the future Temptations' lead singer.

Berry Gordy started Tamla Records around the same time as Anna Records, early Tamla recordings were either blues based or uninspired doo wop - not exactly the "Sound of Young America". When Berry Gordy produced "Money", by Barrett Strong, he negotiated a distribution deal with Gwen and Billy Davis for national distribution, while Tamla handled the record in Michigan. Ironically, it became Anna's biggest record.

Gwen and Harvey Fuqua (with Anna Gordy) continued to develop Anna Records. With a recording by Etta James "All I Could Do Was Cry", (whom Harvey Fuqua had been dating) it explains the drama between Gwen, Billy, Harvey and Etta James. Even with Harvey Fuqua's help Anna Records had problems with cash flow, including the need to borrow $10,000 from Berry Gordy. By 1961, after 28 single releases, Anna Records folded. Gwen and Harvey Fuqua then started Tri-Phi and Harvey Records, taking many of Anna's artists with them, including The Spinners, Shorty Long, Jnr Walker and The All Stars, the Five Quails and Challengers 3. In 1963 the labels where absorbed into Motown along with most of their artists, producers and writers. Gwen's role at the merged company was in Artist Development where artists learn all the rules of etiquette. Staying in the background during Motown's Detroit years, Gwen also worked as a fashion model.

In the late sixties her marriage to Harvey Fuqua ended (after being married in 1961) and Gwen became more involved in the Management side at Motown, Gwen was instrumental in getting G.C. Cameron to stay and not follow the Spinners to Atlantic Records, even with extensive marketing G.C Cameron's solo career was not a success. Gwen then discovered the group High Energy and helped with the hit "You Can't Turn Me On", a prolific songwriter, one of Gwen's major hits was "Distant Lover" for Sandra Green and Marvin Gaye. Gwen also owned the publishing rights to Anita Baker's "Sweet Love."

When Motown Records relocated to Los Angeles, partly based on Berry Gordy's desire to become involved in the motion picture business, most of Berry Gordy's family followed, except for his sister Esther and her husband George Edwards who remained in Detroit. Gwen moved into a fantastic house in Beverly Hills and gave lavish parties when she joined the social scene in Los Angeles. Gwen's health, (aggravated by Los Angeles smog) deteriorated, and worried by this decline Berry Gordy persuaded Gwen to move to a better climate in California where Gwen settled on a ranch and bred horses. Gwen was survived by a son, Glenn Gordy, and was 71 when she died of cancer at her home.

Born on the 27th July 1929 in Louisville, Kentucky

Motown Connection: Married Berry Gordy's Sister Gwendolyn - Songwriter and producer (notably with Johnny Bristol) - Owned Tri Phi and Harvey, with his wife Gwendolyn (bought by Motown) - Introduced Marvin Gaye to Motown.

Producer and songwriter know as lead singer for The Moonglows, who recorded for Chess Records in Chicago in the 1950's. Harvey came to Motown toward the end of 1962 when his own labels, Tri Phi and Harvey, which he co-owned with his wife, Gwendolyn Gordy Fuqua, discontinued and merged with Berry Gordy's Motown. Harvey brought with him such artists as Shorty Long, Jnr. Walker and The All Stars, and The Spinners (later named the Detroit Spinners while in the UK they were known as The Motown Spinners).

Harvey (the nephew of Charlie Fuqua of the Ink Spots) started The Moonglows with lead singer and fellow Louisville Bobby Lester, Alexander Graves, and Prentiss Barnes. Supported by legendary DJ Alan Freed, the group appeared with Freed on his radio show, concerts, and with him in the movies "Rock, Rock, Rock" in 1956. Originally called the Crazy Sounds, it was Alan Freed who changed the name of the group to The Moonglows.

L to R: Maurice King, Billy Davis, Harvey Fuqua and Marvin Gaye.

The Moonglows' first releases were for Freed's Champagne label in 1953. The following year, the group signed with Art Sheridan's Chicago Chance label, scoring a regional hit with a cover of Doris Day's "Secret Love". When Chance records ceased business that same year, label executive Ewart Abner (who would become a future Motown Employee) suggested a move to Chess Records. Their Chess single "Sincerely" was issued in late 1954; other Chess hits include "Most of All" in early 1955, "We Go Together" (later covered by Jan and Dean), "See Saw" b/side "When I'm With You", in 1956, and a cover of Percy Mayfield's 1950 hit "Please Send Me Someone to Love" in 1957.

The first hit to feature Harvey and The Moonglows was "Ten Commandments of Love" in late 1958; the line-up consisted of former members of the Marquees including Marvin Gaye, Reese Palmner, James Knowland, Chester Simmons, and Chuck Barksdale from the Dells. The group also recorded under the name the Moonlighters, while with Chess Records.

In 1958, Fuqua left the Moonglows and label owner Leonard Chess suggested that he join Anna Records in Detroit. (owned by Berry Gordy's sister Anna Gordy). Only Marvin Gaye followed to Detroit, where Harvey began working with Billy Davis (who would become one of the earliest employees at Motown) Harvey still worked with Chess, producing records on Etta James after his move to Detroit.

Harvey had been introduced to Berry Gordy when Berry Gordy asked Chess to lease the rights to The Miracles' "Bad Girl". While with Anna Records, Harvey recorded Lamont Anthony (aka Lamont Dozier) and Johnny Bristol (both future employees of Motown) Harvey rented a room at the home of Berry Gordy's sister Esther Gordy Edwards and her husband George Edwards. In 1961, Harvey started his own labels, Tri-Phi and Harvey Records. On the label was The Spinners who recorded (the Fuqua-lead) "That's What Girls Are Made For" on Tri-Phi, as well as Junior Walker and The All Stars "Good Rockin' Tonight" and Shorty Long.

Harvey then went Motown to head Motown's Artist Development department, Harvey was assisted by Berry Gordy's sisters Gwen (Harvey's wife) and Anna Gordy, with Maxine Powell and Cholly Atkins. While the Artist Development was Harvey's main role at Motown, Harvey still found time to co-produce several hits with Johnny Bristol. Including Marvin Gaye and Tammi Terrell's "Ain't No Mountain High Enough", "Your Precious Love", and "If This World Were Mine" in 1967, in addition to these recordings they produced former Temptation's member David Ruffin's "My Whole World Ended (The Moment You Left Me)" in, early 1969. Next was Jnr. Walker and The All Stars, "Pucker Up, Buttercup" and the Top 10 pop hit "What Does It Take (To Win Your Love)".

Around 1971, Harvey left Motown and signed a production deal with RCA Records, having success particularly with the band "New Birth" and worked with a variety of R&B acts during the 1970's and 1980's. The Moonglows reunited temporarily in 1972, but the venture did not last long.

Harvey also discovered disco artist Sylvester, and "Two Tons O' Fun" (aka The Weather Girls), producing Sylvester's hit singles "Dance (Disco Heat)" and "You Make Me Feel (Mighty Real)" in 1978 as well as his album "Stars" in 1979. Harvey also helped on the 1978 movie "American Hot Wax" featuring a fictional group that was based on The Moonglows and Frankie Lymon and the Teenagers. He also served as Smokey Robinson's road manager. In 1982 he reunited with Marvin Gaye to produce the singer's Midnight Love album which included the single "Sexual Healing". The single "Sanctified Lady". from Gaye's posthumously released 1985 LP "Dream of a Lifetime", was co-produced by Harvey in 1985. Harvey released a version of the Barrett Strong song "Man Up In The Sky" in 1989, followed by the song 'Come To Me' for the Whichway label in 1991.

In 2000, The Moonglows were inducted into the Rock and Roll Hall of Fame, and Harvey set up his own "Resurging Artist Records", and has also acted as a trustee of The Rhythm and Blues Foundation.

Album Track: "If I Could Build My Whole World Around You", Marvin Gaye and Tammi Terrell.

Born Anna Ruby Gordy in 1922 Detroit, Michigan

Motown Connection: Eldest sister of Motown founder Berry Gordy - Owner Anna Records (Who Distributed Early Motown Records) - First wife of Marvin Gaye from 1962 to 1977 - Songwriter - Producer.

Born and raised in Detroit, Michigan to Berry Gordy Snr and Bertha Gordy, both from Georgia, from a family of ten children, which included sisters Esther and Gwen who would help their brother Berry Gordy establish Motown along with brother Robert Gordy. Anna and sister Gwen formed Anna Records, the label would be the national distributor for Barrett Strong's Tamla single, "Money (That's What I Want)", which became Motown's first hit single that went national.

In the late 1950's Anna was involved in various aspects of the music business. From cigarette concessions at local nightclubs, to forming several production companies in Michigan. In the early 1960's Anna Records was absorbed into Berry Gordy's Motown Record label and with that came a number of recording masters and artists including Harvey Fuqua, Lamont Anthony (aka Lamont Dozier), Johnny Bristol and Harvey Fuqua also to Motown was a certain Marvin Gaye. Anna was thirty-eight when she first met Marvin Gaye while the two were at a Christmas party at the Motown studios. At the time, Marvin Gaye was signed to Motown as a session musician. By the time he signed as a solo act for the label in 1961, he and Anna had started a relationship. Anna was considered Marvin Gaye's mentor during the early years of his career at Motown.

Anna Gordy Gaye with her husband Marvin Gaye.
A publicity handout from the artist re-produced in the Detroit Free Press.

Anna and Marvin Gaye married on the 8th January 1962; (with Anna taking the name Anna Gordy Gaye) the couple adopted a son, Marvin Pentz Gaye III, in 1965. The marriage a was not always "rosy", with Anna becoming "increasingly jealous" of the female attention Marvin was gaining from his status at Motown. Marvin Gaye dedicated some of his songs to his wife including "Pride and Joy" and "Stubborn Kind of Fellow", songs Marvin Gaye co-wrote.

The marriage came to an end when Marvin Gaye became involved with Janis Hunter in 1973 and subsequently had two children with her. Anna filed for divorce in 1975 and this was finalised in 1977, one of the conditions of the divorce was that the royalties from Marvin's next album would go to Anna, typically, Marvin Gaye turned his heartaches and divorce into music on the albums "Here My Dear" dedicated to the painful break up of Marvin's marriage to Anna. This almost led to Anna filing a lawsuit for invasion of privacy. That album was not a sales success. It was suspected that both Anna and Marvin Gaye were not faithful, and that these suspicions inspired Marvin Gaye in his performance of "I Heard It Through the Grapevine" and "That's The Way Love Is" in the late 1960's.

Anna was also known for co-writing hits for Marvin Gaye "God Is Love" and "Flying High in the Friendly Sky" from his "What's Going On" album and "Just to Keep You Satisfied" from his "Let's Get It On" album and provided some lyrics to Marvin Gaye's compositions for The Originals', "Baby I'm For Real" and "The Bells".

Anna was still close to her former husband until his 1984 death, and never re-married. Anna currently lives in Los Angeles with her son.

Born Frances Gay on the 5th November 1941 Washington DC - Died 30th December 2001 Los Angeles, California

Motown Connection: Brother of Marvin Gaye - Inspiration for the Marvin Gaye Album "What's Going On" - Background Vocals.

Frankie, whose combat experience during the Vietnam War was credited with influencing his older brother Marvin's legendary album "What's Going On" for Motown Records. Frankie was a radio operator stationed in Vietnam in the 1960's when he wrote letters to his brother expressing his dissatisfaction with the war. Frankie's experiences influenced several of his brother Marvin Gaye songs, including the 1971 album "What's Going On", including the tracks "Save The Children", "Inner City Blues", "Mercy Mercy Me", and of course the title track "What's Going On" Frankie's horrific accounts of his time during the Vietnam War (which included being a radio deejay) would become Marvin's inspiration for the album. Frankie provided background vocals on many of his brother's albums, including "What's Going On" and 1977's "Marvin Gaye, Live at the London Palladium".

Frankie, like his brother Marvin, begun singing in church as a youngster. Frankie also had another brother and two sisters, all of whom grew up in a strict church environment (their father being a preacher). When Marvin and Harvey Fuqua left Washington for Detroit in the early 1960's, Frankie stayed behind and established himself as a singer on the Washington club circuit. In 1964 Frankie was drafted into the armed forces and served in Vietnam, where Frankie was on active service until 1967.

Upon Frankie's release from the armed forces Frankie began working for his brother Marvin Gaye, organising of his live shows and business interests. When Motown relocated to Los Angeles both Marvin and Frankie moved there.

The 1971 "What's Going On" recording project which was based in both Detroit and Los Angeles, Frankie has been credited with, persuading Marvin to work with Al Cleveland and Renaldo Benson to produce the album.

While in Los Angeles, Frankie began his music career composing the soundtrack to the 1972 film, "Penitentiary". Frankie was occasionally part of Marvin Gaye's touring band. Frankie's most notable moment on any of his brother's records was during the live show at Marvin Gaye's Palladium concert in London in 1977.

After Marvin Gaye's death in 1984, Frankie teamed up with Al Cleveland to record an obscure single on Al's Hitsburgh Record Label. Frankie also began a series of visits to the UK, meeting his Scottish wife while on tour in 1980.

Frankie signed up to Ian Levine's the Motorcity Label releasing, "Extraordinary Girl" and "It Takes Two" with Kim Weston in 1989 (Marvin had originally recorded the song with Kim in 1966), next was "My Brother" in 1990. Frankie also released the album of the same name later in the year.

In the late 1990's Frankie worked upon his own release called "The Very Best Of Frankie Gaye".

In 2000, Frankie began work on the autobiography titled "Marvin Gaye: My Brother". There's no telling whether or not he was done with the biography, when on December 30, 2001, Frankie Gaye died of cancer at the age of 60 (other reports suggest complications following a heart attack) in Santa Monica, California. The book was finally released in 2003 to mixed reviews.

Frankie left behind a wife of 23 years, Irene Duncan Gaye, children Frankie Marvin, Fiona; Frankie also had children from his first marriage to Judy Gaye, Denise, and Christy. Marvin Gaye's youngest child, Frankie Christian Gaye (born in November 1975), was named after Frankie.

Born Marvin Pentz Gay on the 2nd April 1939, in Washington DC - Died 1st April 1984 in Los Angeles, California

Motown Connection: Drummer - Solo Artist - Producer - Arranger - Married Berry Gordy's Sister Anna Gordy.

His father, Marvin Gay Sr. of Kentucky, was a minister at a Seventh-day Adventist Church sect called the House of God. It advocated mixed teachings of Orthodox Judaism and Pentecostalism. His mother, Alberta Cooper Gay, of North Carolina, was a domestic worker. Marvin was the eldest son, had a half brother, Michael Cooper, an elder sister Jeanne, brother Frankie, and Zeola "Sweetsie". Raised on the southwest of Washington DC in the Simple City projects. When Marvin turned 14 the family moved to the segregated area of Deanwood Washington, DC in the north eastern part of the city.

A publicity handout from the artist re-produced in the Detroit Free Press.

As a teenager, Marvin caddied at Norbeck Country Club in Olney, Maryland. As a child Marvin's first performances were in his father's church, Marvin sang and played many different types of instruments At Cardozo High School, Marvin joined the DC Tones as a drummer. After dropping out of 11th grade Marvin joined the United States Air Force.

After returning to Washington DC, Marvin reformed the DC Tones as The Marquees and Bo Diddley signed them to the New York Okeh Records, where they recorded "Wyatt Earp", with "Good Morning Little Schoolgirl" as its b/side, the record was not a success. Bo Diddley did introduce the group to Harvey Fuqua, of The Moonglows. Harvey Fuqua signed them as The New Moonglows in 1959 to Chess Records. Marvin and the group sung background on records by Chuck Berry and Etta James and had a modest hit with "The Twelve Commandments of Love". "Mama Loochie" in 1959 which was Marvin's first lead role on a single.

The Moonglows disbanded in 1960, and Harvey Fuqua brought Marvin to Detroit when he moved there, and signed Marvin to the local Anna Records label, founded by Gwen Gordy (Berry Gordy's Sister and Harvey Fuqua's wife). When Motown acquired Anna Records, Marvin was placed on Motown's Tamla subsidiary label. One of Marvin's first tasks was working as a session drummer for The Miracles, The Contours, Martha and The Vandellas, The Marvelettes and many others, one of Marvin's notable recording was on The Marvelettes' 1961 hit, "Please Mr. Postman"

and Little Stevie Wonder's live version of 1963 hit, "Fingertips Pt. 2". Both singles reached number one of the pop singles chart.

Some of Marvin's best solo hits including "How Sweet It Is (To Be Loved By You)", "Ain't That Peculiar", "I Heard It Through the Grapevine" and his duet singles with singers such as Mary Wells and Tammi Terrell, earned Marvin the nicknames "The Prince of Motown" and "The Prince of Soul".

Marvin Gaye with his wife Anna Gordy Gaye. A publicity handout from the artist re-produced in the Detroit Free Press.

While at Motown, Marvin changed his surname to Gaye (from Marvin Gay) adding the 'e' to separate himself from his father, to stop gossip about his sexuality, and to imitate his idol, Sam Cooke, who also added an 'e' to his name.

In June 1961, Marvin issued his first solo recording, "The Soulful Moods of Marvin Gaye", the second album by Motown. The record featured Broadway standards and jazz-rendered show tunes, and the R&B single, "Let Your Conscience Be Your Guide". The record failed to hit the charts. Marvin then released two more singles that were not a success, a cover of The Chordettes' "Sandman" and "Soldier's Plea" in 1962. However, Marvin would find his first success as a co-songwriter on the Marvelettes' 1962 hit, "Beechwood 4-5789". Marvin's first Top 40 singles "Hitch Hike", "Pride and Joy" and "Can I Get a Witness", charted for Marvin in 1963. The success continued with the 1964 singles "You Are a Wonderful One" (which featured background by The Supremes), "Try It Baby" (which featured backgrounds from The Temptations), "Baby Don't You Do It" and "How Sweet It Is (To Be Loved By You)", which became his signature song.

Marvin contributed to writing for Martha and The Vandellas 1964 including the hit "Dancing in the Street". Marvin's work with Smokey Robinson on the 1966 album, "Moods of Marvin Gaye", which produced a consecutive top ten singles with "I'll Be Doggone" and "Ain't That Peculiar", both of which became the singer's first No1 hits of his career. Marvin became a favourite on "American Bandstand", Shindig!, Hullabaloo and The T.A.M.I. Show. Marvin also became one of the few Motown artists to perform at the Copacabana. A live album from the Copacabana performances, however, wouldn't be issued for nearly 40 years.

Marvin married Anna Gordy, sister of Motown Records' Berry Gordy in 1962, but they divorced in 1976 after a 14-year marriage. They had one son Marvin Pentz

Gaye, III (born in 1965) who was adopted by Marvin and Anna. Also in 1962, Marvin's third release, "Stubborn Kind of Fellow", became Marvin's first major hit record. While at Motown Marvin produced for the Originals, "Baby, I'm for Real" in 1969 and "The Bells" in 1970.

A number of Marvin's hits for Motown were with female artists such as Kim Weston and Mary Wells; the first Marvin Gaye/Mary Wells album was in 1964's titled "Together", was Marvin's first charting album. However, it was Marvin's work with Tammi Terrell that became the most memorable. Their first album, 1967's "United", produced two hits, firstly "Ain't No Mountain High Enough" (covered by Diana Ross and former Doobie Brothers singer Michael McDonald) and "Your Precious Love".

It was Nicholas Ashford and Valerie Simpson who provided the writing and production for the Marvin Gaye/Tammi Terrell records. While Marvin and Tammi Terrell were not "lovers" (though rumours did persist) they portrayed themselves as lovers on record. On October 14, 1967, Tammi Terrell collapsed into Marvin's arms while they were performing at the Hampton Institute (now Hampton University) in Hampton, Virginia. Tammi Terrell was later diagnosed with a brain tumour and her health continued to deteriorate. Motown decided to carry on with Gaye/Terrell recordings, issuing the "You're All I Need" album in 1968, which featured "Ain't Nothing Like the Real Thing" and "You're All I Need to Get By". By the final album, "Easy" in 1969, Terrell's vocals were mostly done by Valerie Simpson. Two tracks on "Easy" were vocals from the archives using Tammi Terrell's solo songs, with Marvin's vocals overdubbed.

Tammi Terrell's illness put Marvin into a depression; he refused to acknowledge the success of his song "I Heard It Through the Grapevine", Marvin's first No1 hit and the biggest selling single in Motown history to that point, (with four million copies sold). Marvin's further work with producer Norman Whitfield, who produced "Grapevine", resulted in similar success with the singles "Too Busy Thinking About My Baby" and "That's the Way Love Is".

Marvin Gaye and Tammi Terrell in a 1967 Motown promotional picture. A publicity handout from the artist re-produced in the Detroit Free Press.

Marvin grew more despondent when Terrell died and for a while considered leaving music. In 1970, his 1968 recording of "I Heard It Through The Grapevine" was reissued and featured in the film soundtrack of "The Big Chill". At this time Marvin even tried to play for the Detroit Lions football team, but Marvin was never given a tryout, Lions players Mel Farr and Lem Barney helped Marvin through the period. The phrase "What's Going On" came up during a game of golf between the three.

In 1971, Marvin then made a triumphant comeback with the album "What's Going On," which probably will be remembered as his most important musical album of all time. Many consider the album the first "concept" album by a black artist. The album revealed a poignant and passionate concern with urban decay, ecological crises and spiritual impoverishment. Marvin's mid-1970's work include the "Let's Get It On" and "I Want You" albums.

Marvin Gaye in studio, 1973. A publicity handout from the artist re-produced in the Detroit Free Press.

After the release of "What's Going On", Motown renegotiated a contract with Marvin that allowed him creative control. The deal was worth $1 million, making Marvin the highest-earning black artist at the time. Marvin moved from Detroit to Los Angeles in 1972 after being offered a chance to write the score to a film. Writing, arranging and producing the movie "Trouble Man", Marvin issued the soundtrack and title song in 1972. The soundtrack and single became hits, the single peaking at the top ten in early 1973.

Marvin began working on his final "duet" album, with Diana Ross for the Diana and Marvin project, an album of duets that began recording in 1972, while Ross was pregnant with her second child. Marvin refused to sing if he couldn't smoke in the studio, so the album was recorded by overdubbing Diana Ross and Marvin at separate sessions. Released in 1973, the album yielded the US Top 20 hit singles "You're a Special Part of Me" and "My Mistake (Was to Love You)" as well as the UK versions of Stylistics' "You Are Everything" and "Stop, Look, Listen (To Your Heart)".

By the late 1970's Marvin's career and his marriage to Anna Gordy was coming to an end, Marvin and Anna divorced in 1977 with Anna receiving $600,000 in royalties. Marvin then released the "I Want You" album, which included the title track which became a No1 R&B single, and the more modest, "After the Dance". Album tracks such as "Since I Had You" and "Soon I'll Be Loving You Again" had Marvin using a more funky type material.

In 1977, Marvin released the single, "Got to Give It Up", which went to No1 on the pop chart, and helped his "Live at the London Palladium" album sell two million copies, becoming one of the top ten best-selling albums of the year. After divorcing his wife, Anna, one of the conditions of the divorce was that the royalties from Marvin's next album would go to Anna, typically, Marvin turned his heartaches and divorce into music on the albums "Here My Dear" dedicated to the painful break up of Marvin's marriage to Anna. This almost led to Anna filing a lawsuit for invasion of privacy. That album was not a sales success.

A publicity handout from the artist re-produced in the Detroit Free Press.

Marvin then married Janis Hunter, (who was 17 years younger than Marvin), However, the marriage dissolved within a year. Marvin and Janis Hunter had two children, Nona Marvisa, nicknamed "Pie" by her dad and Frankie "Bubby" Christan Gaye. After attempts at reconciliation, Janis filed for divorce in 1979. The divorce was finalised in February 1981 by 1979, besieged by tax problems and drug addictions; Marvin filed for bankruptcy and moved to Hawaii, where he lived in a bread van. Eventually relocating to Europe in early 1981 (primarily in Ostend, Belgium, but with sometime in London, England) Marvin did a few performances while in Europe, but nothing of substance.

In 1980, Marvin signed with British promoter Jeffrey Kruger to do concerts overseas with the promised highlight of a Royal Command Performance at London's Drury Lane in front of Princess Margaret. Marvin failed to turn up on time and by the time Marvin did arrive, everyone had left. While in London, he worked on "In Our Lifetime?" When Motown issued the album in 1981, Gaye accused Motown of editing and remixing the album without his consent, releasing an unfinished song ("Far Cry"), altering the album art he requested and removing the question mark from the title. A special edition of the album was released in early 2007.

In the early 1980's, after several years of marital, drug and financial problems, Marvin was helped to return to the US (from what he considered to be an exile in Europe). With the help of long-time collaborator Harvey Fuqua, he made a comeback and moved to Columbia Records (working with Larkin Arnold). Marvin recorded his "comeback" the album "Midnight Love" in 1983, this produced the single "Sexual Healing" which became a massive international hit for Marvin and won Marvin two 1983 "Grammy" awards. "Sexual Healing" was Marvin's last hit single which reached No1 on R&B chart, where it stayed for ten weeks, and later No3 on the pop charts. The single sold two million copies in the US (earning a platinum record) in February 1983 it was nominated for Best R&B Song but lost to George Benson. Also February 1983, Marvin performed "The Star-Spangled Banner" at the NBA All-Star Game, held at The Forum in Inglewood, California, accompanied by a drum machine. In March 1983, he gave his final performance in front of a packed theatre for Motown's 25th Anniversary Motown 25, performing "What's Going On". Marvin then embarked on a US tour to support his album. The tour, ending in August 1983, was plagued by health problems and Marvin's bouts of depression, and fear over an attempt on his life.

When the tour ended, Marvin moved into his parents' house in Los Angeles California. Marvin threatened to commit suicide several times after bitter arguments with his father. On April 1, 1984, on the eve of his 45th birthday, Marvin's father shot him after an argument between Marvin's Father and Mother, Marvin attempted to intervene, but was shot (by a gun he had given his father four months earlier). Marvin Gaye Sr. was sentenced to six years of probation after pleading guilty to manslaughter. Charges of first-degree murder were dropped after doctors discovered Marvin Gaye Sr. had a brain tumour. Spending his final years in a retirement home, he died of pneumonia in 1998.

In 1983, the British group Spandau Ballet recorded the single "True" as a tribute to Marvin and the Motown sound he helped establish. A year after his death, The Commodores made reference to Marvin's death in their 1985 song "Nightshift", as did the Violent Femmes in their 1988 song "See My Ships". Diana Ross paid tribute with her Top 10 single "Missing You" in 1985, as did Teena Marie, a former Motown artist, with her album track "My Dear Mr. Gaye". The soul band Maze featuring Frankie Beverly recorded "Silky Soul" in 1989 in honour of their mentor. He was also mentioned in the choral verse of George Michael's "John and Elvis Are Dead", on his album, "Patience".

Marvin was inducted into the Rock and Roll Hall of Fame in 1987. He was inducted to Hollywood's Rock Walk in 1989 and was given a star on the Hollywood Walk of Fame in 1990. In 1995, Madonna, Stevie Wonder, Speech of the group Arrested Development and Gaye's daughter Nona, paid tribute to Gaye with the tribute album, "Inner City Blues" and "The Music of Marvin Gaye", which included a documentary of the same name that was showcased on MTV. In 1999, R&B artists D'Angelo, Erykah Badu, Brian McKnight and Will Downing paid their respects in a tribute album, "Marvin Is 60". In 1996, he was awarded the Grammy

Award for Lifetime Achievement Award and was honoured in song by admirers Annie Lennox and Seal.

In October 2001, a cover of "What's Going On", produced by Jermaine Dupri, was issued as a benefit single, credited to "Artists Against AIDS Worldwide". The single, a reaction to the tragedy of the September 11, 2001 attacks as well as to AIDS, featured Christina Aguilera, Mary J. Blige, Bono, Mariah Carey, Destiny's Child, Fred Durst of Limp Bizkit, Monica, Nelly Furtado, Alicia Keys, Aaron Lewis (of the rock group StainD), Nas, Backstreet Boys, *NSYNC, P. Diddy, Britney Spears and Gwen Stefani. The cover featured Nona Gaye, who sang one of the song's lines, "Father, father/we don't need to escalate". In 2004, Rolling Stone ranked him No18 on their list of the 100 Greatest Artists of All Time.

Marvin's eldest son is a music producer. Marvin also has two grandchildren: Marvin Pentz Gaye IV (born on the anniversary of his grandfather's death) and Nolan Pentz Gaye.

Album Track: "Where Ever I Lay My Hat (That's My Home)", Marvin Gaye.

Dave Godin

Born David Edward Godin on the 21st June 1936 Lambeth, South London, United Kingdom - Died 15th October 2004 Rotherham, South Yorkshire, United Kingdom

Motown Connection: Founder of the Tamla Motown Appreciation Society in the UK - Helped Berry Gordy in establishing Tamla Motown Records in the UK.

Dave Godin was born in Lambeth, London, England, but raised in Peckham, London, England. Dave's father was a milkman. During the war his family moved to Bexley Heath in Kent, England, where Dave gained a scholarship to Dartford Grammar School. It was while at school that his interest in black American music first developed. Dave and a friend visited an ice-cream parlour that had a jukebox. While there, he heard the record "Mama, He Treats Your Daughter Mean" by the R&B singer Ruth Brown this started Dave's lifelong interest in soul music.

One of the UK and international soul music journalists Dave is particularly well known for his "Blues and Soul" magazine column in the 1960's and 1970's. Dave's understanding of Black American social and political life gave him an insight into on the music that made his writing so well received.

Dave's first position was in advertising, a committed pacifist, Dave interestingly refused to do National Service in the UK, even though his father had once been a soldier. In 1957 Dave travelled to Canada and then made his way into the US, where he saw soul stars, La Vern Baker, Fats Domino and Clyde McPhatter. When Dave came back to England, Dave started promoting Berry Gordy's Motown label, Dave is credited with creating the first use of the title Tamla Motown, to use as the new name for Dave's Tamla Motown Appreciation Society. The name would be used by Motown for its UK label (under licence to EMI) which issued the Motown's products in the UK. Dave (while working with Berry Gordy) was instrumental in establishing Tamla Motown in the UK.

Dave had, in 1964, been invited to Detroit by Berry Gordy, who welcomed his views on soul music. Dave met Marvin Gaye, Stevie Wonder and Martha and The Vandellas. Dave is also credited with "coining the phrase", "Northern Soul". Dave also introduced Mick Jagger (of the Rolling Stones) to black music, Jagger was a school acquaintance.

Dave ventured into the record business in the late 1960's when along with David Nathan and Rob Blackmore established the influential "Soul City" record shop in Deptford, England (eventually moving to Monmouth Street in Covent Garden, London). The Soul City label which followed (along with its "Deep Soul" subsidiary) issued singles and LPs many of them being obscure recording of "Northern Soul" classics, the businesses lasted until August 1970.

In the mid 1990's he started to compile a series of CDs of rare (and some not so rare) recordings "Dave Godin's Deep Soul Treasures" for Ace Records, which featured such artists as Loretta Williams, Eddie and Ernie, Jaibi, Ruby Johnson and Jimmy and Louise Tig. The albums were greeted with universal critical acclaim, and Godin described the series as the proudest achievement of his life.

Dave went on to show interests in other areas of entertainment, especially film, becoming involved in the British Film Institute. Having studied art, design and film course at Sheffield Polytechnic, Dave helped found and was director of the Anvil Cinema from 1983 to 1990) in Sheffield, the only cinema in the UK to be funded by a local authority. Dave developed an interest in Esperanto, was also a vegan and an advocate for animal rights. He was also known for his involvement in anarchist and anti-capitalist organisations, including the Freedom Newspaper and Class War. He was the only atheist in his local pro-life organisation. Towards the end of his life he developed an interest in Jainism. Dave along with Guy Stevens, DJ at London's Scene club, Vicki Wickham, the producer of Ready Steady Go, and the pirate radio DJ Mike Raven, helped promote soul music a vital part of British (Mod) youth culture of the 1960's and 1970's.

Godin, who never married, died of lung cancer and passed away in his sleep at the age of 68.

Berry Gordy

Born Berry Gordy Jnr on the 28th November 1929 in Detroit, Michigan

Motown Connection: Founder Motown Records - Founder of the Jobete Music Company publishing - Artist Manager - Songwriter - Producer - Director (Television, Record and Film) - President of Motown Records - Chairman of the Board of Motown Industries - Head of TGC Management LLC - Head of West Grand Media LLC.

Where do you start with this entry? The "Motown Story" is the story of Berry Gordy, who was born in Detroit, Michigan. Berry was the seventh of eight children of Berry, Sr. and Bertha Gordy. His parents had migrated to Detroit from Milledgeville, Georgia in 1922. His father ran a plastering contracting business and his mother sold insurance and real estate. The family also owned a grocery store and print shop. Berry Gordy dropped out of school after his junior year to become a professional boxer; he decided to get out of the fight game in 1950. The Army drafted him in 1951.

Berry Gordy with Martin Luther King in a publicity handout from the artist re-produced in the Detroit Free Press.

By the late 1950's, Detroit was perhaps the largest city in the United States that did not have a strong independent record company.

During his stint in the Army, he obtained his high school equivalent degree. In 1954, he married Thelma Coleman and later that year their first child was born, a daughter Hazel Joy. They had two other children, named Berry IV and Terry, but were divorced in 1959.

When Berry got out of the Army in 1953, using his severance pay and some family help, he and his brother, George, opened a record store called the 3-D Record Mart - House of Jazz. By 1955, the store had failed and Berry was working on the Ford automobile assembly line. While working on the line, Berry constantly wrote songs, His first success as a songwriter came in 1957 when Jackie Wilson recorded "Reet Petite", a song he, his sister Gwen and Roquel Billy Davis (under the pseudonym of Tyran Carlo) had written. "Reet Petite" became a modest hit and over the next two years he co-wrote four more hits for Jackie Wilson, "To Be Loved", "Lonely Teardrops", "That's Why (I Love You So)" and "I'll Be Satisfied". Berry later chose the title "To Be Loved" for his autobiography.

Successful as a songwriter, Berry decided to produce his songs himself. His first production was titled "Ooh Shucks" by the Five Stars, which was released on George Goldner's Mark X label in 1957. Berry had an extraordinary ability to recognize talent. In 1957 while at the offices of Jackie Wilson's manager, he met William "Smokey Robinson" who was the lead singer in a group called The Matadors, who were there for an audition. When they were rejected, Berry caught up with them saying he thought they were really good. This was the start of a lifelong relationship with Smokey in particular. Changing their name to The Miracles, they became Berry's first recording group and Smokey Robinson his first writer.

A publicity handout from the artist re-produced in the Detroit Free Press.

The Miracles consisted of Smokey Robinson, Claudette Rogers (Smokey's future wife), Ronnie White, Pete Moore, and Bobby Rogers. Berry's first production for The Miracles was an answer record to The Silhouettes "Get a Job", titled "Got a Job", which he leased to Goldner for release on End records. The record got some airplay, but then died a quick death, as did The Miracles follow-up on End titled "I Cry".

In 1958, Berry produced a record by Eddie Holland titled "You", which was leased to Mercury records. Also that year, Kudo Records issued four more of Berry's productions, the first Marv Johnson release, titled "My Baby O", and Brian Holland, Eddie's brother (of the future Holland-Dozier-Holland team) single, entitled "Shock". With Smokey Robinson and the Holland brothers, Berry, had by accident discovered three incredible songwriters and producers which would later transform Motown in to the hit making factory Berry had envisaged.

Also in 1958, Berry produced a record by Herman Griffin titled "I Need You" on the H.O.B (which stood for House of Beauty) label. What is notable about this recording is that it was the first song to be published by Berry's publishing company Jobete (pronounced "Jo-bet"), which was named after his first three children, Hazel Joy [Jo], Berry IV [Be], and Terry [Te]. "I Need You" was also the first record to credit the Rayber Voices, a group of background singers put together and named after Berry's second wife, Raynoma, and himself.

The rest is the "stuff of history". With Berry's success in writing and producing for other artists and labels, Berry decided to take total control of his songs and production. On January 12, 1959 Berry borrowed $800 from his family's savings fund to start his own record label, called Tamla. He had originally wanted to call his label "Tammy", after a Debbie Reynolds film, but that title was already taken. Tamla Records was located at 1719 Gladstone Street in Detroit (pre-West Grand Boulevard), and the first release was Marv Johnson's "Come to Me". United Artists distributed the single and it became a moderate hit. After this success United Artists decided to sign Marv Johnson to a recording contract with Berry still continuing to produce him for that label.

After receiving a royalty check for only $3.19, Smokey Robinson told Berry he should start his own label. Berry created Motown Records (after Tamla Records had started), and its first big hit was Barrett Strong's "Money (That's What I Want)", written by Berry and Janie Bradford and produced by Berry. The single appeared on the Tamla label, but distributed by Anna Records (Berry's sister, Gwen's label named after sister, Anna) in February 1960. The Miracles' hit "Shop Around" peaked nationally at No1 on the R&B charts in late 1960 and at No2 on the pop charts, January 1961. This established Motown as an independent record company to take notice of. Later that year, The Marvelettes' "Please Mr. Postman" became Motown's first number one on both charts.

With the creation of Tamla (later to become a subsidiary of Motown Records) Berry was beginning to establish his vision for Motown, based out of a tiny house he dubbed "Hitsville USA" at 2648 West Grand Boulevard incorporating the now famous "Studio A". Berry started with a small rota of artists, which included the Miracles, The Marvelettes, Martha and The Vandellas, The Supremes, Four Tops, solo performers Mary Wells, Marvin Gaye and Stevie Wonder to name a few, an in-house team of writers and producers, which included Smokey Robinson, Mickey Stevenson and Holland-Dozier-Holland. Add to this mix the Andantes as back-up singers and an in-house band of musicians who played on almost every Motown recording in the 1960's, dubbed "The Funk Brothers," and Berry knew he had the right combination to make great pop/R&B records that would appeal to the general market.

In the early days of Motown, (although it certainly wasn't a hard and fast rule), Berry assigned specific artists to specific producers, Smokey would produce Mary Wells, The Temptations and the Miracles and Marvin Gaye. Holland-Dozier-Holland would produce The Four Tops, Martha and The Vandellas and The Supremes, while Mickey Stevenson would also produce Marvin Gaye, Martha and The Vandellas and The Marvelettes. Other producers included Hank Cosby, Sylvia Moy and Clarence Paul who worked with Stevie Wonder. Martha and The Vandellas were produced by both Mickey Stevenson and Holland-Dozier-Holland. Norman Whitfield took over the reins from Smokey on The Temptations and had as tight and successful a hold on them as Holland-Dozier-Holland on The Supremes. Berry also produced many of these artists himself.

In the next few years, Berry signed such artists as Gladys Knight and The Pips, the Jackson 5, The Commodores, Rick James, Teena Marie, DeBarge and more.

Although Berry generally signed black artists, some white artists were signed, such as Nick and the Jaguars, Rare Earth (the most successful), The Valadiers, Debbie Dean and Connie Van Dyke. One of Berry's many gifts was identifying and bringing together musical talent, along with the careful management of his artists' public image. This gift was instrumental in Motown becoming a major national and international success.

Between 1959 and 1972 the Motown operation would establish itself as the largest independent record company in the world (and the largest business of any kind owned by an African American), stemming from a unique assembly line song production process that was as inventive as it was successful. The initial hits by Barrett Strong, The Marvelettes and The Miracles at the beginning of the 1960's and the explosion of the Jackson 5 in the early 1970's were simply bookends to an unprecedented run of commercial and artistic achievements.

In the mid-1960's Motown was especially dominant, and the company more than any other label defined the sixties. The organisation that created these songs was about as close to a musical "hit factory" as popular music has produced. Motown (which of course took its name from the Motor City), in fact, liked to brag

A publicity handout from the artist re-produced in the Detroit Free Press.

that the Detroit auto industry wasn't the only successful assembly line in town. Ford, General Motors, and Chrysler may have produced the classic cars, but Motown produced the classic songs.

By 1972 the Motown era in Detroit came to an end when Berry moved his operation to Los Angeles, California. He resigned as President of Motown Records to become Chairman of the Board of Motown Industries, which included the record, motion picture, television and publishing divisions. Ewart Abner II, a Motown Vice President for six years (and former exec with Vee-Jay Records) became President of Motown Records,

By 1971 Berry was concentrating on movies, particularly on developing Diana Ross's acting career, with the film "Lady Sings the Blues" in 1972 where she starred as Billie Holiday. The film was nominated for five Academy Awards. Then Berry directed her in "Mahogany". In 1985, he produced the cult martial arts film "Berry Gordy's The Last Dragon", which starred martial artist Taimak.

In the 1970's and early 1980's Motown was still a success in promoting the Jackson 5, The Commodores, Rick James, Teena Marie, Lionel Richie, Marvin Gaye and Stevie Wonder who were entering the most successful parts of their career, but Motown's stranglehold on the charts had gone. Diana Ross's solo career was not as successful as first envisioned, and Berry felt that much of the tight-knit family atmosphere that originally made Motown so successful had gone. By the mid 1980's, Motown was losing millions, and in June, 1988, Berry sold Motown for $61 million to a partnership between MCA and Boston Ventures, with Berry retaining the ownership of the Jobete Publishing catalogue, although Berry later sold most of his interests in the Jobete publishing concern to EMI Publishing.

Though retired, Mr. Gordy, is working on a number of projects, including a Broadway musical based on his autobiography, "To Be Loved: The Music, The Magic, The Memories of Motown", published in 1994.

The site of the original Hitsville has been transformed into the Motown Historical Museum in Detroit, visited year-round by tourists from all parts of the world. It features interactive exhibits and memorabilia focusing on the history of Motown and its importance not only in the music industry, but as an institution whose music communicated across a racially divided country and segregated society, around the world, touching all people, regardless of skin colour.

Berry was awarded by the Songwriters' Hall of Fame its coveted Abe Olman Publisher Award in 1993 and their Sammy Cahn Lifetime Achievement Award in 1998; inducted in The Rock and Roll Hall of Fame in 1988; awarded the Grammy's Salute to Industry Icons President's Merit Award by NARAS and numerous other awards and honours. Berry also has a star on the Hollywood Walk of Fame for "Excellence in Music."

Berry delivered the commencement address at Michigan State University on May 5th 2006, and at Occidental College on May 20th 2007, where he received an honorary doctorate degree from each school. He has two other honorary doctorates from Eastern Michigan University and Morehouse College

On February 22, 2007 DreamWorks and Paramount, finally apologised to Berry Gordy in Variety and Hollywood Reporter for Jamie Foxx's thinly veiled and false portrayal of the Motown founder in the Oscar-nominated film "Dreamgirls".

Berry continues to live in a multi-million dollar Tudor-style mansion set in ten acres of the hills of Bel-Air, in Los Angeles, California.

Berry married and divorced three times, to Thelma Coleman, Raynoma Singleton, and Grace Eaton, has eight children: Hazel Joy, Berry Gordy IV, Terry James, Kerry, Sherry, Kennedy, Rhonda and Stefan.

Rhonda Ross Kendrick is his daughter with Motown artist, Diana Ross, with whom he had a long relationship. Kennedy Gordy is better known as the Motown artist, Rockwell. Gordy's daughter, Hazel, was once married to Jermaine Jackson of The Jackson 5.

As good as he was as a judge of talent and hit songs; he was most of all an entrepreneur who transformed an $800 loan into the largest black owned business in United States history.

Album Track: "What's So Good About Goodbye", Smokey Robinson and The Miracles.

Aka Robert Kayli Born in Detroit, Michigan.

Motown Connection: Youngest Brother of Motown founder Berry Gordy - Motown's Engineering Department - Singer - Background Singer - Film Actor ("Hawk" in the "Lady Sings the Blues" - Head of Jobete Music (Motown's Publishing Division).

Robert was the youngest brother of Motown founder Berry Gordy, the youngest child of the Berry Gordy Snr and Bertha Gordy, both from Georgia, from a family of ten children. Robert worked for the Post Office combining this with part-time recording for Anna Records (owned by his sister Anna Gordy) until Berry Gordy's Motown label started to establish itself. Robert left the government job for his first position in Motown's engineering department. Robert recorded under the pseudonym of Robert Kayli for Anna Records including a minor hit in 1958 with the novelty song, "Everyone Was There", (released on Carlton Records) Robert also recorded "Never More" b/side "Peppermint (You Know What To Do)" in 1959.

The next recordings were on Tamla (a subsidiary of Motown Records) called "Small Sad Sam" in 1961, interestingly only a one sided record and then "Tie Me Tight" with "Small Sad Sam" as the b/side (interestingly with backing vocals from Diana Ross), this was an "answer" song to "Big Bad John". Robert then recorded for Gordy (another subsidiary of Motown Records) "Hold On Pearl" b/side "Toodle Loo" in 1962. Bob Kayli was the only member of the Gordy Family to record on three different Gordy labels.

Robert (again as Bob Kayli) had an interesting take on a "duet" with Hattie Littles on two Gordy singles, "Is It Love?" by Hattie Littles on the A side and "Everybody Was There (I Took Care)" on the b/side in 1962. Although scheduled for release in that year, it was never issued. After the death of his sister, Loucye, Robert became Head of Jobete Music, Motown's publishing division. Robert played the character "Hawk" in the film "Lady Sings the Blues" (1972) Motown Production film.

Born Fredrick Gorman on the 11th April 1939 Detroit, Michigan - Died 13th June 2006 Palmdale, California

Motown Connection: Singer - Member of The Originals - Backing Singer - Writer - Producer.

Born and raised in Detroit, Freddie's first performances were on street corners from his early teens. While in high school, he joined the group the Sax Kari and then the Quailtones, and co-wrote "Tears of Love", their only single in 1955 on the Josie label. Next, Freddie formed the group Fidelitones with Brian Holland (a future Motown employee) and knew Berry Gordy from his job as a postman in 1957.

Signed to Motown in 1961 Freddie's first solo release was on the Motown subsidiary label Miracle, called "The Day Will Come" b/side "Just For You". Freddie helped create The Marvelettes' 1961 song "Please Mr. Postman" Motown's first No1 record in the US, originally credited to Georgia Dobbins, (a founder member of The Marvelettes), William Garrett, Brian Holland and Robert Bateman under the name "Brianbert". Freddie's contribution in creating the song was only acknowledged in 1987 when the Songwriters Hall of Fame changed the song writing credits to Brian Holland, Robert Bateman and Freddie Gorman.

This combination ("Brianbert") then went on to write more hits for The Marvelettes like "Twistin' Postman", "Playboy", "Someday, Someway" and "Strange I Know", next came Mary Wells' recording of "Old Love" and The Supremes "I Want a Guy".

Shortly afterwards, he moved to the rival Detroit label Ric-Tic to record "In a Bad Way", "Take Me Back" and "Just Can't Get It Out of My Mind". With Golden World, Freddie co-write the song "(Just Like) Romeo and Juliet", a hit for the Reflections in 1964, this recording became Golden World's biggest success. His final contribution for Golden World was in August 1965 with a song written for the Adorables called, "Devil In His Eyes" which had "Ooh Boy" on the b/side.

When Ric-Tic and Golden World were purchased by Motown, Freddie returned as part of a group called The Originals. From 1965 to 1969, The Originals became the male vocal backing group for Motown artists like Marvin Gaye, Stevie Wonder, and Jimmy Ruffin. In 1966, Motown released their single "Goodnight Irene" b/side "Need Your Loving (Want You Back)" followed by (with vocalist Joe Stubbs singing lead vocals) "Need Your Loving (Want You Back)!"

Their big break came in 1969, when Marvin Gaye co-wrote (with his wife Anna) and produced "Baby, I'm For Real" for the group, at last bringing them recognition at Motown as a group in their own right. The next year, Marvin Gaye co-wrote and produced the hit single "The Bells" which reached No12 on the pop charts. The group's first album was originally issued under the title, "Green Grow The Lilacs", but was reissued as "Baby, I'm For Real" on the back of the success of the single. The Originals disbanded in the early 1970's but did reform in 1975 with Ty Hunter replacing C.P. Spencer. They recorded an album of Lamont Dozier songs, "California Sunset", in 1975; Lamont Dozier was producing for ABC Records at the time. In 1978, they left Motown and released an album on Fantasy Records called, "Another Time, and Another Place". Their second album on Fantasy, "Come A Way With Me" was released in 1979 and featured The Originals as a quintet, with Freddie Gorman, Hank Dixon, Walter Gaines, Ty Hunter and C.P. Spencer.

Freddie returned to The Originals in 1978, three years later, their own version of "Please Mr. Postman" was featured on the album "Yesterday and Today". The group also became involved with the UK producer Ian Levine Motorcity project in the late 1980's and early 1990's, the group made their UK live début in 2002.

Freddie was married with one son before he died aged 67 of lung cancer in Palmdale, California.

Born on the 22nd April 1943 in Fairfield, Texas

Motown Connection: Temptations Musical Director - Writer - Studio Musician - Lectures on Motown.

Cornelius was born and raised in Fairfield Texas and by nine years old had taught himself the guitar although Cornelius first preference was for a piano. Three years later the family moved to Detroit, by 15, Cornelius was playing with some of Detroit's best musicians at clubs, bars, talent shows, and other functions in Detroit though he was still a full-time student at Mumford High.

When Cornelius arrived at Motown he first backed Mary Wells, then Marvin Gaye before eventually working with The Temptations. Cornelius co-wrote (with Eddie Holland and Norman Whitfield), "You're My Everything" by The Temptations. Then, with the late Roger Penzabene (who was a close friend) and Norman Whitfield, he co-wrote "I Wish It Rain" and "I Could Never Love Another." again by The Temptations, tragically Roger committed suicide before he received a royalty check for these songs.

Cornelius next wrote "Take Me in Your Arms and Love Me" and "Ain't No Sun (Since You Been Gone)" both by Gladys Knight and The Pips, Cornelius's next writing credits were with The Temptations on "You Got to Earn It" and "I Got to Find a Way to Win You Back" and then Edwin Starr's recording of "My Weakness Is You" and "I Want My Baby Back". Lulu the British Pop star recorded "Take Me In Your Arms", for her "To Sir With Love" album in the 1960's Cornelius then co-wrote "I'm More Than Happy (I'm Satisfied)" for Stevie Wonder, followed by "Loving and Affection" by Marvin Gaye.

In the 1970's Cornelius became a partner in D.O.C. Productions with Melvin Franklin and Otis Williams of The Temptations, (D.O.C. was an acronym for David, Otis and Cornelius). The company produced two artists, Swiss Movement and Quiet Elegance.

Cornelius was famous for coming up with stunning riffs, a good example being the intro "I Know I'm Losing You" by The Temptations. Produced by Norman Whitfield (after he heard Cornelius playing riffs), Norman Whitfield developed the chord structure, and Eddie Holland supplied lyrics. Cornelius can be heard on selected Motown studio sessions from 1964 to 1970, including Gladys Knight and The Pips No1 hit "I Heard It Through the Grapevine." As a rule Cornelius played on all the sessions that featured songs he co-wrote, except one, "You Got To Earn It", by The Temptations, which Smokey Robinson produced while Cornelius was on the road with The Temptations. Cornelius was not a lover of session work, preferring live performances.

The Temptations (with Cornelius) were invited to the White House by Tricia Nixon Eisenhower. Cornelius also met Reverend Martin Luther King, Jesse Jackson, Elton John, The Beatles, and appeared on many television shows. Cornelius is the Chief Executive of Siege, an entertainment complex that manages and develops new artists. Cornelius also lectures with colleagues from Motown at forums formed to discuss the realities of the music business, teaches guitar at a city college and has written a book entitled: Cornelius Grant's "Guitar For Beginners". Cornelius founded W.A.R.M. (World Academy of Recording Musicians) an organisation to help studio and road musicians gain recognition for their contributions. Cornelius also served as The Temptations' Musical Director for nearly 20 years, travelling all over the world with the vocal group.

Signature sound: Cornelius created the opening guitar riff on "I Know I'm Losing You", stunning.

Born in Detroit, Michigan

Motown Connection: Singer - Performer - Mary Wells' Husband - Recorded the first record published by Jobete Publishing Company.

Born and raised in Detroit, Herman recorded the first song to be published by Berry Gordy's Jobete Publishing Company; Jobete would become Motown's publishing company holding the rights to all the classic Motown recordings. With "I Need You", distributed on HOB Records (HOB was an acronym for the House of Beauty, a hair dresser that Berry's future wife Raynoma Liles used); Berry Gordy laid the foundations for the successful growth of the publishing side of Motown. The single also credited the Rayber Singers (as background singers) for the first time on a recording. It was Berry Gordy's only involvement with Carla Murphy's the owner of HOB Records.

Berry Gordy had been impressed with Herman's exciting performances at a local Detroit Club, where back flips, somersaults, and splits were as much a part of his act as his bluesy tenor voice. Berry Gordy liked his acrobatics and stage craft and offered to record Herman, the result was "I Need You".

Herman's next recording was on Berry Gordy's own Tamla Records (Tamla being established before Motown Records although it would became a subsidiary of Motown Records later) released in October 1960, "True Love" b/side "It's You" was not a commercial success, and did nothing to promote Herman's career. Herman's next release this time on Motown Records was released in July 1962, but "Sleep (Little One)" b/side "Uptight", made no impact on the charts. Interestingly, Herman had been working in the promotions at Motown, which involved "pushing" Motown records with DJs in different cities encouraging them to play Motown releases, this activity made no impact on Herman's records or Herman's signing career.

Herman's credited with being the reason for Mary Wells' departure from Motown. Herman was Mary Well's manager and first husband Herman was trying to gain more control and an increase in Mary's earnings, but it turned out to be more than Motown were willing to concede. Mary Wells turned 21 years old shortly afterwards, just as "My Guy" was becoming a No1 hit, and left Motown almost immediately for a reported advance of several hundred thousand dollars from 20th Century Fox. After signing with 20th Century Fox Mary Well's career never hit the highs of her Motown career. Herman left Motown, (along with Mary Wells) leaving behind "bad feeling" with Berry Gordy and in particular Smokey Robinson who had been writing and producing Mary Wells who thought Mary Wells had been badly advised. As for Herman, Motown staff thought Herman had stopped making a contribution to the company, couldn't read or write music and thought his conduct while conducting the band Mary Wells used while performing (doing back flips while Mary sung ballads) unprofessional.

After Motown, one of Herman's other contributions to the recording industry was as a singer with "The Boys In The Band" group. Herman did participate in Ian Levine's Motorcity label in the late 1980's early 1990's project. Ian Levine recorded a few tracks on Herman, most notably "Not One Chance In A Million".

Junius Griffin

Born on the 13th January 1929 in Stonega, Virginia

Motown Connection: Vice president of Motown - Public Relations Director.

Born and raised in a coal mining town Stonega Virginia, four miles north of Appalachia Virginia, most of the work was in the mining industry (although the area has lost this industry) Junius's father was a coal miner. Junius was an only child and the first school he attended was the Stonega School for Coloured (as it was then called). Graduated from Central High School Appalachia, Virginia, Then Bluefield State College. At seventeen Junius enlisted in the Army Air Corps Reserves (and later became a Marine) he stayed in there until he was almost twenty years then went back to Bluefield for a term, followed by Wayne University for a term.

Junius was public relations director, and a vice president for Motown, also was public relations director for Dr. Martin Luther King Jnr during the 1950's and early 1960's, overlapping with Junius's work at Motown, but during the late 1960's and 1970's, the more radical groups, like SNCC (Student Non-violent Coordinating Committee), started to look to black people only for support, (without any white voice being represented) which Junius thought too radical.

In the 1960's Junius worked as a journalist (after 12 years in the military) beginning his career with the New York Times, (where he remained until 1962). During this time at The New York Times Junius became the first African-American reporter to work on the desk of the Associated Press.

In July 1963, Junius Griffin, Relman Morin, (a two-time Pulitzer Prize winner), and six other Associated Press reporters published a report describing racial prejudice and segregation in the United States. Entitled "The Deepening Crisis", the series attempted to illustrate the social, economic, political, and educational inequalities that were experienced by African-Americans. Griffin's two contributions described the new "Negro" militants that were emerging in urban America and highlighted the diversities between northern and southern racial prejudices (from the perspective of the black American). The series' immense impact eventually led to its nomination for the 1962 Pulitzer Prize in Journalism.

In the mid-1960's, after leaving the New York Times, Junius joined Martin Luther King's staff at the Southern Christian Leadership Conference and spent two years handling public relations. Junius spent the next two years actively engaged in the civil rights movement, travelling everywhere with Martin Luther King. Junius's main work was writing speeches for Dr. Martin Luther King, Junius continued working for Martin Luther King until 1967, interestingly Motown Records (through it's subsidiary Black Forum label), would issue most of Martin Luther Kings speeches (written by Junius in his pre-Motown days), as albums.

While trying to enlist Stevie Wonder for an SCLC rally in 1967, Junius was introduced to Motown Executive Esther Gordy Edwards, who subsequently introduced Junius to her brother Berry Gordy, who offered Junius the position as Vice-president for Motown Records Industries, his main role being Public Relations, handling the day to day operation (which by 1967 was extensive) of all Motown PR issues, Junius was with Motown Records from 1967 to 1982. Suffering from acute ulcers, Junius resigned his position at Motown Records and entered Johnson City's Mountain Home Veteran's Hospital.

While in Hospital Junius pursued a college degree and in 1983 enrolled at East Tennessee State University for a Bachelor's Degree in English and Mass Communications followed by a Masters Degree in English. Junius graduated in 1987 with both his Bachelors and Masters. In 1988 Junius left Tennessee to move back into public relations as an advisor and board member of the Martin Luther King, Jnr. Center for Non-violent Social Change based in Atlanta Georgia.

One of Junius's great interests is the sociological and economic impact Motown has had on African-American business professionals. "Motown was like a graduate school for those of us who didn't have an MBA". Motown's music helped the civil rights movement, now he is a Professor at Emory and Henry College, in Emory, Virginia. He teaches courses in history and African-American studies, including a popular course that studies the origin and history of Motown.

While working in Detroit, Junius met his wife Ragni (who at the time was an Associate Editor of Ebony/Jet Magazine), the marriage ended after 13 years. Ragni who is Swedish, comes from a family of five generations of Baptist ministers, now editor of the "Swedish National Baptist News". They had two daughters from the marriage.

Johnny Griffith

Born John Ellis Griffith Jnr on the 10th July 1936 in Detroit, Michigan - Died on the 10th November 2002 in Detroit, Michigan

Motown Connection: Pianists and Keyboard/member of The Funk Brothers (Motown In House Band).

Born and raised in Detroit, Johnny had developed so rapidly as a piano player that, by the age of 16, he was already backing the blues legend John Lee Hooker. Johnny wrote and produced his first recording "Grand Central Shuffle" with Ernest Kelly for RCA Records. Johnny recorded with many other Detroit soul labels (often moonlighting between his Motown sessions). Johnny also worked for Brunswick Records in Chicago. Before and after his Motown career Johnny worked with such great names as, Sarah Vaughan, Dinah Washington, Aretha Franklin and Lou Rawls.

Johnny gained a musical degree from Wayne State University and the University of Detroit. Johnny was also the artist-in-residence for Indiana University.

Like Motown's other pianists, Joe Hunter and Earl Van Dyke, Johnny had an extensive musical background and education. Originally signed to Motown's Jazz Workshop label, he recorded the albums "Detroit Jazz" a collaboration with a Motown saxophonist, "The Right Side of Lefty Edwards" issued in 1963 and 1964 respectably.

With the establishment and subsequent rise of Motown, Johnny started playing on recording sessions for Motown on an ad-hoc basic. Unlike the other musicians in Motown's "Studio A" who were employees of Motown (resulting in a steady income), Johnny decided to sign a "work to hire contract" (session pay) which at the time was normal for the record  industry. Johnny remained a free lancer through out his career with Motown, allowing Johnny to do sessions for other record labels in New York and Chicago. This different approach did not stop Johnny becoming an integral part of The Funk Brothers. While the other Funk Brothers were stopped from this practice, indeed Johnny was asked to "spy" on the other members (without success).

Johnny must have played on thousands of Motown Records just some of his "roll call" include, Marvin Gaye's "How Sweet It Is (To Be Loved By You)", organ on The Supremes "Stop In The Name Of Love", and "shotgun effects" on Junior Walker and The All Stars "Shotgun" in early 1965. The Temptations "Ain't Too

Proud To Beg" in the summer of 1966. His organ riffs can be heard on "Mercy Mercy Me (The Ecology)" in 1971, using the Wurlitzer electric piano on Marvin Gaye's classic hit "I Heard It Through The Grapevine" in late 1968.

Non-Motown hits include Edwin Starr's "Agent Double 0 Soul" in the summer 1965; interestingly this record became part of the Motown Catalogue with the purchase of Golden World Record by Motown. Working next on "Cool Jerk" by The Capitols and The Artistics' "I'm Really Gonna Miss You" in late 1966. Johnny then did session work with Chicago Soul Producer Carl Davis, working with the other members of The Funk Brothers (without Motown's knowledge) they produced Jackie Wilson's "(Your Love Keeps Lifting Me) Higher and Higher" in late 1967, and Young Holt Unlimited "Soulful Strut, in late 1968 and the The Chi Lites' "Have You Seen Her", in late 1971.

In 1988 he was responsible for directing the Soul Revenue, one of the three performing arts by the African American Arts Institute. Although Johnny will always be know as an integral part of the "Motown Sound", Johnny always through of himself as a jazz musician first. In the 1990's, Griffith was still active on the Detroit club scene.

Johnny moved to Las Vegas, where he lived until sadly, Johnny died of a heart attack only hours before the documentary "Standing in the Shadows of Motown" was premiered. The documentary celebrated The Funk Brother's contribution to the development of the "Motown Sound". Johnny's wife Delma and three children survived him. Johnny's sister pre-deceased him.

Signature sound: is the swirling organ at the beginning of "Stop in the Name of Love" by The Supremes.

Billy Henderson

Born William Henderson on the 9th August 1939 in Detroit, Michigan - Died 2nd February 2007 in Daytona Beach, Florida

Motown Connection: Tenor Singer with The Spinners (aka Detroit Spinners and The Motown Spinners in the UK).

Billy was one of the original members of the group The Detroit Spinners with Pervis Jackson, Henry Fambrough and Bobbie Smith. At school in the suburb of Ferndale, Billy along with other students formed a group they called The Domingoes in 1954. Over the next few years they gave occasional concerts and changed both personnel and group names until, in 1961, they settled on the "The Spinners" named after the large hub-caps of Cadillac cars.

In 1961, they were signed to a recording contract by Harvey Fuqua for his Tri-Phi label, the subsequent single, "That's What Girls Are Made For" became a chart hit. Tri-Phi issued another single which made the US Top Thirty in 1961, called "Love (I'm So Glad) I Found You", on which Harvey Fuqua also appeared, after this recording Bobbie Smith took over the lead vocals with out any further success. However, when Harvey Fuqua sold his Tri-Phi record company to Berry Gordy the consequence of this sale meant The Spinners would became Motown Recording Artists. The Spinners recorded a single for Motown, briefly charting with "I'll Always Love You" in 1965.

By 1968 the Spinners had been moved to VIP (subsidiary label of Motown) working with producer Johnny Bristol, and then Stevie Wonder, who helped them back into the US charts with "It's a Shame". The song was also a Top 20 hit in UK, where the group was renamed The Motown Spinners to avoid confusion with the Liverpool folk group already called The Spinners. Also in that year The Spinners recorded "We'll Have It Made". The Spinners (in their opinion) were promoted behind artists like, The Supremes, Stevie Wonder and The Temptations into international stars, this was reinforced when The Spinners generally opened the show for other Motown artists, and never gained top spot for themselves.

When other labels like Stax expressed an interest in signing The Spinners, Berry Gordy invoked a clause in their contract which tied their lead vocalist G.C. Cameron to a solo deal with Motown. The group's real success came after leaving Motown in 1972 for Atlantic Records, on Aretha Franklin's advice. The label offered the leading Philly Sound producer Thom Bell the opportunity to work with any of its artists and Thom Bell chose The Spinners. Thom Bell and his songwriters created a series of big hits during the seventies, starting with "I'll Be Around", in 1972, (DJs started playing the b/side of "How Could I Let You Get Away", it became the Spinners' first single for Atlantic and their first million-seller. In 1973, "Could It Be I'm Falling in Love", recorded at the same session, also made the US Top Five. Smith and Wynne shared lead vocals on "One of a Kind (Love Affair)" in 1973, while all five Spinners took their turn singing lead on "(They Just Can't Stop the) Games People Play" 1975. The Spinners scored one of their biggest hits in 1976 with "The Rubberband Man", a track co-written by Thom Bell and inspired by his son Mark. The group's only No1 hit in America was "Then Came You", a duet with Dionne Warwick.

By the mid-1980's, Billy and the group were playing on "oldies" circuit with the Four Seasons and the Righteous Brothers. The final album for Atlantic was "Cross Fire", in 1984, although the group was featured in the Atlantic Record Company's 40th anniversary concert in New York in 1988.

Billy remained with the Detroit Spinners until 2004 when he alleged mismanagement and sued the group's corporation and business manager to obtain financial records. The business manager at the time was the wife of Bobbie Smith. On leaving the group, Billy formed The Spinners Part Too, Inc with two of his sons.

In later years, Billy had both legs removed due to diabetes, before he sadly died. Married to Barbara they had three children.

At 2648 West Grand Boulevard housing the famous "Motown Studio A"

Motown Connection: Berry Gordy's House - Original Studio for Motown Recordings 1959 to 1972 - Motown Headquarters 1959 to 1972 - Office and Original Tape Library - Motown Historical Museum.

Hitsville USA "The Sound Of Young America" that title, adorning an unimposing house on West Grand Boulevard in Detroit, served as Motown's headquarters. By the mid 1960's, the company was a musical giant, becoming the largest independent record company in the world; Berry Gordy would be the wealthiest and most successful black businessman in the USA. An instantly recognisable brand name (on a par with Ford and General Motors etc) responsible for some of the most successful and most memorable pop music of that or any other era.

The house that gave birth to the "Motown Sound" is a two-story brick and stucco house, unremarkable except for a sign above the porch identifying it as "Hitsville USA" and a showcase in the front window. Motown founder Berry Gordy lived in an upstairs room in the back of the house, while downstairs, in a small room (that started life as a garage) served as a recording studio christened the "Snake Pit" by the musicians who recorded there. It served as the foundation to what would eventually become the

Motown Record Company. Early recordings at "Hitsville" were made on a simple; two-track tape system when a mistake was made back then, the entire song had to be re-recorded.

The numbers are staggering, the number of superstars who enter "Hitsville" as unknown before becoming all conquering music legends themselves, song after song by Smokey Robinson and The Miracles, The Marvelettes, Mary Wells, Martha Reeves and The Vandellas, The Temptations, The Supremes, The Four Tops, Marvin Gaye, Stevie Wonder, The Jackson 5, The Isley Brothers, add to these the early stars, JJ Barnes The Elgins, Marv Johnson and almost too many others to mention. In the early days all the artists, producers etc worked on the recording, it was normal for Marvin Gaye, Mary Wells, The Miracles and The Temptations and many others to provide background vocals and hand-claps.

Motown recorded all the classic singles released in the 1960's and early 1970's from this building including, "Money (That's What I Want)", "Shop Around", "Please Mr. Postman", "Dancing in the Street", "I Heard It through the Grapevine", "My Girl", "Where Did Our Love Go", "I Can't Help Myself", "Ain't Too Proud to Beg", the list goes on and on. By the end of the 1972 the back catalogue was into the tens of thousands, and to this day more and more recordings are being "discovered" and released in various packages. These songs represent, as described by Berry Gordy, a "body of popular music" that has served as the soundtrack for the lives of at least three generations of music fans.

Unlike other songs from the era, the Motown hits do not now sound dated when played today, evidenced by their continual popularity on radio play lists, movie soundtracks, and the repertoires of performers ranging from bar bands to top recording acts. The Motown era, based around "Hitsville Studio A" and Detroit in the 1960's and early 1970's made music that changed the world, the cast of stars/characters, the company's unique working environment has achieved legendary status with some music fans over the years, but for once the reality lives up to the legend.

A visit to the museum is a must for any Motown fan, evoking a time when Detroit was considered the centre of the music world In addition to gold records on the walls, the museum is full of old album jackets, snapshots, publicity photos and even some old Temptations' costumes. A copy of a loan agreement between Berry Gordy and his family for $800 to start his business hangs on a wall. Nearby is a framed copy of Barrett Strong's single "Money," Motown's first big hit. The museum's existence is down to Esther Gordy Edwards (Berry Gordy's Sister) and her unwillingness to part with Motown memorabilia from the Detroit era.

Motown on West Grand Boulevard

At the height of its influence in Detroit, Motown owned many properties in West Grand Boulevard, below are the key addresses and photographs.

The properties associated with Motown are listed below.

2644/46 West Grand Boulevard Jobete Publishing Company (now the museum entrance) purchased on the 18th April 1961.

2648 West Grand Boulevard recording "Studio A" was at the back of the "Hitsville"

building on the lower ground floor, also the residence of Berry and Raynoma Gordy in upstairs rooms, purchased 2nd August 1959.

2650 West Grand Boulevard Offices of Berry Gordy/Esther Edwards and Ralph Seltzer. This is vacant ground, to the left of Hitsville which burned to the ground in 1971, purchased 23rd January 1962.

2652/54 West Grand Boulevard Motown Administration purchased 23rd January 1962.

2656 West Grand Boulevard Motown Finance (white front) purchased 4th March 1965.

2662/4 West Grand Boulevard Motown Sales and Marketing building purchased 11th July 1966.

2666/8 West Grand Boulevard Motown Sales and Marketing building purchased 11th July 1966.

2670/2 West Grand Boulevard ITMI (International Talent Management Incorporated) purchased 5th July 1966.

2657 West Grand Boulevard Artist Development was located directly Across West Grand Blvd from the Motown Row purchased 12th January 1966.

This was Motown's other building on West Grand Boulevard. It was used for Artist Development, and is situated diagonally across the road from Hitsville. I wonder if the extension to the rear was where choreographer Cholly Atkins worked with those amazing stars. Miss Maxine Powell, who was well respected by all who knew her, was also based in number 2657, where she was in charge of poise and presentation. Veteran bandleader, Maurice King, taught vocal exercises and sophisticated arrangements. Maurice was well known for his work at the Flame Show Bar on John R.

Also working on artist development were Gil Askey (Arrangements) and Johnnie Allen (Rehearsal Pianist).

2657 West Grand Boulevard; Artist Development was located directly across from 2648 West Grand Blvd "Hitsville".

Berry Gordy was so impressed by the quality of the owner's output that he bought out Ed Wingate and Joanne Bratton in September 1966. Although it looks like the sale of the Ric-Tic label was delayed until 1968. In this tiny building many classic Golden World, Ric-Tic and Wingate sides were produced.

The premises then became Motown Studio B and a blue and white sign confirming this was painted on both sides of the building. As you can see, the elements have all but erased the evidence.

Former drummer, George McGregor, recalls that a sign hung across the wall above the entrance proclaiming The Golden World Recording Company. Two large windows sat on either side of the main door. Behind the left hand window was the office of Joanne Bratton. At the rear of the building, on the ground floor, was the recording studio and control room. The ground floor also housed Ed Wingate's office, a mastering lathe room, a tape library and rehearsal rooms.

Now Demolished Motown Studio "B" 3246 West Davison Detroit.

There was also an extension at the back left of the building, which housed the echo chamber, the second floor was used for storing records etc.

Donovan Building 2457 Woodward Avenue

Motown had outgrown West Grand Boulevard by 1967, and Berry decided to move to the city's main thoroughfare, Woodward Avenue. The ten-storey building was only one hundred yards north of the Fox Theatre and on the same side of the street.

Unfortunately, due to the fact that the building had no character it was not liked by Motown employees, (unlike Hitsville). It wouldn't be long before Motown out grew this building and ultimately Motown abandoned this building when the company moved to Los Angeles.

Album Track: "Little Darling (I Need You)", Marvin Gaye.

Now Demolished Donovan Building 2457 Woodward Avenue, Detroit.

Eddie Holland

Born Edward Holland Jnr on the 30th October 1939 in Detroit, Michigan

Motown Connection: Musician - Background Singer - Writer - Producer - Arranger - Part of Holland-Dozier-Holland Team - Record Label Owner (Hot Wax and Invictus).

Eddie Holland had a moderately successful career as a singer, recording for Berry Gordy (as an independent producer) in the late 1950's before Berry Gordy formed Motown. One of Eddie's minor hits was the Berry Gordy produced, but released on Mercury recording in 1958 of "You". This was followed by Merry Go Round in January 1959 (initially released on Tamla, later distributed by United Artists), and three further recordings in 1960 on United Artist (under licence from Tamla) "Because I Love Her", "Magic Mirror" and "The Last Laugh". None of the recordings could be considered a success. Between 1961 and 1964 Eddie recorded for Motown Records starting with Eddie's most popular recordings "Jamie" and "Leaving Here" and ending with "Just Ain't Enough Love" and "Candy To Me" in 1964.

However, Berry Gordy soon spotted that Eddie's talent was for writing lyrics, which led to early collaborations, (co-writing with Norman Whitfield) several songs for The Temptations, Eddie also wrote for other Motown artists and with other collaborators.

Eddie Holland hasn't been as successful on his own, even with his talent writing. By 1962, Eddie replaced Freddy Gorman who at the time was working with Brian Holland (Eddie's brother) and Lamont Dozier and the team made their debut with The Marvelettes' "Locking Up My Heart." As they say the rest is history, going on to become one of the most successful record producing teams in the history of the music industry.

Motown grew to dominate the charts in the 1960's and early 1970's with Holland-Dozier-Holland (and the other producers/writers etc) providing unparalleled (even to this day) recordings of such productivity and consistency it seemed they (and Motown) could not fail. Marvin Gaye recorded several early hits with Holland-Dozier-Holland, including "Can I Get a Witness?", "How Sweet It Is (To Be Loved by You)" and "Little Darling" while Martha and The Vandellas recorded "Heat

Wave", "Nowhere to Run" and "Jimmy Mack". Add to this their relationship with The Four Tops, The Elgins and The Isley Brothers and you get a feel for their hit making potential. However, the team found their greatest successes with The Supremes' recordings of "Where Did Our Love Go?", "Baby Love", "Come See About Me". "Stop! In the Name of Love" and "Back in My Arms Again". All No1 hits (both in the USA and international market).

By the middle of the 1960's, the Holland-Dozier-Holland production moved to another level as the "Motown Sound" truly arrived. Motown was now setting the pace for pop music everywhere, and Holland-Dozier-Holland were there "right in the middle". With recording on The Four Tops including, "Baby I Need Your Loving", "I Can't Help Myself", "(It's The) Same Old Song" and the No1 single "Reach Out I'll Be There", while with The Supreme's records like "You Can't Hurry Love", "You Keep Me Hanging On", "Love Is Here and Now You're Gone" and "The Happening". They stormed the charts.

In 1967 Holland-Dozier-Holland, wanting a share of Motown's success and bitter over their lack of creative control, left Motown with the intention of creating their own record label. However the team quickly became entangled in legal disputes with Motown (at Berry Gordy's instigation) and as a result they were barred from writing and producing any material for the next few years.

However, by 1970, they were able to form their own labels, "Invictus" and "Hot Wax" where they wrote and produced hits for the Chairmen of the Board and Freda Payne. In 1973, Lamont Dozier left the team to follow a solo career, leaving (Brian and Eddie Holland) to run the label. Brian and Eddie Holland carried on for a few more years before finally dissolving the two labels during the mid-1970's.

There can be no doubt of the respect Eddie (and the other members of the team) have gained over the years, just listen to some of their recordings. Regularly featured in radio and television documentaries, they won the prestigious Ivor Novello award in 2004 in London, England.

Brian Holland

Born on the 15th February 1941 in Detroit, Michigan

Motown Connection: Musician - Background Singer - Writer - Producer - Arranger - Part of Holland-Dozier-Holland Team - Record Label Owner (Hot Wax and Invictus).

Born and raised in Detroit, Brian's first role at Motown was to play piano for Barrett Strong in 1960 (after impressing the lead vocalist of the Satintones). Introduced by Barrett Strong to Berry Gordy. Brian joined Motown a year later, and became part of the Holland-Dozier-Holland production and song writing team, (Brian's speciality was record production) Brian helped pioneer the classic Motown sound of the 1960's, scoring hit after hit on artists including, The Supremes, The Four Tops and Martha and The Vandellas. Brian's first input was as "Brianbert" (Brian with Robert Bateman) on The Marvelettes' classic "Please Mr. Postman", with Freddie Gorman, another song writing partner of Brian (pre Holland-Dozier-Holland team). Brian was involved in the final reworking, of what would become Motown's first No1 record.

By 1962, he was partnered with producers and songwriters Lamont Dozier and Freddy Gorman, However within a year Freddy Gorman had been replaced by Eddie Holland's (Brian older brother) and the team made their debut with The Marvelettes' "Locking Up My Heart." As they say the rest is history, going on to become one of the most successful record producing teams in the history of the music industry.

Between 1962 and 1967, Holland-Dozier-Holland would become a "hit factory" within a hit factory, creating a production line that would produce five consecutive No1 hits for The Supremes alone. Their output has never really been matched in the record industry and at the time their production techniques were well ahead of their time. As much as anybody involved with Motown, without doubt a major influence on the creation of "The Motown Sound".

Motown grew to dominate the charts in the 1960's and early 1970's with Holland-Dozier-Holland (and the other producers/writers etc) providing unparalleled (even to this day) recordings of such productivity and consistency. Marvin Gaye recorded several early hits with Holland-Dozier-Holland, including "Can I Get a Witness?", "How Sweet It Is (To Be Loved by You)" and "Little Darling" while Martha and The Vandellas recorded "Heat Wave", "Nowhere to Run" and "Jimmy Mack". Add to this their relationship with The Four Tops, The Elgins and The Isley Brothers and you get a feel for their hit making potential. However, the team found their greatest successes with The Supremes' recordings of "Where Did Our Love Go?", "Baby

Love", "Come See About Me", "Stop! In the Name of Love" and "Back in My Arms Again". All No1 hits (both in the USA and international market).

By the middle of the 1960's, the Holland-Dozier-Holland production moved to another level the "Motown Sound" had truly arrived. Motown was now setting the pace for pop music everywhere, and Holland-Dozier-Holland were there "right in the middle". With recording on The Four Tops including, "Baby I Need Your Loving", "I Can't Help Myself", "(It's The) Same Old Song" and the No1 single "Reach Out I'll Be There", while with The Supreme's records like "You Can't Hurry Love", "You Keep Me Hanging On", "Love Is Here and Now You're Gone" and "The Happening". They stormed the charts.

In 1967 Holland-Dozier-Holland, wanting a share of Motown's success and bitter over their lack of creative control, left Motown with the intention of creating their own record label. However the team quickly became entangled in legal disputes with Motown (at Berry Gordy's instigation) and as a result they were barred from writing and producing any material for the next few years.

However, by 1970, they were able to form their own labels, "Invictus" and "Hot Wax" where they wrote and produced hits for the Chairmen of the Board and Freda Payne. In 1972, Brian released a minor solo hit "Don't Leave Me Starvin' for Your Love", a year later; Lamont Dozier left the team to follow a solo career, leaving (Brian and Eddie Holland) to run the label. Brian (and Eddie Holland) carried on for a few more years before finally dissolving the two labels during the mid-1970's. A handful of solo Brian productions followed, among them the 1978 Donny and Marie Osmond's LP "Winning Combination", but Brian never recaptured the magic of Motown or the Invictus and Hot Wax period. There can be no doubt of the respect Brian (and the other members of the team) have gain over the years, just listen to some of their recordings. Regularly featured in radio and television documentaries, they won the prestigious Ivor Novello award in 2004 in London, England.

Brian Holland still remains active in the music industry and a legendary producer, inducted in 1990, as part of the Holland-Dozier-Holland team into the Rock and Roll Hall of Fame.

Doris Jean Holland

Born Doris Jean Steele in Greenville, Alabama - Died 12th February 1999 in Detroit, Michigan

Motown Connection: Secretary - Typist - Assistant to Personal Managers for Diana Ross, Smokey Robinson, The Four Tops, and The Temptations - Corporate Secretary for the Motown Museum.

Doris graduated from River Rouge High School and was a secretary for the NAACP, the Girl Scouts and the Michigan Employment Security Commission before she began working for the Motown Records.

Jean, started working at Motown in 1962 as a typist and worked in several departments, organising recording sessions, concert tours, recording contracts etc. Doris was always known for her skills in keeping things running smoothly. Jean was knowledgeable about the workings of Motown, and in particular "Hitsville", earning a reputation based on "getting things done". "She was the stabiliser", said Esther Gordy Edwards, for whom Jean was a secretary for more than 20 years.

At Motown, one of Jean's roles was to assist the personal managers of some of the biggest stars, liked by all of the artists, Jean worked with most of the Motown artists including Diana Ross, Smokey Robinson, The Four Tops and The Temptations.

After the company left Detroit in 1972, Jean continued working in the Detroit headquarters in "Hitsville" and helped organise the founding of the museum with Esther Gordy Edwards, as her secretary and undertook the corporate secretary role at the museum until she retired in 1995. Jean was married to Lincoln for 42 years, and is survived by a son Reginald and daughters Deborah, Denise and Reena, Jean died of complications from surgery aged 61 in Detroit.

Formed in 1963 in Detroit Members: Brian Holland - Eddie Holland - Lamont Dozier

Motown Connection: Most Successful In House Writing and Production Team for Motown.

The origins of Holland-Dozier-Holland begin in 1962, when Brian Holland was partnered with producers and songwriters Lamont Dozier and Freddy Gorman, However within a year Freddy Gorman had been replaced by Eddie Holland's (Brian older brother) It was Berry Gordy who put the three together, (Brian, Eddie, and Lamont) after it became evident, that Eddie Holland wasn't going to make it as a solo act, and the team made their debut with The Marvelettes' "Locking Up My Heart." As they say the rest is history, going on to become one of the most successful record producing teams in the history of the music industry.

The list of Holland-Dozier-Holland hits seems endless, they include "Where Did Our Love Go?", "Baby Love", "Reach Out I'll Be There", "Standing in the Shadows of Love", "This Old Heart of Mine", "Nowhere to Run", "I'm a Road Runner" and many others. They produced recordings on The Supremes, Junior Walker and The All Stars, The Four Tops, Martha and The Vandellas, The Isley Brothers, The Elgins and many others before their eventual departure.

Holland-Dozier-Holland started with Marvin Gaye, recording the early hit "Can I Get a Witness?", "How Sweet It Is (To Be Loved by You)" and "Little Darling", the team then moved on to Martha Reeves and The Vandellas, recording a series of singles that included the "Heat Wave", "Nowhere to Run" and "Jimmy Mack". However, Holland-Dozier-Holland enjoyed perhaps their greatest success with The Supremes, producing "Where Did Our Love Go?" the first in a run of five No1 hits between 1964 and 1965 with the singles which included "Baby Love", "Come See About Me", "Stop? In the Name of Love" and "Back in My Arms Again". They next turned to The Four Tops, recording a further run of hits including, "Baby I Need Your Loving", "I Can't Help Myself", "(It's The) Same Old Song" and the No1 international hit "Reach Out I'll Be There" add into the mixture of hits from The Isley Brothers "This Old Heart of Mine", Kim Weston's "Take Me in Your Arms" and The Miracles "Mickey's Monkey", and I have only just "scratched the surface" of hits produced by the team.

By the middle of the decade, Holland-Dozier-Holland were a hit making factory (within Motown's hit making factory) with a mixture of great melodies, rhythms, arrangements and clever lyrics, Holland-Dozier-Holland produced some of the best pop/soul music ever produced.

In 1967, Holland-Dozier-Holland, left Motown; the team quickly became entangled in legal disputes with Motown (and in particular with Berry Gordy), and as a result they were barred from writing and producing any material for many years. They moved to Los Angeles from Detroit and when Motown allowed them to start producing again, created the Hot Wax and Invictus labels. With artists like, Freda Payne, the Chairman of the Board, Laura Lee, 100 Proof Aged in Soul, and the Honey Cone they started to create hit records again in the early 1970's, Brian Holland also produced The New York Port Authority group. They also did outside productions for such artists as Dionne Warwick and issued their own single, "Why Can't We Be Lovers", in 1973. Lamont Dozier then decided to start a solo career, and the most successful writing and production team in music history came to an end. Their record labels, Invictus and Hot Wax remained in business until 1977, with the back catalogue now in the hands of Sanctuary Records.

Inducted into the Hall of Fame in 1990, for their song writing and production achievements.

Album Track: "This Old Heart of Mine (Is Weak For You)", The Isley Brothers.

Brenda Holloway

Born on the 21st June 1946 in Atascadero, California

Motown Connection: Motown First West Coast Artist - The Beatles chose Brenda as their opening act for their US tour in 1965 - The First Ex-Motowner To Take Legal Action Against Motown.

Brenda grew up in the Watts section of Los Angeles where she took up violin and sang in her church choir. At 14, Brenda and sister her Patrice Holloway began working on demonstration records and singing backup for local Los Angeles based R&B acts. In 1962, Brenda made her recording debut with the single, "Poor Fool" composed by Jesse James. Through her church she was introduced to Hal Davis, who became the Motown West Coast rep, Hal Davis worked with Marc Gordon creating Hal and Marc productions. Through this Brenda got her first break singing background on their productions.

Brenda was just 18 when she got her break. In 1964, Brenda sang a version of Mary Well's hit "My Guy" at a Los Angeles disc jockey convention. Hal Davis introduced her to Berry Gordy, who was so taken with Brenda's vocal skills that he wasted no time in signing her to Tamla Records (a subsidiary of Motown Records). Brenda was an exception at Motown as she was a west coast artist (all artists's up until then had been from Detroit) whose debut single "Every Little Bit Hurts" was the first single by Motown to be recorded in Los Angeles.

Next came an offer to appear on American Bandstand with host Dick Clark to appear on his TV show "Caravan of Stars". Brenda performed her blues-styled ballad "Every Little Bit Hurts" which became a hit shortly afterwards. Interestingly Motown tried to get The Supremes a spot on Caravan of Stars, on the back of Brenda's performance, but they were turned down as being not big enough stars. In 1965, the newly arrived British group The Beatles chose Brenda as their opening act for their US tour. Brenda's vocals, (alongside her sister's), were featured in the background of Joe Cocker's hit version of The Beatles', with a "Little Help from My Friends" which was later used as the theme song for "The Wonder Years".

Brenda did travel to Detroit to record, but with not much success. Even working with producer Smokey Robinson did not produce any significant hit recordings although "When I'm Gone" and "Operator." where minor hits for Brenda. Brenda always thought that being from the West Coast (rather than Detroit) was a handicap, even Berry Gordy worked with her on a personal basic, preparing her to take the stage in Las Vegas.

Brenda's sales decreased even with this support, Brenda then turned to song writing, and formed a partnership with her sister Patrice and Frank Wilson, a Motown staff producer. The team produced Brenda's 1968 release, "You've Made Me So Very Happy", which Berry Gordy produced, but the record was not a hit. However, the song did become a hit in 1969, when it was covered by the group Blood, Sweat and Tears. Brenda was a great friend of Tammi Terrell whose illness affected her greatly.

Brenda did have an LP issued by Motown called "Every Little Bit Hurts" a further album "Hurtin' and Cryin" and a live album "Brenda Holloway" were never issued by Motown. In 1968 Brenda's second LP "The Artistry of Brenda Holloway", was released, but that year she announced her retirement from the music business, citing her disillusionment with Motown and her fears of the lifestyle associated with show business (which conflicted with her still-deep religious convictions).in 1969 Brenda married Alfred Davis, a minister, and she became a reborn Christian.

In 1969 Brenda became the first ex-Motowner to take legal action against Motown, over alleged misappropriation of funds. The court ruled in her favour. Brenda had the first catalogue number (1001) on the Eddie and Brian Holland record label Music Merchant, but not the first release.

A new album "Brand New" in 1980 recorded on the gospel Brightright label was, as Brenda stated "not a good idea" however she did work with Gil Askey (former producer at Motown) on the album. In 1987 Brenda divorced, and at the same time joined Ian Levine's Motorcity label, as a result of this collaboration, radio and personal appearances put her back in the spot light and led in 1990, to Brenda issuing the album, "All It Takes".

In 1995, motivated by the death of Mary Wells, she returned to live performance around the Los Angeles area, often with fellow performer Brenton Wood. Brenda performed in the UK in 1997 and 1998 with Kim Weston receiving rave reviews, by 1999 Brenda had signed with the revived Volt label to record "It's a Woman's World". Her most current album being a 2003 recording, "My Love is Your Love".

In the UK, Brenda is regarded as a "Northern Soul legend" while in the US Brenda is often considered one the "lost" Motown artist among other Motown acts that didn't get the recognition they deserved.

Brenda has four daughters Beoir, Unita, Christy and Donteste. Brenda is also a grandmother to five children.

Album Track: "I'll Be Available", Brenda Holloway.

Lawrence Horn

Aka L.T. Born in 1946 in Detroit, Michigan

Motown Connection: Chief Recording Engineer - Producer - Writer.

As a young recording engineer, Lawrence helped create the "Motown Sound" "L.T." as he was known, was one of the first employees of Berry Gordy hired at Motown. However, Lawrence is currently serving a life sentence for hiring a "contract killer" to kill his wife and disabled son.

It is suggested that Lawrence, mixed every Motown release between 1964 and 1967. Lawrence did this remarkable feat by implementing a "3 track recording system" for Motown. The development of the 3 track recording system in 1964, gave "The Motown Sound" its unique quality. With Lawrence doing the transferring and mixing to make the multitrack, he actually did most of the mixing on the material that Motown released. Lawrence also became involved in writing and production at Motown. Until Motown's move to Los Angeles Lawrence had been a key member of Berry Gordy's team, but Lawrence stayed in Detroit and was given less and less work until by 1990 Lawrence was working as a tape librarian in Motown's Detroit office (his last job at Motown).

In 1993 Lawrence's life was to change completely, Lawrence's job was a part-time consultant repairing home computers, virtually un-employed, living in a one-bedroom bungalow with a girlfriend who was the only person helping Horn with his bills etc. Lawrence was behind with child support to his ex-wife. Interestingly, the only luxury Lawrence still had was his white 1976 Cadillac, from his long career with Motown.

On the night of March 2, 1993, Lawrence was watching TV when roughly at the same time, 3,000 miles across the country in Washington, DC, Lawrence's ex-wife, and his 8-year-old invalid son and night nurse, Janice Roberts Saunders were murdered by James Edward Perry. Lawrence had employed James Edward Perry as a "contract killer" to claim the insurance on his wife and child's death, Perry had purchased a how-to manual titled "Hit Man" and followed it almost to the letter when he attacked his victims at their home. Perry was convicted of the murder.

In May 1996 Lawrence was found guilty on three counts of first-degree murder and one of murder conspiracy by a jury that decided the former Motown recording engineer hired Perry to execute his former wife, an overnight nurse and the severely disabled 8-year-old son whose estate he stood to inherit. Lawrence's son Trevor Horn left behind a $1.7 million trust fund from a malpractice settlement that arose from the hospital incident that left him a quadriplegic. Lawrence was fighting in the civil court to inherit that money when he was arrested along with James Edward Perry.

Lawrence was married firstly to Juana Royster, before marrying and divorcing from Mildred Horn (one of the murdered victims) and a son Trevor (also one of the murdered victims).

Ivy Jo Hunter

Born George Ivy Hunter in 1927 in Jackson, Tennessee

Motown Connection: Songwriter - Producer - Singer.

Raised in Detroit a prolific Motown songwriter producer and singer, who worked with all the major stars at "Hitsville". Ivy Jo's early hits included, "Ask The  Lonely", "Dancing In The Street", "Keep Holding" and "Can You Jerk Like Me" all co-written by Ivy Jo. A private person little is known about the mysterious but prolific Motown songwriter producer singer. Ivy Jo's musical gifts came to the front at elementary school, going on to join the Detroit Symphony and the Detroit City Orchestra, excelling on the trumpet, the Euphony, and keyboards. Ivy Jo attended Cass Technical High School undertaking an economics courses, and while at college (aged fifteen) wrote his first song for a group called "The Velveteers", the song helped the group win an amateur talent contest.

After high school Ivy Jo joined the Army, on his return he started singing in local Detroit clubs firstly at the 20 Grand, then Phelp's Lounge. While singing on the club circuit he became a friend of Motown writer/producer Hank Cosby, Hank Cosby introduced Ivy Jo to Motown's A&R Director, William "Mickey" Stevenson. Although Ivy Jo auditioned as a singer, (who wrote his own songs), William "Mickey" Stevenson saw more potential in Ivy Jo as a co-writer at Motown.

His first collaboration with William "Mickey" Stevenson was "Sweet Thing" by The Spinners, this started a long run of hits between the two of them. Writing some of the classic singles to come out of Motown, including "Behind A Painted Smile" and "Got To Have You Race" by The Isley Brothers, The Spinners singles, "I'll Always Love You" and "Truly Yours" add "Yesterday Dreams" by The Four Tops, "Danger Heartbreak Dead Ahead", The Marvelettes and "My Baby Loves Me" by Martha and The Vandellas. The pair also wrote and produced for The Temptations "Born To Love", "Just Another Lonely Night", "Sorry Is A Sorry Word", "It's A Lonely World Without Your Love" and "You" for Marvin Gaye. Even with Ivy Jo's body of work, both Ivy Jo and William "Mickey" Stevenson never received the credit that other Motown writers and producers received. Ivy Jo always said that he would not have his hair cut, until he achieved his first hit with Motown, I've seen very few pictures of Ivy Jo with long hair. Other Ivy Jo compositions include "Loving Country", The Supremes, "Loving You Is Sweeter Than Ever", The Four Tops, and "Seek And You Shall Find" by The Isley Brothers.

Ivy Jo did do some solo recordings for Motown, but they were not released until "I Remember You (Dedicated To Beverly)" b/side "Sorry Is A Sorry Word", in March of 1970. A second recording called "I Still Love You" b/side "I Can Feel The Pain" was released two months later, but neither single hit the charts. Motown released Ivy Jo's album "Is In This Bag" on its VIP label the same year, but again with no success.

When Motown left Detroit for Los Angeles Ivy Jo stayed and contributed to a multitude of musical projects around the Detroit, including playing keyboards on the Funkadelic's "Mommy, What's A Funkadelic?". Co-produced a great album for Wee Gee (William Howard) the then ex-lead singer of the Dramatics, contributing to the classic single "Hold On To Your Dreams" later recorded by Staple Singers, and the recording "You've Been a Part of Me."

Ivy Jo collaborated with Ian Levine Motorcity Label in the 1980's and early 1990's helping produce "Footsteps Keep Following Me" by Francis Nero. There a wonderful scene in Ian Levine's DVD "The Strange World of Northern Soul" issued in the UK, show Ivy Jo running though the song for Francis Nero.

Today, Ivory Joe is best known for his two most enduring compositions, "I Almost Lost My Mind" and the similar, yet more romantic "Since I Met You Baby". Ivy Jo resides in Southfield, Michigan.

Album Track: "Behind A Painted Smile", The Isley Brothers.

Born Joseph Edward Hunter on the 19th November 1927 Jackson, Tennessee - Died 2nd February 2007 Detroit, Michigan

Motown Connection: Pianist/member of The Funk Brothers (Motown In House Band) - Berry Gordy's first hired musician.

Joe moved to Detroit with his parents in his early teens, he played clarinet in the school band, (between 1949 and 1951) he also studied law at the University of Detroit before going into the army as a general's house orderly. In the Army Joe played in bands with the jazz drummer Elvin Jones and Earl Van Dyke (a future leader of The Funk Brothers). Joe started out in Detroit backing up acts such as Jackie Wilson and Hank Ballard and the Midnighters in the early 1950's. Joe could play jazz or Professor Longhair and Fats Domino-style New Orleans piano as well soul/pop tunes.

Pre-Motown Joe's band (The Joe Hunter Band) was the hottest in Detroit with many admirers (including Berry Gordy). Berry spotted Joe at Little Sams, a Detroit club on the back of this Berry Gordy offered (and Joe agreed) to come and work for Berry Gordy's new company Motown. Joe was also instrumental in bringing a third member of his band to the studios, future Motown arranger and saxophonist Hank Cosby.

Joe was Berry Gordy's first hired musician, and was the original bandleader for Motown Records in the early years. Joe was responsible for bringing in the two most important musicians that helped created the "Motown Sound" namely James Jamerson bass player and Benny Benjamin drums who became the core of the House Band "The Funk Brothers". Later replaced by Earl Van Dyke as band leader of The Funk Brothers in 1963, Joe's contribution in putting together the core of the session musician which helped form the "Motown Sound" cannot be underestimated.

Joe Hunter in his early days pre Motown, with future Funk Brothers Benny Benjamin, James Jamerson, Joe Hunter (top of the picture).

Playing a piano or organ, Joe made major contributions to early hits such as Marv Johnson's "Come to Me", "Way Over There" both in 1959. By 1960 "Shop Around" by The Miracles (with Smokey Robinson talking the lead), "Money" by Barrett

Strong 1960, became major international hits for Motown. This was followed up by The Contours' million-seller "Do You Love Me" in 1962, by 1963 "Come and Get These Memories", "Heatwave" both by Martha and The Vandellas and "Pride and Joy" by Marvin Gaye became the next big hits.

Joe left Motown in 1963 and freelanced as an arranger, pianist and bandleader with Jimmy Ruffin, Bobby "Blue" Bland, Junior Parker, Edwin Starr, Big Maybelle and Aretha Franklin. However, by the late Eighties, Joe was playing for "tips" in the lounge of the Troy Marriott Hotel in Detroit.

Like most of the other musicians at the time, when Motown left Detroit in 1972, for Los Angeles California, Joe stayed behind in Detroit performing at whatever gigs there were available. Berts in the Marketplace was a favourite hangout for Joe. Joe published his autobiography, Musicians, Motown and Myself: the dawn of a new sound in 1996.

Joe was encouraged by Allan Slutsky's efforts to produce a documentary about The Funk Brothers' contribution to the "Motown Sound", this was achieved in 2002. This belated tribute was the documentary film "Standing In The Shadows Of Motown", released with this film was a "Funk Brothers'" soundtrack album won which won two Grammy's in 2003. In 2004, Joe and the rest of The Funk Brothers were rewarded with a Lifetime Achievement Award at the Grammys, thereafter the group toured for several years in the US and Europe.

In 2005, prompted by the success of the documentary, the Soul-Tay-Shus label released a CD of Hunter's archive recordings with The Funk Brothers entitled "The Hawk: Rare and Unreleased Transitional Detroit R&B 1960-1963".

Joe was 79 years old when he died while trying to take medicine, Joe was also diabetic. In addition to his son, Joe is survived by a daughter, Michelle, and three grandchildren.

Signature sound: was earthy, boogie style; listen to Joe on "Do You Love Me" by The Contours. "Money" by Barrett Strong and "Heatwave" by Martha and The Vandellas.

The Isley Brothers

Formed in 1954 in Cincinnati, Ohio

Members: O'Kelly Isley, from 1954 to 1955 then between 1957 and 1986 Born 25th December 1937 in Cincinnati Ohio Died 31st March 1986 of a heart attack - Rudolph Isley, from 1954 to 1955 then between 1957 and 1989 Born (as Rudolph Bernard Isley) 1st April 1939 in Cincinnati Ohio - Ronald Isley (1954 to 55 then between 1957 and 1989 again returned 1991 to the present day Born 21st May 1941

Cincinnati Ohio - Vernon Isley from 1954 to 1955 until his death in 1955 Born in 1942 in Cincinnati Ohio Died 1955 car accident - Ernie Isley from 1973 to 1984 then between 1991 to the present day Born 7th March 1952 in Cincinnati Ohio - Marvin Isley from 1973 to 1984 then between 1991 and 1997 Born 18th August 1953 in Cincinnati Ohio - Chris Jasper from 1973 to 1984 Born Christopher Jasper, 30th December 1951 in New Jersey.

An early publicity handout from the artists. O'Kelly Isley, Rudolph Isley and Ronald Isley.

Motown Connection: Group - Background Vocals.

First formed in the early 1950's, The Isley Brothers enjoyed one of the longest, most influential and most diverse careers in popular music. The first generation of The Isley Brothers' group initially formed as a gospel quartet, comprised Ronald, Rudolph, O'Kelly and Vernon Isley. However, after Vernon's 1955 death in a bicycling accident, Ronald became the lead vocalist. Encouraged to begin a singing career by their father, (himself a professional vocalist), and their mother, (a church pianist). Their parents provided the musical background for their early performances. They are one of the few groups to have had a hit single in every decade since 1959.

In 1957, the brothers went to New York City to record a couple of "doo-wop" singles, but with no success, it was not until 1959 that The Isley Brothers came to the attention of an RCA Record executive. While in the audience at an Isley Brothers concert in Washington DC, the group sang the Berry Gordy written "Lonely Teardrops", but with one addition, they introduced the line "You know you make me want to shout", which brought the audience to their feet. Signed to RCA Records shortly afterwards, their first single to be recorded was constructed around this catch-phrase.

"Shout" it failed to reach the pop Top 40 on its initial release; it eventually became a song covered by many stars.

By 1962 their career had still not developed into a hit making group so they left RCA that year. Wanda Records did issue the cover version by the group (originally issued as The Topnotes') "Twist and Shout", which was their first top forty single, although "Twist and Shout" earned greater commercial success when later recorded by The Beatles. After several more releases, the group left Wand Records in 1964 and formed T-Neck Records after moving to New Jersey. Finding only local success with the single "Testify", recorded with a young Jimi Hendrix on guitar, the group temporarily folded T-Neck Records.

The Isley Brothers' big break came when they signed to Motown Records (on subsidiary label Tamla) in 1965, they were teamed with Holland-Dozier-Holland. Their first single, the classic Motown recording "This Old Heart of Mine," was their best record ever produced at Motown, a massive international hit (the song hit No3 in the UK in 1967). The Isley Brothers couldn't come up with a follow-up and complained of being given inferior recordings, even with the help of Smokey Robinson and Holland-Dozier-Holland, no more major hits arrived. In 1968 The Isley Brothers asked to be released from their contract with Motown, and Motown agreed.

On leaving Motown, The Isley Brothers started touring the UK they were hugely popular, three of their Motown singles had reached the Top 40 "This Old Heart", "Put Yourself in My Place" and "Behind a Painted Smile". After touring in the UK, they returned to the US in 1969 with a new image and sound. Signing with Buddah Records, for recording and distribution rights, the group recorded the single, "It's Your Thing", it was released under the group's revived T-Neck label becoming a No2 hit single. It became their biggest chart success selling over a million copies and winning the group a Grammy Award for Best R&B Vocal Performance by a Duo or Group. With the success of "It's Your Thing" Berry Gordy made accusations that "It's Your Thing" was recorded while they were still in Motown, which the group denied. After several years, Berry Gordy settled with the group out of court.

The group released a succession of seven albums for Buddah which ranged from up tempo James Brown/Sly Stone styled funk/soul and classic rock. After which the band released the covers album, "Givin' It Back", which featured revisions of rock hits by WAR ("Spill the Wine") Stephen Stills "Love The One You're With" (their cover was a top forty hit) and even their former band mate Jimi Hendrix ("Machine Gun"). After releasing the rock-tinged "Brother, Brother, Brother" and a live album, the group left Buddah after being offered a long term deal with Epic by Clive Davis, then president of CBS Records.

That year, The Isley Brothers also welcomed a number of new members as younger brothers Ernie and Marvin, brother-in-law Chris Jasper and family friend Everett

Collins became the trio's new backing unit. Spearheaded by Ernie's hard-edged guitar leads, the group began incorporating more and more rock material into its repertoire as the 1970's arrived, and scored a future hit with a cover of Bob Dylan's "Lay Lady Lay".

In 1973, the Isley's scored a massive hit with their rock-funk fusion cover of their own earlier single "Who's That Lady", re-titled "That Lady (Part I)" the album "3 + 3" also proved highly successful, as did 1975's "The Heat Is On", which spawned the smash "Fight the Power (Part I)." As the decade wore on, the group again altered its sound to fit into the booming disco market. While their success on pop radio came to an end, they frequently topped the R&B charts with singles like 1977's "The Pride", 1978's "Take Me to the Next Phase (Part 1)", 1979's "I Wanna Be With You (Part 1)" and 1980's "Don't Say Goodnight."

After the younger brothers split from the group in 1984, the remaining trio continued recording until Kelly's death from a cancer-related heart attack in 1986. In 1985, Isley-Jasper-Isley scored their only big hit with "Caravan of Love"; the song has sometimes been referred to as an "Isley Brothers song" even though it was released by three of the actual group's former members. The same year, the elder original members released "Masterpiece", which featured a cover of Phil Collins' "If Leaving Me Is Easy". However, the brothers found themselves in trouble with the IRS for not paying back taxes and evading payments. To settle, the group agreed to sell their label, though its imprint's logo would still be on Isley Brothers records, all of the group's T-Neck singles are in the control of Sony Music.

In 1987, Rudy and Ron dedicated the Angela Winbush-produced "Smooth Sailin", in Kelly's memory. Nearly two years before the release of 1989's "Spend the Night", also produced by Angela Winbush, whom Ron married soon after, Rudy left the group for a career in the ministry in 1989 disbanding the group once again with Ron releasing solo records, sometimes performing under The Isley Brothers name. Ron found success in a duet with Rod Stewart on a remake of "This Old Heart of Mine".

In 1991, Ron reformed the group with Ernie and Marvin returning to the line-up. Since 1997, after diabetes forced Marvin into retirement, the line-up has been Ron and Ernie, much like the Parliament-Funkadelic, DeBarge and Zapp, The Isley Brothers are among one of the most sampled groups in hip-hop history with their recordings sampled by the likes of 2Pac, The Notorious B.I.G., J Dilla, Bone Thugs-n-Harmony, Ice Cube and Snoop Dogg among others. In 1996, now consisting of Ronald, Marvin and Ernie, they released the album "Mission to Please". Rudolph did release a solo gospel album called "Shouting For Jesus".

In 2000 Michael Bolton unsuccessfully tried to buy The Isley Brothers' catalogue after the Isley's won a lawsuit alleging that Bolton's song "Love Is a Wonderful Thing" plagiarized their 1966 Motown track of the same title.

The group (now consisting of Ron and Ernie) would one have of their biggest selling releases in over twenty years in 2001 with the album "Eternal" and the single "Contagious"; a song written by Kelly which eventually sold more than two million copies. With "Contagious" and "Eternal", they had become the only group to have a single and album in the chart over five decades, longer than any group in recording history. They continued with the 2003 gold disk "Body Kiss", which was their first No1 album in nearly thirty years (since "The Heat Is On") and their first album to go straight to No1 in the charts. It featured the top fifty single, "What Would You Do", followed in 2006's "Baby Makin' Music", which peaked at No5 in the charts.

Over the years The Isley Brothers have not been the luckiest group, Vernon died in 1957 after a car accident, Marvin Isley retired in 1997 due to a bout with diabetes which has since meant amputation of both his legs. Rudolph "Rudy" Isley has had health problems over the years and currently lives in California with Elaine Jasper Isley, his wife of over forty years. Ron Isley was recently convicted of tax evasion charges in 2006 after he was accused of not paying back taxes between 1997 and 2002 and using money from his late brother Kelly's estate to continue his "expensive lifestyle". After divorcing Angela Winbush in 2002, in 2004, Ron suffered a mild stroke during a touring schedule in London and was found to have kidney cancer and failing organs.

Chris Jasper has recorded some solo material over the years since the split of Isley-Jasper-Isley in 1988. Ernie Isley is currently working on his first solo album in nearly twenty years the last being the release in 1990's "High Wire".

The Isley Brothers were inducted to the Vocal Group "Hall of Fame" in 2003. They released their first Christmas album, "I'll Be Home For Christmas", in 2007 on their second release with Island Def Jam Records.

Album Track: "I'll Guess I'll Always Love You", The Isley Brothers.

Formed in 1966 in Gary, Indiana.

Original Line Up: Jackie Jackson - Tito Jackson - Jermaine Jackson - Marlon Jackson - Michael Jackson. **Later joined by:** Randy Jackson (after their Motown career).

Motown Connection: Most Successful Group of the 1970's.

Born and raised in Gary, Indiana, the Jackson brothers were guided early in their careers by their father Joseph Jackson, a steel mill crane operator and former musician, and their mother Katherine Jackson.

In 1964, Jackie, Tito and Jermaine formed The Jackson Brothers, including hometown friends Reynaud Jones and Milford Hite on guitar and drums respectively. By the end of the following year, the group's younger brothers Marlon and Michael joined the instrumental band playing tambourine and congas.

Showing extraordinary talent by the age of eight, Michael began demonstrating his dance moves and singing ability in mid 1966. Michael was allowed to perform his song-and-dance routine at a talent contest held at Jackie's Roosevelt High School in Gary, helping his brothers win the competition. It was at that point that Tito's junior high school orchestra teacher Shirley Cartman began mentoring the group and suggested a name change referring to the boys as The Jackson 5. She also suggested replacing Jones and Hite with more talented musicians Johnny Jackson (no relation) on drums and Ronnie Rancifer on keyboards.

The group then began playing semi-professionally in Indiana, Chicago and other US states, Shirley Cartman then negotiated a record deal with Gordon Keith's local Steeltown label, and the group made their first recordings in October 1967. Their first single, "Big Boy", was released in January 1968 and became a regional hit. The Jackson 5 also recorded "We Don't Have to Be Over 21 to Fall in Love" during their short stay at Steeltown Records, an album was released called "Pre-History: The Steeltown Recordings" (1966-68) on Brunswick Records are available. Steeltown Records was a short-lived record label active only from 1966 to 1972.

The Jackson 5 had a number of admirers in their early days, including Sam and Dave, who helped the group secure a spot in the famous Amateur Night competition at the Apollo Theatre in Harlem. The group won the competitions on the 13th August 1967. In the audience was Motown artist Gladys Knight who then recommended the group to Berry Gordy, but Berry Gordy, (who already had teenager Stevie Wonder on his roster), was hesitant to take on another child act.

The Jackson 5 then opened for Motown group Bobby Taylor and the Vancouvers at Chicago's Regal Theatre. Bobby Taylor was also very impressed with the group, deciding to bring them to Motown. The Jackson 5 had their Motown audition, for which they performed James Brown's then current hit "I Got the Feelin'". However, Berry Gordy was not in attendance, but the audition was videotaped and sent to him in Los Angeles. Berry Gordy's initial reluctance to sign the group disappeared, causing the group signing with Motown, Berry Gordy organised a party at his Detroit mansion on 25th November 1968 to introduce them to the Motown employees and stars.

Motown began negotiations to buy out The Jackson 5's Steeltown contract, completing the deal in March 1969. By the summer, Bobby Taylor began producing the group's first recordings at "Hitsville Studio A" in Detroit. The early Taylor-produced Jackson 5 records were all covers of both contemporary hits and Motown-standards, including Sly and the Family Stone's "Stand!" and their famous rendition of The Miracles' "Who's Lovin' You", written by Smokey Robinson.

Berry Gordy then moved The Jackson 5 (with Joseph Jackson their father) to Los Angeles California, and Berry Gordy and Suzanne de Passe began the process of grooming them as the label's next big act. In the meantime, Motown's marketing

Featuring the originals line-up.
L to R: Jackie Jackson, Tito Jackson, Jermaine Jackson, Marlon Jackson and Michael Jackson.

team began preparing promotional material in readiness for the group's introduction to the music industry. Berry Gordy also decided that Motown star Diana Ross would "discover" the group as was explained in all early press kits. The story was that Diana Ross (and, in some versions of the story, Berry Gordy alongside her) was introduced to The Jackson 5 by Gary, Indiana's mayor, Richard G. Hatcher, at a benefit concert that The Jackson 5 were described as having played for the mayor in 1969.

Diana Ross formally introduced The Jackson 5 to the public on August 11, 1969, at a Beverly Hills, California club called The Daisy. Towards the end of August, The Jackson 5 made their first television appearance, singing The Isley Brothers' "It's Your Thing" at the Miss Black America Pageant in Madison Square Garden, New York City, the rest is History.

The Jackson 5's first single, "I Want You Back", was written and produced by "The Corporation" and released as a single for The Jackson 5, (as Motown decided to officially call the group). The group performed "I Want You Back", as part of their appearance at The Hollywood Palace as special guests of Diana Ross and The Supremes. "I Want You Back" was the only single from The Jackson 5's first album, "Diana Ross Presents The Jackson 5", which was released in December 1969, the song reached No1 in January, 1970. The Jackson 5 became an instant sensation, with "I Want You Back" and its 1970 follow-ups "ABC", "The Love You Save" and "I'll Be There" all going to No1. The Jackson 5 were the first act in the music industry to have their first four singles reach the No1 spot add to this their other early Top 5 hits including "Mama's Pearl" and "Never Can Say Goodbye" and you can see why they became the most successful group of the 1970's.

A publicity handout from the artist re-produced in the Detroit Free Press.

With this success, Joseph Jackson (father to The Jackson 5) moved his wife Katherine and the rest of the family to California in 1970. First moving into a two-story residence, then to a gated mansion they called "Hayvenhurst", in Los Angeles which was purchased by Joseph in March 1971.

Within a year of their debut The Jackson 5 were among the biggest names in popular music. Motown licensed dozens of Jackson 5 related teen products, including The Jackson 5's album covers, stickers, posters, colouring books etc. A new teen magazine called "Right On!", began publication in 1971, and focused heavily on The Jackson 5. Animation producers Rankin/Bass produced The Jackson 5ive, a Saturday morning cartoon which had it's first showing in September 1971 and ran for two seasons on ABC. The Jackson 5 starred in two of their own television specials, "Goin' Back to Indiana" in September 1971 and The Jackson 5 Show in November 1972.

In 1971, Motown began to promote a solo career for Michael Jackson, and issued his first single, "Got to Be There", which to reached No 5 in the charts. Michael Jackson also sang the title track for the 1972 motion picture "Ben". Other brothers to undertake solo projects were, Jermaine in 1972, who had a Top Ten hit with his Shep and the Limelites cover "Daddy's Home", Jackie recorded a solo album, but his releases failed to chart. The solo careers of Michael, Jermaine, and Jackie co-existed with the work in the group, allowing Motown to expand the success and sales of The Jackson 5.

By 1972, The Jackson 5's releases were becoming less successful, but with singles still reaching the upper parts of the charts, it was always going to be difficult to match their initial success. Later chart hits, (mostly written and produced by Hal Davis), included "Lookin' Through the Windows" in 1972 and the disco-styled "Dancing Machine" in 1974, which popularised the "Robot" dance routine. However, Jackson 5 album sales were declining during the latter part of their stay at Motown, although LPs such as "Lookin' Through the Windows" in 1972 and "G.I.T: Get It Together" in 1973 frequently included successful album tracks, including their version of "Hum Along and Dance", a popular number in their live act. The era of The Jackson 5 at Motown was coming to an end, the group would also be the last major group that Berry Gordy would personally work with, although it was without doubt, Suzanne de Passe's influence that helped shape the group's development at Motown. Suzanne was responsible for signing, coaching, and developing the group while at Motown.

In 1975, Joseph Jackson negotiated a new recording contract with CBS Records, who offered a higher royalty rate and would allow the Jackson brothers to write and produce their own records and play their own instruments. After unsuccessfully attempting to keep the group at Motown, Berry Gordy felt the need to sue for breach of contract, although Motown eventually agreed to the termination of their contract, The Jackson 5 were forced to change their name to The Jacksons, because Motown retained the "Jackson 5" trademark during the settlement of the lawsuit. The Jacksons also replaced Jermaine with the youngest brother Randy, since Jermaine chose to stay with Motown. Jermaine at the time was married to Berry Gordy's daughter Hazel. Randy had been an unofficial member of The Jackson 5 since 1972, playing congas onstage as part of their live act.

In summer 1976, CBS television signed the Jackson family (including Michael, Marlon, Tito, Jackie, Randy, Rebbie, LaToya, and Janet) to appear in their own variety show, to compete with ABC's "Donny and Marie" show. Recording first with Philadelphia International Records (a part of CBS), and then Epic Records, The Jacksons continued releasing popular singles such as "Enjoy Yourself" in 1976, produced by Gamble and Huff, two further LPs also produced by Gamble and Huff. However, The Jacksons wanted artistic control, and produced their next LP, 1978's "Destiny". The album included The Jacksons' biggest post-Motown single, "Shake Your Body (Down to the Ground)", which was a major hit, written by Michael and Randy, it sold over two million copies, becoming a double-platinum album.

In 1979, The Jacksons received a star on the Hollywood Walk of Fame for their achievements. In 1980 the group released the "Triumph" album, which featured the hits "Lovely One" and "Can You Feel It". The following year the group started the "Triumph Tour", (which in 1988 was described by Rolling Stone magazine as one of the best 25 tours from 1967 to 1987). The group's success was overshadowed by Michael Jackson's 1982 LP "Thriller"; Thriller went on to become the world's best-selling album of all time.

The Motown 25 television special in 1983, featured a reunion between Jermaine and the other brothers, but was overshadowed by Michael Jackson's performance of "Billie Jean" on the same program, which introduced his trademark "moonwalk" dance. The Jacksons released the album "Victory" in 1984, featuring the hit single "State of Shock" with guest star Mick Jagger, and promoted the album with the successful "Victory World Tour", the Victory album and tour marked the official return of Jermaine to the group's line up.

Shortly after the Victory Tour, Michael left to pursue his solo career; Marlon left the group a year later. The other brothers eventually drifted apart to take on solo projects, although most of them appeared with Michael on the US For Africa single "We Are the World" in 1985. The Jacksons reunited for one last album, "2300 Jackson Street" in 1989. While every Jackson was present (except for LaToya) most of the album featured Jermaine, Jackie, Tito and Randy as the line up. With Michael now as the number one performer of the 1980's as well as the growing career of the group's youngest sister, Janet Jackson, the group had been overshadowed. A CD compilation of hits from the CBS/Epic years, "The Essential Jacksons", was released in 2004, as was a separate compilation by Universal/ Hip-O label.

In 1992, Suzanne de Passe and Jermaine Jackson worked with Motown to produce "The Jacksons: An American Dream", a five-hour television show based on the history of The Jacksons, which won an Emmy Award and was nominated for three more, and won two Awards. The Jackson 5 was inducted into the Rock 'n' Roll Hall of Fame in 1997 and the Vocal Group Hall of Fame in 1999. In addition, two of their songs ("ABC" and "I Want You Back") are among The Rock 'n' Roll Hall of Fame's 500 Songs that Shaped Rock and Roll.

They played at the Michael Jackson 30th Anniversary concert in September 2001; this was their first appearance together for thirteen years.

Album Track: "Never Can Say Goodbye", The Jackson 5.

Chuck Jackson

Born on the 22nd July 1937 in Latta, South Carolina (but was raised in Pittsburgh, Pennsylvania)

Motown Connection: Singer.

Raised in Pittsburgh, Pennsylvania, Chuck spent his early years in the industry performing on such shows as "The Tonight Show", "Soul Train" and "American Bandstand". Chuck sang with one of the best doo wop groups, the Dell-Vikings, in the late 1950's (although he doesn't appear on their hit singles). Chuck was "discovered" when he opened for Jackie Wilson at the Apollo Theatre. After this performance Chuck signed a recording contract with Scepter Records. His first single, "I Don't Want to Cry", which he co-wrote, was in 1961, the song charted on both the R&B and pop charts. In 1962, Jackson's recording of "Any Day Now", the Burt Bacharach-Bob Hilliard classic, became a huge hit.

Early promotional photo of Chuck Jackson.

Chuck was one of the first singers to successfully record Bacharach-David material, also working Leiber-Stoller on one of his best singles, "I Keep Forgettin'" in 1962, it was written and produced by them. Chuck had some success with some duets with Maxine Brown in the mid-1960's, but he left Wand in 1967 for Motown, having been recommended by Smokey Robinson. Chuck was (perhaps understandably) never totally marketed properly by Motown, the company was growing so fast it seemed Chuck was left behind. However Chuck did record a number of successful singles, including "Are You Lonely for Me Baby" and "Honey Come Back." After leaving Motown, Chuck then moved to All Platinum Records and other labels, but with minimal success.

The UK singer and performer Tom Jones was heavily influenced by Chuck, the international hit "It's Not Unusual" was originally written for Chuck on the expectation of Chuck recording and issuing this single. Chuck duetted with Dionne Warwick on the 1997 Grammy-nominated duet "If I Let Myself Go" (for Best Duet) from his CD "I'll Never Get Over You". In addition to his professional commitments, he organises and produces events for New York's world-famous Apollo Theatre. Included in these productions are performances by Smokey Robinson, Dionne Warwick, Tom Jones, Paul Shaffer (The Late Show) and Ashford & Simpson, to name a few.

His latest project, "Chuck Jackson: The Motown Anthology", contains 48 tracks from his early career at Motown. Chuck has received many awards including, the "Apollo Theatre's Hall of Fame" Award, "Heroes and Legends" in 1992: Rhythm and Blues Foundation, "Pioneer Ward".

Chuck is also a permanent member of New York's famous Friars Club. Several of Chuck's earlier songs have became successful hits for other artists, including Ronnie Milsap "Any Day Now" in 1982, which reached No1 on the Country and Adult Contemporary charts. Michael McDonald had a huge hit with his cover of "I Keep Forgettin'".

Jackie Jackson

Born as Sigmund Esco Jackson on the 4th May 1951 in Gary, Indiana

Motown Connection: With his brothers was part of The Jackson 5.

Was given the name "Jackie" by relatives, Jackie's first ambition was to be a professional baseball player, but gave up this dream in 1966 when Jackie and his four younger brothers formed The Jackson 5 in 1966. Jackie and his two younger brothers Tito and Jermaine were early members of the group as The Jackson Brothers in 1964.

Jackie began recording and playing with his brothers at an early age. At the age of 12 when his father finally realised the boys were using his guitar when he wasn't around, Jackie, Michael, Marlon, Tito and Jermaine were given a chance to perform, in front of their father. Encouraged by both parents, The Jackson 5 started to make public appearances, Joe Jackson (who worked part time at a mill at the time) would quickly become their full time manager. At the time Jackie (who was the eldest of the group) was the co-lead singer along with his brother Michael Jackson.

In 1963 the group won a talent contest singing The Temptations' hit "My Girl." Their first professional debut was a local nightclub in Indiana called Mr Lucky's. Keith Gordon had seen the group and signed them to his Steeltown Records. In 1967 the group produced the song "Big Boy" on the label in the summer of 1968 after opening for the likes of Jerry Buffer, the Chi-Lites and Little Miss Soul, The Jackson 5 were signed to Motown Records in Detroit.

On their first hit with "Enjoy Yourself", Jackie did the co-vocals, then Jackie took lead in "Hum Along And Dance", other songs that Jackie took the lead on include "Wondering Who" and "It's Alright", as well as "Wait" and "Torture".

Between 1969 and 1970 the group began recording on Motown and they became an instant success with their first four releases going No1, with "I Want You Back", "ABC", "The Love You Save" and "I'll Be There.". Their first No1 hit, "I Want You Back", sold more than two million records. Jackie often did the co-lead singer role for both The Jackson 5 and The Jacksons. Jackie's lead voice can best be heard on the hit "Love Don't Wanna Lead", where you can easily pick out his voice.

After successfully recording 13 albums with Motown, the group signed with RCA/Epic Records in 1976, they became The Jacksons. Jermaine Jackson had decided to stay on with the Motown record label so Randy Jackson was brought in to replace him.

Jackie released his solo album in 1973 hoping to capitalise on The Jackson 5 name in a similar way to his brothers Jermaine and Michael. The album was not a sales success, and none of the singles that were released were hits. Then Jackie put his a solo career on hold, and did not issue any further recordings until 1989, when Jackie released "Be The One", this album came shortly after the release of the last Jacksons album, "2300 Jackson Street", again with Jackie hoping to use this album to help with the marketing. The album yielded two R&B hits, "Stay" and "Cruzin". These recordings were the last to be issued under Jackie's name, since then Jackie hasn't released an album or single to date. His last performance with his five younger brothers came during a reunion performance at Madison Square Garden in 2001.

Jackie currently lives in California where he runs the record company, Jesco. Artists signed to the label include rappers Mike Street, Emstate, and his son, (also a rapper) DealZ. DealZ released his first "mixtape" in Aug 2007. Jackie is rumoured to be working with some of his brothers on a reunion album for The Jackson 5.

Jackie married Enid Spann, in 1974. They divorced in 1987, Jackie has two children, a daughter Brandi, and Sigmund "Siggy" (who is a rapper and goes by the name DealZ).

Jermaine Jackson

Born Jermaine Lajuan Jackson (aka Muhammad Abdul Aziz) on the 11th December 1954 in Gary, Indiana

Motown Connection: With his brothers was part of The Jackson 5 - Married to Hazel Gordy (the daughter of Motown Founder Berry Gordy) - Worked with Suzanne de Passé produced "The Jacksons: An American Dream".

Jermaine was one of five brothers who made up The Jackson 5, playing bass for the group and background vocals. Jermaine and his two younger brothers Tito and Jackie were part of an early incarnation of the group know as The Jackson Brothers in 1964. Jermaine did occasional leads for the group in 1966 when Jermaine and his four younger brothers formed The Jackson 5. Given a chance to perform, in front of both the parents, The Jackson 5 started to make public appearances, Joe Jackson (who worked part time at a mill at the time) would quickly become their full time manager.

In 1963 the group won a talent contest singing The Temptations' hit "My Girl". Their first professional debut was a local nightclub in Indiana called Mr Lucky's. Keith Gordon had seen the group and signed them to his Steeltown Records. Jermaine became the original lead singer of The Jackson 5 until 1967 when younger brother Michael Jackson took on lead vocals, but Jermaine and Michael Jackson would still record as co-lead on some of The Jackson 5 recording. In 1967 the group produced the song "Big Boy" on the label in the summer of 1968 after opening for the likes of Jerry Buffer, the Chi-Lites and Little Miss Soul, The Jackson 5 where signed to Motown Records in Detroit.

Between 1969 and 1970 the group began recording on Motown and they became an instant success with their first four releases going No1, with "I Want You Back", "ABC", "The Love You Save" and "I'll Be There". Their first No1 hit, "I Want You Back", sold more than two million records. Jermaine contributed occasional lead vocals to their albums in the early 1970's, and his performance of "I Found That Girl" on the third album was one of their best ballads.

After successfully recording 13 albums with Motown, the group signed with RCA/Epic Records in 1976, they became The Jacksons. Jermaine had decided to stay on with Motown, so Randy Jackson was brought in to replace him. Jermaine left the group as he was married to Hazel Gordy, the daughter of Motown owner Berry Gordy and he felt it was important to stay.

Like Michael Jackson, Jermaine also began a successful solo career while in The Jackson 5, and had a hit with the 1972 Shep and the Limelites cover "Daddy's Home". Later releases did not chart, despite a promotion drive from Motown, Jermaine's recordings failed to establish him as a distinctive soul voice and comparisons with The Jacksons' work on Epic did not help. Jermaine's position at Motown was strengthened by his marriage to Hazel Gordy in 1973, also in that year, Jermaine graduated from Birmingham High School.

Jermaine's career was revitalized by Stevie Wonder, who wrote and produced the 1979 hit "Let's Get Serious", this hit increased Jermaine's public profile and won him a more generous contract with Motown in the early 1980's. Jermaine was nominated for the Grammy Award for "Best Male R&B Vocal Performance" for the album "Let's Get Serious".

A duet with his brother Michael, "Tell Me I'm Not Dreamin'", was a No1 hit on the dance chart in 1984. In 1985, Jermaine's duet with Pia Zadora, "When The Rain Begins To Fall", was a No1 in several singles charts in Europe; however his final chart success was in 1989 with "Don't Take It Personal" a No1 hit. Jermaine converted to Islam after a visit to Bahrain in the 1980's, figuring heavily on the Islam Channel in the UK where he talked about his Islamic faith.

In 1992, along with Suzanne de Passé they produced "The Jacksons: An American Dream", an award-winning documentary film about the history of The Jackson 5. While with Motown, Jermaine formed his own production company, with Michael Lovesmith had his first success as a recording artist while overseeing the career development of Syreeta, but this increased freedom was not enough to keep him at Motown and in 1983 he signed with Arista Records.

The following year, he was re-untied with his brothers when he joined the Jackson's on the Victory album and tour. By 1986 Jermaine was working with Whitney Houston on the "Precious Memories" project. In that same year, he formed his own label, WORK Records, and accepted an offer to portray the late Marvin Gaye in a biopic that was never completed and still he continued to work with The Jackson's and as a soloist

The Motown 25 television special in 1983, featured a reunion between Jermaine and the other brothers, which was overshadowed by Michael Jackson's performance of "Billie Jean" on the same program, which introduced his trademark "moonwalk" dance. Jermaine's next appearance with his brothers was not until 2001 for a concert given by Michael Jackson.

During Michael Jackson's child abuse trial in 2005, Jermaine was a great supporter of his brother. Jermaine came to Michael's defence several times on the Larry King show and appeared with Michael in court on numerous occasions.

Jermaine was a housemate in Celebrity Big Brother (UK reality show) in 2007. Jermaine came in second place to Shilpa Shetty in the Big Brother final. Jermaine became a huge favourite in the UK and won many new fans.

Jermaine currently lives in Dubai but has also resided in Bahrain. Jermaine has married three times, first to Hazel Gordy (their children are called Jermaine Jnr, Autumn and Jeremy), to Margaret Maldonado (their children are called Jaimy and Jourdyn) to Alejandra Genevieve Oiaza (ex-wife of Brother Randy Jackson and their children are called Jaffar and Jermajesty). All three marriages ended in divorce. Since 2004, he has been married to Haleema Rasheed. He also has a daughter named Dawn.

Marlon Jackson

Born Marlon David Jackson on the 12th March 1957 in Gary, Indiana

Motown Connection: With his brothers was part of The Jackson 5.

Born as a twin, his older twin brother Brandon died stillborn and Marlon was born several months premature. The second youngest of the Jackson family, Marlon was only one year older than Michael Jackson. Joseph Jackson (Marlon's father) wanted to drop Marlon from the group, but his mother Katherine Jackson insisted that he stay. Marlon was about 6 years old when in 1964 Jackie, Tito and Jermaine formed The Jackson Brothers, including hometown friends Reynaud Jones and Milford Hite on guitar and drums respectively. By the end of the following year, the group's younger brothers Marlon and Michael Jackson joined the band playing tambourine and congas. It has always been rumoured that Marlon was told by his father Joseph that he couldn't sing and wasn't as skilled a dancer as younger brother Michael. While he eventually danced with the group, Marlon was required not to sing during the early years of The Jackson 5 until the group was signed to Motown in 1968.

In 1963 the group won a talent contest singing The Temptations' hit "My Girl." Their first professional debut was a local nightclub in Indiana called Mr Lucky's. Keith Gordon had seen the group and signed them to his Steeltown Records. In 1967 the group produced the song "Big Boy" on the label in the summer of 1968 after opening for the likes of Jerry Buffer, the Chi-Lites and Little Miss Soul, The Jackson 5 were signed to Motown Records in Detroit in 1968.

Due to a contract dispute with a previous manager, it was about a year before Motown could release any Jackson 5 records. Around this time, the Jackson family moved to California. Michael and Marlon stayed briefly with singer Diana Ross until housing could be arranged for the entire family. Once their records started to be released at the end of 1969, The Jackson 5 were an immediate success, with their first four singles going to number one in the US. Marlon and Michael were forced to leave the California public school system due to fans disrupting their classroom. From that point on, most of their education would come from a private tutor.

At the age of 18, in 1975 Marlon eloped with a fan, Carol Parker, marrying without the knowledge of other family members. Marlon lived at home with his parents for five months before they learned what had happened.

After successfully recording 13 albums with Motown, the group signed with RCA/Epic Records in 1976, they became The Jacksons. Jermaine Jackson had decided to stay on with the Motown record label so Randy Jackson was brought in to replace him. Jermaine left the group as well as he was married to Hazel Gordy, the daughter of Motown owner Berry Gordy and he felt it was important to stay.

Marlon took the place of Jermaine as one of the group's co-leaders often taking Jermaine's spot when singing older hits at concert. Marlon took a co-lead spot on The Jacksons' album track "Give It Up" from their "Triumph" album. The return of Jermaine to the group in 1983 after their reunited performance at Motown 25 led to a new album and tour, both titled "Victory" in 1984. Michael Jackson announced he was leaving the group after the Victory tour to pursue his solo career, while Marlon announced he was leaving the group in 1987 to follow a solo career, this left The Jacksons as a quartet of Jackie, Tito, Jermaine and Randy. The Jacksons officially confirmed their break-up in 1990. Marlon didn't participate in much of the Jacksons' final album, the 1989 "2300 Jackson Street" though Marlon and Michael were featured on the title track, which became an R&B hit.

Marlon issued his debut album, "Baby Tonight", on Capitol Records, which was only a modest success. Next, moving on to producing songs for all three of his sisters, including Janet Jackson's 1984 album, "Dream Street", which featured the Top 10 R&B single, "Don't Stand Another Chance", and a song on Rebbie Jackson's debut album, "Centipede". Marlon did rejoin with his brothers for two concerts in 2001 to celebrate Michael Jackson's 30th Anniversary as a solo performer.

Unlike his brothers, Marlon decided to embark on a career outside of show business, becoming a successful real estate agent in Southern California. He also is part owner of Major Broadcasting Corporation, a cable network designed to bring family-friendly programming to the Black community.

Marlon married Carol Parker, (with whom Marlon had eloped when she was a fan), Marlon is the only Jackson brother to avoid divorce, as the couple are still married and have three children: Valencia, Brittany and Marlon Jnr. Marlon is also a grandfather.

Michael Jackson

Born Michael Joseph Jackson on the 19th August 1958 in Gary, Indiana

Motown Connection: With his brothers was part of The Jackson 5 - Singer - Writer.

Often referred to as "The King of Pop" Michael was one of five brothers who made up The Jackson 5, however, Jermaine Tito and Jackie were part of an early group known as The Jackson Brothers in 1964. Michael started to provide lead vocals for the group in 1966 when Michael and his four younger brothers formed The Jackson 5.

The seventh child of the Jackson family, Michael made his professional debut at the age of eleven as a member of The Jackson 5. Michael was identified as the "Most Successful Entertainer of All Time" by Guinness World Records, and holds the record for the best-selling album of all time "Thriller".

Michael showed musical talent early in his life, performing in front of classmates and others during a Christmas recital at the age of five, at the age of eight Michael was performing and taking lead vocals for The Jackson 5.

Between 1969 and 1970 the group began recording on Motown and they became an instant success with their first four releases going No1, with "I Want You Back", "ABC", "The Love You Save" and "I'll Be There". Their first No1 hit, "I Want You Back", sold more than two million records.

As part of The Jackson 5, this made Michael among the most popular artists of the 1970's. While with Motown, Michael issued some solo work which included, Michael's first hit, "Got to Be There" in 1971, subsequent hits included his remake of "Rockin' Robin" and "Ben" in 1972. Michael released a total of four solo studio albums with Motown.

After successfully recording 13 albums with Motown, the group signed with RCA/Epic Records in 1976, and they became The Jacksons. Jermaine had decided to stay on with Motown, so Randy Jackson was brought in to replace him. Jermaine left the group as well, as he was married to Hazel Gordy, the daughter of Motown owner Berry Gordy and he felt it was important to stay, Michael temporarily abandoning his solo career to concentrate on the group.

Marlon took the place of Jermaine often taking Jermaine's spot when singing older hits at concert. The return of Jermaine to the group in 1983 after their reunited performance at Motown 25 led to a new album and tour, both titled "Victory" in 1984. However, Michael announced he was leaving the group after the Victory tour to pursue his solo career, with Marlon announcing he was leaving the group in 1987 to follow a solo career, this left The Jacksons as a quartet of Jackie, Tito, Jermaine and Randy.

In the early 1980's, he became a dominant figure in popular music, the popularity of his music videos together with the growth of MTV, gave the songs and video such as "Beat It", "Billie Jean" and Thriller a whole new "young" audience. Videos such as "Black or White" and "Scream" made Michael a star on MTV well into the 1990's. With all this solo work it was inevitable that Michael's future was as a solo artist, with this The Jacksons officially confirmed their break-up in 1990. Michael didn't participate in much of The Jacksons' final album, the 1989 "2300 Jackson Street" though Marlon and Michael were featured on the title track, which became an R&B hit.

The Jackson 5 signed a new contract with CBS Records in June 1975, joining first the Philadelphia International Records and then Epic Records. As a result of legal proceedings, the group was renamed The Jacksons after Motown successfully won the right to the name Jackson 5. After the name change, the band continued to tour internationally, releasing six more albums between 1976 and 1984. Michael also undertook the role as lead songwriter of the group, writing hits such as "Shake Your Body (Down to the Ground)", "This Place Hotel" and "Can You Feel It".

In 1978, Michael starred as Scarecrow in the film musical "The Wiz" The music was arranged by Quincy Jones, who formed a partnership with Michael, they jointly produced the solo album "Off the Wall". Michael received songwriter credits along with, Rod Temperman (of the group Heatwave), Stevie Wonder and Paul McCartney.

Released in 1979, "Off The Wall" was the first album to generate four US Top 10 hits, including the chart-topping singles "Don't Stop 'Til You Get Enough" and "Rock with You". The album reached No 3 on the charts and sold over seven million copies in the US and eventually sold over fifteen million copies worldwide.

In 1982, Jackson contributed the song "Someone In the Dark" to the storybook for the film "E.T. the Extra-Terrestrial"; the record won a Grammy for "Best Album for Children". On the back of the success of "Off The Wall" Michael issued his second Epic album, "Thriller". The album broke every music industry record, it remained in the Top 10 for 80 consecutive weeks and 37 of those weeks at No1, It was the first album to have seven Top 10 singles, including "Billie Jean", "Beat It" and Wanna Be Startin' Somethin', it sold twenty seven million copies in the US, (making it a Double Diamond Album). It is said to be the best-selling album of all time, with worldwide sales between forty seven million and one hundred and four million copies. Thriller did not have an official tour to promote it, but the 1984 "Victory Tour", by The Jacksons, used much of Michael's new solo material, Michael donated his $5 million share from the Victory Tour to charity.

Thriller became an industry within an industry, with record breaking profits from CD's and the sale of "The Making of Michael Jackson's Thriller" a documentary produced by Michael and John Landis. (Funded by MTV), the documentary sold over 350,000 copies in a few months of sale. On 25th March 1983, Michael performed live on the "Motown 25: Yesterday, Today, Forever" a television special, appearing with The Jackson 5 and on his own, Michael performing "Billie Jean". It was the only "non-Motown" song performed, it included Michael's public performance of his moonwalk.

While in Los Angeles in 1984 Michael was involved (while filming a Pepsi Cola commercial at the Shrine Auditorium) in an accident suffering second degree burns to his scalp after pyrotechnics accidentally set his hair on fire. PepsiCo settled a lawsuit out of court, and Michael gave his $1.5 million settlement to the "Michael Jackson Burn Center" which was a piece of new technology to help people with severe burns. Also in 1984, Michael was a guest at the White House to receive an award presented by American President Ronald Reagan. The award was given for Jackson's support of charities that helped people overcome alcohol and drug abuse. In that year Michael co-wrote the charity single "We Are the World" with Lionel Richie, which was released worldwide to aid the poor in Africa and the US. He was one of 39 music celebrities who performed on the record. The single became one of the best-selling singles of all time, with nearly 20 million copies sold and millions of dollars donated to famine relief.

Michael then purchased Northern Songs, a music publishing company which held thousands of songs, including, The Beatles' back catalogue and songs by Elvis Presley. Michael outbid Paul McCartney and Yoko Ono at a cost of $47.5 million. The idea came to Michael while working with McCartney on the two hit singles "The Girl Is Mine" and "Say Say Say" a few years prior.

In 1988, Michael released his first autobiography, "Moonwalk", which took four years to complete. Michael told of his childhood, his experience in The Jackson 5 and the abuse he suffered as a child. Michael also spoke of his plastic surgery, saying he had two rhino plastic surgeries and the surgical creation of a cleft in his chin. In the book, he attributed the change in the structure of his face to puberty, weight loss, a strict vegetarian diet, a change in hair style and stage lighting. Moonwalk reached the top position on The New York Times best sellers' list. Michael then released a film called "Moonwalker", which featured live footage, music videos, and a feature film, staying there for 22 weeks. It was eventually knocked off the top spot by Michael Jackson: "The Legend Continues".

Michael brought his Neverland Ranch in 1988 (and lived there until 2005), where he built an amusement park and private zoo that was frequently attended by disadvantaged and terminally ill children. Rumours of sleepover parties received both negative media coverage and public attention after it was revealed that children had slept in his bed or bedroom. This first came to light when he was accused of child sexual abuse in 1993. Michael Jackson's relationship with children was brought into the spotlight again in 2003 when the TV documentary "Living with Michael Jackson" was broadcast. Shortly afterward, Jackson became the first Westerner to appear in a television advert for Russia.

In March 1991 Michael renewed his contract with Sony for $65 million; a record breaking deal at the time recording the album "Dangerous", which sold four million copies and spawned the hits "Black and White", "Remember the Time", "In the Closet" and "Jam." This coincided with Michael's second world tour, launched in Europe in June 1992, continued into 1993.

Michael throughout his career had managed to keep his reputation, which remained clean cut, but in 1993 Michael suffered serious damage to his image. A teenage friend accused Michael of child abuse, although Michael always denied the accusations, Michael settled the civil case "out of court" in early 1994.

Michael then began working on "HIStory" double album, "HIStory" contained one disc of Michael's greatest hits and one disc of new material, and it was released in 1995.

In 1997, another collection was issued, "Blood on the Dance Floor: History in the Mix", which collected dance remixes of several of the new compositions on "HIStory", as well as a few brand new tracks.

In March of 2001, Jackson was inducted into the Rock 'n' Roll Hall of Fame, but a broken foot prevented the 'King of Pop' from performing at the ceremony. Later in the year, a star-studded Michael Jackson tribute concert was booked for Madison Square Garden in New York City, including performances by Whitney Houston, Britney Spears, and Destiny's Child, among others, as well as appearances by such celebrities as Marlon Brando, Elizabeth Taylor, and Shaquille O'Neal. The concert's biggest draw for many fans was when a full Jackson 5 reunion set was announced to be part of the show. Still, the show created some controversy when Jackson's brother Jermaine criticised Michael for the concerts bloated ticket prices (top seats were $2500). A month before the show, a new Michael Jackson single was released to radio, "You Rock My World", with an all-new studio album, "Invincible", followed on the 30th October 2001.

On 18th December 2003, Michael was charged with seven counts of child molestation and two counts of administering an intoxicating agent in order to commit that felony, with Gavin Arvizo, who was under fourteen at the time of the incident. Michael denied these allegations, saying that the sleepovers were in no way sexual in nature. The People v. Jackson trial began in Santa Maria, California, on January 31, 2005, and lasted until the end of May 2005, with Michael being acquitted on all counts in June.

In 2005 Sony negotiated with a loans company on behalf of Michael. Two hundred million in loans were due in December 2005 and were secured on the music catalogue he purchased in 1985. Jackson failed to pay and Bank of America sold them to Fortress Investments, a company dealing in distressed loans. However, Michael has not as yet sold any of the remainder of his stake. The possible purchase by Sony of twenty-five percent of Sony/ATV Music Publishing is a conditional option; it is assumed the singer will try to avoid having to sell part of the catalogue of songs including material by other artists such as Bob Dylan and Destiny's Child. As another part of the deal Jackson was given a new three hundred million loan and a lower interest rate on the old loan to match the original Bank of America rate. When the loan was sold to Fortress Investments they increased the interest rate to twenty percent. An advisor to Jackson, however, did publicly announce he had "restructured his finances with the assistance of Sony".

To celebrate Jackson's 50th birthday, Sony BMG released a compilation album called "King of Pop" in various countries. These albums included tracks from Jacksons and Michael's solo career, all voted for by fans. Sony added a previous "MegaMix" by Jason Nevins. The albums had different track lists, according to how the fans of each nation voted. Although it was not released in the US or France, "King of Pop" did reach the Top 10 in the vast majority of countries it was issued in. In early 2008, he released Thriller 25 (a special edition of the "Thriller" album), which became a commercial success selling more than one and a half million copies worldwide in eight weeks.

In 1980, Michael won three awards at the American Music Awards for his solo efforts: Favourite Soul/R&B Album, Favourite Male Soul/R&B Artist and Favourite Soul/R&B Single (for "Don't Stop 'Til You Get Enough"). Also in that year, he also won Billboard Music Awards for "Top Black Artist" and "Top Black Album" and a Grammy Award for "Best Male R&B Vocal Performance" for "Don't Stop 'Til You Get Enough".

Michael has also received thirteen Grammy Awards (eight on a single night in 1984) and two of his solo albums have been inducted into the "Grammy Hall of Fame". Michael had thirteen number one singles in the United States, more than any other male artist. In November 2006, the World Music Awards announced that Michael had sold over seven hundred and fifty million units worldwide and given several hundred million dollars to charity, making Michael one of the best-selling music artists and one of the most philanthropic performers of the twentieth and twenty-first century.

In 2003, the TV network VH1 named "Off The Wall" the No36 greatest album of all time. Rolling Stone ranked it No68 in their list of the 500 Greatest Albums of All Time. In 2008, the album "Off The Wall" was inducted into the "Grammy Hall of Fame".

Michael married Lisa Marie Presley, the daughter of Elvis Presley, in 1994. They divorced less than two years later, although they still remain friends. In November 1996 (during the Australian leg of the HIStory World Tour), Michael married his dermatologist's nurse Deborah Jeanne Rowe, with whom he had a son called, Michael Joseph Jackson, Jnr. (also known as "Prince"), and a daughter, Paris Katherine Jackson. Jackson and Rowe divorced in 1999. Jackson's third child, Prince Michael Jackson II (a.k.a. Blanket) was born in 2002.

Born on the 17th May 1938 in New Orleans, Louisiana - Died 18th August 2008 in Detroit, Michigan

Motown Connection: Bass and Vocalist Singer with The Spinners (aka Detroit Spinners and The Motown Spinners in the UK).

Born in New Orleans, Louisiana, Jackson was perhaps best known for his line of "12:45" from the group's chart, Top 10 hit, "They Just Can't Stop It (Games People Play)", Pervis was still undertaking an active part of The Detroit Spinners recording and stage performances up to his death. The group was formed by a group of high school students in Detroit.

Pervis formed the bass vocal foundation for the group. He was, additionally, one of the original members of the group with Henry Fambrough and Bobbie Smith the other original Spinner, Billy Henderson, died last year.

At school in the suburb of Ferndale, Pervis along with other students formed a group they called The Domingoes in 1954. Over the next few years they gave occasional concerts and changed both personnel and the group name until, in 1961, they settled on The Spinners, with Bobbie Smith as the high tenor lead singer, the tenor George Dixon and the baritones Henry Fambrough and Billy Henderson. "The Spinners" name came from the large hub-caps of Cadillac cars.

 In 1961, they were signed to a recording contract by Harvey Fuqua for his Tri-Phi label, the subsequent single, "That's What Girls Are Made For" became a chart hit. However, when Harvey Fuqua sold his Tri-Phi record company to Berry Gordy the consequence of this sale meant The Spinners would became Motown Recording Artists. With the signing to Motown, The Spinners (in their opinion) were promoted behind artists like, The Supremes, Stevie Wonder and The Temptations who went on to become international stars, this was reinforced when The Spinners generally opened the show for other Motown artists, never gaining the top spot for themselves.

Although they had several R&B successes at Motown, their only pop hit was "It's a Shame" in 1970, written and produced by Stevie Wonder. It was also a Top 20 hit in UK, where the group was renamed The Motown Spinners to avoid confusion with the Liverpool folk group already called The Spinners.

The group's real success came after leaving Motown in 1972 for Atlantic Records, on Aretha Franklin's advice. It was Thom Bell who gave Pervis the key line to sing

"12.45" on the 1975 hit "They Just Can't Stop It (Games People Play)", Pervis was subsequently known as "Mr 12.45".

That record was one of five million-sellers produced by Thom Bell during the seventies, starting with "I'll Be Around", in 1972, and "Could it Be I'm Falling in Love", a Top 20 hit in UK, where the group was now known as The Detroit Spinners. Other hits included "One of a Kind (Love Affair)", "The Rubberband Man" and "Ghetto Child". The group's only No1 hit in America was "Then Came You", a duet with Dionne Warwick.

In 1977 Wynne left for a solo career and was replaced by John Edwards. His departure coincided with the Philly Sound's loss of popularity to disco and, in 1980, the group switched producers from Thom Bell to Michael Zager. He created two best-selling medleys for the Spinners. The first recording was the old Four Seasons hit "Working My Way Back to You" with Zager's own composition "Forgive Me Girl" interestingly turning the medley into one recording. This recording was the group's final million-selling record and their only No1 hit in the UK The second recording used the same formula with Sam Cooke's "Cupid" and "I've Loved You for a Long Time".

By the mid-1980's, Pervis and the group were playing the "oldies" circuit with The Four Seasons and the Righteous Brothers. The final album for Atlantic was "Cross Fire", in 1984, although the group was featured in the Atlantic Record Company's 40th anniversary concert in New York in 1988.

For the next two decades, The Spinners performed their repertoire of hits, averaging 200 concerts a year at venues throughout America and Europe. Besides Pervis, the two other original members, Henry Fambrough and Bobbie Smith, were still with the group completing a half a century of performing together in The Spinners.

Pervis's last onstage appearance was 19th July 2008, when The Spinners performed in La Habra, California. Pervis died aged seventy; he had been suffering from cancer.

Pervis married his wife Claudreen in 1968; they had two sons, two daughters and eight grandchildren.

Tito Jackson

Born Toriano Adaryll Jackson on the 15th October 1953 in Gary, Indiana

Motown Connection: With his brothers was part of The Jackson 5.

Tito was one of five brothers who made up The Jackson 5, was the guitarist and lead and background vocals. Tito and his two younger brothers Jermaine and Jackie were part of an early incarnation of the group know as The Jackson Brothers in 1964. Tito did occasional leads for the group as well the guitarist when in 1966 Tito and his four younger brothers formed The Jackson 5.

In 1963 the group won a talent contest singing The Temptations' hit "My Girl". Their first professional debut was a local nightclub in Indiana called Mr Lucky's. Keith Gordon had seen the group and signed them to his Steeltown Records. Jermaine became the original lead singer of The Jackson 5 until 1967 when younger brother Michael Jackson took on lead vocals, but Jermaine and Michael Jackson would still record as co-lead on some of The Jackson 5 recording. In 1967 the group produced the song "Big Boy" on the label in the summer of 1968 after opening for the likes of Jerry Buffer, the Chi-Lites and Little Miss Soul, The Jackson 5 were signed to Motown Records in Detroit. Tito was considered the "serious" one in the band, but contributed to the group's success by adding his musical knowledge to the group.

Between 1969 and 1970 the group began recording on Motown and they became an instant success with their first four releases going No1.

After successfully recording 13 albums with Motown, the group signed with RCA/Epic Records in 1976, they became The Jacksons. The Jackson 5 were forced to change their name, because Motown retained the "Jackson 5" trademark during the settlement of the lawsuit. Jermaine had decided to stay on with Motown, so Randy Jackson was brought in to replace him. Jermaine left the group as well as he was married to Hazel Gordy, the daughter of Motown owner Berry Gordy and he felt it was important to stay.

In 1978 he co-wrote the songs "Everybody", "Destiny" and "Push Away" for his new record label. As the group The Jacksons, including Tito, they self-produced the "Destiny" album. Later, for the "Victory" album Tito produced, wrote, and sang on "We Can Change The World".

Tito was involved with the live performance on the "Motown 25: Yesterday, Today, Forever" (a television special), with The Jackson 5 the first time in many years the brothers performed together. Their last commercial work was the 1989 album "2300 Jackson Street". The Jacksons officially confirmed their break-up in 1990, Tito did rejoin with his brothers for two concerts in 2001 to celebrate Michael Jackson's 30th Anniversary as a solo performer.

Projects undertaken after the split from The Jacksons included collaborations with his son's Taj, Taryll and TJ, on the group 3T, in addition to working with sisters Janet, Rebbie and La Toya, Tito has worked with countless great musicians, singers, and producers, such as the production team of Gamble and Huff, LA Reid and Baby Face, and Howard Hewitt. Tito also has produced songs for Sister Maureen's solo album, "Centipede".

In 1997 Tito and his brothers were ceremonially honoured as inductees of the well-respected Rock 'n' Roll Hall of Fame. In 2005 he started on a new musical project for a 2006 release.

Tito married Delores "DeeDee" Martes in June 1972, and later divorced in 1988. The couple had three sons, who compose the musical group 3T , and one daughter, Toriano Adaryll, "Taj" II, Taryll Arden, Tito Joseph "TJ" and Royal (ty).

Born on the 29th January 1938 in Charleston, North Carolina - Died 2nd August 1983 in Los Angeles, California

Motown Connection: Bassist/Member of The Funk Brothers (Motown In House Band) - One of the Greatest Bass Players in Music History.

James's father (James Lee Jamerson Sr) worked in shipyards and his mother (Elisabeth) was a domestic worker. In 1953, Jamerson's mother moved to Detroit to find work and a year later James joined his mother. When his parents divorced, James divided his time between his grandmother, who played piano, an aunt who sang in the church choir and practising piano at his cousin's house.

After a bicycle accident, James spent a year in a wheelchair, forced to wear high topped shoes in order to walk, the incident left James with a slight limp and a shyness James found hard to hide.

While attending Northwestern he started playing upright bass and James honed his skills playing in the high school jazz band and playing with some of Detroit's top jazz musicians like Kenny Burrell, Yusef Lateef and Hank Jones. As his reputation grew, James began playing at dances, weddings and parties with schoolmates, pianist Richard "Popcorn" Wylie and drummer Clifford Mack. James married Annie Wells but turned down a music scholarship from Wayne State University reasoning that he was already working in the music field playing with Washboard Willie and the Superstuds of Rhythm.

In 1958, Johnnie Mae Matthews, owner of Northern Records employed James to play on sessions for the label, James's other work included Fortune, Tri Phi, Anna Records. James would often travel to nearby Chicago to do session work for VeeJay or Brunswick Records. James can be heard on John Lee Hooker's single "Boom Boom".

James played on a hit record of a song written by Wylie, "With This Ring" by The Platters on Musicor in early 1967.

James's next assignment was a session at "Hitsville Studio A" the rest as they say, is Motown history. James quickly became part of the studio-recording band (eventually becoming The Funk Brothers), but James also toured with Smokey Robinson and The Miracles. The bassist found his musical "soul mates" in pianist Earl Van Dyke, drummer Benny Benjamin, guitarists Robert White, Joe Messina and the rest of The Funk Brothers. In 1961, Jamerson switched to the newly created electric Fender Precision bass, this move made his bass lines stand out more on records.

Motown wasn't too keen about James and the rest of The Funk Brothers recording for other labels. Several music entrepreneurs, local and otherwise, took advantage of the situation offering the band more money, leading to The Funk Brothers being heard on a lot of "backdoor sessions" for the local Golden World and Ric-Tic label owned by Ed Wingate. The band can be heard on "Agent Double 0 Soul" by Edwin Starr in 1965 and "Stop Her On Sight" in 1966, on Ollie McLaughlin's Karen label, "Cool Jerk" by The Capitols in July 1966. Making the trips to nearby Chicago, The Funk Brothers played session on several records for producer Carl Davies. "I Just Wanna Testify" by The Parliaments in 1967.

Also in 1967 The Funk Brothers did background sessions for "Just Be Sincere" and "(Your Love Keeps Lifting Me) Higher and Higher" which set the stage for Jackie Wilson's mid-1960's comeback and was his second No1 R&B in October 1967, followed by "Since You Showed Me How to Be Happy" a hit in November 1967, "I Get The Sweetest Feeling" in June 1968, "Can Feel Those Vibrations" and "This Love Is Real" in November 1970. The Funk Brothers also travelled south to record in Muscle Shoals and Atlanta among other cities.

In 1968 James lost one of his closest friends, Motown drummer Benny Benjamin to heroin addiction, also because of high demand, Motown hired bassist Bob Babbitt in an effort to keep up with the ever-expanding recording schedules. At least when the company moved to Los Angeles in the early 1970's, James was offered session work (most of the other Funk Brothers were not).

Despite having some "no show" at record dates, because of his alcoholism (in the opinion of some Motown staffers). In 1971, against the advice of other Motown employees, Berry Gordy refused to fire James, Berry's loyalty paid off when Marvin Gaye enlisted James to play on his 1971 multi platinum "What's Going On". The next year, James's schedule seemed to be his busiest ever, touring with Marvin Gaye, Joan Baez, Maria Moulder, also recording jingles, movie scores, TV themes ("Starsky and Hutch") and of course, million selling records. Al Wilson's "Show and Tell" in late 1973, The Hues Corporation's "Rock The Boat", a No1 record in early 1974. Another massive hit that featured James was "Then Came You" by

Dionne Warwick and The Spinners in late 1974, The Sylver's "Boogie Fever" another No1 record, in late 1975, and the "Theme From SWAT" by the studio group Rhythm Heritage a No1 hit also in 1975. Late in 1975, James worked with Marilyn McCoo and Billy Davis, JR's "You Don't Have To Be A Star (To Be In My Show) No1 hit in late 1976, James can also be heard on Robert Palmer's "Which of Us Is the Fool" from his 1976 Island LP, "Pressure Drop".

Things began to sour for James as chronic alcoholism, and medication led to his exclusion from the "A list" of call session players. Many of the last years of James's life were spent in and out of hospitals and mental institutions.

Just four months after the May 1983 NBC TV broadcast of "Motown 25: Yesterday, Today and Forever", Jamerson died of complications stemming from cirrhosis of the liver, heart failure and pneumonia in Los Angeles. Overlooked in "Motown 25" The Funk Brothers finally got their reward in the excellent 1997 ABC/TV special, "Motown 40". For the Motown fans and the countless musicians that he inspired, he's remembered as the genius whose contribution helped define the "Motown Sound". Annie Jamerson, widow of Motown bassist James Jamerson, received (on his behalf) in New York on March 8, 2000 his induction to the Rock 'n' Roll Hall of Fame.

One of his children, James Jamerson Jnr grew up to be in demand as a studio bassist, scoring a hit with his group Chanson, "Don't Hold Back" in late 1978. James is survived by Annie, sons James Jnr, Ivey, Derek and a daughter Doreen.

Signature songs: Must be "What's Going On" by Marvin Gaye and one of my favourite's "My World Is Empty Without You" by The Supremes.

Album Track: "What's Going On", Marvin Gaye.

Formed in 1958 in Detroit, Michigan

Motown Connection: The publishing company name (pronounced "Jo-BET"), is named after his three children, Hazel Joy (Jo), Berry IV (Be) and Terry (Te).

Jobete Music Company Incorporated was formed by Berry Gordy in 1958 and became the music publishing arm to his Motown Records label. Its catalogue contains the classic songs of the "Motown Sound", including Stevie Wonder, Diana Ross and The Supremes, Smokey Robinson and The Miracles, Martha Reeves and The Vandellas, Marvin Gaye, The Temptations, The Four Tops, The Jackson 5 and Lionel Richie and The Commodores.

The initiative for the establishment of the Jobete was that the then struggling songwriter, Berry Gordy was forced to split his royalties with the publisher, on top of that, many of the records (and the way they were produced) he didn't particularly like. Therefore, with advice from Smokey Robinson, Berry Gordy formed both his own Record label and publishing company.

The first Jobete song was Herman Griffin's "I Need You," produced by Berry Gordy, released on the HOB label (HOB stands for House of Beauty), the name of a beauty parlour in Detroit whose owner established the label based on profits from the business. The beauty parlour was where Berry Gordy's second wife Raynoma Gordy had her treatment.

The first song published by Jobete Motown Publishing Company.

Over the years Jobete would hold the rights to all the classic Motown songs of the Detroit era, in the 1960's and early 1970's Jobete did partner some of the Motown artists who produced their own recordings, including "Stone Agate Music", Stone Diamond Music Corporation, Black Bull Music. This part of Berry Gordy's Motown business has proved an invaluable asset over the years, and generated massive income, firstly when wholly owned by Berry Gordy, and subsequently when sold in parts to EMI. In July 1997 EMI Group plc acquired a 50 per cent equity interest in "Jobete Music" and its associated companies for approximately $132 million. The assets held consisted of 15,000 music copyrights. After increasing its share from 50 per cent to 80 per cent, in March 2004 EMI Group PLC finally completed the acquisition of Jobete songs by increasing its shareholding from 80 percent to 100 percent, the price was approximately $80 million. With this, Berry Gordy was able to get $300 million for the Jobete music catalogue sale in total.

Berry Gordy remained active in the development and creative direction of Jobete Music for a period, working on several projects relating to the development of the catalogue. Berry Gordy was involved with the production of "Ain't No Mountain High Enough", the working title of a Broadway musical play for which Berry Gordy is writing the book. Berry Gordy is also looking at a proposed major network television mini-series based on his autobiography, "To Be Loved: The Music, The Magic, The Memories of Motown".

Born on the 3rd November 1930 in Bastrop, Texas

Motown Connection: Was the first female signed by Berry Gordy to Motown's Tamla label - Singer - Background Singer.

Mable was born in Bastrop, Louisiana, but moved from the south to Detroit to find employment. After graduating from Pershing High School. The family lived in the Dequindre projects across the street from the Stubbs family (Levi Stubbs going onto become lead singer with The Four Tops) Mabel's brother was Little Willie John. Mabel took a job as an insurance representative at a company run by Berry Gordy's mother, Bertha. Meeting Berry Gordy in 1959 Mabel began recording for Berry Gordy in that same year. Mable John was the first woman to record on Berry Gordy's Tamla label, which later merged with Motown. One of Mabel's first performances was to open for Billie Holiday.

Mabel released her first single, "Who Wouldn't Love a Man Like That," on the Tamla Label,

Early publicity shot and record label.

but with no success. Mabel followed with "No Love" and then with "Actions Speak Louder Than Words" the following year. Motown eventually found Mabel's niche at Motown, promoting her as a R&B singer (using a smoother production, rather than a more gritty blues style), even after Berry Gordy started to move away from this type of production by letting go many of his early blues artists, Berry Gordy decided to keep Mabel on the next year as a background singer but did not renew her contract in 1962.

After leaving Motown, Mabel spent several years as a Raelette, backing many Ray Charles hits. In 1966 Mabel started her solo career again, signing with Stax Records. Mabel's first single with the Stax was, "Your Good Thing is About to End" which became a soul classic as a result of its lyrics and Mabel's emotional performance. The song peaked at No6 on the R&B charts, and even managed to be a minor hit on the main charts. Mabel released six more singles for the label, none of which were a commercial success, as her first singles had been.

Leaving Stax Records in 1968, Mabel rejoined The Raelettes for several years, again with limited success. Mabel left mainstream music in 1973, and began managing Christian gospel acts, occasionally returning to the studio as a singer. Mabel was well known for her performances and song writing skills, particularly with Ray Charles becoming director of The Raelettes. At the same time Mable organised her own business, Fourth House Music, a publishing company and talent management agency.

During her long career, Mable has performed with some of the greats of the business, people like the late Billie Holiday, B.B. King, Bill Doggett, and David Newman. Mabel was inducted into the Rhythm and Blues Hall of Fame in 1994.

Mabel splits her time between Los Angeles and Detroit, where her family is. Mabel maintains a home in Detroit. Mable married a minister, had four sons, of which three pre-deceased her within the past two years. Two of her sons, Joel and Limuel, launched their own show business careers, while also serving as Executive Vice Presidents of Mabel's publishing companies.

Marv Johnson

Born Marv Earl Johnson on the 15th October 1938 in Detroit, Michigan - Died 16th May 1993 Columbia, South Carolina

Motown Connection: First artist for the Tamla label - Singer - "You've Got What It Takes" by Marv Johnson was the first Berry Gordy production to reach the Top 10.

Marv was born in Detroit, and was raised in a musical environment that mixed the gospel music of the Baptist church with the jazz of Louis Jordan and his group the Tympany Five. Marv graduated from Detroit's Cass Technical High School in 1957 and was a member of a group called the Serenaders that toured with carnival shows in Florida and the South, playing rhythm and blues in the summer's term. In the summer of 1957, Marv was involved in a serious car accident that put him out of circulation for about a year. In 1958, Marv recorded his first single, "My Baby-O" and "Once Upon a Time"; the recording session resulted in a meeting with songwriter and record producer Berry Gordy. Berry Gordy produced the record (with Sonny Woods co-producing) released on the Detroit based gospel label, Kudo Records, run by Robert West, who also operated Lupine Records, however the single failed to sell.

After this recording session, Marv played a song originally written by him "Come to Me" for Berry Gordy and his future wife Raynoma, on the strength of this Marv became the first artist for their record label, Tamla. The new label didn't have a distribution system outside of Detroit, so "Come to Me" (co-produced by Berry Gordy and Marv) was released nationally by United Artists, and rose to No6 on the R&B charts and No30 on the pop charts. On hearing the singer perform, Berry Gordy lost control of Marv when United Artists offered him a contract, but Berry Gordy did continue for a while as the singer's manager. His subsequent records were released on United Artists until 1965, while Marv was with United Artists, Berry Gordy wrote and produced his material, usually making the master recordings in Detroit.

Marv's second single was not a success, however his third single, in 1959 "You've Got What It Takes", the song was written by Berry Gordy, Gwen Gordy and Tyran Carlo (pseudonym for Billy Davis), and published by Jobete, it became a Top 10 hit earning Marv a gold record. Making it the first Berry Gordy production to reach pop's Top 10, it stayed in the chart for twenty-two weeks.

The 1960 follow-up "I Love the Way You Love" also was a Top 10. Other recordings included "You've Got To Move Two Mountains" was another Top 20, while "Happy Days" got to No7 on the R&B charts late in 1960. "Merry-Go-Round," issued in early 1961, was Marv's last significant chart success.

Although contracted to United Artists, Marv toured with Motown acts such as The Miracles, in addition he appeared on Alan Freed's "Rock 'n' Roll Revues" such as "American Bandstand", and was part of the early package tours and stage shows with his idols Sam Cooke and Jackie Wilson.

In 1965, with the British Invasion in full swing, Marv's contract with United Artists came to an end. Finally signing formally to record on the Gordy label (a subsidiary of Motown), he never enjoyed another American hit, although he earned a UK gold record with "I'll Pick a Rose for My Rose" for Tamla Motown in 1968. While at Motown Marv did a front-office job, also wrote songs with Tyrone Davis and Johnny Taylor. Marv's recording career really ended in the late 1960's, but Marv never stopped performing, and remained active on stage into the 1990's.

Marv did not move with Motown Records to Los Angeles from Detroit in 1972, and was sadly not included in the company's 25th anniversary show in 1983. Marv did become involved in Ian Levine's Motorcity records project in the late 1980's and early 1990's, and recorded some great material before his death from a heart attack.

Album Track: "I'll Pick a Rose for My Rose", Marv Johnson.

Uriel Jones

Aka Uriel 'Possum' Jones Born on the 13th June 1934 in Detroit, Michigan - Died 24th March 2009 in Dearborn, Michigan

Motown Connection: Drummer/member of The Funk Brothers (Motown In House Band).

Uriel was the drummer in The Funk Brothers formed in Detroit (under the name of The Joe Hunter Band), they performed at the Chit Chat club, the Twenty Grand, and the other venues that grew out of Detroit's booming nightlife scene of the late 1950's and early 1960's.

Uriel's association with Motown started when he toured with Marvin Gaye and at various live Motown performances in the early 1960's, with this success Uriel was offered session work at the "Hitsville Studio A" in Detroit in 1964, he became a lifelong friend of Earl Van Dyke. Originally Uriel was used as a replacement for Benny Benjamin (until his death in 1969). With Richard "Pistol" Allen he shared the role of lead drummer until the closure in 1972 of the studio.

A particular favourite of Motown arranger Paul Riser who thought Uriel was the "funkiest" of the three drummers in the studio. Uriel played the drums on some of the most successful Motown recordings such as "The Tracks of My Tears" by The Miracles and on Gladys Knight and The Pips recording "I Heard it Through the Grapevine." which would become one of Motown's most famous international hits when recorded by Marvin Gaye.

When Norman Whitfield moved the "Motown Sound" into "psychedelic soul", Uriel became an indispensable component of that sound. Also, in recordings with Ashford & Simpson, they used him on many of the Marvin Gaye Tammi Terrell duets, including "Ain't No Mountain High Enough".

The long awaited recognition of the contribution The Funk Brothers gave to the creation of the "Motown Sound" came with the documentary "Standing in the Shadows of Motown". The film, released in 2003, gave a new lease of life to Motown's session musicians, focusing on thirteen musicians, who were credited as being the core of the musician who collectively became known as "The Funk Brothers" going on to win two Grammy awards.

Uriel was the one of the last surviving drummers of the group, he passed away after suffering complications from a heart attack, and he was 74. Uriel is survived by his wife, June, and three children.

Signature sounds: listen to him on The Temptations' "Ain't Too Proud To Beg" and "Cloud Nine".

Born Edward James Kendrick aka Eddie "Cornbread" Kendricks on the 17th December 1939 in Union Springs, Alabama - Died on 5th October 1992 in Birmingham, Alabama

Motown Connection: Background Singer - Member of The Elgins (not to be confused with the Motown Group of the same name) - Member (and occasional lead vocalist) of The Temptations - Solo Artist - Eddie dropped the "s" from his stage name during the 1980's.

Eddie's family moved to Birmingham when he was a young child, where he met and began singing with his best friend Paul Williams (a future member of The Temptations) in their church choir in the late 1940's. In 1955, Eddie, Paul Williams, and friends Kel Osbourne and Willie Waller formed a doo-wop group called The Cavaliers, starting with performances around the Birmingham area. The group decided in 1957 to move (hopeful for better musical opportunities), to Cleveland Ohio, the group now included Eddie, Paul Williams, and Kel Osbourne with Willie Waller staying in Alabama. While in Cleveland, they arranged to be managed by Milton Jenkins, and when he moved to Detroit, Michigan, the group followed. With this move came a change of name for the group, The Cavaliers renamed themselves "The Primes". Under Milton Jenkins' management, The Primes started to create a name in the Detroit area, including forming a female spin-off group called "The Primettes" (later they would become the Motown artists The Supremes). His favourite food was cornbread, and as a result he was nicknamed "Cornbread" (or "Corn" for short).

In 1961, Kel Osbourne moved to California, and with this move the Primes disbanded after only a few years, Eddie and Paul Williams (Paul Williams would commit suicide in 1973 and this had a profound effect on Eddie) then joined a group called The Distants (which included Otis Williams as lead, Elbridge Bryant and Melvin Franklin), the new group took the name The Elgins, (not to be confused with the future Motown group of the same name), as The Elgins they signed to Motown, before changing the name to The Temptations and signed to Motown subsiduary, Miracle.

The Temptations began singing background for many of the Motown artists already signed to Motown, including early Mary Wells's recordings. Eddie sang lead vocals on the groups break though hit "The Way You Do the Things You Do" their first US Top 20 hit, followed by "I'll Be in Trouble", "Girl (Why You Wanna Make Me Blue)", "Get Ready", "Just My Imagination", and "Please Return Your

Love to Me", Eddie also shared lead vocals with notably David Ruffin on "You're My Everything". Without doubt the most successful Temptations' recording from this time was the Smokey Robinson (who wrote and produced their No1 hit) "My Girl".

The first phase of The Temptations career was guided by Smokey Robinson, who usually wrote and produced their material, next came the collaboration with Norman Whitfield and Barrett Strong who wrote and produced the psychedelic soul recordings where all five Temptations undertook lead vocals, with such recordings as the Grammy winner "Cloud Nine" and "I Can't Get Next to You". Eddie was responsible for creating most of the group's vocal arrangements, and also served as wardrobe manager, including the suits etc created to complement the "new" psychedelic soul sound.

It is suggested that Eddie was uncomfortable with the psychedelic style that Norman Whitfield and Barrett Strong were producing with the group, as opposed to the romantic ballads of Smokey Robinson. Also at this time, his friend and group member, Paul Williams was often too ill to perform with the group, and Eddie often found himself at odds with other members of the group, Otis Williams and Melvin Franklin.

With this tension in the group Eddie began to develop his relationship with ex-Temptation David Ruffin, and started to consider leaving the group, but not before Eddie recorded one last single with The Temptations, the 1971's "Just My Imagination (Running Away with Me)". However, by the time the record was released Eddie left the group, signing instead a solo contract with Motown (recording on the Tamla Label), "Just My Imagination" was a No1 US hit in April 1971.

In 1972, Eddie released the album "People... Hold On" which became a New York Disco hit, included on the album was the eight minute take on "Girl, You Need A Change Of Mind". Eddie's collaboration with veteran Motown producer Frank Wilson, produced several pop hits, including "Boogie Down" a No2 US hit and "Keep On Truckin' (Part 1)", a No1 US hit, "Shoeshine Boy" a US No18 hit, and "He's a Friend" a minor US hit. Other noteworthy solo hits followed, including "Get The Cream Off The Top" and "Happy" in 1975 and "He's A Friend" in 1976, most of his solo albums were released on the Motown label.

Eddie left Motown in 1978, forced to sign away the rights to his royalties on any Temptations and solo material while at Motown, as part of the deal to leave. After Motown, Eddie signed firstly with Arista Records, recording "Ain't No Smoke Without Fire" and "The Best of Strangers Now" and "Something More" for "Arista" in 1979 and the 1980: "I Just Want To Be the One In Your Life", moving next to Atlantic Records recording the 1981: "Oh I Need Your Loving" single and "Love Keys" .

By the middle of the 1980's Eddie's solo career had stalled, and he was gradually losing his voice as a result of his chain smoking. Eddie and David Ruffin briefly re-joined The Temptations for a 1982 reunion tour an album. In 1985, Eddie became involved in the Hall and Oates live album "Live at The Apollo" recorded at New York City's Apollo Theatre featuring David Ruffin and Hall and Oates, next performing with the same individuals at the Live Aid concert in Philadelphia on the 13th July 1985 and also in 1985, at the MTV Video Music Awards in New York. Eddie did participate in the Artists United Against Apartheid's Sun City project in 1985 and recorded with David Ruffin. After these performances Hall and Oates credited Eddie and the rest of The Temptations as a major influence on their music. John Oates later wrote a minor hit single for David and Eddie Kendrick, but the relationship came to an end that year, allegedly due to Daryl Hall's objections to David's heavy drug use.

Recorded as a duo (with David Ruffin) for RCA in 1988 and in 1989, Eddie along with the original members of The Temptations was inducted into the Rock 'n' Roll Hall of Fame. After meeting at this ceremony Eddie along with David Ruffin and Denis Edwards started the project to record and tour under the name "Ruffin/Kendrick/Edwards. However, the project ended in 1991, when Eddie was diagnosed with lung cancer and David Ruffin had died of a drug overdose.

In late 1991, Eddie (now living in his native Birmingham), underwent surgery to have one of his lungs removed, Eddie continued to tour through the summer of 1992, but became ill again stopping his performing. Eddie died of lung cancer aged 52 in Birmingham. Eddie was survived by three children Parris Kendrick, Aika Kendrick and Paul Kendrick.

Born Clarence Maurice King in Renshaw, Mississippi (raised in Greenwood, Mississippi) - Died 23rd December 1992 in Detroit, Michigan

Motown Connection: Musical Director of Artist Development - Independent Musical Director.

Maurice was the youngest of six children, (raised in the heart of the Mississippi Delta). After he graduated from high school he moved to Nashville in the early 1930's to study music at Tennessee A&I State College (now Tennessee State University). While there he was given the job of assistant Music Director for the school's band Tennessee State Collegians. Maurice then joined a Works Progress Administration (WPA) concert band around 1940, with LeRoy

L to R: Maurice King, Billy Davis, Harvey Fuqua and Marvin Gaye.

Smith, (a pioneering black Detroit society bandleader) spending three years in the band, at the time Maurice was also working full time as a musician in Nashville. Maurice's future wife arrived in Detroit after her father got into a serious fight with a white man and, as a result, he and his family moved to Detroit and stayed with relatives.

In 1943 King became the Music Director of the International Sweethearts of Rhythm, one of several "girl" bands at the time. King composed their signature tune ("Galvanising"), wrote and arranged most of their music, guiding them through film appearances. In April 1950 King took charge of the band at the famous Flame Show Bar in Detroit and remained for eleven years. With artists like Billie Holiday (the first well known artist to perform), including T-Bone Walker, Wynonie Harris, Sarah Vaughan. Berry Gordy's sister Gwen owned the photo concession at the Flame. Gwen Gordy introduced Berry Gordy to the Flame Show Bar Manager, Al Green, who had Maurice and several other artists, like LaVern Baker, Johnny Ray and Jackie Wilson, signed to personal contracts. When Maurice left the Flame Show Bar in 1961, he was replaced with an organ trio led by Detroit saxophonist George Benson that included future Motown bandleader Earl Van Dyke, however within two years The Flame Show Bar closed.

Maurice's next role was the Music Director at the Fox Theatre, a position he held for six years. Interestingly, Elvis Presley (making his first Detroit appearance, in 1956) was among the many entertainers accompanied by the Fox orchestra when Maurice was employed there.

In 1963, Maurice was hired by Berry Gordy to work as Motown Record's Musical Director of Artist Development. Maurice had a reputation at Motown as a father figure, and Maurice spent more time with the Motown acts than with his family. Maurice's role was bringing a certain style and presentation skills to the artists, demanded by Berry Gordy to transform his stars into "superstars". Berry Gordy's vision was to have his stars perform at the best cabaret clubs in the US (and eventually internationally) with Cholly Atkins, Maxine Powell, and Harvey Fuqua among the employees hired by Berry Gordy, to fulfil this dream. Without doubt the Artist Development Department "put Motown on the map" with performers like, Gladys Knight and The Pips, Martha Reeves and The Vandellas, The Four Tops, The Supremes, as well many other Motown Stars, would all be grateful to Maurice for his support and guidance over their Motown years and beyond it in many cases.

Maurice left Motown as an employee in the 1970's, but continued to work with the company as an independent musical director. Maurice continued his association with Gladys Knight, and The Detroit Spinners who employed Maurice as their music director.

Maurice started to cut back on his activities during the 1980's, but kept in touch with music through his association with The Detroit Spinners, and Maurice did mentor the group "DC Drive", teaching them stage craft and offering music advice.

Maurice continued his music activities but the death of his wife Eddie Mae in 1988, hit Maurice hard and curtailed a lot of Maurice's activities. Maurice married Eddie Mae in 1933. Their children were Clarence King Jnr, followed by Evans Waller and Karen Diane, a fourth child, Gregory, died shortly after birth. Maurice married his long-time friend Nellie Foreman just a few months before his death in Detroit.

Gladys Knight

Born Gladys Maria Knight on the 28th May 1944 in Atlanta, Georgia

Motown Connection: Lead Singer Gladys Knight and The Pips.

Gladys was born into a musical family. Her parents were singers in the "Wings Over Jordan" gospel choir. She began singing gospel music at the Mount Moriah Baptist Church and had her first recital in 1948. Gladys then toured southern churches with the Morris Brown Choir of Atlanta, Georgia from 1950 through 1953, and she also performed in recitals at local churches and schools. By age seven, with her mother's encouragement, Gladys appeared on Ted Mack's "The Original Amateur Hour" in 1952, where she won the first prize of $2,000 for singing Nat King Cole's "Too Young". Gladys formed Gladys Knight and The Pips with her brother Merald and a couple of cousins.

In 1952 Gladys often entertained her family singing with ten-year-old brother Merald (known as "Bubba"), sister Brenda, and cousins William and Elenor Guest. Another cousin, James "Pip" Wood later suggested that they turn professional. It was James's nickname that produced "The Pips" as a stage name.

Their first major tour for "Gladys Knight and The Pips" was nationally with Jackie Wilson and Sam Cooke just before Gladys's thirteenth birthday. Making their recording debut on Brunswick in 1957 the recording did not chart or have any success. In 1960 Gladys married her high school sweetheart James Newman and after a miscarriage, Gladys decided to return to performing with The Pips. In 1960 the group recorded a version of Johnny Otis's "Every Beat of My Heart," on Vee-Jay it became their first R&B Top 20 hit in 1961, after scoring a second hit, "Letter Full of Tears", Gladys had a son, Jimmy III she retired for a short while, and The Pips toured on their own. Then in 1963 her daughter, Kenya was born, Gladys returned to recording with The Pips in order to support her family. Once reunited as a quartet, although the group signed a long-term deal with Fury Records, they then switched to the Maxx label in 1964 but without any recording successes.

Gladys (with The Pips) moved to Motown in 1966, Gladys Knight and The Pips developed into one of Motown's most soulful acts, although Gladys resisted being moulded into another "A La Ross" artist. They never quite scaled the commercial or artistic heights of fellow stars on the label including, Marvin Gaye, The Supremes and The Temptations. In their early Motown career Gladys Knight and The Pips toured as the opening act for Diana Ross and The Supremes.

While at Motown it was producer Norman Whitfield who provided most of the production and song writing support. Scoring big hits with "Friendship Train" and the original version of "I Heard It Through the Grapevine", "It Should Have Been Me" and "The End of Our Road," One of her best recording's was the ballad "If I Were Your Woman." In 1970, Gladys used her influence to help The Jackson 5 become Motown artists, It was Gladys (not Diana Ross as the PR people at Motown suggested) who wrote to Berry Gordy suggesting that he sign the group. Gladys's biggest Motown hit was "Neither One of Us" in 1973 which made No2.

Shortly afterwards, Gladys and The Pips left Motown for Buddah Records where the group suddenly became international stars in 1973 with their recording of "Midnight Train to Georgia" (their only No1), "I've Got to Use My Imagination" and "Best Thing That Ever Happened to Me." In 1974 the group performed on Curtis Mayfield's soundtrack for the film "Claudine", which included the hit single, "On and On". The following year, the title track of "I Feel A Song" was another No1 R&B hit. The group successfully continued with the recording of "The Way We Were/Try to Remember", which was included on their Second Anniversary album in 1975. During this same year, the group hosted their own American television series and, the following year, Gladys made her acting debut in "Pipedreams", for which the group recorded a soundtrack. The subject of this film involved love among the Alaskan oil pipelines employees.

The remainder of the 1970's was a difficult time for Gladys as a result of their attempt to switch labels to Columbia Records (from Buddah), also in the background were unsettled legal proceedings with Motown. Therefore, Gladys was not allowed to record with The Pips for three years (though they sang live). However, Gladys did record solo albums including, "Miss Gladys Knight" in 1978 for Buddah and "Gladys Knight" in 1979 on Columbia Records, while The Pips released two albums on the Casablanca label. An out of court settlement in 1980, resulted in a new contract with Columbia Records for Gladys Knight and The Pips. The group recorded "All About Love" the R&B hit, "Landlord" and "Touch" in 1981. During this period, it was rumoured that Gladys had a gambling addiction to the game baccarat, which Gladys overcame. In the early 1980's, Johnny Mathis invited Gladys to record two duets - "When A Child Is Born" (previously a hit for Johnny Mathis) and "The Lord's Prayer".

In November of 1982, the group performed with a variety of musicians at the first Jamaican World Music Festival in Montego Bay Jamaica. Gladys then recorded the Grammy award winning gold single "That's What Friends Are For" with Dionne Warwick, Stevie Wonder and Elton John in support of AIDS in 1986. The album "Visions" also produced a hit single, "Save the Overtime" In 1988, the title cut of the group's "Love Overboard" album became their biggest selling single in decades. This song earned them a Grammy award in early 1989 for the Best R&B

Performance, following this success Gladys Knight and The Pips decided to break up the group. In 1989 Gladys had her first hit as a solo artist in the UK with the top ten hit from the James Bond film theme song, "License to Kill".

Gladys then released an album in late 1991, "Good Woman", featuring guest stars Patti LaBelle and Dionne Warwick, with the recording, "Superwoman" performed by Gladys, Pattie LaBelle and Dion Warwick. Gladys recorded a successful duet with David Peaston entitled "Give Me A Chance". Gladys also contributed to writing several songs on the album, including the ballad, "Waiting on You".

By 1997 Gladys, along with Ron Winan opened "Chicken and Waffles", the Atlanta-based fast food restaurant chain. Jimmy Newman, Gladys's son and long-time manager, died in his sleep in 1996, Gladys's daughter Kenya became her manager after Newman's death, son Shanga-Ali Hankerson, is head of operations for "Chicken and Waffles". After her divorce from Les Brown in 1997, Gladys converted to the Mormon religion.

Gladys continues to perform on stage and record including the album "At Last" released in 2001. Now married to William McDowell, Gladys created and now directs the Mormon-themed choir "Saints Unified Voices", SUV has released a Grammy Award-winning CD titled "One Voice, in 2008, a duet between Gladys and Johnny Mathis was released on Mathis' album "A Night to Remember". In the spring of 2008, Gladys appeared alongside Chaka Khan, Patti Labelle and Diana Ross at the 'Divas with Heart' concert in aid of cardiac research, at New York's Radio City Hall, also in that year, Gladys, Jack Black, Robert Downey Jnr. and Ben Stiller performed on American Idol to raise money for charity.

Awards include, in 1986 Best Pop Performance by a Duo or Group with Vocal - "That's What Friends Are For" with Dionne Warwick, Elton John and Stevie Wonder. Gladys Knight and The Pips were inducted into the Georgia Music Hall of Fame in 1989 and into the Rock and Roll Hall of Fame in 1996 by Mariah Carey. In 1995, Gladys received the Whitney M. Young Award, and in 2001 Best Traditional R&B Vocal Album - "At Last" in 2004 Best Gospel Performance - "Heaven Help Us All" with Ray Charles 2005 Best Gospel Choir Or Chorus Album "One Voice" with The Saints Unified Voices. 1995 Gladys Knight was awarded a star on the Hollywood Walk of Fame in Los Angeles.

Gladys married in 1960 then divorced from James Newman, she married Barry Hankerson in 1974 but divorced in 1979, married Les Brown 1995 then divorced in 1997, and then married William McDowell in 2001, has three children, James (deceased), Kenya and Shanga-Ali.

Album Track: "If I Was A Woman", Knight Gladys and The Pips.

Born Fredrick Long on the 20th May 1940 in Birmingham, Alabama - Died 29th June 1969 in Detroit

Motown Connection: Singer - Songwriter - Producer.

Raised in Birmingham Alabama, Shorty's musical inspirations were Alvin "Shine" Robinson and W. C. Handy. Apart from being an early Motown singer, Shorty could play piano, organ, drums, guitar, trumpet, and harmonica, as a background performer Shorty provided hand claps to many Motown recording. While living in Birmingham Shorty worked as a DJ, toured with the Ink Spots, and performed at a local club called Old Stables. Shorty was only five feet tall (hence the nickname).

In 1959 Shorty moved to Detroit and caught the attention of Harvey Fuqua, recording two singles for Harvey Fuqua's Tri-Phi label, firstly "I'll Be Here" b/side "Bad Willie" which was released in 1962, but was not a chart success, the follow up "Too Smart" released later in the year suffered the same fate. With the sale of Tri-Phi records to Motown. Shorty became a Motown recording artist when all the stars contracts to Tri-Phi, transferred to that label.

Shorty was not known for recording what would be described as the normal Motown recording, Shorty relied on a more "funky" arrangement. His first release "Devil With the Blue Dress On" was a slow bluesy recording with a great solo guitar break, Shorty and William "Mickey" Stevenson wrote "Devil with the Blue Dress On" and although the producers thought they had a hit record for some reason it didn't chart. However, a cover version by Mitch Ryder from Detroit recorded the song at a much faster pace; it reached No4 in the charts.

Motown then released "Function At The Junction" written by Shorty and Eddie Holland everybody at Motown thought (again) that they had a million-seller, the recording was more soulful, had a great beat, and good lyrics, however it only made No97 position on the chart in 1966. His next offering the cover of the Big Boppers' "Chantilly Lace" received some airplay, but failed to impact on the charts. Shorty's next release "Night For Last" went to No75 on the charts, even though it was felt to be an inferior recording. Shorty's first big hit came in 1968 with "Here Comes the Judge" which at the time was a popular catch phrase, this recording went to No8 on the charts.

Motown released an excellent LP that included his hit recordings and some new recordings including "Don't Mess With My Weekends" and "Here Comes Fat

Albert." Omitted from the LP were the minor hits "It's a Crying Shame" and "Chantilly Lace". Also none of Shorty's Tri-Phi recordings were included. Motown released a second LP, the "Prime of Shorty Long" and like the first, highlighted the many talents of the singer. Motown allowed Shorty to produce himself; the only other Motown singer allowed to do this was Smokey Robinson.

Sadly, just when many thought Shorty was about to establish himself as a solo performer Shorty died in a boating accident with friend Oscar Williams in 1969 on the Detroit River.

Formed in Detroit in 1957 Aka The Del-Phis, The Vels, and Martha Reeves and The Vandellas formed 1957 in Detroit, Michigan

Original Members: Martha Reeves Born 18th July 1941 - Rosalind Ashford-Holmes Born 2nd September 1943 - Annette Beard-Helton Born 4th July 1943 - Gloria Williams Born 1942 Died 2000.

Later Additions: Betty Kelly Born 16th September 1944 - Lois Reeves Born 12th April 1948 - Sandra Tilley Born 6th May 1946 Died 9th September1981.

Motown Connection: Background Singers - Group.

Martha and the Vandellas

L to R: The classic line-up of Rosalind Ashford, Betty Kelly and Martha Reeves.

In 1957, Martha Reeves along with Rosalind Ashford, Gloria Williams and Annette Beard formed the group The Del-Phis named after Edward "Pops" Larkins. The Del-Phis performed initially at local venues but lasted only a short time until the group temporarily disbanded. In 1960, Martha Reeves and the other members of the group re-formed, but with Gloria Williams taking the lead singer role, they then signed with the Chess Records subsidiary, Checkmate, and recorded the single, "I'll Let You Know", in 1961. Under the name The Vels, they recorded (with Gloria Williams on lead vocals) "There He Is (At My Door)" while another Detroit singer, Sandra Mallett (a future member of Motown group The Elgins), recorded "Camel Walk"; (The Elgins would eventually record for Motown). After those two singles failed to chart, Gloria Williams left the group and the group disbanded.

Martha Reeves, while performing solo at Detroit's Twenty Grand club, was asked by Motown executive and staff songwriter/producer William "Mickey" Stevenson to come to the label to audition (Martha Reeves unexpectedly took the job of secretary at the label after showing up to audition on the wrong day). Around this time, Martha Reeves and her former The Vells, Rosealind Ashford and Annette Beard were recruited to perform background work for Marvin Gaye on his second album, "Stubborn Kinda Fellow". Gaye's first hit records "Stubborn Kind of Fellow", "Hitch Hike" and "Pride and Joy", prominently featured the girls. After

Mary Wells failed to make a recording session and with The Andantes out of town performing for another Motown act, Martha Reeves, Rosalind Ashford and Annette Beard were asked to record a demo recording, "I Have to Let Him Go". On hearing the demo Berry Gordy decided to sign the group, in September 1962, Martha chose the name Vandellas after a street her family grew up around and after idol Della Reese, herself a native of Detroit, so from then the group would be known as Martha and The Vandellas.

Following their signing to Motown, Martha and The Vandellas' second release, the first collaboration with Holland-Dozier-Holland, titled "Come and Get These Memories" became their first hit record. Their second recording was, "(Love is Like A) Heat Wave", which became an international hit for the group, reaching No4 on the charts and reaching No1 on the R&B singles chart for five weeks. It became their first million-seller and eventually won the group their only Grammy Award nomination for Best R&B Vocal Performance by a Duo or Group.

The group's success continued with their second Top 10 recording called "Quicksand" in 1963, again written and produced by Holland-Dozier-Holland. Annette Beard (who was pregnant with her first child) left the group in 1964, with Betty Kelly, (formerly of the Velvelettes), replacing her. The next two singles, "Live Wire" and "In My Lonely Room" were less successful, failing to reach the Top 40. However, their next single, "Dancing in the Street", rose up to No2 on the charts and was another massive international hit, reaching No21 on the UK chart in 1964. In 1969,

L to R: Rosalind Ashford, Betty Kelly and Martha Reeves.

"Dancing in the Street" was re-issued and reached No4 in the UK, making the song one of the all time favourite Motown single releases ever, the song became a million-seller. "Dancing in the Street" was covered by many artists, one of the most famous was the 1985 duet by David Bowie and Mick Jagger, The Vandellas' popularity gained them performances on The Ed Sullivan Show, The Mike Douglas Show, American Bandstand and Shindig! At this point in time Martha and The Vandellas became Motown's most successful artists.

By 1967, the Motown in house team of Holland-Dozier-Holland were in the process of leaving the label and this affected their recording output, also another important Motown connection for the group Martha Reeves' mentor William "Mickey"

Stevenson also left label abruptly. Even after these important supporters left. The Vandellas did find some success with the Richard Morris produced "Love Bug Leave My Heart Alone" and "Honey Chile" which did reach the lower part of the carts. In the summer of 1967, the group did perform with, The Supremes, The Temptations, The Four Tops and Marvin Gaye at the Copacabana live albums from The Four Tops and Marvin Gaye were issued, but a live album of their performance was never released.

From 1967, Berry Gordy started to focus much of his attention on Diana Ross's solo career and as a consequence The Vandellas' support started to go and their recording suffered as a result. Soon the makeup of the group started to change with Betty Kelly being the first to leave in 1967 (reportedly for missing shows and as well arguments with Martha Reeves) and was replaced by Martha Reeve's sister Lois. The group's name was officially changed to Martha Reeves and The Vandellas; Martha Reeves suffered a nervous breakdown in the late 1960's and for a short time needed medical help to overcome this problem. The breakdown led to a brief disbanding of the group and at this time Rosalind Ashford departed from the group later becoming a nurse. During this time, The Vandellas recorded "(We've Got) Honey Love", "Sweet Darlin'" and "Taking My Love and Leaving Me" were issued in Martha Reeves absence.

With Martha Reeves returning to the group in the early 1970's, Rosalind Ashford was replaced by another former member of The Velvelettes, Sandra Tilley, and the group continued to release albums and singles into the early 1970's, although the releases did not hit the heights achieved in their early years at Motown, they did have a minor hit with "I Can't Dance to That Music You're Playing", (with Syreeta Wright singing the chorus). In 1970, the group issued Motown's first recognised protest song, "I Should Be Proud", which was a modest hit on the R&B charts.

In 1971, the group scored a minor international hit with "Bless You" (produced by The Jackson 5's producers The Corporation). The song was a minor hit, although it turned out to be the highest placed chart record of the 1970's for Martha Reeves and The Vandellas, "Bless You" was their first UK Top 40 hit since "Forget Me Not". Two further releases which became successive Top 40 R&B hits, were the ballad "In and "Out of My Life" and the Marvin Gaye cover, "Tear It On Down", with these issue's the group's career at Motown came to an end, they performed a farewell concert, at Detroit's Cobo Hall on 21st December, 1972.

Sandra Tilley retired from show business in the late 1970's, dying of a brain aneurysm in 1981 at the age of thirty-six. In 1978, Martha Reeves and original members Rosalind Ashford and Annette Beard-Sterling reunited at a Los Angeles benefit concert for actor Will Geer. In 1983, Martha Reeves successfully sued for royalties from her Motown hits and the label agreed to have the songs credited as Martha Reeves and The Vandellas from then on.

In 1989, original members Rosalind Ashford and Annette Beard also sued Motown for royalties; this brought the original members together to re-form the group, both as a recording act and in performances. They recorded with Ian Levine's Motorcity, issuing the group's first single for seventeen years called "Step Into My Shoes". While Rosalind Ashford, (now Rosalind Ashford Holmes), and Annette Beard (now Annette Beard-Helton), continue to perform with other singers, Martha Reeves sings with her sisters Lois and Delphine performing as Martha Reeves of Martha Reeves and The Vandellas.

L to R: Rosalind Ashford, Betty Kelly and Martha Reeves.

In 1993, the group were awarded the "Pioneer Award" at the Rhythm and Blues Foundation. Except for pre-Vandellas member Gloria Williamson, all members of the group were inducted to the Rock and Roll Hall of Fame in 1995, becoming just the second all-female group to be inducted. They were inducted to the "Vocal Group" Hall of Fame in 2003. Two of their singles, "(Love Is Like A) Heat Wave" and "Dancing in the Street" were included in the list of The Rock and Roll Hall of Fame's 500 Songs that Shaped Rock and Roll. In 2004, Rolling Stone Magazine ranked the group No96 on their list of the 100 Greatest Artists of All Time.

Album Track: "(Love Is Like A) Heatwave", Martha Reeves and The Vandellas.

The Marvelettes

Formed in 1961 aka The Marvels Inkster, Michigan

Original Members: Wanda Young Rogers - Gladys Gorton Born - Katherine Anderson Shaffner.

Group has also consisted of Juanita Cowart Motley - Georgeanna Tillman - Gladys Horton - Georgia Dobbins - Ann Bogan.

Motown Connection: Group - First Motown Record to reach No1 - Background Singers.

The original members in an early publicity photograph.

The Marvelettes are the sixth most successful female recording act in the music industry (at the time of publishing). They were the first Motown group whose first record not only sold over one million records, but also went on to become a number No1 hit. In the early years of the group, all three had to leave the act at various times although Wanda Rogers and Gladys Horton continued to make frequent "guest appearances". While at Motown The Marvelettes helped Berry Gordy move the "Motown Sound" from a more blues based recording sound to the crossover recording which would appeal to both the Black and White buying public.

Gladys Horton and Georgia Dobbins formed The Casinyets in their hometown, Inkster, Michigan, with backing vocalists from Georgeanna Tillman, Wyanetta (aka "Juanita") Cowart, and Katherine Anderson. In 1961 as a quintet, called The Marvels, they entered the Inkster High School talent show, resulting in an audition for Motown. The audition in April 1961 was to Motown executives Brian Holland and Robert Bateman, with the girls alternating lead parts. They then auditioned for Berry Gordy and Smokey Robinson, with "He's Gone" and "I Met Him On A Sunday". But Berry Gordy was more interested in whether the group had any original material.

With this request in mind Georgia Tillman, asked pianist William Garrett if he had any songs, He showed her a blues song called "Please Mr. Postman" that had only a few lyrics and no music. William Garrett agreed to Georgia Dobbins rewriting the song, as long as he was given song writing credit. Georgia, who had no previous song writing experience, reconstructed the song, keeping only the title. The recording became (credited to Georgia Dobbins and William Garrett) the Marvelettes' first Motown single and their greatest hit, called "Please Mr. Postman". Berry Gordy then renamed them The Marvelettes and "Please Mr. Postman" was released on the Tamla label (a subsidiary of Motown Records) in the summer of

1961. Soon after the release of the single Georgia Dobbins left the group to be replaced by Wanda Young, the reason given at the time for Georgia Dobbins' departure was her father (a religious man) who was against the idea of his daughter singing in night clubs.

The Marvelettes' next song "Twistin' Postman" had a heavily accented blues beat. It would ultimately reach number thirty-four pop and number thirteen R&B. The group was becoming popular on tour, but underlying tensions and internal competition were taking their toll. The Marvelettes' next record "Playboy" was a hit reaching No7 pop and No3 R&B.

Shortly after this recording was "Beechwood 4-5789" late 1962 which reached No17 on the pop chart and No7 R&B chart. In 1963 singles issued included "Strange I Know" and "Locking Up My Heart" again only minor hits. The Marvelettes then turned down a song in 1964 which would have been written and produced by Holland-Dozier-Holland, the song was called "Baby Love" and was instead given to The Supremes, which became the group's second number one record.

However, there was a turnaround in 1965, the group was having hits again with "Too Many Fish In the Sea", "I'll Keep Holding On" and "Don't Mess With Bill", written by Smokey Robinson and with Wanda Rogers on lead. Also in 1965 Wyanetta (aka "Juanita") Cowart left the group reportedly following a nervous breakdown. When Georgia Dobbins fell ill she also left the group, leaving the remaining members to continue as a trio. In 1967 The Marvelettes had three charts hits in a row beginning with "The Hunter Gets Captured by the Game", "When Your Young and in Love", and "My Baby Must Be a Magician" after this success Gladys Horton then left the group to get married and was replaced by Anne Bogan. Their run of hits came to an end with their last chart record in late 1968 with the recording of "Destination Anywhere", Wanda Young completed the group's recording commitments with an album, "The Return Of The Marvelettes", which saw her supported by session vocalists.

By 1969 the group disbanded, Motown did release four more singles up until 1971, the last issue for the group was "Breathtaking Guy". Then Georgia Tillman married Billy Gordon of the Contours, but sadly died of sickle cell anaemia in 1980, Wanda Young married Bobby Rogers of The Miracles, Katherine Anderson (who subsequently had a stroke) married Joe Schaffner, the road manager for The Temptations. Gladys Horton is single and lives in Los Angeles where she cares for her handicapped son.

In 1989 original members Wanda Rogers and Gladys Horton, with Echo Johnson and Jean McLain providing vocals, recorded for Ian Levine's Motorcity project, releasing "Holding On With Both Hands" and "Now" after these recordings, Jackie and Regina Holliman replaced Echo Johnson and Jean McLain.

The Marvelettes have been honoured by the Rock and Roll Hall of Fame, with commemorative collector postage stamps. In the UK "Please, Mr. Postman" is the only record in the last 25 years to reach number one for three different groups (The Beatles and The Carpenters).

Album Track: "Destination Anywhere", The Marvelettes.

Van McCoy

Born Van Allen Clinton McCoy on the 6th Jan 1940 in Washington DC - Died 6th July 1979 in Englewood Cliffs, New Jersey

Motown Connection: Writer - Producer - Arranger.

Van was the younger of two very talented brothers, his parents were active members of the Metropolitan Baptist Church, which in Van's early life developed his musical talents by singing and performing in the choir. Van attended the local public schools, and sang in the school choirs, Van at the time also performed at local events with his brother, Norman, Jnr. and learnt to play piano in the family home.

Van's musical career started with his brother Norman, Jnr. and a few high school friends who formed a group called "The Starlighters". Van became the lead singer, writer, and music director for the group. Van was also involved with another group called The Marylanders. The Starlighters first recording was the single, "The Birdland" on End Records, named after a popular dance of the late 1950's they recorded a total of three singles for End in 1959. The group appeared on stage in Washington, DC, Philadelphia and New York and were introduced to Vi Burnsides, of "Sweethearts of Rhythm" who took the group to many of their performances.

The group disbanded when members started to either be called into the army, or become married etc. After the group disbanded Van enrolled at Howard University, but only stayed two years before he moved to Philadelphia and then later to New York with the hope of making a career of the music business. Van had his own label, Rock 'N, but in 1960 Van became an A&R director at Scepter/Wand this lasted from 1961 to 1964. Florence Greenberg as a staff writer at Scepter Records hired him. Van also worked with Lieber and Stoller and David Kapralik, who hired Van as a composer for April Blackwood Music. Van wrote for many artists including, Chuck Jackson, The Shirelles, Jackie Wilson's international hit "I Get the Sweetest Feeling", and Ruby and the Romantics "When You're Young and in Love" which would become an international hit for The Marvelettes at Motown. Van produced sessions for The Shirelles, Gladys Knight, and the Drifters, add to this Vando and Share and Maxx labels which Van owned during the 1960's, working with such artists as Chris Bartley and the Ad-Libs.

Next Van started working with Columbia Records as a singer. The producer Mitch Miller, produced an album of ballads, called "Night Time is Lonely Time" by Van. He later created Van McCoy Productions in 1968, and formed Faith, Hope and Charity in the early 1970's before becoming a solo artist and signing with Avco.

"The Hustle" was a number one R&B and pop hit in 1975, as well as a gold single. McCoy also had a Top 10 R&B hit with "Change with the Times" that same year, also on Avco, Van continued on H&L and MCA through to 1976.

In the 1970's Van wrote the music for the TV classic, "Woman Called Moses", the story of Harriett Tubman. His next project was with Mae West, for the film "Sextette", Van was to write the theme song, and to make a cameo appearance in the film. The last eight years of his life were spent working in partnership with writer and producer, Charles Kipps, forming McCoy-Kipps Productions, forming his own orchestra, Soul City Symphony, and producing several albums on Faith, Hope and Charity. Then followed the Grammy nominated "Disco Baby" album and the Grammy winning, Gold single, "The Hustle". The Disco explosion of the mid-1970's brought international success and Van and "The Hustle" went into a world tour.

Van wrote for Aretha Franklin, Gladys Knight and The Pips, Roberta Flack, Vikki Carr, Tom Jones, Nina Simone, Jackie Wilson, Gloria Lynn, Brenda and the Tabulations, Nat Cole, Melba Moore, Stacey Lattisaw, David Ruffin, The Shirelles, Chris Bartley, Chris Jackson, before he died in 1979 at home of heart failure.

Born in Detroit, Michigan

Motown Connection: Producer - Engineer - Writer.

Born and raised in Detroit, before he started in the music industry, Clay was working for an insurance company; with a college student Clay submitted Spyder Turner's cover of "Stand By Me" as a demo to MGM Records. The demo consisted of Clay trying to imitate (using Spyder Turner) soul stars like Jackie Wilson, David Ruffin, Smokey Robinson, and Chuck Jackson. MGM issued the demo as a record, giving Spyder Turner a major chart hit in February 1967; this was followed by an album also released on MGM of the same name, "Stand By Me". The follow-up single, "I Can't Make It Anymore", was only a minor hit only reaching the lower end of the charts, released in the same year. Clay's next move was into music distribution as a promotions manager with Arc-Jay-Kay Distribution in Detroit.

Three years later, Clay was hired to work in Motown's quality control department; part of the role was to listen to every Motown recording to check if the recording met the stringent quality demanded by Motown, before it was released. After two years, Clay undertook the role of record producer, taking over from Norman Whitfield for a number of artists. However, the first artists Clay began working with was Gladys Knight and The Pips, and the first major production was with Pam Sawyer who had submitted a song to Clay called "If I Were Your Woman," Pam Sawyer and Gloria Jones had written the song and asked Clay to produce it on Gladys Knight and The Pips.

On hearing it Norman Whitfield urged Clay to produce the song, Norman Whitfield thought it had the feel of a No1 record, Gladys Knight rejected it but was pursued by Berry Gordy to complete the recording. The recording was issued on Motown's subsidiary Soul label, and as Norman Whitfield had predicted it went to No1 on the R&B in January 1971, became a Top 10 pop chart hit in February 1971 becoming a gold record for the group. An album, "If I Were Your Woman", was released April 1971 and included the excellent ballad "I Don't Want to Do Wrong" and covers of Sly and the Family Stone's "Everybody's a Star" and Joe Cocker's "Feelin' Alright".

Clay's next production and writing assignments for Motown, included The Miracles' "Nowhere to Go," (co-written with Gary Fears and Dennis Jackson) first album after Smokey Robinson left the group called "Renaissance" then Clay moved on to working with Kiki Dee on her 1971 Motown debut album "Great Expectations", the run of production success continued with, The Four Tops, The Spinners, The Supreme's and further recordings on Gladys Knight and The Pips. Clay also co-produced The Temptations' "Christmas Card" album; Undisputed Truth's "Girl You're Alright". Outside of Motown Clay also produced and wrote songs for folk rocker Paul Parrish's "Forest of My Mind" album.

Moving to LA with Motown when the label moved there, however, after Norman Whitfield left Motown, Clay also left to accept a position as the A&R director at Norman Whitfield's new label "Whitfield Records". Working with Norman Whitfield, Clay helped mix the movie soundtrack of the 1976 Universal Pictures release "Carwash". The sound track from "Carwash" was released as an album by MCA Records and went on to become a platinum record. The title track, recorded by the band Rose Royce, was a No1 R&B hit in December 1976, and a No1 pop hit in January 1977, two other singles were released "I Wanna Get Next to You" a Top 10 chart and R&B hit and "I'm Going Down" a Top 10 R&B hit. Spyder Turner was also involved with Rose Royce, writing the 1978 hit called "Do Your Dance" and an album, called "Music Web" released in January 1978, for Whitfield Records but distributed by Warner Brothers. Three other singles were issued by the group "Is It Love You're After", "I've Been Waitin'" and "Tomorrow's Only Yesterday". At this time when the group disbanded, Clay began working with his wife as a solo artist.

In May 1977, Clay started their own record production company called, "Love 'n Comfort Entertainment Corporation", and music publishing companies "Claka Music" and "Farrah Music". In June 1977, MCA released a solo production on Karen Pree, which was produced by Clay it included a cover of "Cry Me a River", Clay also in that year co-produced an album for Rick West on the MCA, later that same year, the group New Birth covered one of his songs, "Your Love Is in My Veins" this time on RCA, the album "Reincarnation", involved Clay working with ex-Motown colleague Frank Wilson.

Clay is currently Executive Director of Mytown Records, Claka Music Publishing and Love n' Comfort Entertainment Corp, Clay married Karen Pree of The Pree Sisters.

Barbara McNair

Born on the 4th March 1934 Chicago, Illinois (Raised in Racine, Wisconsin) - Died 4th February 2007 in Los Angeles, California

Motown Connection: Singer - Actress - TV Performer.

Born in Chicago, but raised in Racine Wisconsin, her parents were Horace and Claudia McNair, and Barbara had four brothers, and sisters Horace, Sam, Juanita, and Jacqueline. Barbara began her singing career while still at school, after spending a year at UCLA Barbara moved to New York with a view to developing her career further. Barbara's first job was as a secretary giving her a steady income, while pursuing her show business career, by auditioning at as many night clubs as she could. Barbara's first break came when Max Gordon of "The Village Vanguard" club offered a week of appearance's on "The Arthur Godfrey Talent Scout Show".

Then followed a performance at "The Purple Onion" in New York, and this convinced Barbara to leave her secretarial job and concentrate on her show business career. Barbara then came to the attention of columnist Walter Winchell who saw her perform in Las Vegas and started "pushing" Barbara in his column, with this exposure came a record contract with Coral Records. Barbara's first movie role was a small part as a singer in the Henry Fonda film, "Spencer's Mountain" in 1963.

In 1965 Berry Gordy wanted to add to the roster of stars at Motown with an artist who had a "middle of the road" appeal in terms of record sales and some Hollywood sophistication. Placing Barbara on the Motown labels, interestingly Berry Gordy also signed Tony Martin and Billy Eckstine at the same time. Barbara produced some great recordings, but Berry Gordy refused to release some of the recordings including "Baby A Go-Go" and an album of Smokey Robinson songs. However, Barbara did release two great albums, "Here I Am" in 1966 and "The Real Barbara McNair" in 1969, Barbara recorded many tracks, but Motown seemed reluctant to release these recordings (although many have now appeared on albums like "The Cellar Full Of Motown" series).

Although Barbara did not have the commercial success Berry Gordy thought would happen with Motown, many of Barbara's hits became part of the Northern Soul Scene in the UK. "You're Gonna Love My Baby" and "You Could Never Love Him" became some of the favourite singles played at venues specialising in this type of music. A double album of released and un-issued material, "The Ultimate Motown Collection" issued in 2003, highlighted the quality of her work in particular some of the un-released material. It was suggested that Motown could have marketed Barbara better taking into account her own TV show "The Barbara McNair Show" in 1969, with such guests as Johnny Mathis, B.B. King and Bob Hope. Barbara actually toured in Vietnam with Bob Hope, the series ran until 1971.

Barbara's next album featured the minor hit "It Happens Every Time", the final Motown recordings came in 1968, with the singles "Where Would I Be Without You" and "You Could Never Love Him" on the album. While at Motown, Barbara also recorded the original version of the song "For Once In My Life", that later became an international hit for Stevie Wonder. Barbara's nude appearance in the film "If He Hollers Let Him Go" in 1968 caused some controversy, featuring in a Playboy Magazine. Barbara also made a couple of TV appearances around this time, including "I Spy", "Hogan's Heroes" and "Mission: Impossible".

In 1969 Barbara played Sister Irene, one of three nuns (with Mary Tyler Moore and Jane Elliot), in "Change Of Habit", this was Elvis Presley's last film as an actor, in 1970, Barbara played one of her most memorable roles, as Valerie, the wife of Lt. Virgil Tibbs (Sidney Poitier) in "They Call Me Mister Tibbs" the follow-up to the classic "In The Heat Of The Night". Barbara played the role in this sequel, as well as in the third and final film, "The Organisation" in 1971.

In the 1970's Barbara performed with Nat King Cole, during his stage shows, "I'm With You" and "The Merry World Of Nat King Cole". Some of her other stage appearances included Richard Rogers' "No Strings", "Pyjama Game" with Hal Linden, and "Sophisticated Ladies", a Duke Ellington tribute.

In 1976, Barbara's husband, Rick Manzi, was murdered, and Mafia boss Jimmy "The Weasel" Frattiano later claimed in his book "The Last Mafioso" that Rick Manzi had been a Mafia associate. In 1984, she accepted a role on the daytime soap opera 'General Hospital'.

In the late Nineties, Barbara recorded for the Ian Levine Motorcity project, recording "Face To Face With Love" in 1990. This was followed by a few TV guest appearances, and her last film appearance was in the 1996's "Neon Signs". In recent years, she had been performing in night clubs and opening for Bob Newhart, also appeared in a touring tribute to Duke Ellington, called the "Sophisticated Ladies".

Barbara was married four times; her marriage to Charles Blecka lasted twenty years before Barbara died after a battle with throat cancer in February 2007.

Born on the 13th December 1928 in Detroit, Michigan

Motown Connection: Guitarist/member of The Funk Brothers (Motown In House Band).

Messina started playing jazz at Detroit nightclubs in addition to local TV and radio work. Joining Motown in the early 1960's Joe quickly settled into the in house band The Funk Brothers. Through Joe's contacts in the Detroit music scene Joe became highly sought after because of his skill in being a good sight-reader (he could read music notation quickly) and his steady hand while playing guitar rifts. He was often used when an arranger wanted someone to double James Jamerson's bass lines, as on Marvin Gaye and Tammi Terrell's "Your Precious Love" issued in late 1967.

Joe was a key member of The Funk Brothers, the Motown's in house studio band. The group also included fellow guitarist Robert White and Eddie Willis and this combination produced the background to most of the recording coming out of "Hitsville Studio A", nicknamed the "white brother with soul".

Joe started playing guitar in his early teens, before Motown (in his mid-twenties), Joe was playing in the ABC Television studio band, accompanying guests that included Sonny Stitt, Charlie Parker, Stan Getz, Jack Teagarden, Lee Konitz, Jimmy Giuffre, Pepper Adams, Donald Byrd, Eddie (LockJaw) Davis, Frank Rosolino and Dizzy Gillespie, among others. While at ABC, he played on the nationally televised Soupy Sales Show alongside notable guests such as Miles Davis and Charlie Parker.

In 1958 Berry Gordy recruited Joe to Motown to record for his new venture, with fellow studio musicians (who would eventually be known as The Funk Brothers) Joe worked on all the major releases. During his time at Motown, Joe would work with performers such as Diana Ross and The Supremes, The Temptations, Marvin Gaye, The Four Tops, Stevie Wonder, and Smokey Robinson and The Miracles. Among Joe's most notable performances are hits including, "Dancing in the Street" by Martha and The Vandellas in 1964, "I Can't Help Myself (Sugar Pie, Honey Bunch)" by The Four Tops in 1965, and "Your Precious Love" by Marvin Gaye and Tammi Terrell 1967.

The guitarist was also proficient on keeping time on the backbeat, (a key ingredient of the Motown Sound); Joe created many of his guitar rifts while bouncing ideas off

Robert White and Eddie Willis, when producers would ask the band to add the right groove to a song. This helped when recording with the members of The Detroit Symphony Orchestra, the band and everyone had to be "tight". In the early days of "Hitsville Studio A" everything was recorded live in one take; one mistake and the recording tape would have to be rewound and everyone would have to start all over again.

Motown Records relocated to Los Angeles, partly based on Berry Gordy's desire to become involved in the motion picture business and the era of The Funk Brothers (based on Hitsville Studio A) was coming to an end. A few years after Motown moved to Los Angeles; Joe retired from the music business and opened up a couple of businesses. Joe is featured in the classic book of "Standing In The Shadows Of Motown: The Life and Music Of Legendary Bassist James Jamerson" by Allan "Dr. Licks" Slutsky and the subsequent documentary.

Among Messina's influences are Charlie Parker, Les Paul, and George Barnes. In his early days, Messina played a Gibson L5 guitar, and later moved over to an early 1960's Fender Telecaster with a Jazzmaster neck strung with flatwound strings.

Messina is the creator of an alternative music technique known as The Interval Study Method, which uses the chromatic and diatonic scales to create music. He still resides in Detroit, where he performs as a jazz musician.

Signature songs: "Dancing in the Street" by Martha and The Vandellas in 1964 and "I Can't Help Myself (Sugar Pie, Honey Bunch)" by The Four Tops in 1965.

Ron Miller

Born Ronald Norman Miller in 1933 in Chicago, Illinois - Died 23rd July 2007 in Santa Monica, California

Motown Connection: Songwriter - Producer - Arranger.

Ron was born in Chicago and his talent for writing came via his first song about his baseball team, the Chicago Cubs. After serving in the marines, Ron's next job was selling washing machines in the day and performing in clubs by night. Next, was a job delivering pizzas where Ron met William "Mickey" Stevenson Motown's A&R

Director, at a Chicago Hotel. Ron explained about his writing skills convincing William "Mickey" Stevenson to offer him a position at Motown. Ron began the next day although his early efforts were not successful; Ron would go on to write numerous hits for Motown artists particularly with Stevie Wonder.

In 1966 Ron wrote the seasonal song for Stevie Wonder, called "Someday At Christmas", However, Ron's first major hit was "For Once in My Life" (co-written with Orlando Murden). On first presenting the song, many of the artists at Motown weren't interested. The song had been written to celebrate the birth of Ron's daughter and it was first recorded by The Temptations for their album "In a Mellow Mood" issued in 1967. Stevie Wonder then recorded it as a more up tempo tune, but Berry Gordy felt that it was too sophisticated for a Stevie Wonder release.

Then it was released by Jean DuShon as a single for a rival label, Chess Records. On hearing this version, the singer Carmen McRae recommended the song to her friend Tony Bennett, and his recording was the first to enter the pop charts. The breakthrough came when Stevie Wonder did his own up-tempo arrangement and Ron gained his first major success for Motown. Stevie Wonder's version was released in October 1968, prior to that, Jackie Wilson also released his version of the song. Stevie Wonder's version would be the chart success, with Tony Bennett making No91 on the charts, Jackie Wilson made No70, but Stevie Wonder had a No2 hit. Stevie Wonder also had a No3 hit in the UK in January 1969. The song would become one of Motown's most covered songs and placed Ron on the map.

On the back of this success Ron wrote a number of songs for Stevie Wonder, including four hit singles, up until 1971 when Stevie Wonder decided to take control of his own recordings after his re-negotiation of his contract with Motown after his twenty first birthday. These hits included, "Yester-Me, Yester-You, Yesterday" in 1969 and "Heaven Help Us All" in 1970. Ron also wrote "Touch Me in the Morning" for Diana Ross in 1974, Ron's biggest success was the song by Charlene's called "I've Never Been to Me", which Ron wrote and produced. When first issued in 1977 it never reached the charts, but was re-issued in 1982 to become a massive international hit.

In 1973 Ron produced the musical "Cheery" based on the Marilyn Monroe film "Bus Stop" and it included "I've Never Been A Woman Before". One of the show's numbers was recorded by Barbara Streisand for her album "The Way We Were" the musical was not a success. Ron then worked on a musical based on the book "Daddy Goodness", starring Freda Payne in 1979; however, it closed before it reached Broadway.

Ron disappeared from the music scene in the 1980's and Died in July 2007 of cardiac arrest after a long battle with emphysema and cancer. Ron is survived by his wife Aurora Miller and two sons, four daughters; one daughter is singer Lisa Dawn Miller.

Album Track: "For Once In My Life", Stevie Wonder.

Formed in 1957 in Detroit, Michigan aka Smokey Robinson and The Miracles from 1967 to 1972

Original Members: Bobby Rogers - Claudette Rogers - Smokey Robinson - Ronnie White - Pete Moore - Marv Tarplin (guitarist in original pictures-not a member of the singing group).

Other Members: (pre-Miracles and post Smokey Robinson departure) Clarence Dawson - James Grice - Emerson "Sonny" Rogers - Donald Griffin - Billy Griffin - Dave Finley - Sidney Justin -Tee Turner - Mark Scott.

Motown Connection: First Motown group (aka The Matadors) from 1957 to 1972.

The Miracles began with two young Detroit students, William "Smokey" Robinson and Ronald White, who had become friends and started singing together while in school. Smokey Robinson, nicknamed "Smokey" because of his love of cowboy movies, started a doo-wop group called The Five Chimes in 1955 at Northern High School with Smokey Robinson as lead singer, Ronnie White vocal's, bass singer Pete Moore, a childhood friend who had known Smokey since he was aged eleven years old, Clarence Dawson, and James Grice. Within six months, Clarence Dawson and James Grice had been replaced by cousins Emerson and Bobby Rogers, and the group's name had been changed to The Matadors. Emerson Rogers was drafted into the army in 1956, to be replaced by his sister Claudette Rogers, (who would later marry Smokey Robinson.

The Chimes (1954). L to R: Clarence Dawson, Pete Moore, Ron White, Smokey Robinson and James Grice (in the front).

In 1958 Marv Tarplin was the band director of The Primettes (Diana Ross, Mary Wilson, Florence Ballard and Barbara Martin); Smokey asked the girls if he could use their guitar player on tour, in return he would set up an audition at Motown when he got back from touring. The girls agreed, and Tarplin has performed with Robinson ever since. The Primettes went on to become The Supremes.

In 1958, The Matadors auditioned for the manager of Jackie Wilson, Nat Tarnapol, who turned the group down because he felt their sound and four-man-one-woman line up were too similar to The Platters, a popular vocal group. On their way out the group met Berry Gordy, who at the time was Jackie Wilson's songwriters, Berry Gordy eventually became the group's manager.

Berry Gordy and his colleague Billy Davis had written a song called "Got a Job" as an answer song to "Get A Job", a recent hit by The Silhouettes. The Matadors recorded the single, written and produced by Berry Gordy and Billy Davis, Berry Gordy then arranged a distribution deal with End Records. At this time, they changed their name to The Miracles, Berry Gordy and Smokey Robinson then wrote another Miracles single, "Bad Girl". This time issued on Chess Records, "Bad Girl" became the group's first national charting single, other early recordings included "Way Over There" another minor national "I Need A Change", "I Cry", "Whatever Makes You Happy", "Would I Love You", "Happy Landing" and "You Can Depend On Me".

Smokey Robinson and the Miracles

Signed Photograph. L to R, (back row): Pete Moore, Ronnie White, (front row): Bobby Rogers, Claudette Robinson and Smokey Robinson.

With the disappointment of the amount of royalties received from the record "Got A Job" (a cheque for just over $3.00) it was Smokey who suggested to Berry Gordy that he start a label of his own. Berry decided to take total control of his songs and production and in January 1959, Berry borrowed $800 from his family's loan fund to start his own record label, called Tamla; within a year of the company's conception another label was created in April of 1960 called Motown Record Company, with The Miracles as the label's first signed artist.

After three unsuccessful singles, The Miracles' fourth Tamla single, "Shop Around" became their first Motown hit. "Shop Around" was the first Motown song to reach No1 on the national R&B charts, and the first to sell over a million copies. In the light of this success, The Miracles became the first Motown act to perform on Dick Clark's "American Bandstand" in February 1961. "Shop Around" was followed by many more hits, including in 1962 "You Really Got a Hold on Me" in 1962, "What's So Good About Goodbye", "I'll Try Something New", next in 1963 came "Mickey's Monkey", "I Gotta Dance to Keep From Crying", by 1964 they released "I Like It Like That", followed in 1965 by "Going to a Go-Go", "My Girl Has Gone", "Ooo Baby Baby" and the first major international hit "The Tracks Of My Tears".

The group became the headline act for the "Motor Town Special", a nationwide concert show which showcased Motown artists. The concerts name was changed to the Motor Town Revue, and during the first Motor Town Revue tour, Smokey Robinson caught the Asian flu, requiring Claudette Robinson to take over his role as lead singer until he recovered.

In addition to writing their own material, Smokey Robinson, Ronnie White, Bobby Rogers, Marv Tarplin, and Pete Moore collaborated on other Motown artists, including songs for The Temptations "The Way You Do The Things You Do", "My Girl", "Since I Lost My Baby", "Get Ready", Mary Wells "My Guy", "The One Who Really Loves You", "Two Lovers", Marvin Gaye "I'll Be Doggone", "Ain't That Peculiar", The Marvelettes "Don't Mess With Bill", The Contours "First I Look at the Purse, and Brenda Holloway "When I'm Gone".

Despite their success, The Miracles had a number of personal changes during the early and mid-1960's, Pete Moore was drafted into the US Army and remained away for over a year. Smokey and Claudette Robinson tried for a family, but Claudette was to have several miscarriages and decided to retire from the touring in early 1964, Claudette did not tour with The Miracles or appear in any official group photographs or on television after this date, although she continued to sing backup with the group in the studio until 1972.

By 1967 the group's name was changed to Smokey Robinson and The Miracles, although they were billed as "The Miracles" on the 1967 recording of "The Love I Saw in You Was Just a Mirage", on the b/side was "Come Spy with Me"; which The Miracles sang as the original theme to the film of the same name. Also in 1967 they recorded a few more major hits such as "(Come 'Round Here) I'm The One You Need". The next run of hits started in 1967 with "I Second That Emotion", and "More Love".

Although The Miracles' career began fall away by the late 1960's, the group still continued to reach the lower parts of the chart, the hits included in 1968 "If You Can Want", and "Special Occasion", "Here I Go Again" was a Top 10 in 1969 and "Baby, Baby Don't Cry" also charted in that year. When their 1966 recording of "The Tears of a Clown" was released as a single in 1970, it became a No1 hit in both the U S and the UK. The single was spotted by an employee at Motown Record label headquarters in London and released on this recommendation. They had one more Top 20 hit in late 1971, "I Don't Blame You At All" before it was confirmed that Smokey Robinson would be leaving the group for a solo career.

With the surprise success of "The Tears of a Clown", Smokey decided to remain with The Miracles for a few more years. In 1972 Smokey did decide to leave the group, and The Miracles began a six-month farewell tour. On 16th July 1972,

Smokey and Claudette Robinson and the rest of the group gave their final performances as The Miracles in Washington DC, at this performance Smokey introduced the group's new lead singer, Billy Griffin. The group's final studio album with Smokey Robinson was "Flying High Together" in 1972. The single, "We've Come Too Far To End It Now", became their last Top 10 R&B hit. Billy Griffin's

L to R: Claudette Robinson, Bobby Rogers, Marv Tarplin, Ronnie White and Smokey Robinson.

arrival marked the departure of not only Smokey Robinson, but Claudette Robinson and Marv Tarplin as well. Marv's replacement was Billy Griffin's brother Donald, who became the new guitarist. However, there was no direct replacement for Claudette.

The group's first post-Smokey Robinson album was the 1973's album, "Renaissance". The Miracles continued, with three more Top 40 hits in 1973's "Do It Baby", and in 1976's No1 hit "Love Machine (Part 1)", which turned out to be the group's biggest hit, and the Top 10 R&B hit "Don't Cha Love It". However, from the mid-1970's the group's releases failed to chart and they left Motown in 1977, signing for Columbia Records, but again where their releases failed to make an impact on the charts.

In 1978, the group decided to dis-band, with Billy Griffin and Pete Moore retired from performing to concentrate on song writing. Billy Griffin would start to perform again later, enjoying a brief and successful solo career in the 1980's, scoring a hit with "Hold Me Tighter in the Rain" in 1982. Ronnie White and Bobby Rogers recruited new member Dave Finley. They reunited with Smokey Robinson on the "Motown 25: Yesterday, Today, Forever TV special in 1983, (minus Ronnie White, Ronnie did not participate in the 1983 television special, "Motown 25: Yesterday, Today, Forever", because at the time his first wife, Earlyn, who had been diagnosed with breast cancer several years earlier had recently died).

Motown organised a 35th anniversary performance for The Miracles in 1993, and Ronnie White and Bobby Rogers decided to reunite with the group. The two of them and Dave Finley recruited Sidney Justin (formerly of Shalamar) as the new fourth member, and began making personal appearances and touring. Ronnie White, the last founding member remaining in the group, died of leukaemia in 1995, and the other three members carried on as a trio for some time. In 1987, Smokey Robinson was inducted into the Rock and Roll Hall of Fame as a solo artist. The Miracles as a group were honoured with the national "Rhythm and Blues Foundation's Pioneer Award" in 1997, and inducted into the "Vocal Group Hall of Fame" in 2001.

A video retrospective of The Miracles' work, Smokey Robinson and The Miracles: The Definitive Performances was released on DVD by Motown Records and Universal Home Video in late 2006. It featured new interview footage with original Miracles Smokey Robinson, Pete Moore, and Bobby Rogers. In early 2007, "The Tracks of My Tears" became the fourth Miracles song to be inducted into the Grammy Hall of Fame. The other inducted songs are "Shop Around" (inducted 2006), "The Tears of a Clown" (inducted 2002), and "You've Really Got a Hold on Me" (inducted 1998).

Today, the Miracles are still performing with a line comprising of Bobby Rogers, along with Dave Finley, Tee Turner, and new lead singer Mark Scott, Claudette Robinson makes occasional appearances. On March 20, 2009 The Miracles were honoured with a star on the Hollywood Walk of Fame.

The group also influenced a significant number of performers who were not contracted to Motown, in particularly The Beatles, who covered The Miracles' "You Really Got a Hold on Me" on their second album, "With the Beatles". John Lennon stated that Smokey Robinson was one of his favourite writers, and said that The Miracles' "I've Been Good To You" was one of his favourite songs. Another Beatles song, "Ask Me Why", written by John Lennon, was influenced by The Miracles' hit "What's So Good About Goodbye". George Harrison also greatly admired Robinson and paid tribute to him in his 1976 song "Pure Smokey". Other artists to record either, Smokey Robinson or Miracle songs was The Rolling Stones who covered "Going to a Go-Go", The Hollies covered the 1963 recording of "Mickey's Monkey", The Who covered The Miracles' hit, "I Gotta Dance to Keep From Crying".

Still touring with the line up of Bobby Rogers, Mark Scott, Dave Finley and Tee Turner, with occasional appearances with Claudette Robinson, Pete Moore and Billy Griffin.

Born Alphonso Mizell on the 15th January 1943

Motown Connection: Songwriter and Record Producer as a member of The Corporation.

Fonzie and his brother Larry were born and raised in Harlem New York, and later moved to Englewood, New Jersey. At college, they formed a singing group known as The Vanlords, with the other member being John Butler. Some years later, Larry and Fonce both graduated from Howard University in Washington DC. Among their teachers was Dr. Donald Byrd, who recognised their talent and played an instrumental part in the development of their careers.

When Motown moved to Los Angeles, Fonzie was then recruited as songwriter, and record producer by Berry Gordy to work as a member of The Corporation, the hit making production team that wrote and produced all The Jackson 5's essential early hits, including "I Want You Back", "ABC", "The Love You Save", "Mama's Pearl", and "Maybe Tomorrow". The Corporation was Berry Gordy's answer to Holland-Dozier-Holland's departure from Motown. This group of individuals would not be easily recognised by the public (as H-D-H had been), but would fill the gap left by Holland-Dozier-Holland.

Larry worked with Donald Byrd on his Grammy nominated 'Black Byrd' album, which became the biggest-selling album in Blue Note history at the time. From then on, having moved to California, the brothers were working together, producing a string of fantastic records with their company, Sky High Productions. Most albums featured the same musicians, including Harvey Mason Sr. on drums, Chuck Rainey or James Jamerson on bass, Melvin "Wah Wah Watson" Ragin on guitar, Jerry Peters on piano and Stephanie Spruill on percussion.

Most of the releases were on either Blue Note, Fantasy or CTI, they include classic jazz-funk like Donald Byrd's "Street Lady" Bobbi Humphrey's "Blacks And Blues" and Johnny Hammond's "Gears", (a deep soul-funk and R&B), Gary Bartz's "The Shadow Do". LTD's "Love To The World" and Rance Allen's 'Say My Friend', were huge disco hits which also included A Taste Of Honey's "Boogie, Oogie, Oogie". Fonzie produced LTD (with lead vocals by Jeffrey Osborne) "Love Ballad" a No1 R&B, and No20 Pop charts record in late 1976. The record "Love To The World" in early 1977.

On most of the Sky High Productions records, the Mizell Brothers accompanied the artists (Byrd, Humphrey, Hammond and Bartz) on their own instruments. While Fonzie played clavinet and trumpet, Larry can be heard on piano and synth. In addition, Larry and Fonce often provide the backing vocals and vocal arrangements, which are a distinctive feature of many Sky High Productions recordings.

By the end of the decade and after some A&R work with Elektra, the Mizell Brothers disappeared from the scene. They kept writing songs occasionally, but became much less active than during the 1970's. Today, they still run their publishing company Alruby Music in Pasadena, California (named after their parents Alphonso and Ruby).

The Mizell Brothers' 1970's productions have become popular sampling objects for todays artists.

Formed in 1964 in Detroit, Michigan aka The Majestics

The first album release by The Monitors.

Original Members: Richard Street (later of The Temptations) - Sandra Fagin - John "Maurice" Fagin - Warren Harris.

Motown Connection: Group.

The Monitors played a small part in Motown, a minor act from the 1960's. The group, which consisted of lead singer Richard Street, Sandra Fagin, John "Maurice" Fagin, and Warren Harris, had only one minor hit, a cover of the Valadiers' "Greetings (This is Uncle Sam)", which reached number 21 on the R&B charts, "Greetings (This is Uncle Sam)" explores the feelings felt by many young African American men, as they were drafted into the army to serve in the Vietnam War. The Valadiers originally cut the groups biggest hit for Motown's Miracle label in 1961.

Their first release as The Majestics was to have been "Hello Love" on Motown's VIP label in 1964, but release was cancelled. A year later, "Say You" was released initially as The Majestics, but a name change to The Monitors was made after it was found there was another group already recording as The Majestics for another company. Recording the one major hit "Greeting (This Is Uncle Sam)" produced by William "Mickey" Stevenson who looked on them as more The Contours than The Temptations. Two more singles appeared on the VIP label "Since I Lost You Girl" in November 1966 and "Bring Back The Love" in January 1968. They were then switched to Motown's Soul label and released "Step by Step (Hand in Hand)" in the summer of 1968, but this was to be their final single with Motown.

Lead singer Richard Street had been with The Distants, which became The Temptations (without him), wrote the Contours hit "Can You Do It" before joining The Monitors.

Without any commercial success The Monitors' group members held other positions within Motown, Richard Street, worked in the Quality Control department, and later travelled as a stand in for Paul Williams of The Temptations who was becoming increasingly ill during the late 1960's and early 1970's due to his alcoholism. When Paul Williams left The Temptations because of these problems, Richard Street replaced him and the Monitors were then dissolved.

Pete Moore

Born Warren Moore on the 19th Nov 1939 in Detroit, Michigan

Motown Connection: A member of Motown group The Miracles (aka The Matadors) from 1956 until 1978 - Writer - Producer.

Born and raised in Detroit, Pete became a member of another vocal group while in high school in the mid 1950's. Pete then became a key member of one of Motown's first successful groups The Miracles from 1957, this group which included William "Smokey" Robinson, cousins Bobby Rogers and Emerson, Emerson would eventually be replaced by his sister Claudette Rogers (Smokey Robinson's future wife), later joined by guitarist Marv Tarplin in 1958. They auditioned for Jackie Wilson's manager Nat Tarnapol, but the group was unsuccessful, but the group did catch the attention of Jackie Wilson's songwriter Berry Gordy. Berry Gordy was at a Detroit talent show, when Berry was introduced to Smokey Robinson and the rest of The Miracles, on the back of this meeting Berry Gordy offered The Miracles a recording contact, The Miracles became Motown's first real recording group.

The Miracles were placed on the Tamla label, with their string of hits starting in 1960 the hits included "Going to a Go-Go", "I Second That Emotion", "(Come Round Here) I'm The One You Need" and "If You Can Want". In 1967, The Miracles changed the name to Smokey Robinson and The Miracles, and Smokey then started to contemplate a solo career at Motown, however, their 1969 recording "Baby Baby Don't Cry" became a Top 10 hit, and when their 1966 recording of "The Tears of a Clown" was released as a single in 1970, it became a No1 hit in both the US and the UK. The single was spotted by an employee at Motown Record label headquarters in London and released on this recommendation.

In 1972 Smokey did decide to leave the group, and The Miracles began a six-month farewell tour. On 16th July 1972, Smokey and Claudette Robinson and the rest of the group gave their final performances as The Miracles in Washington DC, at this performance Smokey introduced the group's new lead singer, Billy Griffin.

By 1978 Pete had left The Miracles and ventured into composing, writing the Pearl & Dean theme song, "Asteroid", and the platinum album from which it came, "City of Angels", as well as many other compositions. In addition to his role as singer and songwriter, Pete worked as a producer, and continued to work in Detroit even after The Miracles split. Among the stars he produced albums for, were Smokey Robinson, Marvin Gaye and Diana Ross and The Supremes. Pete then moved to being a record company owner in Detroit.

In 1983, The Miracles reunited with Smokey Robinson for Motown's 25th anniversary TV special. In late 2006, Pete re-united with original Miracles members Smokey Robinson and Pete Moore for the group's first - ever extended interview on the Motown DVD release, "Smokey Robinson and The Miracles: The Definitive Performances".

Sylvia Moy

Born in Detroit, Michigan

Motown Connection: Songwriter - Producer - First female record producer at the Motown,

Born and raised in Detroit Sylvia came from a family of nine, with her eight brothers and sisters, graduated from Detroit's Pershing High School and attended Highland Park Community College after not being accepted into Wayne State University's music school. With her brothers and sister they started performing, using pots and pans as instruments. At school Sylvia started to learn how to play jazz and classical music.

Motown discovered Sylvia in 1964 while she was singing in supper clubs in the Detroit/Windsor area. Sylvia worked for Motown from 1964 to 1970, writing between 150 and 200 songs. The artist Sylvia is most associated with, was Stevie Wonder, who recorded many of her songs in his early days at Motown. Sylvia was also the first female to have the title of "record producer" at Motown, but achieved her greatest success at Motown as a songwriter.

According to Berry Gordy's autobiography "To Be Loved" Sylvia was directly responsible for keeping Stevie Wonder at Motown. Berry Gordy wrote that, after Stevie's voice began to change as a result of puberty, he was going to drop him from the label. Sylvia, was convinced she could write a hit for Stevie Wonder, went to Berry who agreed with her. So was established a working relationship which produced a string of hits with Stevie Wonder sharing song writing credit's with her on, "Up Tight", "My Cherie Amour", "My Baby Loves Me", "I Was Made To Love Her" and "Nothing's Too Good For My Baby", all recorded by Stevie Wonder.

Other hit singles Sylvia wrote or produced for Motown include "This Old Heart of Mine (Is Weak for You)" by The Isley Brothers, and "Honey Chile" and "Love Bug Leave My Heart Alone" by Martha and The Vandellas and "It Takes Two" by Marvin Gaye and Kim Weston. Sylvia's writing has been recognised with many awards, and Sylvia received seventeen gold records for songs she wrote at Motown.

Sylvia went on to write the theme songs for many television shows like "Blossom", "The Wonder Years", and "Growing Pains". Sylvia was also involved with the theme music for the films, "It Takes Two", "Mr. Holland's Opus" and "Dead Presidents.

In 1972, she built her own studio and became an independent producer, which is used to help young people develop their own musical talents. Sylvia has had six Grammy nominations, 20 BMI awards, and a place in the National Songwriters "Hall of Fame". Sylvia co-founded the "Center for Creative Communications", also known as "Masterworks", which trains young adults in the field of telecommunications and media arts.

In the late 1980's and early 1990's Sylvia became involved in the Motorcity project organised by the UK producer Ian Levine, helping to produce many recordings of early Motown artists.

Album Track: "It Takes Two", Marvin Gaye and Kim Weston.

Frances Nero Born of African American and Cherokee Heritage on 13th March in Asheville, North Carolina

Motown Connection: First Female Artist on the Soul Label - Solo Artist.

At the age of three, Frances sang on a table top in the neighborhood "juke joint" and achieved money in a saucer, which awarded her first paid entertainment work. Frances attended Stephens-Lee High School in Asheville becoming a member of the Glee Club. Her love of music (influenced by Dinah Washington, Sarah Vaughn, Etta James and Doris Day) had her simultaneously singing with two high school bands as featured female vocalist with both The Tams and The Untils, the group included Stanley Baird, Bynum Griffin, who later worked with such artists as Chuck Jackson and James Brown.

Frances Nero with Joe Hunter, 1964 Chappy's Lounge.

In 1960, influenced by the music of "Little" Willie John and Marv Johnson (they later would became friends and toured Europe together) Frances moved to Detroit in the express hope of joining the Motown, at first Frances found it difficult to get an audition. She sang at local nightclubs.

In June 1965 after entering a "WCHB Talent Show" Frances came first out of 5,000 contestants singing her own rendition of The Shirelles "Everybody Love a Lover". Berry Gordy, founder of Motown Records, was a judge and co-sponsored the contest. Frances won $500.00, a dozen long stemmed roses and a one year recording contract with Motown. She became the first female artist on the Motown Soul Label, and her first release was played on "WCHB" radio every 1-1/2 hours for one month.

After three years, Frances not being promoted enough by Motown, asked to be released from her contract. Frances was not permitted to perform in local clubs due to contract stipulations by Motown, which did not allow her to work for any other promoter or label. Frances did appear on several local Detroit television programs and on the Canadian television programme, "Swinging Time" the recording of "Keep On Loving Me" was picked four days in a row by their panel of judges, but the eventual winner was a recording by Gary U.S. Bonds.

Frances next had to put her career on hold for several years while providing care for her mother, following her mother's passing, her son was involved in a car accident and was diagnosed with extensive brain damage in 1986.

In 1989 Frances became involved with Ian Levine Motorcity project, she agreed and recorded what the UK would call the "Anthem of the Nineties" the recording "Footsteps Following Me" became a massive hit in the UK, and also a favourite of mine, reaching No3 (behind Cher at No1 and Michael Bolton at No2). Frances appeared British television including "Top of the Pops" and "The Terry Wogan Show", and was competing with artists such as Madonna and Luther Vandross in the charts. Frances recorded a number of cover songs and wrote three of her own recordings, eventually becoming Motorcity's No1 UK recording artist. After recording constantly and receiving no royalties from Ian Levine Motorcity project, the relationship with Ian Levine came to an end and Frances decided to pursue other projects.

One of these ventures was establishing her own record label "AJA Records" named after her granddaughter Aja (pronounced "Asia"). She wrote, produced and provided the vocals for "Love Ride" and "It Ain't The Same Without You" on that label.

Frances next collaborated with Jeremiah Yisrael, a high school friend (former actor and stuntman) in producing a script entitled "Menegerie A-Fowl". The title was later changed to "Reject Island" and eventually became a film of the same name. Jeremiah Yisrael directed the movie and Frances created the costumes, wrote the soundtrack and appeared in a cameo role.

In March 2005, Frances was filmed performing at the Sands Hotel in Atlantic City with other former Motown artists, including Martha Reeves, Mary Wilson, The Velvelettes, The Contours, Brenda Holloway and Gladys Horton, members of The Andantes (Pat Lewis and Louvain Demps) for a PBS project managed by TJ Lubinsky which was for release in 2005.

In 2007, Frances completed a comedy film, called "The Passing of Ezra Hazlette", based around a ghetto funeral; Frances also wrote the script, the soundtrack, directed and starred in this film. She produced and performed on an album titled "Frances Nero salutes Dinah Washington - Queen of the Blues" in June 2007. Frances has completed the DVD which chronicles her life story in her own words, called "Mountains, Motown and Motion Pictures" which is now available.

Formed in 1966 in Detroit, Michigan

Members: Freddie Gorman - Walter Gaines (ex-Five Stars, ex-Voice Masters) - C.P. Spencer (aka Crathman Spencer, aka Spencher Craftman ex-Five Stars, ex-Voice Masters) - Henry "Hank" Dixon - Joe Stubbs (left in 1966 to join 100 Proof Aged in Soul) - Ty Hunter (ex-Voice Masters; replaced C.P. Spencer in 1975).

Motown Connection: Group - Backing singers - Writers.

Although the group didn't record on their own until 1966, members of the group had sung in "doo-wop" groups in the 1950's. C P Spencer and Walter Gaines had recorded together for Anna Records (owned by Anna Gordy, Berry Gordy's sister) as members of Anna Gordy's recording group, the Voice Masters;  this brought them into contact with both Berry Gordy and Harvey Fuqua (a future Motown Employee).

When Ric-Tic and Golden World were purchased by Motown, it included Freddie Gorman as a solo artist, along with Walter Gaines, C.P. Spencer and Henry Dixon Motown then formed the group The Originals. From 1965 to 1969, The Originals became the male vocal backing group for Motown artists like Marvin Gaye, Stevie Wonder, and Jimmy Ruffin. In 1966, Motown released their single "Goodnight Irene" b/side "Need Your Loving (Want You Back)" followed by (with vocalist Joe Stubbs singing lead vocals) "Need Your Loving (Want You Back)!".

The Originals found their biggest recording success with Marvin Gaye, who co-wrote (with his wife Anna) "Baby; I'm For Real" at last bringing them recognition at Motown as a group in their own right. The next year, Marvin Gaye co-wrote and produced the hit single "The Bells" which reached No12 on the pop charts. The group's first album was originally issued under the title, "Green Grow The Lilacs", but was reissued as "Baby; I'm For Real" on the back of the success of the single. The group released later that year two minor chart hits, "We Can Make It Baby" and "God Bless Whoever Sent You". The Originals' released two further single in 1971 and 1972, without any commercial success, called "Keep Me" and "I'm Someone Who Cares", both failed to chart. They tried to revive their careers in 1973 with the recordings, "Be My Love" and again in 1975 with "Good Lovin' Is Just a Dime Away" but without success.

When Motown relocated from Detroit to Los Angeles, the group followed and in 1976 teamed with Lamont Dozier for the album "Communique", this album topped the disco charts, producing the hit "Down to Love Town" (the first-ever 12" single released by Motown), the follow-up, "(Call on Your) Six Million Dollar Man," did not chart. The Originals disbanded in the 1970's, but did reform in 1975 with Ty Hunter replacing C.P. Spencer. They recorded an album of Lamont Dozier songs, "California Sunset", in 1975; Lamont Dozier was producing for ABC Records at the time.

While the group went on to have more modest success in the disco era in the late 1970's the songs they did with Marvin Gaye became their most memorable. Their two most famous songs have been covered by various artists including, in 1992 the R&B group "After 7" recorded "Baby; I'm For Real", while another 1990's R&B group Colour Me Badd re-recorded "The Bells" for one of their albums.

In 1978, they left Motown and released an album on Fantasy Records called, "Another Time, and Another Place". Their second album on Fantasy, "Come A Way With Me" was released in 1979 and featured the Originals as a quintet, with Freddie Gorman, Hank Dixon, Walter Gaines, Ty Hunter, and C.P. Spencer. Freddie Gorman returned to The Originals in 1978, three years later, their own version of "Please Mr. Postman" was featured on the album "Yesterday and Today" on the Phase II label.

Apart from a subsequent remake of "Baby I'm for Real", the group's recording career essentially ground to a halt by the mid-1980's, although they continued touring for years to follow. In 1997, Freddie also issued a solo album "It's All About My Love". The group also became involved with the UK producer Ian Levine Motorcity project in the late 1980's and early 1990's, the group made their UK live début in Manchester in 2002

Of the originals members Ty Hunter died in 1981, Joe Stubbs, (brother of Four Tops' lead Levi Stubbs) died on 5th February 1998, C.P. Spencer died on the 20th October 2004 and Freddie Gorman died on the 13th June 2006.

Album Track: "Baby; I'm for Real", The Originals.

Born Clarence Otto Pauling on the 19th March 1928 in Winston-Salem, South Carolina - Died 6th May 1995 in Los Angeles, California

Motown Connection: Producer - Writer - Stevie Wonders Mentor.

During the 1950's, Clarence sang with the gospel groups the Coleman Brothers and Wings Over Jordan. He served in the US army in the Korean War. When his tour of duty was over, he returned to the US and began recording secular songs for various record labels including, Federal, Roulette and Hannover.

At this time Clarence shortened his name to Clarence Paul to avoid confusion with his brother (who had also begun recording secular songs). Clarence with his brother Lowell Pauling, formed The Royal Sons which became the 5 Royales after Clarence left, the group recorded the No1 R&B hit, the double a/side "Baby Don't Do" and "Help Me Somebody" another No1 R&B hit "Crazy, Crazy, Crazy". Some of Clarence's releases from this time include, "I'm In Love Again", "Operation Breadbasket" credited to Clarence Paul and The Members on Chi Sound. Next, turning to song writing, Clarence co-wrote with Will S Jennings and Andrea Woods, and produced the single "I Need Your Lovin", in 1959 a minor hit for singer Roy Hamilton.

Relocating to Detroit in the early 1960's, Paul met a pre-Motown Stevie Wonder (still known as Steveland Morris), this developed into a close relationship, becoming almost like father and son. Clarence was responsible for teaching Stevie Wonder his vocal techniques. Clarence brought Stevie Wonder to the attention of Berry Gordy who signed Stevie Wonder to Motown subsidiary, Tamla Records in 1961.

Clarence was made a Motown staff producer and songwriter and assistant to Motown's A&R Director William "Mickey" Stevenson. They produced Stevie Wonder's first single at Motown, "Thank You (For Loving Me All The Way)" in November 1962. It wasn't until the live recording of the single in 1963, was release called "Fingertips-Pt.2 "(written by Clarence and Henry Cosby) that Stevie Wonder's talent was recognised. The song originally on his album, "The Jazz Soul Of Little Stevie Wonder" featured Stevie Wonder's harmonica playing, hit the No1 in the R&B charts and was a No1 pop hit in summer 1963. The follow up (another harmonica flavoured song) co written by Clarence called, "Work Out Stevie Work Out" was a minor R&B hit in late 1963. Other collaborations with Stevie Wonder included the hits are "Hey Love"(with Morris Broadnax) (covered by 1990's R&B

star R. Kelly), in the early 1967, "Travelling Man" with on the b/side "Wondering" (with Joey Di Benedetto).

Clarence worked with William "Mickey" Stevenson, co-producing and writing for Marvin Gaye on "HitchHike" then working with Marvin Gaye on the Mary Wells hit "What's The Matter With You Baby" b/side "Once Upon A Time" (with William "Mickey" Stevenson, Barney Ales and Dave Hamilton), in spring 1964. Next was Martha Reeves and The Vandellas, "You've Been In Love Too Long" (with Mickey Stevenson and Ivy Jo Hunter), the b/side of the hit, "Love (Makes Me Do Foolish Things)".

Stevie Wonder would often use non-Motown songs, particularly those of singer songwriter Bob Dylan. One good example was Bob Dylan's "Blowin in The Wind" Clarence collaborated with Stevie Wonder on the track with Clarence providing vocal riffs It went on to become a No9 Pop hit in late 1966, also in that year Stevie Wonder, Clarence and Morris Broadnax co wrote, "Just A Little Misunderstanding" a hit for The Contours.

In 1967 came their next co-production, "I'm Wondering", another pop hit. The next recording in that year was "Until You Come Back To Me (That's What I'm Going Do)" with Morris Broadnax joining Stevie Wonder and Clarence, however, this recording wasn't released until it was included on Stevie Wonder's 1976 greatest hits album. Aretha Franklin's version of the song became a gold record, reaching No1 on the R&B charts, No3 in the Pop Charts in early 1974. The song has also been covered by Johnny Mathis & Denise William's (on the album "That's What Friends Are For"). Clarence also helped Motown develop new talent including, singer songwriter Ronnie McNeir, helping him on his 1976 album, "Love's Comin' Down".

During the late 1970's, Clarence left Motown to become A&R director of William "Mickey" Stevenson's new label, Venture Records (a subsidiary of MGM records). William "Mickey" Stevenson was offered a reported million-dollar deal to assume control of the MGM Venture subsidiary. However, Clarence and Mickey Stephenson could not make a success of the label and Clarence disappeared from the music industry for a time.

Clarence did work with Motown again, helping compile, Marvin Gaye's "The Master 1961/1984 Lost and Found" and "Love Starved Heart" (Expanded Edition), in 1995 for The Temptations "The Temptations Anthology" and the "Ultimate Collection, Emperors of Soul", the "Early Classics, The Four Tops Anthology" their 16 No1 hits of the Early 1960's album and Smokey Robinson "The 35th Anniversary Box".

Clarence eventually retired to Las Vegas, California, and died after a short illness in Los Angeles with Stevie Wonder at his bedside, he was 67. Clarence was survived by his daughter Alexis, two other daughters and two boys, one child pre-deceased him his eldest son, Darryl.

Album Track: "Pretty Little Baby", Marvin Gaye.

Born in Detroit, Michigan - Died 31st December 1967 in Detroit, Michigan

Album cover from The Temptations release which included the single "I Wish It Would Rain" written by Roger Penzabene.

Motown Connection: Writer.

Roger was the childhood friend of Cornelius Grant, The Temptation's musical director, and through this connection Roger became involved with both Norman Whitfield and Barrett Strong. Roger is best known for the collaboration with Norman Whitfield and Barrett Strong on the hit single "I Wish It Would Rain" for The Temptations. Roger also wrote for many other Motown Artists including "The End of Our Road" by Gladys Knight and The Pips, and Marvin Gaye, other hits for The Temptations were "You're My Everything" and "I Could Never Love Another (After Loving You)", but it is "I Wish It Would Rain" for which he will always be remembered, released 21st December 1967, by The Temptations on the Gordy Label (a Motown subsidiary), the record was produced by Norman Whitfield.

The song was based on Roger's failing relationship with his wife, Roger had found out that his wife was having an affair, but could not bring himself to leave her, and his emotions are there for all too see on both, "I Wish It Would Rain" and "I Could Never Love Another". Rather than confront his wife Roger committed suicide on New Year's Eve 1967, a week after the release of "I Wish It Would Rain", another interesting fact about this recording was that "I Wish It Would Rain" was the first Motown release, to incorporate the use of sound effects.

Issued with the Melvin Franklin on lead vocals for The Temptations with the b/side "I Truly, Truly Believe" it reached No4 on the charts, and No1 on the R&B charts. The single was the main track on The Temptation's 1968 album "I Wish It Would Rain".

"I Wish It Would Rain" has been covered by a number of artists, including Gladys Knight and The Pips minor chart hit, a No15 R&B charts in late 1968, Marvin Gaye, Aretha Franklin, Little Caesar and The Faces, whose 1973 cover was a hit in the UK. The song was the b/side to Marvin's No1 hit, "Let's Get It On".

Freddie Perren

Born Frederick J Perry on the 15th May 1943 in Englewood, New Jersey - Died 16th December 2004 Chatsworth, California

Motown Connection: Member of The Corporation Production Team (a Motown In House Writing and Production Team).

Freddie lived in California from 1968, but grew up in Englewood, New Jersey. He graduated from Englewood's Dwight Morrow High School in 1961. He played in the school's marching band and orchestra, and sang in its choral ensemble, "The Chansoneers". He attended Howard University in Washington DC. After graduating in 1966 with a degree in music education, he taught in the district's high schools, played keyboards for Chubby Checker and served as Jerry Butler's road conductor.

Joining Motown Records Freddie became a member of "The Corporation," a song writing-producing quartet that also included Berry Gordy, Deke Richards and Fonce Mizell. The team wrote and produced The Jackson 5's early hits, including "I Want You Back", "ABC", "The Love You Save", "Mama's Pearl" and "Maybe Tomorrow". The Corporation was formed after the departure of Holland-Dozier-Holland. Berry Gordy was looking for individuals who would not be easily recognised by the public (as H-D-H had been), but would fill the gap left by Holland-Dozier-Holland.

In 1968, Freddie and a friend from Howard University, Fonce Mizell, moved to California and met Deke Richards, (who had already done some work for Motown). The three came up with a song, "I Wanna Be Free", which they thought would be good for Motown artists Gladys Knight, and The Pips or Diana Ross. Berry Gordy, suggested some lyrical revisions, and gave the reworked song, called "I Want You Back", to his new group, The Jackson 5.

The Corporation was formed, and it became the quintet's breakthrough hit, in 1969. The Corporation was also responsible for The Jackson 5's next two hits, "ABC" and "The Love You Save", and they produced Michael Jackson's first No1 single as a solo artist, "Ben". Freddie (as a solo producer) also produced G.C. Cameron "It's So Hard to Say Goodbye To Yesterday" from the film Cooley High, Freddie further extended his songwriting and production works to include hits for Gloria Gaynor "I Will Survive" and Peaches and Herb "Reunited". Freddie won a Grammy for "I Will Survive" (best disco recording) in 1980.

The Corporation didn't stay together long, and after leaving Motown, Perren was feeling a bit down about the music business, when an old college friend, Larkin Arnold, vice president of Capitol Records suggested that he work with The Sylvers, Freddie being familiar with the group from Memphis, (through their friend Jerry Butler). Freddie produced hits for the group on Pride Records, (a MGM Records subsidiary) including "Fool's Paradise" and "Wish That 1 Could Take You", in late 1972.

Freddie soon established himself as a leading figure in the funk/disco era, working on the soundtracks of the movies "Hell Up In Harlem" in 1973 and "Cooley High" in 1975. Freddie worked on hits like "Love Machine" by The Miracles in 1975, "Heaven Must Be Missing An Angel" by Tavares in 1976 and "If I Can't Have You" by Yvonne Elliman in 1978. Freddie won a Grammy in 1979 for producing two songs from the "Saturday Night Fever" soundtrack (album of the year) by the Bee Gees.

In 1977, Freddie produced a cover of Jesse Belvin's 1956 hit, "Goodnight My Love". In 1978 Freddie created his own production company MVP Productions. One of Freddie's first signings was his old friend from DC Herb Fame and his colleague Linda "Peaches" Greene, using Polydor Records to distribute any records released. Their first Polydor single, "Shake Your Groove Thing" went gold in late 1978. The soulful ballad, "Reunited" followed, at the time it was an unlikely follow-up to the disco-oriented "Shake". However, "Reunited" earned platinum status, (totally unexpected) going to the No1 spot (for 4 weeks on both the R&B and Pop charts) after its release in early 1979.

Other Freddie related releases on Polydor are "The Best of Peaches and Herb", Jerry Butler's 1994 "Valley Vue/Navarre" album, "Simply Beautiful" Gloria Gaynor's 1998 best of set, "I Will Survive: The Anthology", Tavares' greatest hits CD, "It Only Takes a Minute: A Lifetime with Tavares", "The Best of Michael Jackson" in 1990, the hip hop remix Blue Break Beats CDs on Donald Byrd and Bobbi Humphrey and Kenny Nolan's 1999 MCA LP, "Head To Toe".

It's no exaggeration to say that the 1970's wouldn't have been the same without him, as he contributed to some of the decade's signature songs, particularly in the dance field. "He was an up-tempo guy," said his widow, Christine. "He thought all the up-tempo songs should have the heartbeat of somebody who was dancing, and he always checked his rhythms to that."

His career faded along with the disco craze, although he remained active in the music industry throughout the 1980's, notably with the group New Edition.

He met Christine Yarian in 1967, and they married in 1970. She was a budding playwright, not a songwriter, when they met, but they ended up collaborating on many songs, including the frequently covered holiday tune, "Give Love On Christmas Day" and "It's So Hard To Say Goodbye To Yesterday", a No2 hit for Boyz II Men in 1991.

In the 1990's, he suffered a massive stroke and died 11 years later in 2004 at the age of 61 at home, his wife Christine survived him with his son, Derek, daughter, Amy, and sisters, Florence and Esther.

Maxine Powell

Born Maxine Blair on the 30th May 1924 in Texarcana, Texas

Motown Connection: Motown etiquette director in the artist's development division.

Maxine was born in Texarcana, but raised in Chicago, the daughter of Clarence and Gladys Blair, but at six months was raised by her aunt and uncle in their house. Maxine attended the John Robert Powers School in Chicago and eventually developed an entertainment career becoming an actress, a dramatic reader and later on, a professional dancer, also producing and directing debutante balls, parties and fashion shows.

By 1948, Maxine had moved to Detroit and within two years, had opened the "Maxine Powell Finishing and Modelling School" in the Ferry Centre, in Detroit. During the late 1940's Maxine joined the Zontas Business and Professional Organization, a black civic group dedicated to the desegregation of Detroit's theatres, ballrooms and other public venues.

Maxine came to know Berry Gordy through his sister, Gwen Gordy who was one of Maxine's students. Maxine first met Berry Gordy during the early 1950's, when she hired their family printing business to prepare programs for her annual Las Vegas-style fashion show. Since the early 1960's, Berry Gordy had sought Maxine's views on some of the young talent Berry Gordy was beginning to sign to Motown. Gwen Gordy convinced her brother that they should hire Powell to teach etiquette to the performers.

In 1964 Maxine was offered a position at Motown and closed her business to join the label. Firstly as a special company consultant, then to work full time in the Artist Development as Etiquette Director. Maxine, initially worked with the artists in one of the storefronts owned by the Gordy family at St. Antoine and Farnsworth, before moving to a house opposite "Hitsville USA" on West Grand Boulevard. Maxine's main role was to instruct the label's artists, many of whom came from Detroit's housing projects, on the fine points of stage presence and public speaking. The list of stars Maxine worked with would include almost all the Detroit era girl groups and solo artists including, The Marvelettes, Martha and The Vandellas, The Supremes, Tammi Terrell and Mary Wells.

Maxine taught the performers a new set of rules, never turn your back on the audience; don't hold the mike like you're going to swallow it. Maxine gave instructions on how to give interviews, how to conduct themselves in public, reminding them that their every move was being watched. Maxine would spend two hours a day with each performer, teaching them that they were being trained to perform in two places,

"The White House and Buckingham Palace". Although Motown employed Cholly Atkins for choreography, Maxine did work on dance technique. With Maurice King coaching on the art of singing and choreographer Cholly Atkins on the art of movement, the team was complemented with Maxine coaching on the art of grace. So was formed the nucleus of the Artist Development division.

Maxine prepared all the Motown artists to be able to perform at top class concerts around the US including, the Copacabana, Latin Casino, the Ed Sullivan Show, and concert halls throughout UK.

Maxine left Motown in 1968, four years before Berry Gordy moved Motown to Los Angeles. Artistic development continued, in Detroit and in Los Angeles. In 1971 she began teaching a course in personal development at Wayne Community College; the class featured Powell's own textbook Development and Professional Development. Maxine's most memorable tributes came in 1975, when Diana Ross introduced her to a Broadway audience as the "lady who taught me everything I know."

Since the 1980's Powell has been interviewed in a number of popular publications: People Magazine, Look and Time. She has also appeared on several television programs in the US, Canada and Europe. Since retiring in 1985, Maxine continued to teach, has undertaken occasional requests for interviews about working with the original Motown stars. Maxine is expected to complete writing her memoirs soon. Maxine recently had a tribute provided, (which drew hundreds) at the Roostertail in Detroit, which helped renew interest in her story and led to a People magazine article and producers calling from England and Australia for interviews.

There is little doubt that such recognition of Maxine's vital role in establishing Motown, not just as a record label, but as a major force in the entertainment business was in part due to Maxine's influence. Maxine influenced the lives and careers of most of the Motown stars from the Detroit era.

Barbara Randolph

Born 5th May 1942 in Detroit, Michigan - Died 15th July 2002 South Africa

Motown Connection: Singer - Married Eddie Singleton whose first wife had been Raynoma Gordy (Berry Gordy's second wife).

Born and raised in Detroit, Barbara's mother was the actress Lillian Randolph, Barbara was a member of The Platters in 1964 before she was signed to Motown as a recording artist working with the label during the mid-to-late 1960's. She never became a household name at Motown, and because of this never received the support to push her career.

Barbara was briefly considered as a possible replacement for "Supreme" Florence Ballard in 1967, but it was Diana Ross who wanted Jean Terrell instead. Barbara's biggest success at Motown was the recording by Holland-Dozier-Holland "I Got a Feeling" in 1968 regarded as a classic among Motown fans. Another minor hit was when she recorded her own version of Marvin Gaye's "Can I Get a Witness". Did duet with Marvin Gaye when Tammi Terrell became ill and toured briefly with Marvin Gaye until Tammi Terrell's death in 1970.

She left Motown in the early 1970's but did record for other labels, in the early 1980's she made a mini-comeback in UK performing at Northern Soul events. She married Eddie Singleton. Barbara and Eddie formed a production company which was not a commercial success, which led to their retirement from the music industry, although Barbara re-recorded "I Got A Feeling" for Ian Levine's Motorcity project in 1989. Eddie Singleton also became involved with the project and was a great supporter of Ian Levine at the time.

Barbara sadly died from cancer in 2002 in South Africa. Barbara's husband Eddie Singleton died about ten years after her.

Album Track: "I've Got A Feeling", Randolph Barbara.

Formed in Detroit 1958

Motown Connection: Backing Singers - Raynoma a member of the Rayber Voices would become Berry Gordy's second wife - Uses Ray (Raynoma) Ber (Berry Gordy) to form the name.

Members included: Robert Bateman - Gwendolyn Murray - Brian Holland - Raynoma Liles (aka Raynoma Gordy, Raynoma Gordy Singleton) - Sonny Sanders - Louvain Demps.

In 1958 two young teenagers auditioned for Berry Gordy, called Raynoma Liles and Alice Mayberry, Berry was not impressed with the two teenagers, but thought Raynoma Liles could help him with song writing duties and preparing cord sheets (Raynoma unusually had perfect pitch). Berry Gordy and Raynoma Liles then moved onto developing the "Rayber Music Writing Company" a combination of Rays and Berry Gordy's first name, the business idea was to charge budding artists who wanted to make a record using their facilities.

The first incarnation of the Rayber Voices was Raynoma Liles, Robert Bateman, Brian Holland and Sonny Sanders who would provide background vocals for the new clients. Advertising on a local radio station one of their first clients was Louvain Demps, closely followed by William "Mickey" Stephenson who was an ex-neighbour of Raynoma Liles. Louvain Demps would eventually sing as part of the Rayber Voices.

A selection of record labels.

When Berry Gordy founded Motown in 1959 the Rayber Voices became a "ready made" background singers. Used as a backing vocal group on early Motown records as well on other local Detroit labels, their first record credit was in 1958 backing Herman Griffin on Berry Gordy's production of "I Need You" on the House of Beauty label, but the first recording linked to Jobete Publishing.

Eventually, Jackie Hicks and Marlene Barrow (who had worked with Louvain Demps on occasions), joined Motown and in early 1962 they were put with Louvain Demps and Anne Bogan to form The Andantes. These singers became the main backing group at Motown. One of their first recordings was back up to Marvin Gaye on "Mr. Sandman".

A number of the members of the Rayber Voices would go on to playing significant roles at Motown these included, William "Mickey" Stephenson A&R Director, Raynoma Liles would become Berry Gordy's second wife, and help prepare all the early sessions (chord sheets, production etc), Robert Bateman would become an In House producer, Motown audio engineer, songwriter, Brian Holland would become part of the legendary writing production team Holland-Dozier-Holland.

Born Martha Rose Reeves on the 18th July 1941 in Eufaula, Alabama

Motown Connection: Lead of Martha Reeves and The Vandellas (aka Martha and The Vandellas, The Del-Phis, and The Vels) - Background Singer - Secretary to Mickey Stevenson A&R Director.

Martha Reeves was born to Elijah Joshua and Ruby Lee Gilmore Reeves, the third of eleven children, the Reeves family moved to Detroit, Michigan right after Martha's birth. Martha's grandfather was Elijah Reeves who was the minister at Detroit's Metropolitan Church. Martha attended the Northeastern High School, and Martha's first influence was Abraham Silver who became her vocal coach. Abraham Silver would also work with future Motown stars Florence Ballard and Mary Wilson (original members of The Supremes) and Bobby Rogers (of The Miracles).

In 1957, Martha along with Rosalind Ashford, Gloria Williams and Annette Beard formed the group The Del-Phis named after Edward "Pops" Larkin's. The Del-Phis performed initially at local venues but lasted only a short time until the group temporarily disbanded. Martha then performed with other groups including the Sabre-Ettes and The Fascinations. In 1960, Martha and the other members of the group re-formed, but with Gloria Williams taking the lead singer role, they then signed with the Chess Records subsidiary, Checkmate, and recorded the single, "I'll Let You Know", in 1961, however the song failed to make the charts.

Later on that year, Motown A&R director and songwriter William "Mickey" Stevenson was in the audience while Martha was performing at the Twenty Grand club in Detroit. Using the stage name Martha LaVaille, William "Mickey" Stevenson asked her to attend for audition for Motown. Attending the audition on the wrong day. William "Mickey" Stevenson asked Martha to look after his office while he was busy, and accidentally Martha found herself as his secretary.

When not working as William "Mickey" Stevenson's secretary, Martha recorded with the Del-Phis (also performing as the Vels), recording on Mel-O-Dy (a Motown subsidiary label). The first single was, "There He Is (At My Door)", with Gloria Williams taking lead vocals, which didn't chart. When Gloria Williams left the group in 1962, Martha took on the lead vocals, Martha and the group now consisting of Rosalind Ashford, and Annette Beard, provided background vocals for other Motown artists, particularly in Marvin Gaye's early career on, "Stubborn Kind of Fellow", "Hitch Hike" and "Pride and Joy".

After Mary Wells failed to make a recording session and with The Andantes out of town performing for another Motown act, Martha, Annette and Roz were asked to record a demo recording, "I Have to Let Him Go". On hearing the demo Berry Gordy decided to sign the group, in September 1962, Martha chose the name Vandellas after a street her family grew up around and after idol Della Reese, herself a native of Detroit, so from then the group would be known as Martha and The Vandellas.

Martha then became one of the first super stars of Motown moving from background singing to early hit recordings including, "Come and Get These Memories" and "(Love Is Like a) Heat Wave" often suggested as the first song to define the "Motown Sound". Their style hit a chord with the musicians The Funk Brothers, "Heat Wave" became the group's first million-seller. The hit singles continued with signature recordings including, "Quicksand", "In My Lonely Room", "Live Wire", "Nowhere to Run", "A Love Like Yours (Don't Come Knocking Everyday)", "I'm Ready for Love", "Jimmy Mack", "Honey Chile" and the group's most popular international single, "Dancing in the Street". In the 1960's one of Martha best known performances was with UK soul singer Dusty Springfield, on the UK show, "Ready, Steady, Go".

Martha's time at Motown produced some highs, producing some of the best recording ever, under the banner of the "Motown Sound", but also some lows, despite the success of the Martha and The Vandellas, Martha thought that Berry Gordy promoted The Supremes (particularly Diana Ross) more so than The Vandellas. A relentless recording and touring schedule led Martha to a drugs and alcohol addiction. Martha suffered a nervous breakdown in the late 1960's and for a short time needed medical help to overcome this problem. The breakdown led to a brief disbanding of the group and at this time Rosalind Ashford departed from the group.

After Martha recovered she re-formed the group by recruiting, Lois Reeves (her sister) and Sandra Tilley and this line-up continued until 1972, when the group disbanded again, shortly after issuing the "Black Magic" album. In 1973, Martha planned developing her solo career with Motown, but with the planned move to Los Angeles California Martha made the decision to stay in Detroit, and the glory days for Martha at Motown came to an end. Martha began negotiations to end her contract with Motown, so ending her twelve-years with the label.

With the move to Los Angeles California by Motown confirmed, Martha then signed for MCA Records in 1974, recording her debut solo effort, "Martha Reeves", produced by Richard Perry, featuring the singles, "Power of Love" and "Wild Night", the album was well received by the music industry, but failed to be a commercial success. Other recordings included her 1976 album "The Rest of My Life" and the 1978 album "We Meet Again". In 1970's, Martha also recorded on other labels including Arista and Fantasy, Martha was also successful in gaining an acting position in the movie "Fairytales". In 1977, with the help of good friend, David Pesnell, Martha ended her drug and alcohol addiction and became a born-again Baptist. Recording one more album in 1980, Martha cut back on her schedule concentrating on performing her old hits, with David Pesnell promoting her concerts. In 1983, Martha successfully sued Motown, for back royalties and in the same year, performed a solo spot singing "Heatwave" for the Motown 25 TV special.

Martha's next performance was in a Broadway production of "Ain't Misbehavin", followed by a reunion with the original members of The Vandellas (Martha, Annette Beard and Rosalind Ashford) in 1989, recording for the Ian Levine Motorcity Records issuing the single "Step Into My Shoes" and following the recording with a national tour. David Pesnell and Martha ended their business relationship in 1989. A factor also complicating the business relationship was that David Pesnell's wife, who was Martha's songwriter and producer found it difficult to work together.

In 1995, Martha Reeves and The Vandellas were inducted to the Rock and Roll Hall of Fame and eight years after that were inducted to the Vocal Group Hall of Fame in 2003. In 2004, Martha released her first album in 24 years, "Home to You"; with records she had written and produced herself except for a Billie Holiday cover and an updated version of her big hit, "Jimmy Mack". Martha was an early contributor to the music newspaper, Soul, for which she was honoured by the "Black Women in Publishing" organisation. She was also honoured for her best-selling 1995 autobiography.

Martha continued as a solo artist, and in addition performed as Martha Reeves and The Vandellas in the 1990's, which now consisted of Lois Reeves and a third sister, Delphine Reeves. In 2005, Martha was elected to the Detroit City Council; Martha was instrumental in getting West Grand Boulevard changed to "Berry Gordy Jnr. Boulevard" in 2007. Also a board member of AFTRA Detroit chapter. In 2007, she testified before Congress on behalf of musicians, session singers and recording artists for better wages and royalties. Martha was honoured for her hard work and courage by the delegates and members of AFTRA. Also in that year, Martha returned to the "Hitsville USA Motown Studio A" in Detroit to sing "(Love Is Like A) Heat Wave" with Australian group Human Nature for their "Get Ready" album.

Martha was the one consistent member of the group, staying throughout. All the group's original members Annette Beard and Rosalind Ashford were replaced over the years with, Betty Kelly, Sandra Tilley, Martha's sister Lois Reeves and Delphine Reeves. Martha has one child called Eric.

Born in Los Angeles in 1944

Motown Connection Member of "The Clan" Production Team (a Motown In House Writing and Production Team) - Member of "The Corporation" Production Team (a Motown In House Writing and Production Team) - Ran the Motown's West Coast office.

Deke's father was a screenwriter, and Deke expected he would follow his father into film, that was until he heard "Heartbreak Hotel" by Elvis Presley, this inspired him at 12 to start learning guitar and he wrote his first song "Bubblegum" at 14.

In the 1960's, Deke played in an R&B band, Deke and The Deacons (later The Four Sounds), they toured as backup for many artists, including Dobie Gray, but the band split up in 1965. Richards formed a new band, backing singer Debbie Dean, one of the first (and only) white artists on Motown. Deke wrote a song for Debbie Dean, and with $300 borrowed from 10 different people, cut the instrumental track at Podolor's American Recording studio, but Deke didn't have enough money to lay down the vocals.

While Berry Gordy was accompanying The Supremes to a show at the Hollywood Palace in 1966. Debbie Dean gave Berry Gordy a call who invited them to bring the record over. Dean sang live to the tape in the hotel room, and Berry Gordy offered Debbie Dean her second artist's contract with Motown and Richards a producer/writer contract on the spot. Deke and Debbie Dean (working out of the L.A. office), did put out a few singles together, but with no success.

While working for Motown in Los Angeles in 1968 Deke teamed up with writer/ producer Frank Wilson. Finding themselves under used they contacted Berry Gordy. In response to their letter Berry Gordy flew Richards and Wilson to Detroit to work with lyricists R. Dean Taylor and Pam Sawyer. Working under the title of "The Clan" they were given the task of producing a hit single for The Supremes. The result was "Love Child", a return to No1 spot for Diana Ross and The Supremes. The follow-up was the similarly themed "I'm Living In Shame", which became a Top 10 hit.

By 1968 Deke met Freddie Perren and Fonce Mizell, who had recently moved to California, The Corporation was then formed after the departure of Holland-Dozier-Holland. Berry Gordy was looking for individuals who would not be easily recognised by the public (as H-D-H had been), but would fill the gap left by Holland-Dozier-Holland. Incidentally The Corporation proved the high point of Deke Richards' musical career.

Their first challenge was The Jackson 5 who had been signed to Motown in March 1969. The Corporation wrote and produced three No1 hits in a row for The Jackson 5: "I Want You Back", "ABC" and "The Love You Save". With not just these songs, but with many others, The Corporation created a brilliant update of soul music.

Richards' next effort was Diana Ross' second solo album, "Everything Is Everything", which produced a huge hit in England, "I'm Still Waiting", that never made it in the USA. It was heavily backed by an English disk jockey Tony Blackburn. Tony pursued Tamla Motown to issue it in England where it became a No1 hit for Diana Ross in November 1971.

After the break-up of The Corporation, Deke ran the Motown's West Coast office, also producing, and writing and supervising recording. Deke left Motown in 1973, a successful dealer in film posters and memorabilia.

Lionel Richie

Born Lionel Brockman Richie, Jnr on the June 20th 1949 in Tuskegee, Alabama

Motown Connection: Saxophonist - Lead Vocals The Commodores - Solo Artist - Writer - Producer - Member of the last Motown Group or Solo Artist to Record in "Hitsville Studio A" in 1972 - Recorded the album "Can't Slow Down", which became the biggest selling album in Motown's history.

Lionel grew up on the campus of Tuskegee Institute; his grandfather's house was across the street from the home of the president of the Institute. He next moved with the family to Illinois were he attended the Joliet Township High School in Joliet. Lionel became a star tennis player in Joliet, he was so successful at his tennis that he was offered and accepted a tennis scholarship to go back to Tuskegee Institute where Lionel later graduated with a major in economics.

Back as a student in Tuskegee, he formed a succession of R&B groups in the mid-1960's culminating in a group called "The Mystics", before The Commodores came into being. The Commodores came together as a result of two groups "The Mystics" and "The Jays", performing for one year as the "The Mystics" in 1968 then changing the name to The Commodores in 1969, between then and 1972, they started performing from their regional base, which included Tuskegee, Montgomery and Birmingham, before moving onto the New York funk scene, the place at which they became most well known was at "Small's Paradise" in Harlem. There is one pre-Motown album on Atlantic, the result of a one off deal (Walter "Clyde" Orange gave King a dictionary and told him to pick a name, the name he picked was The Commodores) the original line-up consisted of William "Clyde" King, Thomas McClary, Ronald LaPread, Walter "Clyde" Orange, Lionel Richie and Milan Williams. Interestingly, Lionel Richie was the group's saxophonist in the group's early days, not the group's lead vocalist.

Bennie Ashburn, their manager (who died 1982), introduced them to Motown executive Suzanne de Passé in 1972, their signing to Motown in that year came after the group was told to be in New York City for an audition, the group did not know the audition was for The Jackson 5 tour, and two weeks later they were informed that they had been selected for the tour with The Jackson 5. They opened for The Jackson 5 for two and a half years. The group's first release on Motown was the instrumental dance recording taken from the album of the same name called "Machine Gun", written by Milan Williams, the recording became their first Top 10 hit. This was the last commercial recording undertaken at "Hitsville Studio A". This recording is now used at many of the biggest American sporting events, and was featured in many films, including "Boogie Nights" and "Looking for Mr. Goodbar".

Their second No1 R&B hit single and No7 chart hit was "Fancy Dancer" followed by one of their best known chart hits "Easy". Which reached No1 on the pop charts, however, their soul/funk style of recording was more evident on their next release and would become the group's anthem, "Brick house". The arrangement and vocals are by Clyde Orange. Two consecutive No1 singles would follow, the dance recording "Too Hot Ta Trot" and the Ballard "Three Times a Lady". Next was the recording of "Still", which would become the last No1 hit for the group with Lionel before his departure.

In 1976, they played a forty-two-city tour with the O'Jays, followed in early 1977, with a successful Australian tour and a world tour in 1977 and 1978. Also in 1978, they toured the US, and performed with the Rolling Stones and Earth, Wind, and Fire. In 1977, they played themselves in the movie, "Thank God It's Friday", which was released by Columbia in 1978; Motown co-produced the film with Casablanca Records. In 1978, The Commodores were named the No1 R&B group by Rolling Stone magazine. Three albums were released in between 1975 and 1976, "Caught in the Act", "Movin' On" and "Hot On The Tracks" and are considered the height of their funk style music period.

While still a member of the group, Lionel started his song writing career, with the song "Lady" for Kenny Rogers, which hit No1 in 1980, and he produced the Kenny Rogers, "Share Your Love" album the following year. Lionel also recorded "Endless Love" with Diana Ross the single reached No1 on the charts, the success of the single then prompted Lionel Richie to leave the group to follow a solo career. Before Lionel Richie's departure, the group had a string of hits, which included "Old Fashion Love", "Lady (You Bring Me Up)" and "Oh No" which was used in the film "The Last American Virgin", the single reached No4 on the US charts. The Commodores also recorded many songs that were not releases and never charted, the most famous being "Zoom", later covered and made into a chart hit by the group, Fat Larry's Band.

In 1982, Lionel officially left The Commodores to pursue his own solo career. His first solo album, "Lionel Richie", yielded three hits: "Truly", "You Are" and "My Love". For "Truly", Lionel received his first Grammy Award. In early 1983, Lionel made his first major solo tours, to Japan and then a three month, tour of the US later that year. Several more Top 10 hits followed, the most successful of which was the

No1 hit "Hello" in 1984, also in 1984 he released his second solo album, "Can't Slow Down", and it became the biggest selling album in Motown's history. It won Lionel two Grammy's for "Album of the Year" and "Producer of the Year" (with co-producer James Anthony Carmichael).

In 1985, he was the host for the 11th annual American Music Awards, where he won six awards, later that same year he co wrote with Michael Jackson "We Are the World", which won two Grammy awards, and participated in the Live Aid concerts. "Say You, Say Me" which became a No1 pop hit and appears on his 1986 album, "Dancing on the Ceiling". "Say You, Say Me" won the 1985 Oscar for Song of the Year; it was the title song from the film, "White Nights".

In 1986, Lionel released "Dancing on the Ceiling" album, which produced a run of US and UK hits including "Say You, Say Me", "Dancing on the Ceiling" and "Se La". Lionel then collaborated with the country group Alabama on "Deep River Woman" project which produced a different sound for him.

By 1987, Lionel was exhausted from his extensive work schedule and took a year out to care for his father in Alabama, sadly his father, Lionel Sr., died in 1990. Lionel then made a return to the recording studio and live performances following the release of his first greatest-hits collection, Back to Front, in 1992. Lionel was semi-retired until 1996 when he released the album "Louder Than Words", and "Time" both failed to achieve the previous decade's commercial success. Some of his recent work such as the album "Renaissance" achieved success in Europe, but had only modest attention in the US. With the UK now his main outlet for recordings, he has since 2004, produced a total of six Top 40 singles in the UK.

In November 2005, Lionel performed with Kenny Rogers on a CMT Crossroads special; the show provided an insight into their friendship both in and out of the music world. Lionel was also the headline act at a 2000 4th July tribute concert with Fantasia Barrino at the Philadelphia Museum of Art. Lionel then released his eighth studio album entitled "Coming Home" in September 2006. The first single of the album was "I Call It Love" and was issued in July 2006, becoming his biggest hit in the US in ten years, the album also proved successful for Lionel in the US, reaching No6 on the album charts. His adopted daughter Nicole Richie stars in the music video for this track.

On 9th December 2006, Lionel hosted and performed live on the British television show An Audience with Lionel Richie. In February 2007, Lionel performed his 1980's hit song "Hello" on the televised Grammy Awards show, in November of that year, he made a surprise appearance on the Australian Idol grand finale performing "All Night Long (All Night)" at the Sydney Opera House. On 2nd May 2008, Lionel was the 21st recipient of the "George and Ira Gershwin Lifetime Achievement Award". Lionel continues to be very popular as a solo artist and as a composer, his popularity is due largely to the ballads he writes and sings. He divorced in 1997, and withdrew from the music business for a while, after this and his father's death. Now he is back in the limelight making hit records once again.

Richie married college sweetheart Brenda Harvey in October 1975. During their marriage, Lionel began a relationship with Diane Alexander in 1986. In 1988, while separated, Brenda allegedly discovered Lionel and Alexander together in a Beverly Hills apartment. A confrontation ensued, and Brenda was then arrested for spousal abuse, trespassing and vandalism. Lionel and Brenda divorced in August 1993.

In 1983, Lionel and wife Brenda informally adopted the 2-year-old daughter Nicole Richie as their daughter and adopted her legally when she was nine years old.

Lionel married Alexander in December 1995 they have a son, Myles Brockman born in 1994 and a daughter, Sofia born in1998, Lionel and Alexander divorced in January 2004.

Lionel became a grandfather in January 2008 when his daughter Nicole Richie had a baby girl named Harlow Winter Kate Madden. Her father is Joel Madden, lead singer of the band Good Charlotte.

Born in Detroit, Michigan

Motown Connection: Arranger - Trombone player.

The unbroken string of Supremes hits may have been supplied by Holland-Dozier-Holland, but with their departure, a new hit making team was needed. A marathon writing session was held involving, R. Dean Taylor, Frank Wilson, Pam Sawyer and Deke Richards producing the hit, "Love Child". For Diana Ross and The Supremes, Paul was the arranger for this recording.

Paul has consistently generated hit after hit for the past five decades, Paul's influence on "The Motown Sound" has influenced most of the recording that came out of the Detroit era. Although Paul worked quietly, outside of the public's eye, along with The Funk Brothers, The Andantes, etc in the studios of Motown, Paul was instrumental in producing the "Sound Of Young America".

Among Paul's biggest hits as an arranger are, "My Girl" "Papa Was A Rollin' Stone" by The Temptations, for which he won a Grammy Award, both versions of "I Heard It Through The Grapevine" by Marvin Gaye and Gladys Knight and The Pips, for Stevie Wonder "My Cherie Amour," both versions of "Ain't No Mountain High Enough" for Diana Ross and Marvin Gaye and Tammy Terrell, "If I Were Your Woman" by Gladys Knight and The Pips and "Tears of A Clown" by Smokey Robinson and The Miracles. Paul composed "What Becomes of The Brokenhearted" for Jimmy Ruffin.

Other Motown recordings include one of my favourites "It's A Shame" by The Spinners (aka Detroit Spinners and The Motown Spinners in the UK), working on all the major Motown labels, Gordy, Soul, VIP, Rare Earth, Motown and the UK label Tamla Motown.

On leaving Motown in the 1970's, (although Paul occasionally still provided arrangements for Motown) Paul worked with the Holland-Dozier-Holland team at their Hot Wax label (renewing his ties with them), Volt (the subsidiary of Stax records) with Otis Reading and again renewing an acquaintance from his Motown days Kim Weston on her album "Kim Kim Kim". Paul also worked with the famous Detroit group The Dynamics on Black Gold Records of Detroit (Distributed by PIP Records, a division of Pickwick) in 1973. Following this work Paul worked with many other labels including, Epic in 1972, Sussex Records in 1973, ABC Records 1973, Atlantic Records in 1976.

Two more old colleagues from his days at Motown featured in Paul's career, firstly with Jack Ashford (from The Funk Brothers) on Blaze records in 1975 recording as Jack Ashford and The New Detroit on the recording "Do The Choo-Choo", and then with Norman Whitfield on his Whitfield label in 1976 on both the film and sound track to the successful film "Car Wash" featuring the group Rose Royce.

In 1978 Paul worked with A&M Records on the recording "Just The Way You Are" a hit for both Barry White and Billy Joel. An interesting aspect of Paul's career was working with a USSR state label Мелодия, it was the only label existing during that time in the USSR, but ceased to exist when the USSR fell apart, although it has since been revived. Export releases were shipped with full colour sleeves and with English translation; copies sold domestically have generic paper sleeves. The label was also known as Melody, Melodia or Melodiya.

Over the years Paul has worked in both the film and television industry, providing the musical scores for "Mad About You", "Bamboozled", "Space Jam", "Four Brothers", "Which Way Is Up", "Mother" and "Jugs and Speed." One of Paul's later contributions was the 2002 documentary on The Funk Brothers "Standing In The Shadows Of Motown" Paul had known most of The Funk Brothers personally from his involvement with "Hitsville Studio A" in Detroit. The documentary celebrated The Funk Brother's contribution to the development of the "Motown Sound" and won a Grammy award.

Paul's other his in the 1990's include, "Never Too Much" by Luther Vandross, "Two Hearts" by Phil Collins and "I Believe I Can Fly" by R. Kelly. Paul continued to work with Motown/Universal Records through out the 1990's and early 2000's helping put together greatest hits type packages, and most noticeably the box sets of all the Motown singles released from the Detroit era called "The Complete Motown Singles" on Hip-O-Select (a subsidiary of Universal). Paul's arrangements have been used on recordings for The Carpenters, Carly Simon, Quincy Jones, The Doobie Brothers, Tom Jones, Natalie Cole, Pharoah Sanders, Kiki Dee, Johnny Mathis, Patti LaBelle, Stephanie Mills, Anita Baker, Roberta Flack, Michael McDonald, Aretha Franklin and many others.

Jimmy Roach

Born Jimmy Basil Roach on the 10th February 1944 in the Bedford-Stuyvesant area of Brooklyn, New York

Motown Connection: Producer - Songwriter - Arranger.

Jimmy's first introduction to music was at fourteen years old when he took piano lessons along with his four sisters; Jimmy also learned keyboards as well, and joined a neighbourhood group called the Lyrics (Little Anthony's early group), but the group never recorded any singles.

By 1963, Jimmy had become a staff writer with Chardon Music, working there for two years before being called up to the army in 1965. At Chardon Music, Billy's main writing partners were Carl Smith and Gary Klein their composition "The Kitty Kat Song" was the b/side of Lee Dorsey's first major hit "Ride Your Pony".

After national service, Jimmy resumed writing with Rosemary McCoy; she introduced him to Pam Sawyer (a future Motown writer and producer). Pam Sawyer had recently split with ex-partner Lori Burton and was seeking a new partner, even though they did have some minor hits, including the O'Jays' "It Won't Hurt".

In 1965 Jimmy played keyboards, for Pam Sawyer on "I'm By Your Side" for Brenda and The Tabulations, and collaborated on the Persians' "Too Much Pride" and the O'Jays' "I Miss You". Jimmy's next move was to Motown in 1969 to become a staff writer and arranger at "Hitsville Studio A". His first big success was a song he wrote with Pam Sawyer called, "My Whole World Ended", recorded by David Ruffin, Jimmy had to share credits with Harvey Fuqua and Johnny Bristol as the producers, to get tunes recorded at the time. It is suggested that the Motown's archives may contain many unreleased songs by Jimmy, including an album on Jimmy Ruffin, who became a close friend of Jimmy while at Motown. Next arranging most of the tracks on The Four Top's album's "Still Water" and "In Changing Times" and The Miracle's Christmas album in 1970. When Motown moved to Los Angeles, Jimmy remained in Detroit and started to work with producer and writer Don Davis.

Jimmy helped the Spinners (aka The Detroit Spinners and Motown Spinners in the UK) when they moved to Atlantic Records. Jimmy helped produce a four-song demo tape, featuring new lead singer, Philippe Wynne. However, a planned album was scrapped when Thom Bell was chosen to produce the group for the label, so Jimmy was dropped from the production team. One of the four songs "Oh Lord I Wish I Could Sleep" was placed on The Spinners' double-disc anthology album years later.

Jimmy wrote for another Detroit group the Dramatics including "And I Panicked", "I Made Myself Lonely" and "Learning to Love You Was Easy" with William "Wee Gee" Howard on lead vocals before he left the group, followed by "I Dig Your Music" and "I Get Carried Away". So Billy recorded them with Larry "L.J." Reynolds on lead vocals.

In the 1980's Jimmy went into managing artists and promotions, securing a deal for a Detroit group called, Everlife, on 20th Century Fox Records, but the label did not release the album, so Jimmy released it locally on his own Jibaro Records. In the 1990's Jimmy wrote, "Hit and Run" for a young, Roz Ryan, who became a Broadway actress and later landed the choir director role in the 1990's sitcom "Good News".

Jimmy's songs have been recorded by The Supremes, Esther Philips, James and Bobby Purify, The Dells, Gloria Gaynor, Houston Pearson, The Sins of Satan, Five Special with many of the tracks produced and arranged by him for these artists.

By the mid-1980's Jimmy pulled away from the music business (apart from the Roz Ryan work) stating that the rise of rap music, and other changes in music was not for him. Jimmy still lives in Detroit, his adopted home, and ran the Accessories Boutique store for many years.

Claudette Robinson

Born Claudette Marie Rogers Born September 1942 in Detroit, Michigan

Motown Connection: A member of Motown group The Miracles (aka The Matadors) from 1957 to 1972 - The Miracles were Motown's first group.

Was the first female artist ever signed to a Motown related label "Tamla".

Born and raised in Detroit, Claudette was not an original member of The Miracles, it was actually her brother, Emerson "Sonny" Rogers who was an original member of the group, which started life as The Matadors before The Miracles were formed in 1957. It was Claudette who took her brother's place after he was drafted into the US Army in that year.

In November 1959, Claudette married The Miracles lead singer Smokey Robinson, he would become one of the major influences at Motown with his work with The Miracles and other Motown artists. In early 1964, Claudette decided to retire from touring with the group and remain at home in Detroit. Claudette did not appear in any official group photographs or on television, although she continued to sing backup with the group in the studio until 1972 when she formally retired from the group.

Claudette was the inspiration for Smokey Robinson's No1 recording of "My Girl" by The Temptation's, the song was originally intended to be recorded by The Miracles. In 1983, The Miracles reunited for the successful "Motown 25" TV special to celebrate Motown's 25th Anniversary, singing with Smokey and the rest of the group for the first time since 1972.

Claudette and Smokey Robinson were divorced in 1986, after 27 years of marriage. Berry Gordy gave Claudette the title of "First Lady of Motown", in his autobiography, as a member of The Miracles, (Motown's first group), she was the first female artist ever signed to a Motown-affiliated record label Tamla. Claudette also began writing her autobiography, "A Miraculous Life", a book of her memoirs and of her life with The Miracles, as of 2008, it has yet to be released. Today, she is a board member of the national Rhythm and Blues Foundation; Claudette also still makes selected appearances with The Miracles today. A volunteer teacher and still a source of knowledge on the great years at Motown in particular the Detroit years.

Smokey and Claudette had two children, both with a Motown connection, their oldest boy was called Berry William, and a daughter, Tamla Claudette who was named after Berry Gordy's first label Tamla Records.

Rudolph Victor Robinson

Born on the 21st December 1940 Detroit, Michigan - Died 18th February 2002 Detroit, Michigan

Motown Connection: Composer - Arranger - Performer - Producer.

Rudolph was part of the group called the Hungry Five, a local Detroit group, known for its live shows at venues such as the 20 Grand and the Fox Theatre. The group had the lead singer Misty Love, along with Rudolph in the group. Rudolph was happy playing all types of music with a particular emphasis on gospel, jazz, blues, and R&B.

Rudolph achieved five gold albums and one platinum single over his musical career his biggest hit being Marilyn McCoo and Billy Davis Jnr's "I Hope We Get to Love in Time". While at Motown Rudolph arranged, produced and played keyboards for artists such as The Supremes, The Temptations. Working with also some of the great Motown singers, including Marvin Gaye, Levi Stubbs of The Four Tops and non Motown Artists The Dramatics and Martha Reeve's when Martha Reeves left Motown. Rudolph' career also included music scores for films and was an independent producer in his own right.

Co-founded the record label D-Town Records and owned the labels New Moon Records and Nadia Records. Worked on the album with Martha Reeves called "Home To You" Rudolph was producer, arranger (for the horn section) and played keyboards for the recording in 2004.

Rudolph Victor died of a heart attack at his home in Detroit, he was 61 and gave his last performance, at the MGM Grand Detroit Casino.

William "Smokey" Robinson

Born William Robinson on the 19th February 1940 in Detroit, Michigan

Motown Connection: A member of Motown group The Miracles (aka The Matadors) from 1957 to 1972 - Berry Gordy second signing to Management Company, (the first being Eddie Holland) - Singer - Producer - Writer - Arranger - Vice President 1961 to 1987 - Life long friend of Berry Gordy.

Smokey is regard as one of the key personnel involved with Motown, second only to the company's founder, Berry Gordy. At the age of six or seven Robinson's uncle Claude nicknamed him "Smokey Joe", after coming from a cowboy movie matinee with his nephew; it is suggested he did not want William to forget that he was Black. William at that time was light skinned, with blonde hair, and blue eyes. In his teens, this was shortened to "Smokey".

Smokey was born and raised in Detroit, Michigan's North End neighbourhood. In 1955, Robinson founded a group he called The Five Chimes with his best friend Ronald White, and Northern High School classmates Pete Moore, Clarence Dawson, and James Grice. By 1957, the group was called the Matadors and included cousins Emerson and Bobby Rogers in place of Dawson and Grice. Later Emerson was replaced by his sister Claudette Rogers (Smokey's future wife). In 1958 Marv Tarplin was the band director of The Primettes (Diana Ross, Mary Wilson, Florence Ballard and Barbara Martin); Smokey asked the girls if he could use their guitar player on tour, in return he would set up an audition at Motown when he got back from touring. The girls agreed, and Tarplin has performed with Smokey ever sense. The Primettes went on to become the Supremes.

With Smokey as lead singer, The Matadors began touring the local Detroit clubs. In 1957, Berry Gordy (who had an extraordinary ability to recognise talent), was at a Detroit talent show, Berry Gordy was introduced to Smokey and this was the start of a lifelong relationship. The Miracles became Berry Gordy's first real recording group. Smokey and Berry Gordy then co-wrote the single for the group called, "Got a Job", an answer song to The Silhouettes' hit single "Get a Job". Also in this year Smokey married Claudette.

After this success the group renamed itself The Miracles, and issued singles on both End Records and Chess Records. With disappointment in the amount of royalties received from this record (a cheque for just over $3.00) it was Smokey who suggested to Berry Gordy that he start a label of his own. Berry Gordy decided to take total control of his songs and production and in January 1959, Berry borrowed $800 from his family's loan fund to start his own record label, which soon became the Motown Record Company with The Miracles were among the label's first to sign. By 1961, Berry Gordy had appointed Smokey vice-president of Motown Records, a title Smokey held for as long as Berry Gordy remained with the company.

The first success for The Miracles was "Shop Around" in late 1960. Berry Gordy withdrew the original single in favour of a faster, more fully produced version of the song, this version went onto become a No2, helping to establish The Miracles, and also Motown itself, it became Motown's first million seller. The 1962 Top 10 hit "You've Really Got a Hold on Me", established Smokey (and The Miracles) as a chart topping group. Around this time Bob Dylan was impressed enough to call him "America's greatest living poet". While successfully developing The Miracles as a songwriter and producer, he was also working with numerous other artists especially for Mary Wells and The Temptations. Other famous hits included "Mickey's Monkey", a 1963 Top 10 hit, "Going to a Go-Go" and lesser known hits like "I Gotta Dance to Keep from Crying".

While The Miracles were never Motown's biggest act, they were one of its most consistent groups at Motown in it's heyday of the 1960's. Other great recordings included "I Second That Emotion", "The Love I Saw in You Was Just a Mirage", "The Tracks of My Tears", "Ooo Baby Baby", "Baby, Baby Don't Cry" all written and produced by Smokey.

Smokey's success with other Motown artists were the No1 singles "My Guy" by Mary Wells and "My Girl" by The Temptations (with Ronnie White), and Smokey also worked with The Marvelettes and Marvin Gaye. Smokey continued to tour with The Miracles, while supporting these artists. Smokey's wife Claudette stopped touring with the group in the mid-1960's, although she continued to record on their recordings. For a time Smokey was the main songwriter and producer for The Temptations (from 1963 to 1966), with hits such as "The Way You Do the Things You Do", "Since I Lost My Baby" and "Get Ready". Other Motown artists hit singles included, "Still Water (Love)" by The Four Tops, "Don't Mess With Bill" and "My Baby Must Be a Magician" by The Marvelettes, "When I'm Gone" by Brenda Holloway, "Ain't That Peculiar" and "I'll Be Doggone" by Marvin Gaye, and "First I Look at the Purse" by The Contours.

In 1967, The Miracles changed the name to Smokey Robinson and The Miracles, and Smokey then started to contemplate a solo career at Motown, however, their 1969 recording "Baby Baby Don't Cry" became a Top 10 hit, and when their 1966 recording of "The Tears of a Clown" was released as a single in 1970, it became a No1 hit in both the US and the UK. The single was spotted by an employee at Motown Record label headquarters in London and released on this recommendation.

With the surprise success of "The Tears of a Clown", Smokey decided to remain with The Miracles for a little longer. In 1972 Smokey decided to leave the group, and The Miracles began a six-month farewell tour. On 16th July 1972, Smokey and Claudette Robinson and the rest of the group gave their final performances as The Miracles in Washington DC, at this performance Smokey introduced the group's new lead singer, Billy Griffin.

Smokey had a low-key start to his solo career, concentrating on his duties as Vice President of Motown, however, Smokey did release his first solo LP, "Smokey", in 1973 with the first hit single, "Sweet Harmony" dedicated to The Miracles. Then in 1975, Smokey's decided to dedicate time to his solo career, after the success of the No1 R&B hit "Baby That's Backatcha". Smokey then issued the single "Quiet Storm" in 1976, and its accompanying album of the same name. Smokey also recorded the soundtrack to the film "Big Time" in 1977. Other Smokey recordings were, "Cruisin'" in 1979, "Being With You", a UK No1 in 1981, "Tell Me Tomorrow" in 1982, and "Ebony Eyes", a duet with label mate Rick James in 1983.

In 1986 after 27 years of marriage Smokey and Claudette divorced although they are still firm friends, also during the mid-1980's, Smokey became addicted to cocaine. This addiction caused his recording schedule to slow, but with the help of a friend, Leon Kennedy, Smokey was able to stop the addiction. Smokey then started to record again, having hits in 1987 with the Grammy Award-winning "Just to See Her" a US No8 recording, and "One Heartbeat" another US No10 hit, also in that year, the UK band ABC recorded a US and UK hit with their tribute to Smokey entitled "When Smokey Sings".

In 1988, Robinson published his autobiography, "Smokey", and was inducted into the Rock and Roll Hall of Fame. However, the other original members of The Miracles, Bobby Rogers, Ronnie White, Pete Moore, Marv Tarplin, and Claudette Robinson, were not. Also in 1988, he resigned his Motown vice presidency and left Motown in 1990 as both artist and employee. Smokey signed with SBK Records, recording in 1991 the album "Double Good Everything".

Smokey's next release was on the 11-track album, "Intimate," released in 2001, working with Detroit-born producer Michael Stokes in Los Angeles, with support also from Patti Labelle and Jesse Powell, on (you guessed it) Motown Records. Helped by his personal manager and ex-Motown executive Suzanne de Passe Smokey returned to Motown to release the album. Perhaps even more amazing is the executive producer, a certain Berry Gordy, the album became a genuine "labour of love" for Berry Gordy and Smokey a collaboration which found the two working shoulder to shoulder, much like they did during their Detroit heyday.

In 2003, Robinson served as a guest judge for American Idol during "Billy Joel Week." Smokey issued a gospel album, "Food for the Spirit" in 2004. Next was an album of pop standards, called "Timeless Love", released in June 2006. In 2004, Smokey's company, SFGL Foods, launched a special brand of gumbo called "Smokey Robinson's 'The Soul is in the Bowl' Gumbo". Smokey appeared on "Friday Night with Jonathan Ross" a UK BBC programme, the NBC daytime drama "Days of our Lives", and on The Rachael Ray Show.

In May 2006, Howard University conferred on Smokey the degree of "Doctor of Music", in December of that year, Smokey was one of five Kennedy Centre honourees, along with Dolly Parton (with whom Robinson had recorded a 1987 duet, "I Know You By Heart"), Zubin Mehta, Steven Spielberg and Andrew Lloyd Webber. Also in 2006, Smokey sang "The Tracks Of My Tears" as a cameo in the film "Last Holiday". By the end of the year, Smokey reunited with fellow members of The Miracles (Bobby Rogers and Pete Moore) for the group's first extended interview. This interview forms the basis of the Universal Music DVD release "Smokey Robinson and The Miracles: The Definitive Performances", a DVD retrospective of the group's music and career.

February 2007, saw Smokey singing "Tracks Of My Tears" at the 49th annual Grammy Awards, as part of a tribute to R&B music. In November 2007, Smokey toured Australia and performed with Australian band Human Nature on the programme "Dancing With The Stars". In August 2008, Smokey appeared at Harlem's legendary Apollo Theatre with the UK singe/songwriter Elvis Costello to record a television special.

Smokey married Claudette Rogers in 1957, they had two children, a son Berry (named after Berry Gordy), and a daughter, Tamla (named after the Tamla record label). Smokey had a child with a girlfriend while still married to Claudette called Trey.

Album Track: "Don't Look Back", The Temptations.

Bobby Rogers

Born Robert Rogers on the 19th February 1940 in Detroit, Michigan

Motown Connection: A member of Motown group The Miracles (aka The Matadors) from 1956 until the present time – Songwriter.

Born and raised in Detroit, Bobby was a key member of one of Motown's first successful groups The Miracles. Bobby's cousin was Claudette Rogers, who became a member of the group, and later married The Miracles lead singer Smokey Robinson. Bobby was born on the exact same day as Smokey Robinson, in the very same Detroit hospital, though the two didn't meet until 15 years later when forming the group. In 1957, The Miracles were called The Matadors, and included cousins Bobby Rogers and Emerson, Emerson would eventually be replaced by his sister Claudette Rogers (Smokey Robinson's future wife), later joined by guitarist Marv Tarplin in 1958.

In addition to his work in The Miracles, Bobby became a songwriter, working with Smokey Robinson to produce The Temptations' first hit single, "The Way You Do the Things You Do". Bobby also co-wrote Mary Well's hit, "What Love has Joined Together", the minor hit for The Contours'1965 called "First I Look At The Purse", Marvin Gaye's 1966 Top 40 hit, "One More Heartache" and The Miracle's 1966 hit recording called, "Going To A Go Go".

The first success for The Miracles was "Shop Around" in late 1960's; it became Motown's first million seller. The 1962 Top 10 hit "You've Really Got a Hold on Me", established The Miracles as a chart topping group. While The Miracles were never Motown's biggest act, they were one of its most consistent groups at Motown in it's heyday of the 1960's, other great recordings included "I Second That Emotion", "The Love I Saw in You Was Just a Mirage", "The Tracks of My Tears", "Ooo Baby Baby", "Baby, Baby Don't Cry" all written and produced by Smokey Robinson.

In 1967, The Miracles changed the name to Smokey Robinson and The Miracles, with the expected news that Smokey Robinson would announce his intention to leave the group for a solo career. However, when their 1966 recording of "The Tears of a Clown" was released as a single in 1970, it became a No1 hit in both the US and the UK. With the surprise success of "The Tears of a Clown", Smokey decided to remain with The Miracles for a few more years. In 1972 Smokey did decide to leave the group, and The Miracles began a six-month farewell tour. On 16th July

1972, Smokey and Claudette Robinson and the rest of the group gave their final performances as The Miracles in Washington DC, at this performance Smokey introduced the group's new lead singer, Billy Griffin.

The Miracles then started to tour and record with the line up of Bobby, Billy Griffin, Pete Moore and Ronnie White, Claudette Robinson had retired from the music business. They recorded the hits, "Love Machine", "Do It Baby" and "Don't You Cha Love It" in 1978. In this year, the group decided to disband. In the late 1990's Bobby re-formed the group with Sidney Justin (formerly of Shalamar), Dave Finley and Tee Turner (as background singer and musical director). Tee was soon moved to the frontline, thus continuing the four-man group. Mark Scott replaced Sidney Justin as lead singer in 2005 and this line-up continues performing today.

In 1983, The Miracles reunited for the successful Motown 25 TV special to celebrate Motown's 25th Anniversary concert, singing with Smokey and the rest of the group for the first time since 1972.

In late 2006, Bobby re-united with original Miracles members Smokey Robinson and Pete Moore for the group's first - ever extended interview on the Motown DVD release, "Smokey Robinson and The Miracles: The Definitive Performances".

Bobby still lives in Detroit with his wife Joan, and is the former husband of Wanda Young, the lead singer of the Motown group The Marvelettes, but they divorced.

On March 20, 2009, Bobby Rogers, Pete Moore, Claudette Robinson, Billy Griffin and Smokey Robinson were presented with a star on the Hollywood Walk of Fame.

Born Arthur Ross on the 1st January 1949 in Detroit, Michigan - Died 22nd April 1996 in Detroit, Michigan

Motown Connection: Song writer - Younger brother of Diana Ross.

Born and raised in Detroit Arthur always wanted to become a star and was introduced to Motown via his sister Diana Ross. Diana recruited him to Motown as a songwriter in 1972 as the company was moving from Detroit to Los Angeles. Arthur's first collaboration was with fellow songwriter Leon Ware and together they wrote hits for acts such as Michael Jackson, The Miracles and Marvin Gaye. Among their many hits were, "I Wanna Be Where You Are" and "I Want You".

Album Cover of Arthur "T-Boy" Ross release.

Never easy to deal with because of his drugs and alcohol addiction these addictions eventually led to the break up of his partnership with Leon Ware. The relationship came to an end when recording the Marvin Gaye album "I Want You" because of these difficulties. Arthur left Motown in the early 1980's after failing to establish himself as a solo artist; one album was recorded and released by Motown in 1979 called "Changes". The album was not a commercial success, and Arthur retired from the music industry, deciding on cutting himself off from his family (including Diana Ross). Arthur's work with Leon Ware continues to be covered by many artists the most famous Arthur/Leon Ware recording, "I Want You", has been covered by Robert Palmer, Madonna. Diana Ross released a covers album called "I Love You" in tribute to Arthur.

Arthur had a tragic end to his life, on the night of 22nd April 1996, Arthur and his new wife were found dead in another house in Detroit. The two of them were reportedly bound and gagged and died of suffocation, Arthur was 47 years old.

Diana Ross

Born Diane Ernestine Ross on the 26th March 1944 in Detroit, Michigan

Motown Connection: Background Singer - Member of The Supreme's - Solo Artist - Part Owner in 1989 of Motown - Former Partner to Berry Gordy - Mother of Berry Gordy's child Rhonda Suzanne.

Diana was born in Detroit, but was raised in Bessemer Alabama by relatives in her early years, moving back to Detroit to live not far from Woodward Avenue (where Motown would eventually have their administration headquarters), and living near to a future Motown star Smokey Robinson. The next family move was when Diana was fourteen years old to the Brewster-Douglass Housing project in Detroit. Diana was the second of six children born to a Fred Earl Ross, Snr, and Ernestine Ross. Her sisters were Barbara Ross who became a doctor, and Rita Ross who became a schoolteacher. Younger brother Arthur "T-Boy" Ross was a successful songwriter for Motown, Diana's youngest brother, Wilbert "Chico" Ross, was a dancer on Diana's tours, and

Early promotional photograph of Diana Ross when the singer started her solo career.

another brother Fred Jnr. During Diana's teenage years, Diana's parents separated and divorced, with her mother remarrying many years later, Diana attended Detroit's Cass Technical High School.

In 1959 Diana began her music career, with neighbourhood friends Mary Wilson, Florence Ballard, and Betty McGlown (who would leave shortly after its formation) they formed the group The Primettes as a "sister group" to local Detroit group The Primes. After unsuccessfully auditioning for Berry Gordy at Motown (for the reason that they should first finish school before trying for a musical career), however, after hanging around "Hitsville" for many months, they eventually signed to Motown in 1960.

By 1961 they had changed their name to The Supremes (with prompting from Berry Gordy) to reflect a more "up beat" name, at this time Barbara Martin (who had replaced Betty McGlown) then left, and the group continued with the same line up until Florence Ballard was forced to leave in 1967.

Between 1961 and 1963, The Supremes released eight singles, none of which charted, becoming known as the "no-hit Supremes" in this period the group provided background vocals, hand claps etc for the established artists at Motown including Marvin Gaye, The Temptations (who they had known and worked with when they were called The Primes). During these years, all three took turns singing lead vocals, but with Florence Ballard looked on as the "lead vocalist" of the group. Most of their early material was written and produced by Berry Gordy and or Smokey Robinson. Then in December 1963, Berry Gordy decided to try The Supremes with his production team of Holland-Dozier-Holland on a single called "When the Lovelight Starts Shining Through His Eyes" this recording became their first chart entry, reaching No23 on the charts.

With this success, Berry Gordy allocated Holland-Dozier-Holland to produce their next recordings; this resulted in almost five years of unparalleled success. By early 1964, The Supremes had recorded and released the single "Where Did Our Love Go" (with Diana Ross confirmed by Berry Gordy as the lead vocalist) interestingly the song had been originally intended to be recorded by The Marvelettes. In August 1964, while The Supremes were appearing on Dick Clark's "Caravan of Stars", the single "Where Did Our Love Go?" went to No1 on the US pop charts, it was also their first recording to chart in the UK, where it reached No3. Followed by four consecutive US No1's "Baby Love" (which was also their first No1 hit in the UK), "Come See About Me", "Stop! In the Name of Love" and "Back in My Arms Again". "Baby Love" was nominated for the 1965 Grammy Award for Best Rhythm and Blues Recording, and "You Keep Me Hangin' On" was awarded the 1966 Grammy for Best Pop single. They would go on to have twelve No1 hits in the US, with all these singles being international hits around the world (in particular the UK, Europe and Japan).

In 1967 the first major changes to the line up and name of the group occurred, renamed "Diana Ross and The Supremes", this coincided with Cindy Birdsong replacing Florence Ballard. Their last recording was "Someday We'll Be Together" in October 1969, with Mary Wilson and Cindy Birdsong surprisingly not providing background vocals (these were supplied by the Jones Girls) during the session, Johnny Bristol (the producer) coached Diana Ross through the recording. Berry Gordy liked the song so well, that he decided to leave the recording as it was with Johnny Bristol's coaching track included. This would be Diana Ross and The Supremes final No1 chart hit.

On the back of the success of this recording, Diana launched her solo career, Motown initially paired her with writer and producer's Nicholas Ashford and Valerie Simpson, who gave her four Top 40 pop hits, including the No1 hit "Ain't No Mountain High Enough" in July 1970.

With Motown's move to Los Angeles in 1972, Berry Gordy's other aspiration for Diana, apart from her solo singing career, was to develop her and Motown into films. Diana's first acting role was, starring in a film biography of Billie Holiday, "Lady Sings the Blues" in November 1972, produced by Motown Production a separate company formed by Berry Gordy, this gave Diana her first nomination for an Academy Award, it also boosted her musical career when the sound track to the film went to No1 in the charts. In between her next film role Diana issued the Top 10 album "Touch Me in the Morning" in June 1973, with the title track also becoming a No1 hit. A duet album followed with Marvin Gaye, titled "Diana and Marvin" in October 1973, which produced three chart hits, most of the recording on this album was done separately, as Diana was pregnant at the time and Marvin's constant "smoking" she felt could affect the unborn child.

Diana's next film was "Mahogany" in October 1975, playing a fashion model, the film may not have been as well received as "The Lady Sings The Blues" but it brought her another No1 single for the theme song, "Do You Know Where You're Going To?". That and her next No1, Diana's first attempt at a disco recording "Love Hangover" in March 1976, were featured on her second album to be titled simply "Diana Ross" released in February 1976, and which became a Top 10 hit.

Diana's third film role was The Wiz in October 1978, featuring Michael Jackson as the Tin Man, again this film was not well received, but compensation came in May 1979 with the album "The Boss" which became a gold-selling album, followed by the platinum-selling album "Diana" in May 1980 (Diana had already had a solo album with that name, a 1971 TV soundtrack). From the album, came her next No1 single "Upside Down" followed by "I'm Coming Out" an other Top Ten hit.

The 1980's started well for Diana, when another film sound track, became a third Top Ten hit for her called "It's My Turn" in 1980, next came Diana's biggest hit of her career so far, with another film sound track, a duet with Lionel Richie on "Endless Love" in June 1981. This proved to be her last big hit for Motown, when after more than 20 years, Diana unexpectedly (and without Berry Gordy's blessing) left Motown for a new recording contract with the RCA record label.

The move to RCA had an immediate effect, with a million-selling album, called "Why Do Fools Fall In Love" with the cover of Frankie Lymon and The Teenagers hit, "Why Do Fools Fall In Love" a single from the album, becoming her next Top 10 hit, "Mirror, Mirror", another single from the album also became a Top 10 hit. Diana's next album with RCA, "Silk Electric" released in October 1982 was another gold album, featuring the Top 10 hit "Muscles", written and produced by Michael Jackson.

The next album "Swept Away" released in September 1984 was another commercial success for Diana, it contained the hit "Missing You", recorded as a tribute to Marvin Gaye who had recently been shot by his father and had died in April 1984, Diana's recordings did slow down towards the end of the 1980's, but there was the No1 UK hit produced by the Bee Gees "Chain Reaction", and the 1985 worldwide No1 "We Are The World". The 1987 album "Red Hot Rhythm and Blues" was not a commercial success and "If We Hold On Together", the theme to the Steven Speilberg animated film of the same name in 1988 was a No1 single in Japan, also becoming a UK Top 20 in 1992.

In 1983, Diana reunited with The Supremes, Mary Wilson and Cindy Birdsong for the television special "Motown 25: Yesterday, Today, Forever". They performed their 1969 No1 hit "Someday We'll Be Together", although altercations on stage between Diana and Mary Wilson became an issue during the taping of the special, but were left out of the final edited performance. After this performance Diana did a solo of "Ain't No Mountain High Enough" (while suffering from a heavy cold) and brought the show to an end by asking Berry Gordy to join her on stage to receive his applause from the audience.

In 1989, leaving RCA, Diana returned to Motown, becoming, both an executive and a recording artist for the label. Diana released her first Motown album in eight years, the Nile Rodgers-produced "Workin' Overtime", the title track became a Top 10 R&B hit, but the album failed to reach the pop charts. Her last major R&B hit was "No Matter What You Do" a duet with Al B which reached No4 in early 1991. Subsequent follow-up albums in 1991 was "The Force Behind the Power", in 1995 "Take Me Higher" and 1999 "Every Day is a New Day" again produced no chart success.

However Diana did have some success in the UK and Europe with some of her Motown albums, having a Top 10 UK hit with "When You Tell Me That You Love Me" in 1991, also in 1991, Diana was the main star at the UK Royal Variety Performance.

"One Shining Moment" in 1992 and "Heart (Don't Change My Mind)", another major highlight of her in career was in the same year with an appearance at "Christmas in Vienna", with two of the world's greatest tenors, Placido Domingo and Jose Carreras.

In 1994 Diana released the albums "Your Love" and "The Best Years of My Life", and made her dramatic television debut in "Out of Darkness," and earned a Golden Globe nomination for her role, serving as executive producer for the production, other albums and television work followed, by the end of the decade Diana released "Not Over You Yet" in 1999. Also in 1999, Diana was voted the most successful female singer in United Kingdom charts, although fellow Detroit singer Madonna would eventually beat Diana.

Diana was the guest when the late Billie Holiday was inducted into the Rock and Roll Hall of Fame in March 2000. Diana performed Billie Holiday's signature tune, "God Bless the Child", at the same ceremony Motown bassist James Jamerson was also inducted with his widow Annie Jamerson receiving the award. Also in 2000, Diana re-united with The Supremes, Mary Wilson and Cindy Birdsong, for a concert tour called "Return to Love". Mary Wilson and Cindy Birdsong did not become involved or join the tour, instead Lynda Laurence and Scherrie Payne, both of whom were members of the group after Diana Ross had left The Supremes filled in. Despite a respectable opening in Philadelphia and a sell out show at Madison Square Garden in New York (ironically, the final show they would play), the "Return to Love" tour lasted only nine shows.

In December 2002, Ross was arrested in Tucson, Arizona for drunk driving, serving a two day jail sentence near her home in Greenwich, Connecticut. Also in 2002, Diana left Motown although they would release recordings Diana had made after her departure.

Diana next returned to the charts in 2005, with a duet, "I Got a Crush on You" with Rod Stewart for his album "The Great American Songbook". Another duet, recorded with the UK boy band Westlife, a remake of Diana's 1991 No2 UK single, "When You Tell Me You Love Me", this also reached No2 in the UK and was a No1 hit in Ireland.

In 2006, Motown released the album "Blue", and it became a major jazz hit. In August, Diana released a new studio album of classic rock and soul standards on the EMI label Angel Records, The album, "I Love You", was released on Manhattan Records EMI label, it became Diana's first Top 40 US pop album since the 1984 "Swept Away". In January 2007, Ross appeared on a number of TV shows promoting the album and touring the US. Diana also appeared on "American Idol" TV show, as a mentor to the contestants.

At the 2007 BET Awards, Diana was presented with a Lifetime Achievement Award by singer Alicia Keys and her five children. Stevie Wonder, Erykah Badu, and Chaka Khan performed a tribute to Ross, covering several of her hits. Later that year, the prestigious Kennedy Centre Honours committee named Diana as one of the honourees. In February 2008, Diana Ross was the guest speaker at the

Houston-based Brilliant Lecture series, at The Hobby Center, Houston. In early May 2008, Diana headlined at New York's Radio City Hall at the 'Divas with Heart' event, which also featured fellow R&B legends Gladys Knight, Chaka Khan and Patti LaBelle. In July 2008, Diana Ross performed at two major events in the UK; the famous "Liverpool Pops Festival" and the "National Trust Summer Festival" at Petworth House, East Sussex. In October 2008, Diana was announced as the headliner for the Nobel Peace Prize Concert in December of the same year.

Diana married her business manager Robert Ellis Silberstein in January 1971, they divorced in March 1977, Diana then married Norwegian tycoon Arne Naess Jnr in February 1986, and they divorced in 1999.

Diana has five children, one to Berry Gordy, two to Robert Silberstein, and two to Arne Naess. Rhonda Suzanne Silberstein born in August 1971, (aka Rhonda Ross Kendrick), Rhonda is the daughter of Berry Gordy, but has the Silberstein name because Diana was married Robert Silberstein at the time, although the pregnancy was confirmed before Diana married Robert Silberstein, also Berry Gordy was married at the time.

Tracee Joy Silberstein born in October 1972, (aka Tracee Ellis Ross) and Chudney Lane Silberstein born in November 1975, (aka Chudney Ross) are the children of Robert Silberstein. Ross Arne Naess born in October 1987 and Evan Olav Naess born in August 1988, (aka Evan Ross) are the children of Arne Naess.

Album Track: "I'm Still Waiting", Diana Ross.

David Ruffin

Born Davis Eli Ruffin aka as Ruff on the 18th January 1941 in Whynot, Mississippi - Died on 1st June 1991 in Philadelphia, Pennsylvania

Motown Connection: Background Singer - Member of The Temptations - Solo Artist.

Born in Whynot (although some references suggest it could be Meridian, Mississippi) David was in a family of five, he had two older brothers, Quincy and Jimmy, (who would later have a successful Motown career of his own) a sister Rita Mae, and younger brother Garfield "G" Fleming), David's early introduction to the music industry was travelling with his father and their stepmother as a family gospel group, his mother had died when he was two years old. By the mid 1950's David left home at the age of fourteen years old, and moved firstly to Louisiana to a horse farm, and then to Memphis and the next stop was Arkansas were he joined The Dixie Nightingales.

In the late 1950's David would next join his brother Jimmy Ruffin in Detroit, who was trying to develop his solo career, while holding down a job at the Ford Motor Company. David first came to the attention of the Detroit music scene when he sang with The Voice Masters, which included future Motown producer Lamont Dozier and members of the singing group The Originals.

The group was signed to the Anna label, owned by Berry Gordy's sister, Gwen Gordy Fuqua, and David sang lead on two recordings "I'm In Love" and "Action Speaks Louder Than Words". On the label David is credited with lead vocals, and the Voice Masters as background singers. It's believed to be David first credit on a recording. The Anna label was absorbed into Motown Records in 1961 when purchased by Berry Gordy.

After the Voice Masters disbanded, David was signed by Billy Davis' (a future Motown employee) to his Checkmate Records in 1963. While with Checkmate Records, David recorded the single "Mr. Bus Driver, Hurry", a minor Detroit hit, and David then established his first connection with The Temptations playing gigs as a drummer for the group. David performed at shows around Detroit, and even lived with Berry Gordy's parents for a brief period. At the same time Jimmy Ruffin had been offered and accepted a contract with Miracle Records, at the time a subsidiary of Tamla (which later became a subsidiary of Motown).

David became an official member of The Temptations after one of the original members Elbridge "Al" Bryant was asked to leave the group. Interestingly, his brother Jimmy Ruffin was initially offered the opportunity, but Jimmy Ruffin declined in favour of David. One of the main reasons for The Temptation's strong appeal was the charisma and stage presence of David Ruffin. Though not what was traditionally thought of as a sex symbol, David with his large dark glasses and tall lean body, could command the attention of an audience with his raspy and sexual voice and his unique and exciting stage presence. It was David that came up with the idea of the four headed microphone stand that allowed each of The Temptations go though their dance routines without all crowding around the same mike.

David initially sang background vocals on The Temptations' recordings while the role of lead singer generally alternated between Eddie Kendricks and Paul Williams. In November 1964, Smokey Robinson wrote a single especially for David to sing lead on and also producing the recording. "My Girl", which became the group's first No1 single (and international hit) and its signature song, with this success David was installed as the lead vocalist (although Eddie Kendricks in particular would still undertake lead vocals when required). The lanky, 6'3" Ruffin's passionate and dramatic performances endeared him to The Temptations' audiences and fans.

The success of "My Girl" started a run of hit single including, "Since I Lost My Baby" in 1965, "Ain't Too Proud to Beg" in 1966, "All I Need" in 1967, and "I Wish It Would Rain" in 1967, however in that year, David became addicted to cocaine, and began missing rehearsals and performances. Refusing to travel with the other Temptations, David and Motown artist Tammi Terrell (his then-girlfriend) decided to travel in a limo (with the image of his trademark black rimmed glasses painted on the door). At this time David was pushing for recognition by Motown of his lead vocal role with The Temptations, citing how Motown had allowed the name change for The Supremes (to Diana Ross and The Supremes in early 1967). David felt that the same should apply to The Temptations, and began demanding that the group name be changed to David Ruffin and The Temptations. This led to conflict in the group (in particular with recognised group's leader, Otis Williams), in addition David started inquiring into The Temptations' financial records, demanding an accounting of the group's money, causing further friction between David and Berry Gordy.

In mid-1968, The Temptations agreed that David should leave the group when he missed a 1968 concert to attend a concert being performed by his new girlfriend, Barbara Martin (daughter of Dean Martin). After taking a vote, The Temptations decided for the good of the group that David would have to leave, recruiting former Contour's singer Dennis Edwards as his replacement. David was at first happy to become a solo act, but when the time came for the group to start performing without him, David just couldn't accept the change. He continued to show up at

Temptation's performances uninvited and would join them on stage. Eventually security guards had to be used to keep him away.

At the same time, David started legal proceedings against Motown, seeking a release from the label and a statement of the money owed to him. Motown countersued to keep the singer from leaving the label and eventually the case was settled. The settlement required David to remain with Motown to work out his contract (David had kept his solo contract with Motown even after joining The Temptations), and produce solo recordings for the company.

David's first solo recording after officially leaving the group was interestingly, a song originally intended for The Temptations, "My Whole World Ended (The Moment You Left Me)", the single reached the US charts and was a R&B top ten hit. David continued releasing solo material into the 1970's. In 1971, David recorded an album with his brother Jimmy Ruffin, for which they did a popular cover of the Ben E. King song "Stand By Me". However, David's final Top 10 hit was the 1975's "Walk Away From Love", produced by Van McCoy, which reached No9 on the US chart. While his solo career initially showed great promise, David never regained the popularity with the public he had with The Temptations in part because of his cocaine addiction and (as David always suggested) the lack of support from Motown.

Leaving Motown in 1977, David recorded for Warner Brothers Records, and later signed with RCA, accompanied by former Temptations colleague Eddie Kendrick, after Eddie Kendrick had started experiencing problems with The Temptations. In 1982, David joined The Temptations' Reunion tour, in 1985, long time Temptations fans Hall and Oates teamed up with David and Eddie Kendrick to perform at the re-opening of the Apollo Theatre in New York. Their performance was released as a relatively successful live album and single. The four singers also sang a medley of Temptations hits at Live Aid on 13th July 1985. John Oates later wrote a minor hit single for David and Eddie Kendrick, but the relationship came to an end that year, allegedly due to Daryl Hall's objections to David's heavy drug use.

In 1989, The original members of The Temptations were inducted into the Rock and Roll Hall of Fame, in that year David, Eddie Kendrick, and Dennis Edwards began touring and recording as "Ruffin/Kendrick/Edwards: Former Leads of The Temptations". The project, never really materialised. Before his death David also become involved with Ian Levine's Motorcity project, recording the single "Hurt the One You Love".

There is some controversy over the details of David's death, including the suggestion that David's body was randomly found in the middle of the street, and laid unclaimed in a morgue for over a week. However, his children did come to the hospital a few days later to claim the body. The case was considered an accidental overdose, although there were some questions surrounding the circumstances.

David had a stormy relationship with singer Tammi Terrell before her death in 1970; David married twice, firstly Sandra Ruffin and then Joy Hamilton. While married to Sandra, they had three daughters Cheryl, Nedra and Kimberly (aka Mone). David also has a son, David Jnr (now also a recording artist), by a former girlfriend.

David died from a drug overdose in 1991, in a hospital in Philadelphia, Pennsylvania, at the age of 50, Michael Jackson covered some of the expenses of his funeral, at which Aretha Franklin and Stevie Wonder performed.

Jimmy Ruffin

Born on the 7th May 1939 in Collinsville, Mississippi

Motown Connection: Older Brother of David Ruffin (The Temptations) - Singer - Background Singer.

Jimmy Ruffin is the older brother of David Ruffin (from The Temptations). As children, Jimmy and David Ruffin began their career with a gospel group called the Dixie Nightingales. Beginning his career with Anna Records (which would later be bought by Motown), following the release of the first album, the brothers switched to another Detroit label, Checkmate, where they produced two singles, which were written and produced by Billy Davis (who would become writer and producer for Motown). Jimmy then had a forced absence from music with his call up to the army, on Jimmy's return to Detroit (he had first signed with the Motown on the subsidiary, but short-lived Miracle label in 1961) to re-sign with Motown placed on the Soul label (a subsidiary of Motown) in 1964.

Jimmy's first major hit was in 1966 with "What Becomes of the Brokenhearted" which became his signature song. A follow up release had been recorded called "East Side West Side", but was released only in Australia, (due to a disagreement with Berry Gordy over its hit potential), the song had been written by Ron Welser and Terry Johnson (of The Flamingos'). Jimmy recorded and released (with his brother David Ruffin), a cover version of "Stand By Me" by Ben E. King, the single was taken from the Ruffin Brother's album, "I Am My Brother's Keeper".

Jimmy's other major Motown hits include "I've Passed This Way Before", "Gonna Give Her All The Love I've Got", "Don't You Miss Me A Little Bit Baby", "I'll Say Forever My Love", "It's Wonderful To Be Loved By You" and the 1974 recording "Tell Me What You Want".

In the 1980's, Jimmy decided to move the UK, where his popularity on the Northern Soul scene and his huge fan base helped Jimmy to his own talk show. Also in the 1980's, Jimmy made an impressive comeback on RSO Records with a major pop hit called, "Hold On to My Love", produced by Robin Gibb of the Bee Gees. Jimmy's next collaboration was in 1986, with the UK pop group Heaven, with "A Foolish Thing To Do" and "My Sensitivity" on their EP release.

In 1997 Jimmy performed in England at Summerbreeze 97, held on the weekend of

July 18-20, along with over 100 musicians in some 20 acts with four international headline names. Next, he performed at the concert to honour Princess Diana, he has now retired from the music scene.

In addition to his brother David who died from a drug overdose in 1991 aged 50, he had three children Quincy, Rita Mae (deceased) and Rosa (deceased).

Album Track: "I'll Say For Forever My Love", Jimmy Ruffin.

The Satintones

Formed in Detroit in 1957

Original members: James Ellis - Sony Saunders - Robert Bateman - Chico Leverrette.

Later Members: Veron Williams - Sammy Mack.

Motown Connection: Background singers - First Group to Sign to Motown - "My Beloved" was the first commercial release on the new Motown label.

Formed in Detroit in 1957, The Satintones claim to fame was that they were the first group to be signed to the Motown label. Starting from three groups from the Detroit area called The Quailtones, Five Sounds and The Fidelitones, they first rehearsed in Chico Leverrette's house in the late 1950's. Their first record under The Satintones name was the single "Motorcity", now a very rare recording from Motown with James Ellis on  lead vocals. The Satintones signed to Tamla in 1959, the group's first single was "Going To The Hop", this was followed by the first single on Motown Records, called "My Beloved", credited to Berry Gordy, Sony Saunders, Robert Bateman and Chico Leverrette.

An interesting footnote in Motown history was the single "Solid Sender" released by Chico Leverette on the Tamla label. It is the first known release on the Tamla 54000 series, and is most likely the first recording produced by Berry Gory on his own Tamla Label. Berry Gordy did have a few earlier releases on the very rare three digits and one digit on Tamla and Motown, but "Solid Sender" was probably his first original release.

Next came their second release called "My Beloved" the first commercial release on the Motown label, at this time, they also started touring the Midwest as a Motown act. Added to the group were Veron Williams and Sammy Mack. Then the group was sued for using a song by The Shirelles "Tomorrow and Always", after that dispute James Ellis decided to leave the group, after three further singles for Motown the group disbanded, with Robert Bateman becoming a producer for the Motown. Robert Bateman's most known work is with The Marvelettes on the hit single "Please Mr. Postman" in 1962, before leaving Motown and setting up as an independent producer in Detroit. There is one album that was unreleased on Motown called "The Satintones Sing" from 1961.

After Robert Bateman, Sonny Sanders had the most impressive post Satintones career, working as an arranger, producer and bandleader in Detroit and Chicago. In Detroit, he arranged and produced several big hits for Ric-Tic, notably Edwin Starr's "Stop Her On Sight" with The Funk Brothers providing the background session musicians, and The Reflections' "Just Like Romeo And Juliet". Moving on to Chicago, working with producer Carl Davis, he arranged such hits as Mary Well's "Dear Lover", the Artistics "I'm Gonna Miss You", Barbara Acklin's "Love Makes A Woman" (with also credits as a co-writer), and Gene Chandler's "The Girl Don't Care". Sonny Sanders was heavily involved with the Brunswick label during the late 1960's and early 1970's. Next, moving on to support the career of Sydney Joe Qualls, producing most of his 1970's recordings.

In 1990, The Satintones reformed to work with Ian Levine's on the "Motorcity" project in the Detroit, recording and helping with production on this label.

Born Raynoma Mayberry Liles on the 8th March 1937 in Detroit, Michigan

Motown Connection: With Berry Gordy started the Rayber Voices - Second Wife of Berry Gordy - An early influence in the creation of Motown - Organiser of Studio Musicians - Creative Assistant - Administrator.

Born and raised in Detroit, Raynoma was the daughter of a janitor who worked at the Cadillac plant in Detroit. She was first introduced to Berry Gordy through his sister's music interests, Berry Gordy at the time was a singer and songwriter, mainly making his name through Jackie Wilson. Raynoma was auditioned by Berry Gordy on behalf of his sister for her Anna records; eventually Raynoma would become a major partner of the Berry Gordy Motown business. It is often stated that in the early days of Motown, Raynoma had a 50% stake in the label, and it was Berry Gordy who persuaded Raynoma to relinquish this stake.

Before the formal incorporation of Motown, Raynoma, Berry Gordy and his musicians, used the small apartment she owned to launch the Rayber Music Company, a combination of Ray's and Berry Gordy's first name. The business idea was to charge budding artists who wanted to make a record using their facilities.

The next venture that Raynoma and Berry Gordy started after the Rayber Music Company was their first label Tamla (which would become eventually Motown records). Their first major hit would be The Miracle's with "Shop Around". Raynoma had the unusual gift of "perfect pitch" which proved invaluable in the early days of Motown when the number of employees was small and everybody was multitasking, Raynoma was also heavily involved in arranging recordings. Raynoma went on to working and developing the first major stars at Motown like, The Miracles and The Satintones. Around this time Raynoma and Berry Gordy became romantically involved even though at the time Berry Gordy was married and had three children. When their son, Kerry, was nearly a year old, Berry Gordy divorced his first wife and married Raynoma.

The marriage to Berry Gordy had ended by 1963, but Raynoma continued working for Motown in Detroit, working with Diana Ross for a short time, until she moved to the Motown office in New York, however, her employment with Motown ended when Raynoma pressed 5000 copies of Mary Well's No1 hit single "My Guy" without the knowledge of Motown, with the intention of selling these "pirate" copies to record stores in New York. Raynoma decided, rather than face prosecution, she would sign a "general release" from Motown and all its associated companies and labels and left Motown. Raynoma then married Eddie Singleton and founded with him the short-lived soul label, "Shrine Records", in Washington DC which would issue some classic Northern Soul recordings.

One of Raynoma's most controversial projects was her book "Berry, Me and Motown" not well received by Berry Gordy and his family, with claim and counter claim going between both parties for many years. However, what was never in doubt was her contribution to the early days at Motown, and her support given to the early stars at Motown.

Raynoma then moved to Los Angeles with Eddie Singleton, and his family, before divorcing (interestingly Eddie Singleton would later marry Barbara Randolph an ex-Motown singer). Raynoma then concentrated on developing the performing careers of two of her four children, Cliff Lyles and Rea Singleton, her son Ed Singleton Jnr worked in the A&R Department at Warner Brothers records.

Raynoma had a son Cliff, from a teenage marriage, and then she married Berry Gordy which produced a son Kerry, this married ended in 1963, and Raynoma then married Eddie Singleton which produced two son's Rea and Eddie Jnr.

Eddie Singleton

Born William Edward Singleton in New Jersey, New York State - Died in South Africa

Motown Connection: Writing - Producer.

Eddie's mother Mary was a gospel singer, and through this she encouraged Eddie to develop his musical abilities. Eddie's first entry into the music business was organising concerts at the local army base in New Jersey. Eddie moved to New York in 1956, which brought him into contact with Hy Weiss, the owner of Old Town records, and was offered and accepted a recording contract with the label, Eddie recorded a few solo singles, but these were never released. Eddie's next move was to Brunswick Records recording with a group he had formed called "The Chromatics", their only release "Too Late" and "My Heart Let Me Be Free" released in 1958, was a moderate hit and became a collector's item for collectors of early Brunswick label recordings.

The group did perform at shows, but Eddie wanted to move on to producing his own material and left the group. In 1959, Eddie decided to open his own office in New York in the Broadway area. For the next three years Eddie built up an impressive roster of artists and became well connected with all of the major entertainers in New York.

Eddie began writing and producing for Barbara Lewis in the late 1950's and early 1960's, also included on this list was The Matadors (which would become The Miracles, one of Motown's first groups) and Marie Knight. Next moving on to work with Motown, Eddie wrote "Don't Bring Back Memories" for The Four Tops and produced one of the great Northern Soul classics "The La Rue" for Lada Edmund Jnr.

Eddie married Berry Gordy's ex-wife Raynoma in the early 1960's while both were still associated with Motown. On leaving Motown Eddie and Raynoma would start the short lived "Shrine" recruiting Harry Bass as his right-hand man, Harry Bass would work with Eddie for most of his musical career and contributed songs and business skills to the label. Artists associated with the label include, Ray Pollard, Eddie Daye, The Cautions, The Cairos, Shirley Edwards, The Prophets and JD Bryant. Although commercially unsuccessful, "Shrine" would eventually become more appreciated in the UK than the US. A detailed history was documented in the booklets to the two volumes of Kent CDs "Shrine: The Rarest Soul Label". The quality and rarity of the Shrine records combined to make the label a Northern Soul collector's item.

Next, working with Ian Levine's Motorcity project, Eddie was a great supporter of this work in the late 1980's and early 1990's, helping Ian Levine with production and promotion. Eddie's second marriage was to the ex Motown singer Barbara Randolph who sadly pre-deceased him by about ten years. He was a warm, talented man who was very happy that his commercially unsuccessful work at Shrine was eventually appreciated overseas.

Eddie had been living in South Africa for several years, before his death, he is survived by his son Eddie Jnr who is still involved in films, music and production.

Born Crathman Plato Spencer on the 13TH January 1938 in Detroit, Michigan - Died 20th October 2004 in Oak Park, Michigan

Motown Connection: Tenor Singer with The Spinners (aka Detroit Spinners and The Motown Spinners in the UK) - Singer with The Originals - Songwriter - Producer.

C P Spencer first sang doo-wop on street corners in Detroit as a teenager with his friend Walter Gaines. In 1954 a group of friends in Ferndale High School in Ferndale Michigan formed a group consisting of C P Spencer, Billy Henderson, Henry Fambrough, Pervis Jackson, and James Edwards calling themselves The Domingoes. James Edwards lasted only a few weeks; he was replaced by Bobbie Smith, who sang lead on most of The Spinners' early records (and many of their biggest Atlantic hits), C P Spencer left the group shortly afterwards. C P Spencer along with Walter Gaines joined the 5 Jets, the group which evolved into the 5 Stars for a single on the Mark-X label in 1958. Next C P Spencer teamed up with Ty Hunter, Lamont Dozier and David Ruffin to form the group The Voicemasters.

The group came to the attention of Gwen Gordy, the sister of Berry Gordy, who released the single "Hope and Pray" their first recording on her Anna label in 1960. The group had a local hit with the ballad "Needed (For Lovers Only)" and released further singles, but without too much success.

By 1964, David Ruffin had moved to join The Temptations and Ty Hunter had signed a recording deal with Chess Records in Chicago. Lamont Dozier was now a songwriter in the newly established Holland-Dozier-Holland team at Motown, Next Lamont Dozier introduced C P Spencer, Walter Gaines and Hank Dixon to Freddie Gorman, who then formed The Originals, added to this group was Joe Stubbs (brother of The Four Tops lead vocalist Levi Stubbs) in 1966 the Originals recorded a cover of the Leadbelly song "Goodnight Irene". Following Joe Stubbs' departure, they carried on as a four-piece, recording the singles "We've Got a Way Out of Love" and "Green Grow the Lilacs" for Soul (a subsidiary of Motown), at this time The Originals were also providing backing vocals for the majority of the Motown Stars including, Jimmy Ruffin, Stevie Wonder and Marvin Gaye.

Marvin Gaye then suggested they should record "Baby I'm For Real" and helped produce the recording, interestingly, The Originals all sang some of the lead parts on this 1969 million-seller. The following year, they recorded another million-seller called "The Bells", again produced by Marvin Gaye, and the single reached No12 in the United States. Further singles, "We Can Make It Baby" and "God Bless Whoever Sent You", struggled in the lower reaches of the charts and Spencer left the group in 1972.

Having contributed to four of the eight albums The Originals issued on Soul, the group then embarked on a disco recording career and C P Spencer returned in 1978 for two albums on Fantasy; three years later they cut "Yesterday and Today" in 1981, dedicated to Ty Hunter, who died that year.

The Originals. L to R: Freddie Gorman, Hank Dixon, Walter Gaines and C P Spencer.

Often described as Motown's best-kept secret, the Originals worked with the British producer Ian Levine on his label Motorcity in the late 1980's and early 1990's and made their belated UK live début in Manchester. In 2002 C P Spencer died of a heart attack.

Formed in 1954 in Ferndale, Michigan Aka The Spinners and The Motown Spinners in the UK

Original Members: Henry Fambrough Born 10th May 1935in Detroit, Michigan - Robert 'Bobbie' Smith Born 10th April 1937 in Detroit Michigan - Billy Henderson Born 8th September 1939 in Detroit, Michigan Died 2nd February 2007 - Pervis Jackson Born 17th May 1938 in New Orleans, Louisiana Died 18th August 2008 in Detroit Michigan - C P Spencer (Born Crathman Plato Spencer) Born 13th January 1938 in Detroit Michigan Died 20th October 2004 in Oak Park Michigan - G C Cameron (Born George Curtis Cameron) Born 21st September 1945 in Jackson Mississippi - James Edward (who only lasted a few weeks before being replaced by Bobbie Smith).

Later members: George Dixon Philippé Soul Wynn (a.k.a. Phillip Walker) Born on the 3rd April 1941 Detroit, Michigan - Died 14th July 1984.

Motown Connection: Group - Background Singers.

Formed In 1954 a group of friends in Ferndale High School in Ferndale, Michigan, just outside Detroit, came together to make music. Billy Henderson, Henry Fambrough, Pervis Jackson, C P Spencer, and James Edwards called themselves The Domingoes. James Edwards lasted only a few weeks; he was replaced by Bobbie Smith, who sang lead on most of The Spinners' early records (and many of their biggest Atlantic hits). C P Spencer left the group shortly afterwards, and would later go on to be a member of the Voice Masters and The Originals. He was replaced by George Dixon. The group renamed themselves The Spinners in 1961. This name was chosen after looking at car hubcaps and noting how they spun around on a car's wheel. Known as The Motown Spinners in the UK (to avoid confusion with the The Spinners folk group), and Detroit Spinners, after they left Motown.

In 1961, they were signed to a recording contract by Harvey Fuqua for his Tri-Phi label, the subsequent single, "That's What Girls Are Made For" became a chart hit. Tri-Phi issued another single which made the US Top Thirty in 1961, called "Love (I'm So Glad) I Found You", on which Harvey Fuqua also appeared, after this recording Bobbie Smith took over the lead vocals with out any further success. However, when Harvey Fuqua sold his Tri-Phi record company to Berry Gordy the consequence of this sale meant The Spinners would became Motown Recording

Artists. The Spinners recorded a single for Motown, briefly charting with "I'll Always Love You" in 1965.

By 1968 the Spinners had been moved to VIP (subsidiary label of Motown) working with producer Johnny Bristol, and then Stevie Wonder, who helped them back into the US charts with "It's a Shame". The song was also a Top 20 hit in the UK, where the group was renamed The Motown Spinners to avoid confusion with the Liverpool folk group already called The Spinners. Also in that year The Spinners recorded "We'll Have It Made". The Spinners (in their opinion) were promoted behind artists like, The Supremes, Stevie Wonder and The Temptations into international stars, this was reinforced when The Spinners generally opened the show for other Motown artists, and never gained top spot for themselves, although the Spinners had some R&B hits at Motown during their stay at Motown including "I'll Always Love You" and "Truly Yours". Before the band signed with Atlantic Records, Philippé Wynne replaced Cameron as the groups lead vocalist. Wynne had previously sung with Catfish and Bootsy Collins.

When other labels like Stax expressed an interest in signing The Spinners, Berry Gordy invoked a clause in their contract which tied their lead vocalist G C Cameron to a solo deal with Motown. The group's real success came after leaving Motown in 1972 for Atlantic Records, on Aretha Franklin's advice. The label offered the leading Philly Sound producer Thom Bell the opportunity to work with any of its artists and Bell chose The Spinners. Thom Bell and his songwriters created a series of big hits during the seventies, starting with "I'll Be Around", in 1972, (DJs started playing this b/side of "How Could I Let You Get Away", it became The Spinners' first single for Atlantic and their first million-seller. In 1973, "Could It Be I'm Falling in Love", recorded at the same session, also made the US Top Five. Smith and Wynne shared lead vocals on "One of a Kind (Love Affair)" in 1973, while all five Spinners took their turn singing lead on "(They Just Can't Stop the) Games People Play" in 1975. The Spinners scored one of their biggest hits in 1976 with "The Rubberband Man", a track co-written by Thom Bell and inspired by his son Mark, the groups only No1 hit. In 1977 Phillip Wynne left to pursue a solo career, being replaced by John Edwards.

Wynne's departure coincided with the Philly Sound's loss of popularity to disco and, in 1980, the group switched producers from Bell to Michael Zager. He created two best-selling medleys for The Spinners. The first combined the old Four Seasons hit "Working My Way Back to You" with Zager's own composition "Forgive Me Girl". The second used the same formula with Sam Cooke's "Cupid" and "I've Loved You for a Long Time". The first recording was the group's final million-selling record and their only No1 hit in Britain. During the early 1980's, they had several minor hits before touring on the "oldies" circuit, became their main focus, with the Four

Seasons and the Righteous Brothers. The final album for Atlantic was "Cross Fire", in 1984, although the group was featured in the Atlantic Record Company's 40th anniversary concert in New York in 1988.

In 1989, the group signed for the Fantasy distributed Volt label releasing the album "Down To Business". In early 2000 the Elton John and Thom Bell collaboration, of "Are You Ready For Love?" became a No1 hit in the UK. The song originally had been recorded by The Spinners on their album 'From Here To Eternally' on Atlantic Records in 1978/79.

The group did re-record some of their earlier material for the 1999's new studio album "At Their Best". In 2004, Billy Henderson alleged mismanagement of the group's finances and sued the group's corporation and business manager to obtain financial records. The business manager at the time was the wife of Bobbie Smith. Only two original members, Henry Fambrough and Bobbie Smith, are still with the group after fifty years in the music industry.

The Spinners were nominated for six Grammy Awards and they received a star on the Hollywood Walk of Fame, the second star for a musical group consisting of Black people.

Album Track: "It's a Shame", Motown Spinners.

Born Charles Hatcher on the 21st January 1942 in Nashville, Tennessee (raised in Cleveland, Ohio) - Died 2nd April 2003 Bramcote, Nottingham, England

Motown Connection: Singer - Duets with Motown Artist Blinky - Writer.

Edwin and his cousin's future soul singers Roger and Willie Hatcher moved to Cleveland, Ohio at an early age. In 1957, Edwin formed a "doo-wop" group called, The Future Tones, which started Edwin's singing career. By the early 1960's Edwin had moved to Detroit and was signed to his first label Ric-Tic, (which would eventually be bought by Motown) in 1968.

In 1960, Edwin joined the army performing with a special group of servicemen, after the Army, Edwin decided to turn professional and toured for two years as the vocalist with the organist Wild Bill Doggett's band. While in the band, Edwin was spotted in Detroit by Eddie Wingate and signed Edwin in 1966 to his Golden World records, one of Eddie Wingate's labels at Golden World was the Ric-Tic which is where Edwin's releases would be issued from.

Edwin's first record was released on this label called, "Agent Double 0 Soul", a hit in the pop charts in August 1965. Ed Wingate used The Funk Brothers on this recording, initially without Berry Gordy knowing, it is rumoured when Berry Gordy found out about the recording he fined The Funk Brothers. Next came "Back Street" which was not a commercial success, but Edwin's most famous recording came next, with the Top 10 hit, "Stop Her On Sight (S.O.S)" in early 1966 (again using The Funk Brothers as backing musicians). During this period, Edwin also developed his performing career with appearances on many television shows, including "Shindig", "Where The Action Is" and "Hollywood A Go Go!"

Berry Gordy would buy the Ed Wingate labels and turned the studio used by Golden World into "Motown Studio B" to help accommodate the extra recording space needed by the ever increasing roster of stars signed to Motown.

Edwin was in England when he discovered his contract had been sold to Motown and that he was now a Motown artist. On Edwin's return to the US, he was booked to perform at The Apollo Theatre in New York, including a welcome by The Temptations to Motown. Edwin refused to record for Motown for two years, although his single recordings work at Ric-Tic and Golden World was re-issued now under the Gordy label, with a Motown album called "Soul Master", released in 1968.

In February 1969, he had a major tour of the US to promote his newly released song, "Twenty-Five Miles" which became a No6 on the pop charts the single was produced by Johnny Bristol and Harvey Fuqua. Tours of the UK followed this, where Edwin had over the previous years, built a large fan base on the Northern Soul scene. In 1970 he recorded the albums "War and Peace", and "Involved" from the albums came the biggest single hit of his career. "War" would reach the No1 position on the US pop charts and become a major international hit for Edwin. The song was produced by Norman Whitfield and written by Norman Whitfield and Barrett Strong, the song had been intended for The Temptations, but was deemed too controversial by Motown for the group. The album "Involved" also featured another song of very similar a type called, "Stop the War Now", which was a minor hit in its own right.

Adopted as an anti-Vietnam song "War" would go on to sell over 3.5 million records by the end of the year, and a further 1.5 million sales since that time, When the 1991 Gulf War started the BBC decided to ban the record and it was again banned by American radio networks after the 11th September 2001 attack on the World Trade Centre. In 1971, Edwin moved away from the protest song and recorded the cover of "Raindrops Keep Falling On My Head" Edwin also recorded a few songs with the Motown artist Blinky.

In 1974, Edwin recorded the song "Hell Up In Harlem" for the film, of the same name, which was the sequel to "Black Caesar", an earlier hit with a soundtrack by James Brown. Edwin stayed with Motown until 1975, but after "War" his Motown career never reached those heights again. Edwin always had a strong following when it came to his live shows, Edwin became involved with many R&B shows featuring artists like, Jackie Wilson, Otis Redding, and Sam and Dave.

Edwin made a brief comeback during the disco craze, with recordings like, "(Eye to Eye) Contact" and "H.A.P.P.Y. Radio" in 1979, combining this with touring the UK and Europe and playing the "oldies" circuit. In 1984 (after the death of Marvin Gaye) he recorded a tribute album called "Marvin Gaye" for UK based Streetwave label. Further recordings were issued on the record label such as 20th Century Records, Avatar, Calibre, 10 Records, Motown (a return to his former label for a 1989 remix of "25 Miles") and Hippodrome.

Edwin had relocated to Britain and moved to Nottingham, and signed with the Hippodrome label and issued a couple of singles on that label in 1985 and 1986 including "It Ain't Fair", a minor hit. Next moving to the UK label Virgin, Edwin was produced by the hit making team Stock Aitken and Waterman, for the club hit "Whatever Makes Our Love Grow".

In the late 1980's early 1990's Edwin was a major supporter of Ian Levine's Motorcity project and helped Ian Levine promote the venture, releasing six singles and the album "Where Is the Sound?", as well as co-writing several songs for other artists on the label. Also at this time Edwin had a recording contract with WEA in Germany. Edwin had some songs featured on the Walt Disney film "Mousersize".

In 1989, a No17 UK hit by the Cookie Crew called "Got to Keep On" sampled a portion of "25 Miles". The previous years remix of "25 Miles" appeared on the UK charity No1 single "Let It Be" by Ferry Aid, recorded by various artists who gave their contribution and waved their royalties for the charity.

Edwin returned to recording in 2000, teaming up with the UK band Utah Saints to record a new version of his song "Funky Music Sho Nuff Turns Me On". In 2002, Edwin recorded a song with the UK musician Jool's Holland, singing "Snowflake Boogie" on his album, "More Friends". Edwin's last recording was with Utah Saints, on a so far unreleased version of his No1 hit "War".

Edwin is also a noted songwriter. Among his song writing credits are "Oh How Happy" (recorded by the Shades of Blue), "Agent Double 0 Soul," "Stop Her On Sight (S.O.S.)" and 'Twenty Five Miles", as well as numerous other songs he recorded himself.

I last saw Starr appear on a New Years Eve TV show on 31st December 2002 and before that a couple of months before at Woking in Surrey with, Martha Reeves and May Wilson. Edwin was a great live performer and remained a hero on England's Northern Soul circuit until his death from a heart attack not long after performing a live show.

Edwin, who had been previously been married, had a son and daughter and was living with his partner Jean at the time of his death.

Album Track: "Stop Her On Sight (S.O.S.)", Edwin Starr.

William "Mickey" Stevenson

Born William Stevenson in Detroit, Michigan

Motown Connection: Writer - Producer - Arranger - A&R Director.

Mickey began his musical career singing in gospel choirs and doo-wop groups in the Detroit area. One of the first employees at Motown starting around 1959. Mickey co-produced Marv Johnson, Motown's first recording artist, but his place in Motown history would probably be the putting together of the in house musicians which would go onto become the core of The Funk Brothers. Starting with pianist Joe Hunter as the first recognised bandleader, Mickey brought to Motown what would become a truly remarkable group of Detroit jazz and club musicians, including bassist James Jamerson, guitarists Robert White and Joe Messina, and drummer Benny Benjamin, these individuals would be the first "building blocks" to establishing the "Motown Sound".

Mickey was Motown's first A&R director, helping to discover many of the future stars at Motown like Martha Reeves, Marvin Gaye and future wife Kim Weston. In 1961 Mickey teamed up with co-writer Barrett Strong to score his first major hit, Eddie Holland's (of the future production team Holland-Dozier-Holland) called "Jamie". Next came the hit for The Marvelettes' "Beechwood 4-5789," this time with Motown founder Berry Gordy, a few weeks later, Motown released Marvin Gaye's first hit single, "Stubborn Kind of Fellow", which Mickey co-wrote as well. Using Martha Reeves, (at the time Mickey's secretary), and The Vandellas to produce the backing vocals on the record.

When Mary Wells failed to arrive for a planned recording session, Mickey instead asked Martha Reeves to record the song, with The Vandellas, resulting in the group's 1963 recording called "I'll Have to Let Him Go". In that same year, Mickey produced The Miracles hit record "Mickey's Monkey", followed in 1964, by the Mickey Stevenson, Marvin Gaye and Ivy Hunter recording on Martha and The Vandellas' titled "Dancing in the Street", this became his biggest song writing hit for the Motown. Also in 1964 he recruited Norman Whitfield as his A&R assistant, and by doing so brought to Motown an individual who would become one of Motown's most influential and successful producers. Mickey's last major hit for Motown was in 1966 with the classic "It Takes Two", by Marvin Gaye and by then his wife, Kim Weston. Mickey used the name Avery Vandenburg when writing for Jobete's subsidiary "Stein and Van Stock" while at Motown.

Other inputs from Mickey as a writer and producer using many different co-writers and producers, included "Ask the Lonely", "What Becomes of the Brokenhearted", "My Baby Loves Me", and "Uptight (Everything's Alright)" Mickey also wrote "Devil With The Blue Dress On" in 1964 for Shorty Long, which became a major hit for Mitch Ryder and the Detroit Wheels in 1966.

341

By early 1967 both Mickey and Kim Weston had left Motown to form their own label called People. At the time Kim Weston signed to MGM records, and Mickey was offered a reported million dollar deal to assume control of the company's floundering Venture subsidiary, but his influence was not a success and the label did not have any major hits.

In 1969, Mickey decided to go into producing music for films the first piece of work was for the film "Changes". Next came a series of theatrical musicals including "Swann", "Showgirls", "Wings and Things", "The Gospel Truth", "TKO" and "Chocolate City".

For 1999's recording "Sang, Sista, Sang", a tribute to legendary vocalists Bessie Smith, Billie Holiday and Josephine Baker. Mickey also reunited with ex-colleague and ex-Motown star Smokey Robinson. Now divorced from Kim Weston.

Album Track: "Danger Heartbreak Dead Ahead", The Marvelettes.

Born in 1942 in Detroit, Michigan

Motown Connection: Member of The Temptations (Replacing Paul Williams 1971) - Quality Control - Writer.

Born and raised in Detroit. Richard began his music career at the age of 12, playing piano and singing with his mother who has been a professional entertainer for over 47 years. By 1955, Richard along with his cousin Melvin Franklin was invited to join a vocal group called Otis Williams and The Distants. When the group subsequently signed to Motown not as Otis Williams and The Distants, but as The Primes adding Paul Williams, Eddie Kendrick and Eldridge Bryant the new group took the name The Elgins, (not to be confused with the future Motown group of the same name) before the change to The Temptations.

Richard undertook the lead vocals for, Otis Williams and The Distants, and sang lead on their local hit "Come On", co-written by Otis Williams and Detroit manager and producer Johnnie Mae Matthews, she had Richard briefly lead a new Distants group in the early 1960's.

This led to an introduction to Motown where Richard was given the role as lead singer of The Monitors, which were already signed to Motown. Interestingly, at the time Richard was also coaching a girl group, (which consisted of Florence Ballard, Mary Wilson and Diane Ross) called The Primettes a sister group to his cousin Melvin Franklin's The Primes. Richard's valuable experience in vocal coaching, choreography and his knowledge of the music industry helped Richard gain a position in Motown's Quality Control Department.

The Monitors played a small part in Motown, their first release as The Majestics was to have been "Hello Love" on Motown's VIP label in 1964, but the release was cancelled. A year later, "Say You" was released initially as The Majestics, but a name change to The Monitors was made after it was found there was another group already recording as The Majestics for another company. Recording the one major hit "Greeting (This Is Uncle Sam)" produced by Mickey Stevenson, two more singles appeared on the VIP label "Since I Lost You Girl" in November 1966 and "Bring Back The Love" in January 1968. They were then switched to Motown's Soul label and released "Step by Step (Hand in Hand)" in the summer of 1968, but this was to be their final single with Motown.

By 1969, The Temptations' lead singer David Ruffin, left for a solo career and was replaced by former Contours lead vocalist Dennis Edwards. In 1971, singer Eddie Kendricks left for a solo career as well. Paul Williams, suffering from the effects of alcohol abuse, left the group (he later committed suicide), and Richard was his replacement. Choosing Richard, then lead singer of The Monitors and known from his days as lead singer of The Distants, to travel with The Temptations and sing all of Paul's parts from behind a curtain, except for Paul's solo contributions, such as "Don't Look Back" and "For Once in My Life". Richard firstly started to perform on stage as a member of The Temptations, then taking his place on recording sessions, before officially taking over from Paul in 1971.

With the arrival of Richard and new lead singer Dennis Edwards for The Temptations the musical style changed from love songs to looking at topical subjects such as the Vietnam War and urban poverty with songs such as take "Superstar (Remember How You Got Where You Are)" in 1971, "Masterpiece" in 1973, and his featured solo, "Hey Girl (I Like Your Style)" in 1973, "A Look Around", "Ball Of Confusion (What The World Is Today)" and the international award winning "Papa Was A Rolling Stone" in 1972, which earned the group three Grammy awards. It wouldn't be until 1985, that a ballad "Treat Her Like A Lady" would give The Temptations their next softer hit.

Richard has appeared on television, stage and radio, Richard's notable lead vocals are on "Heavenly", "The First Time Ever I Saw Your Face", "Firefly", "Hey Girl", "Masterpiece", "Every Time I Close My Eyes", "I'll Keep My Light In My Window", "Super Star", "Show Me Your Love", "Bare Back", "Standing On the Top", "Love Comes At Christmas", from The Temptations Christmas album "Everything for Christmas" and "Papa Was a Rolling Stone". Among the awards Richard has received are three Grammy Awards, two American Music Awards, and an NAACP Award. Richard was in attendance when The Temptations were inducted into the Rock and Roll Hall of Fame in 1989.

Following the death of his cousin Melvin Franklin in 1995 of heart failure, Richard felt it was time to leave the group. Animosity between Richard and Otis Williams, the group's only surviving original member surfaced and it is alleged that the group's finances revealed mis-management of funds resulting in Richard being significantly underpaid along with other members of the group.

While Richard has spent most of his post-Temptations years as a producer for Los Angeles-based artists, Richard and former Temptations lead singer Ali-Ollie Woodson formed the Temptations Review and recruited singers Willie Green, Perry Moore and Chris Arnold to the group. Richard and the new group have no official rights to the Temptations name; it belongs to Motown with Otis Williams having control of the use of the name. Interestingly, Otis Williams won a court settlement against former lead singer Dennis Edwards and forced him to stop using the name the New Temptations. It was decided that Dennis's group would be called

"The Temptations Review featuring Dennis Edwards", the name that Dennis Edwards tours under to this day. Otis Williams has been exerting legal pressure to stop Richard using any variants of the name.

With a book planned called "Ball of Confusion", Richard chronicles his years with the group. Richard also continues to perform in his own show that includes the legendary music of The Temptations along with other classic hit songs as a solo artist to this day. At times, he performs as a duo with former Temptations Damon Harris, who had joined the group at about the same time he did, also Richard has put together a tribute group called "The Voices starring Richard Street".

Richard married The Velvelettes' lead singer Carolyn "Cal" Gill in 1969, divorcing in 1983; they have one son, Richard Jnr.

Born on the 5th Feb 1941 in West Point, Mississippi

With Norman Whitfield in the background.

Motown Connection: Singer - Writer - Producer.

Born in West Point, but moved to Detroit in his teenage years, Barrett is a cousin of fellow Detroit soul singer Nolan Strong. Barrett became one of the first employees at Motown, working with Janie Bradford, and Berry Gordy as one of the first writing production teams to establish themselves at the then "New Hitsville Studio" in Detroit. While working with and bouncing ideas around with Janie Bradford and Berry Gordy a tune would emerge that would shape the first big push by Motown into the pop chart. With Berry Gordy initially on vocals, and Barrett and Janie Bradford providing lyrics and structure, it was then that Barrett took over vocals and the song "Money (That's What I Want)" was recorded. Released on Anna records (Berry Gordy's sister Anna Gordy label) the single would provide both chart exposure and cash to Berry Gordy to further establish his Motown label.

Although "Money (That's What I Want)" was Barrett's only major hit as a singer, reaching No2 on the R&B charts and just missing the pop chart Top 20. Barrett was without doubt a key person in helping Berry Gordy establish Motown as a force in the record business, both as a close friend and as a producer, singer, and arranger.

Barrett's next collaboration at Motown, during the late 1960's and early 1970's, was with Norman Whitfield, on some truly classic Motown songs. These included, Marvin Gaye's major hits "I Heard It Through the Grapevine", "Too Busy Thinking About My Baby", next with Edwin Starr's "War", "Take Me in Your Arms and Love Me" for Gladys Knight and The Pips, and "Smiling Faces Sometimes" by The Undisputed Truth, all of which Barrett co-wrote with Norman Whitfield.

A leading figure (with Norman Whitfield) on the introduction of "Psychedelic Soul" by Motown, (primarily by The Temptation's) Motown issued a string of hits including, "Cloud Nine", "I Can't Get Next to You", "Psychedelic Shack", "Ball of Confusion (That's What the World Is Today)", and "Papa Was a Rollin' Stone", as well as many other international hits. Barrett, along with Norman Whitfield, received a Grammy Award for Best R&B Song in 1973 for co-writing "Papa was a Rollin' Stone".

When Berry Gordy decided to leave Detroit and move Motown to Los Angeles in 1972, Barrett stayed in Detroit and signed with Epic records. After only one single which failed to chart, Barret then moved to Capitol records, which culminated in the release of the album "Stronghold" in 1975 next, in 1976 came "Live and Love". Although the album was not a commercial success, there was one single hit, called "Man up in the Sky" which did make the charts, with Johnny Bristol (an ex-colleague from Motown) covering the song which again became a minor hit.

Though out the 1980's Barret continued to recorded and produce for many different independent labels recording "Rock It Easy" as a solo artist. Barrett wrote and produced "You Can Depend on Me," which was included on The Dells' album called "The Second Time" in 1988. In the mid-1990's Barrett decided to launch his own recording studio in Detroit to help develop the local talent in the city, located in the Southfield area of Detroit, the studio was opened in 1995. This also incorporated a new record label called Blarritt Records, and Barrett's first project was developing the artist Eliza (born Elizabeth Thomasian).

Barrett's first album in over twenty five years was released in 2008 called "Stronghold II", co-written with rocker/songwriter Eliza Neal in 2008 in digital format only, sounding surprisingly like some of the early Motown recordings with eight original tracks and a cover of The Temptations "I Wish it Would Rain", written and produced with colleagues, Norman Whitefield and Roger Penzabene.

"Money (That's What I Want)" was covered by many artists including The Beatles (as an album track) The Kingsmen in 1964, fellow Motown artist Jnr Walker and The All Stars in 1966, and the UK group the Flying Lizards in1980.

Barrett is currently recovering from a stoke.

Album Track: "Money (That's What I Want)", Barret Strong.

Aka The Primettes formed in Detroit in 1959, disbanded 1977

Original members: Betty McGlown (when with the group as the Primettes) but left in 1961 - Florence Ballard - Diana Ross (aka Diane Ross) - Mary Wilson - Barbara Martin (was with the group when the name was changed to The Supremes) but left in 1961.

Secondary members: (joined the group while at Motown) - Cindy Birdsong (ex-Patti LaBelle and the Blue Belles) replaced Florence Ballard in 1967, returned in 1974 to replace Susaye Green - Jean Terrell replaced Diana Ross in 1969 - Lynda Laurence replaced Cindy Birdsong in 1972 - Sherrie Payne replaced Jean Terrell in 1974 - Susaye Green to 1975.

Motown Connection: Background Singers - Most Successful Female Group at Motown.

Motown's most successful performers of the 1960's, with five US No1 singles in a row, and twelve No1's in total (from the original line up). At the age of fourteen, Florence Ballard along with a group of friends (from the Brewster Housing Project) formed the group The Primettes as a "sister group" to local Detroit group The Primes (later to become The Temptations) and started to perform at gigs in Detroit. Florence Ballard was the lead in forming the group with Mary Wilson,

Original Supremes members from L to R, (front): Barbara Martin, Mary Wilson, and Florence Ballard, (top): Diane Ross (the spelling "Diana" was used as a stage name).

(who had lived in the same neighbourhood), and had performed at the same talent show, with Betty McGlown, Barbara Martin and Diana Ross. However, the trio that would become famous as The Supremes was Diana Ross, Mary Wilson and Florence Ballard.

The Primettes did release a one record "Tears of Sorrow" b/side "Pretty Baby" for Lupine Records in 1960, they also sang backing vocals for other singers on that label, before unsuccessfully auditioning for Berry Gordy at Motown. Berry Gordy gave the reason that they should first finish school before trying for a musical career, however after hanging around "Hitsville" for many months, they eventually signed to Motown in 1960. Shortly after they signed for Motown, they had been renamed The Supremes, Barbara Martin had left (after replacing Betty McGlown) reducing the group to a trio, and the group continued with the same line up until Florence Ballard left in 1967.

With the group's name changed to The Supremes, (with prompting from Berry Gordy) they had their first release on Tamla label in April of 1961. The Supremes' first Motown recordings were much more girl group oriented than their later hits. Additionally, not all of them featured Diana Ross on lead vocals, both Mary Wilson and Florence Ballard were considered to have as good a voice. Their first few releases brought a series of unsuccessful recordings, earning The Supremes the nickname "The No Hit Supremes", although Berry Gordy remained confident that the group would eventually prove to be one of Motown's biggest.

Florence Ballard sang lead vocals on the group's second release, "Buttered Popcorn" following the trend at the time to share lead vocals among the three members. Florence Ballard never again sang lead vocals on a single release, but did on future Supremes albums, most notably "It Makes No Difference Now" from The Supremes "Sing Country, Western and Pop", and "Ain't That Good News" from "We Remember Sam Cooke" album, Florence also recorded lead vocals for a two tracks on a Christmas album, "Silent Night" and "O'Holy Night".

Signed Photograph. L to R: Florence Ballard, Mary Wilson and Diana Ross.

By the time they finally did get their first Top 40 hit, "When The Lovelight Starts Shining Through His Eyes", in late 1963, produced by the Holland-Dozier-Holland team, Diana Ross had officially taken over the lead vocals for the group. Berry Gordy's patience paid off in 1964, when the single "Where Did Our Love Go" (interestingly the song had been originally intended to be recorded by The Marvelettes) was issued in August 1964, while The Supremes were appearing on Dick Clark's "Caravan of Stars", the single went to No1 on the US pop charts; it was also their first recording to chart in the UK, where it reached No3. This song was again written and produced by Holland-Dozier-Holland, starting a trend at Motown that would last for the next few years, in which the production team with the last hit on an artist would always have first chance with the next recording on that same group or individual. It also established the "sound" for The Supremes which would result in their run of five consecutive number one hits between 1964 and 1965. Starting with "Where Did Our Love Go" followed by "Baby Love", "Stop! In the Name of Love", "Come See About Me" and "Back in My Arms Again".

Along with Diana Ross's lead vocals, the backup vocals provided by Mary Wilson and Florence Ballard, they would also "perfect" the highly stylised choreography and visual style performances for television and live performance and move Motown into the major cabaret clubs in the US. The hard work of both the production team of Holland-Dozier-Holland and artist development came together to produce Motown's first truly international stars. "Baby Love" was nominated for the 1965 Grammy Award for Best Rhythm and Blues Recording, and "You Keep Me Hangin' On" was awarded the 1966 Grammy for Best Pop single.

The line-up after the departure of Florence Ballard from L to R: Mary Wilson, Jean Terrell and Diana Ross.

In 1967, Motown had decided to change the line up of The Supremes, Florence Ballard was asked to leave by Motown, with the reason for her departure being that the strain of touring had become too great for her. However, it is widely reported that Berry Gordy thought Florence Ballard's behaviour, drinking heavily, late for recordings etc, was deemed increasingly to be unprofessional behaviour by her. The removal from the group only pushed Florence further into a chronic depression and alcoholism. These were taken into consideration, and again it is widely reported that these factors weighed heavily on Berry Gordy as he took the decision to dismiss Florence Ballard from the group in July 1967. Florence was replaced by Cindy Birdsong (from Patti LaBelle and the Bluebells). Florence's final performance with the group was their first appearance at the Flamingo Hotel in Las Vegas.

After Florence Ballard's departure from the group another name change was announced by Motown, the group would now be known as "Diana Ross and the Supremes", adding to the speculation that Diana Ross was planning a solo career shortly. Interestingly, The Supremes had a good year in 1967, with the mildly psychedelic influences on the single "Reflections" being the high point. However, when Holland-Dozier-Holland left Motown in late 1967, the quality of The Supremes' records suffered (as some would suggest, did the Motown organisation as a whole). It was now obvious, that the days of "Diana Ross and The Supremes" as a group were coming to an end, but not before the post Holland-Dozier-Holland production "Love Child" (in 1968 Motown created the writing production team The Clan consisting of Deke Richards Frank Wilson, R. Dean Taylor and Pam Sawyer) which became another No1 hit. Their last recording was "Someday We'll

Be Together" in October 1969, with Mary Wilson and Cindy Birdsong surprisingly not providing background vocals (these were supplied by the Jones Girls) during the session, Johnny Bristol (the producer) coached Diana Ross through the recording. Berry Gordy liked the song so well, that he decided to leave the recording as it was with Bristol's coaching track included. This would be "Diana Ross and The Supremes" final No1 chart hit.

In November 1969, Diana Ross formally announced she would be leaving to develop her solo career, (although she played a few more dates with them), the last performance was in Las Vegas in January 1970. Jean Terrell officially replaced Diana Ross at the performance, Jean Terrell along with Mary and Cindy Birdsong, recorded much of The Supremes' material in the studios (both in Detroit and Los Angeles), and rehearsed the group's "new style" performances during the day (with Mary Wilson and Cindy Birdsong) in preparation for the eventual final performance of Diana Ross and The Supremes.

The group now reverted back to the original name of "The Supremes" and continued to record with Motown. The group scored three major hits in the early 1970's with Jean on lead vocals, "Stoned Love" was a No1 R&B and chart hit in 1970, " while both "Nathan Jones" and "Up the Ladder to the Roof" were Top 10 hits on both the pop and R&B charts. Also recorded at the time was "River Deep Mountain High" with The Four Tops "Automatically Sunshine" and "Floy Joy." After the success of "Floy Joy", Cindy Birdsong decided to leave the group to start a family and was replaced by Lynda Laurence (a former member of Stevie Wonder's group Wonderlove). Toward the end of 1973, Jean decided to leave the group along with Lynda Laurence, (who was pregnant). At the same time, Mary announced that her husband (Dominican businessman Pedro Ferrer who she married in 1974) would be the new manager for the group. When The Supremes disbanded in 1977, Mary Wilson was the only surviving member of the original group.

"Mary, Scherrie and Susaye" is the final 'official' studio album by The Supremes, released in 1976 on the Motown label. The album featured the final line-up for The Supremes, comprised of original Supreme Mary Wilson and latter-day members Scherrie Payne and Susaye Greene. All three Supremes take leads on the album. Regarded as something of an overlooked disco gem, the album was a mixture of hard-driving, high energy dance tracks and ethereal R&B ballads. Scherrie Payne and Susaye Greene mostly took over the dance tracks while Mary Wilson performed the ballads. Released to the public in October 1976, the album was released nine months before the trio broke up. A later line up made an album of re-recordings in the 1990's, but this album remains the last collection of all-new material.

The Supremes have been inducted into the "Rock and Roll Hall of Fame" had commemorative collector postage stamps issued showing original members, Diana Ross, Mary Wilson, Florence Ballard and Barbara Martin. A portion of the proceeds from stamps sold in the US will go to Florence Ballard's three daughters Lisa, Michelle and Nicole Chapman.

Album Track: "When the Lovelight Starts Shinning in His Eyes", The Supremes.

Formed in 1965 for UK and European Market

Motown Connection: Motown's Overseas label - Issued all Motown (and subsidiary) Recordings.

The British/European label established by Motown for its European Sales, loved by all British Mods, and was the coolest label. The name Tamla Motown came from the use of two existing labels Berry Gordy had started in the US. Tamla and Motown a (shortened version of Detroit Michigan nickname Motor Town), add these together and we have "Tamla Motown".

All the major groups and artists' material from the US Motown labels were issued on Tamla Motown, including the groups The Four Tops, Temptations, Supremes, Marvelettes, Martha Reeves and The Vandellas and JR. Walker and The All Stars, and of Stevie Wonder, Mary Wells, Marvin Gaye, Jimmy Ruffin and The Isley Brothers.

Signed programme from the 1965 Tamla Motown Tour.

In the UK, early Motown records were issued recording on a variety of labels, "Come to Me" by Marv Johnson was the first Tamla Motown production (not yet a separate label) record to be issued in the UK, it was released by the London American in May 1959, London American also issued the first EP (extended play, usually 4 tracks two on each side, in a picture sleeve) "Shop Around" by The Miracles in 1961, in total London put out 11 Tamla Motown productions. Next, Fontana issued around four singles up until March 1962, these included The

Marvelettes "Please Mr. Postman" and "Jamie" by Eddie Holland, (now a very rare single). Then Fontana decided not to issue more Tamla Motown records and Oriole, an independent label took over the distribution, including promoting the Tamla Motown records on Radio Luxembourg. Mary Wells made a significant contribution to the early of success of Oriole with recordings like "You Beat Me To The Punch", "The One Who

Tour Bus from the 1965 Tamla Motown Tour.

Really Loves You" and "Two Lovers", which were written and produced by Smokey Robinson. Mary Wells was also the first Motown artist to tour the UK.

Next came the Stateside label which issued around forty singles from 1963 until March 1965, including early hits for The Supremes with 'Baby Love' and 'Where Did Our

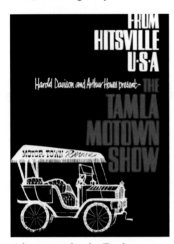

Love Go'. Many of the Stateside releases have become quite rare and therefore very collectable with demo copies even more sought after. By March 1965, Berry Gordy had decided on a one label approach for the market outside of the US. With EMI, Berry Gordy launched the Tamla Motown label to issue recordings from Berry Gordy's US Motown labels including, Tamla, Motown, Gordy, Soul and VIP. The first issue was TMG 501 "Stop In The Name Of Love" by The Supremes. The distinctive black and silver colour would stay as a separate label until 1982, when all Motown issues use the "famous" blue "M" style label.

Advertising for the Tamla Motown Show.

Some of the early Tamla Motown records have become much sought after collector items, Earl Van Dyke's only album issued in 1960's on Tamla Motown called "That Motown Sound". Another is an instrumental by Choker Campbell, called "Mickey's Monkey" and Dr Martin Luther King (who was assassinated in 1968) tribute album called "The Great March To Freedom" which included extracts from his speeches, this album is now one of the rarest Tamla Motown recordings.

Motown also used the Tamla Motown label to issue recordings from the back catalogue of record labels they had purchased in Detroit like Ric-Tic, and Golden World (the label had been owned by Ed Wingate). These included artists and recordings by Rare Earth, Laura Lee, J J Barnes, Edwin Starr and the Fantastic Four.

Tamla Motown Tour 1965

In 1965, to supplement the decision to launch the Tamla Motown label, Arthur Howes in association with Harold Davidson presented the first Tamla Motown Touring Revue to appear in the UK. The show featured The Supremes, Smokey Robinson and The Miracles, Stevie Wonder, Martha and The Vandellas, and the Earl Van Dyke Sextet, the UK recording star "Georgie Fame and The Blueflames" were asked to support the tour, Motown booked Tony Marsh to act as compère for the tour. The tour built on the previous performances by Motown artist Kim Weston who supported "Gerry and The Pacemakers" tour in the same year, it has been suggested that this was possibly to test the reaction of the UK public for a full scale Motown Tour.

Malcolm Cook the tour manager remembers a wonderful moment featuring Kim Weston; during rehearsals, (which were held at the Seville Theatre in the West End), when asked by compère Bryan Burdon how he should introduce Kim, Malcolm told Bryan to ask her and she told him to 'Just tell them I'm Tamla Motown'. Bryan was a variety artist and not into popular music, so you can image the look on

Kim's face when, having been given the OK to proceed he introduced Kim "Now ladies and gentlemen, please welcome from Detroit City in the US of A, Miss Pamela Motown".

Marv Tarplin

Born Marvin Tarplin on the 13th June 1941 Atlanta, Georgia

Motown Connection: A member of Motown group The Miracles (aka The Matadors) from 1957 to 1978 - Guitarists - Writer.

Born in Atlanta, Georgia and raised in Detroit, Marv began his career working with The Primettes (who would become a future Motown group) as a teenager. The Primettes would later change their name to The Supremes. The Primettes (consisting of Diana Ross, Barbara Martin, Mary Wilson and Florence Ballard) were given an audition by Motown Records, with Marv playing guitar to Smokey Robinson (by then Motown Vice-President as well as the lead singer, writer and producer for The Miracles). Smokey Robinson was so impressed with Marv's guitar playing and attitude, that Smokey offered Marv the opportunity to work with The Miracles. Marv left The Primettes to join The Miracles in 1958, working with the group both in the studio and as their touring guitarist. This relationship with The Miracles and in particular Smokey Robinson turned into a lifetime of collaboration, both at Motown and their subsequent recordings.

Marv's main contribution to The Miracles music was the ability to produce interesting melodies and catchy guitar riffs. Marv would play to Pete Moore and Smokey Robinson who would listen until they heard something that they thought would form the basis of a recording. The recording was then taped or Smokey Robinson and Pete Moore would take the recording into the studio and start the process of expanding this into a single.

Remaining with The Miracles while Smokey Robinson was their lead singer, Marv was not given a high profile in the group; indeed Marv is only present on the cover of three Miracles albums. Marv does get a credit (though not pictured), on the back cover of the group's very first album, "Hi... We're The Miracles" in 1961, and is listed as an original group member, on the 1962 album's "Cookin' with The Miracles", "I'll Try Something New" and "The Fabulous Miracles" released in 1963. As a songwriter, Marv co-wrote many of The Miracles' hit singles, like "I Like It Like That" in 1964, then in 1965 came a string of hits, including their most famous international recording "The Tracks of My Tears", also in that year came, "My Girl Has Gone", "Going to a Go-Go" followed by the 1967 hit "The Love I Saw in You Was Just a Mirage", from the album "Tears of a Clown". In addition, Marv co-wrote several Smokey Robinson produced hits by Marvin Gaye, including the Top 10 million selling hits, "Ain't That Peculiar" and "I'll Be Doggone". Marv's guitar work is featured prominently on Gaye's Top 40 hit, "One More Heartache", which he also co-wrote.

Marv came up with the melody for "Ain't That Peculiar" while travelling in UK as part of the Motown Motortown Revue. The Miracles Pete Moore and Robinson arranger Willie Shorter who did the basic musical charts was used as the basis of arranger Paul Riser's string arrangement. Marvin Gaye's version became Marvin Gaye's second No1 R&B single, (credited to Pete Moore, Smokey Robinson Bobby Rogers and Marv Tarplin),

Marv left the Miracles in 1973, shortly after Smokey Robinson left to pursue his solo career; Claudette Robinson had left the group the year before. Marv's replacement in The Miracles was Donald Griffin, brother of Billy Griffin, Smokey Robinson's replacement in the group.

When Smokey Robinson launched his solo career in 1972, Marv co-wrote some of his most memorable tunes, including "Baby Come Close" the ballad "Silent Partner in a Three-Way Love Affair" on the b/side of the single "Open," next came "Cruisin'", from the album "Where There's Smoke...", and "I've Made Love to You a Thousand Times". In 1978 the recording "Love Breeze" was a feature on "Madam X" radio show. Next came one of Smokey Robinson's best works with "Just My Soul Responding" the b/side of "It's Her Turn to Live", featuring the full-length album version which received substantial airplay. The No1 R&B recording was released called "Just Passing Through" b/ side of "Baby That's Backatcha" from his "Storm" album. In 1972 Smokey Robinson produced the Motown album by The Supremes, "Floy Joy". Included on this album was "Precious Little Things", a Smokey Robinson favourite. Smokey Robinson and Marv continued to collaborate as writers on Smokey Robinson's solo recordings, including the Top 10 1981 hit "Being with You".

In the 2006 Motown DVD release, Smokey Robinson and The Miracles: "The Definitive Performances 1963-1987", Smokey Robinson and original members, Pete Moore and Bobby Rogers commented that Marv's unique guitar-playing was reminiscent of the late Curtis Mayfield, and was actually the inspiration behind many of the group's greatest hits. Marv continues to this day to work and tour with Smokey Robinson. In 2007, musician Paul Cebar paid tribute to Marv with his song "Marv's Fluttering Guitar (For Marv Tarplin)" from the album "Tomorrow's Sound Now For Yes Music People".

Bobby Taylor and The Vancouvers

Formed in the Early 1960's in Vancouver, Canada

Original Members: Bobby Taylor Born February 18 1936 in North Carolina and raised in Washington, DC - Robbie King - Ted Lewis (aka Duris Maxwell) - Tommy Chong. One of Motown's most racially mixed groups, the members included a Black Canadian, White American, and an Aboriginal, Bobby Taylor himself had African-American, Puerto Rican, and Native American roots.

The album cover for of the only LP by Bobby Taylor and the Vancouvers released in 1968.

Motown Connection: Bobby Taylor would become The Jackson 5's first producer - Bobby Taylor would be a solo artist at Motown - Group.

Bobby Taylor moved to New York City, and performed in doo-wop groups around the city, with members who would perform in successful acts such as "Frankie Lymon and the Teenagers" and "Little Anthony and the Imperials". Next, after a move to Vancouver, Bobby Taylor joined a group known as The Four Pharaohs in 1958, where he recorded his first single to be issued, but only locally in the Vancouver area. In the early 1960's, Bobby Taylor joined a group called "The Calgary Shades", made up of vocalist Tommy Melton, bassist Wes Henderson, and drummer Floyd Sneed and guitarist Tommy Chong (who would become a key member of the group). The word Shades referenced the fact that the band was racially integrated. This group would later change it's name to "Little Daddy and The Bachelors" and the group moved to San Francisco California and built up a small local following there.

Now with Bobby Taylor as lead vocalist and producer of the group, Bobby Taylor replaced Tommy Melton for keyboardist Robbie King and Floyd Sneed for drummer Ted Lewis (aka Duris Maxwell). Bizarrely, on the suggestion of Tommy Chong, the group changed its name again to "Four Niggers and a Chink" not surprisingly the groups was not successful after this name change. Deciding to return to Vancouver, the group name changing came to an end when the group finally decided on "Bobby Taylor and the Vancouvers". One interesting footnote, the group's early career was the inclusion of guitarist Jimi Hendrix, whose father and grandparents were from Vancouver.

In 1965 the group signed to Motown, The Supremes' members Mary Wilson and Florence Ballard heard the band, whose performances consisted primarily of Motown covers, in Vancouver. On their suggestion Berry Gordy offered an audition and signed them to the Gordy label (a subsidiary of Motown records). The group's debut album, and their debut single of the same name, was released in 1968 (co-written by Tommy Chong) "Does Your Mama Know About Me?", reached No29 on the charts. The group released two further singles, "I Am Your Man", produced by Nickolas Ashford and Valerie Simpson, and the Smokey Robinson written and produced "Malinda".

In July 1968 Bobby Taylor and The Vancouvers were booked to perform at Chicago's Regal Theatre, they had decided to use The Jackson 5, as their opening act. Bobby Taylor was so impressed by the group he personally brought them to Detroit, arranging an audition for them with Motown executive Suzanne de Passé and Berry Gordy. Suzanne de Passé was more impressed with The Jackson 5 than Berry Gordy, who was unsure about signing an act with young children, however, Suzanne de Passé assured Berry Gordy that she would take care of the group personally and the group was signed to the label within a year.

Bobby Taylor became The Jackson 5's first producer, producing a number of soul covers, including their famous rendition of The Miracles' "Who's Lovin' You". When Berry Gordy later moved the group to California, Bobby Taylor would briefly join The Jackson 5 there, although Bobby Taylor worked with the group, he did not receive any credit, particularly on the early singles such as "I Want You Back" and "ABC" alongside Berry Gordy's team known as The Corporation.

"Does Your Mama Know About Me?" turned out to be the high spot in the group's career at Motown, their only other high spot was supporting Motown artist Chris Clark on a national tour. However, Tommy Chong and Wes Henderson were fired by Chris Clark and Johnny Bristol on this tour when they did not arrive for a performance (instead applying for Green Cards to settle permanently in the US). The group disbanded shortly afterwards this incident, Bobby Taylor did audition for the lead singer position in The Temptations (following David Ruffin's departure from the group), but was not successful. Tommy Chong went on to become famous as one-half of comedy duo Cheech and Chong.

As a solo artist, Bobby Taylor was moved to V.I.P (a Motown subsidiary label), although his recording "Oh, I've Been Blessed", became a major club hit, his other singles failed to reach the charts. In 1971, Bobby Taylor left Motown, and signed with some small independent labels, including Philadelphia International, Tommy Zs7, Sunflower, Playboy, but these contracts resulted in very few singles or albums being issued through out the 1970's. Bobby Taylor did successfully sue Motown for a substantial amount of money for back royalties etc in the late 1970's.

Moving to the UK, Bobby Taylor started a new group, Bobby Taylor and the New Vancouvers, and recorded an album for Ian Levine's Motorcity Records project called "Find My Way Back" in 1990. Bobby Taylor's later musical career was affected by bouts of throat cancer, which he had treated by various holistic doctors over the years.

Born Richard Dean Taylor in 1939 in Toronto, Canada

Motown Connection: Singer - Writer - Producer.

R Dean made his first performance at the age of 12, singing at various open-air Country and Western shows in the Toronto area, and began his musical career in 1961, as a pianist and singer with several bands in Toronto. He recorded his first record at Bert Hunt's studio for the Audio Master label. Next came the release "At The High School Dance" in 1961 a single for Amy-Mala Records, which was a minor success. Next, came a single which reached No23 on the Toronto rock and roll station CHUM-AM, "I'll Remember", followed by "It's A Long Way to St. Louis", "We Fell In Love As We Tangoed" and "Beautiful Dreamer", by now R Dean had moved to New York in 1962 with this success R Dean decided to move to Detroit in 1964 to further his career.

In 1963 a friend from Detroit called him about a newspaper article featuring an "up-an-coming record" company called Motown Records and said he could arrange an audition. R Dean was fortunate enough to meet with Brian Holland and Lamont Dozier of Motown's top producing team, Holland-Dozier-Holland. They liked his material and R Dean was immediately signed as a writer and artist on the V.I.P label (a Motown subsidiary label). R Dean's first single in March 1964 was the topical satire "My Ladybug (Stay Away From That Beatle)", but was felt not to have a commercial sound and was never issued.

It was not until November 1965 that R Dean's single, "Let's Go Somewhere", a subtle war protest song was issued, co-written by R Dean in conjunction with Brian Holland, and produced by the team of Holland-Dozier-Holland, however, the song was only a regional hit in several US cities and Toronto.

R Dean's next single in 1967 was "There's A Ghost In My House" again co-written by R Dean with Brian Holland, and produced by the team of Holland-Dozier-Holland. It was not a commercial success, not reaching a good position in the US charts, but it was a No3 hit in the UK. At this time R Dean was also developing his skills as a songwriter for other acts, with notable success with, "I'll Turn to Stone" by The Four Tops, and "All I Need" by The Temptations (both charting in US in 1967) and "Just Look What You've Done" by Brenda Holloway.

In 1968, R Dean again hit the UK Chart with his own production of the single "Gotta See Jane", (co-written with Brian Holland), which became a Top 20 hit. However, his real success came as a member of the Motown writing and production team known as "The Clan". This production group briefly took over as the providers of material for Diana Ross and The Supremes after the Holland-Dozier-Holland left Motown in the same year. Among R Dean hits in 1968 and 1969 (as a member of The Clan) was the Diana Ross and The Supremes' No1 US hit "Love Child" and their Top 10 hit "I'm Livin' in Shame".

R Dean resumed his recording career in 1970, becoming one of the first artists assigned to Motown's new Rare Earth (a Motown subsidiary label), which had been created for white artists at Motown. His first Rare Earth single "Indiana Wants Me" became a No1 hit in both the United States and his native Canada. He appeared on CKLW's "The Robin Seymour" TV Show a number of times to promote the single. "Indiana Wants Me" became a million-seller and climbed to No1 on the US charts, making him the first white artist in the history of Motown to do so. With this success "Gotta See Jane" was reissued in 1971, and became a Top 10 hit in Canada. R Dean continued recording for Rare Earth, working as a writer producer for other artists until the Rare Earth label was closed in 1976. Though he never again reached the high end of the charts (as he had done with "Indiana Wants Me"), his releases did quite well, especially in Canada. R Dean did issue an album on Polydor in 1975 called LA Sunset without much success.

Dean attempted a comeback in the early 1980's, with the 1983 release "Let's Talk It Over" on the C&W label, but it became a poor seller only reaching No90 on the charts, after which he took a break from the music industry. Dean came back into the music scene in the late 1990's as one of the headliner acts at several UK Northern Soul shows. Dean then set up his own record label, the appropriately named Jane Records, and built a recording studio in his home in Los Angeles and is working on a new CD and writing a book about his Motown memories.

Album Track: "Indiana Wants Me", R Dean Taylor.

Formed in 1960 in Detroit, Michigan from two groups Otis Williams and The Distants and The Primes

Original line up - Otis Williams and The Distants: Eldridge "Al" Bryant - Albert Harell - Richard Street - Melvin Franklin.

Original line up - The Primes: Eddie Kendricks - Paul Williams - Kel Osborn.

Original line up - The Temptations: Otis Williams - Eldridge "Al" Bryant (quickly re-placed by David Ruffin) - Melvin Franklin - Eddie Kendricks - Paul Williams - Eddie Kendricks.

Later members - while still with Motown: Richard Street - Denis Edwards - Ron Tyson.

Later members: Ricky Owens - Damon Harris - Glenn Leonard - Louis Price - Ali-Ollie Woodson - Theo Peoples - Ray Davis - Harry McGilberry - Barrington "Bo" Henderson - G C Cameron.

Current line up: Otis Williams - Terry Weeks - Joe Herndon - Ron Tyson - Bruce Williamson.

Motown Connection: Background Singers - Group - Most Successful Male Motown Group.

The Temptations were formed in 1960 in Detroit by combining two groups, firstly Otis Williams and The Distants, founded by Otis Williams, and featuring Eldridge Bryant, Albert Harell, Richard Street and Melvin Franklin, secondly the group The Primes featuring Eddie Kendrick's, Paul Williams and Kel Osborn.

Johnnie Mae Matthews promotional material.

After Richard Street's departure from The Distants, the groups combined and now consisted of Eddie Kendrick's, Paul Williams, Melvin Franklin, Eldridge "Al" Bryant, and Otis Williams. David Ruffin became an official member of The Temptations after Elbridge "Al" Bryant was asked to leave the group, and so the "classic" line up for the future Temptations was in place.

In 1961, Kel Osbourne (who had kept the name The Primes) moved to California, and with this move the Primes were formally disbanded after only a few years, however, Detroit manager and producer

Johnnie Mae Matthews, who had worked with the original Primes did ask Richard Street (a future Temptations) to briefly lead a new Distants group in the early 1960's, but with no success. The Primes also had a "sister" group called The Primettes, who later evolved into The Supremes.

THE TEMPTATIONS
Gordy Recording Artists

International Management Company
2457 Woodward Avenue
Detroit, Michigan 48201

Melvin Franklin started to use his mother's basement as a rehearsal room for a new group in 1960, the new group took the name The Elgins, (not to be confused with the future

Signed Photograph. L to R: Paul Williams, Dennis Edwards, Melvin Franklin, Eddie Kendricks and Otis Williams.

Motown group of the same name). Gaining an audition, with Berry Gordy at his first studio on St. Antoine in Detroit as The Elgins they signed to Motown, before changing the name to The Temptations and being signed to Motown subsidiary label Miracle.

They recorded their first record for Motown "Oh Mother Of Mine" with Paul Williams on lead, though not a commercial success the recording did showcase the group's talent. Using perfectly timed choreography, arranged by Paul Williams, and their ability to share the lead vocals amongst themselves the group looked to have it all.

The Temptations began singing background for many of the Motown artists already signed to Motown, including early Mary Wells' recordings. Towards the end of 1963, Berry Gordy and the Motown writing staff had all attempted to record the song that would give The Temptations their first major hit, but with no success. Berry Gordy then had the idea of a contest among the Motown Producers to see who could be the first to come up with a number one hit for The Temptations. While on tour, Smokey Robinson along with fellow Miracle member Bobby Rodgers wrote a song for the group which Smokey Robinson was sure would be a hit if recorded on the group. Meanwhile, back in Detroit Berry Gordy had written a song he thought would be a hit also, both songs (along with three others) were recorded by The Temptations and later, when put to a vote at the Friday quality control, the result went to the Smokey Robinson production.

While all of this was going on The Temptations were on tour and upon their return they were greeted with the news that they had made the charts. "The Way You Do the Things You Do" their first US Top 20 hit, followed by "I'll Be in Trouble", "Girl (Why You Wanna Make Me Blue)", "Get Ready", "Just My Imagination" and "Please Return Your Love to Me". Without doubt the most successful Temptations recording from this time was the Smokey Robinson (who wrote and produced) the No1 hit "My Girl". The success of "My Girl" started a run of hit singles including, "Since I Lost My Baby" in 1965, "Ain't Too Proud to Beg" in 1966, "All I Need" in 1967 and "I Wish It Would Rain" in 1967. The Temptations sang "My Girl" when asked to appear on the Ed Sullivan Show and their career was now taking off.

Over the next few years, The Temptations would find huge success in record sales, television appearances and tours of the US and Europe. However, with all this success came conflict within the group. The group perceived the major problem to be David Ruffin, in 1967 David Ruffin became addicted to cocaine, and began missing rehearsals and performances. Refusing to travel with the other Temptations, David and Motown artist Tammi Terrell (his then-girlfriend) decided to travel in a limo (with the image of his trademark black rimmed glasses painted on the door). At this time David was pushing for recognition by Motown of his lead vocal role with The Temptations, citing how Motown had allowed the name change for The Supremes (to Diana Ross and The Supremes in early 1967). David Ruffin felt that the same should apply to The Temptations, and began demanding that the group name be changed to David Ruffin and The Temptations. This led to conflict in the group (in particular with recognised group's leader, Otis Williams), in addition David Ruffin started inquiring into The Temptations' financial records, demanding an accounting of the group's money, causing further friction between David Ruffin and Berry Gordy.

In mid-1968, The Temptations agreed that David should leave the group when he missed a 1968 concert, to attend a concert being performed by his new girlfriend, Barbara Martin (daughter of Dean Martin). After taking a vote, The Temptations decided for the good of the group that David Ruffin would have to leave, recruiting former Contours' singer Dennis Edwards as his replacement. He continued to show up at Temptations' performances uninvited and would join them on stage. Eventually security guards had to be used to keep him away.

With the induction of Dennis in to the group, The Temptations' music, along with the times began to change. The first phase of The Temptations' career was guided by Smokey Robinson, who usually wrote and produced their material, next came the collaboration with Norman Whitfield and Barrett Strong who wrote and produced the "psychedelic soul" recordings where all five Temptations undertook lead vocals, with such recordings as the Grammy winners "Cloud Nine" and "I Can't Get Next to You".

Their music began to reflect the times and changing attitudes of the music buying public, with the release of "Cloud Nine" which introduced the concept of using drugs to get "high". Although Norman Whitfield always maintained the song was not about drugs and drug taking, there was to be no doubt as to the meaning within the recording of "Cloud Nine". "Cloud Nine" was an instant success and would go on to win Motown's first ever Grammy Award.

As the 1960's came to an end The Temptations further developed the "psychedelic soul" style with recording such as "I Can't Get Next to You" (another Grammy Winner), "Ball Of Confusion", "Psychedelic Shack", "Papa Was A Rolling Stone" and "Runaway Child". With the strong lyrics of Norman Whitfield and Barrett Strong the group was expressing the feelings 1970's protest songs, The Temptations and Motown had entered the 1970's in a new sound. The success of "Papa Was A Rolling Stone" led Norman Whitfield to create more psychedelic influenced recording, including the Top 10 hit "Masterpiece" in 1973 and several of the tracks on the resulting "Masterpiece" album. Tensions developed between Norman Whitfield and the group, who found him arrogant and difficult to work with. Otis Williams complained about Norman Whitfield's actions between him and The Temptations' Berry Gordy intervened and reassigned them to Jeffrey Bowen, who had been co-producer of the 1967 "In a Mellow Mood" album.

The final Norman Whitfield produced Temptations' album was released in late 1973, and included the Top 30 single "Let Your Hair Down". Norman Whitfield left Motown in 1975 and established Whitfield Records.

Though successful with this new sound, one member of the group Paul Williams was unhappy with the diminishing role he played in the group. Paul was the lead singer on several of their earlier songs and was also the group's main choreographer, before the addition of Cholly Atkins and the Artist Development Department. Paul Williams' alcoholism and poor health (he had Sickle Cell Anaemia) contributed to his decline and influence in the group, Otis Williams and the other Temptations decided to look for a replacement for when Paul was unavailable. Choosing Richard Street, then lead singer of the Motown act The Monitors and known from his days as lead singer of The Distants, Richard Street was recruited to travel with The Temptations and sing all of Paul's parts from behind a curtain, except for Paul's solo contributions, such as "Don't Look Back" and "For Once in My Life".

Eventually, Paul became too ill to perform, and Richard Street firstly started to perform on stage as a member of The Temptations, then taking his place on recording sessions, before officially taking over from Paul Williams in 1971. However, Paul Williams was still involved with the group as a way of "showing support" for the group, being employed as an advisor and choreographer, for the next two years.

Next to leave the group was Eddie Kendricks who became increasingly unhappy with the direction their music had taken the group. The loss of his friend Paul Williams from the group and his feelings of being overshadowed by Dennis Edwards, Eddie Kendricks decided to pursue a solo career. Eddie Kendricks did leave the group on a high note with the release of "Just My Imagination (Running Away with Me)", which was a No1 US hit in April 1971. However, by the time the record was released Eddie Kendrick had already left the group, signing instead a solo contract with Motown (recording on the Tamla Label). Eddie Kendricks' original replacement was Ricky Owens, from the Los Angeles-based vocal group The Vibrations. However, Owens gave poorly-received performances during the few shows he performed with the group, and he was dropped after only a few weeks. During most of the spring of 1971, The Temptations remained a quartet, and re-recorded the single "It's Summer" without a fifth member.

Jeffrey Bowen's first LP with The Temptations was in January 1975 with "A Song for You", with the pop Top 40 and R&B No1 hit "Happy People" (featuring The Commodores as the instrumentalists), at this time Damon Harris was asked to leave the group during the recording of "A Song for You", his replacement was Glenn Leonard, formerly of the Unifics. A number of other producers, including Brian Holland, James Carmichael began producing albums for the group including the next three album's, "House Party" in November 1975, "Wings of Love" in March 1976, and "The Temptations Do The Temptations" in August 1976. None of these recordings were as commercially successful as "A Song for You", and none of their associated singles entered the charts. After "The Temptations Do The Temptations" was recorded Dennis Edwards was asked to leave the group, and was replaced by new lead Louis Price, shortly after this replacement The Temptations left Motown for Atlantic Records.

Their releases on Atlantic "Here to Tempt You" in 1977, "Bare Back" in 1978, and the singles released from these albums were unsuccessful in 1979, Atlantic released the group from its contract. Shortly afterwards, The Temptations met with Smokey Robinson and Berry Gordy, and the group re-signed with Motown in 1980, Louis Price departed from the group and joined The Drifters, Dennis Edwards, who had been unsuccessful in his solo career for the previous three years (despite remaining with Motown as a solo act), returned to the line up. Berry Gordy co-wrote and produced The Temptations' first single under the new contract, "Power", from the album of the same name. Two years of underperforming singles and albums followed, including an album with Philadelphia based producer Thom Bell, until Motown began planning a Temptations reunion tour in 1982.

Eddie Kendricks and David Ruffin agreed to rejoin the group for the "Reunion" album and tour. Melvin Franklin's nephew, Motown funk star Rick James (who had previously used The Temptations as backup vocalists on his 1981 hit "Super Freak"), wrote, produced, and appeared on the "Reunion" album's hit single, "Standing on the Top", which featured David Ruffin, Eddie Kendricks and Dennis Edwards sharing lead vocals, the single went to be No6 on the R&B charts. At the conclusion of the "Reunion" tour, David Ruffin and Eddie Kendricks left the group for the final time, but did start to tour and perform together as a duo.

One more album, "Surface Thrills", was released in 1983, the R&B Top 20. "Love on My Mind Tonight", a single from "Surface Thrills", made it to number 17. "Sail Away", produced by Norman Whitfield (who briefly returned to Motown) and featuring Ron Tyson's first lead vocal, reached at No13 on the Charts. Following the release of "Surface Thrills", Glenn Leonard left and was replaced by Ron Tyson, who was with the Philadelphia groups The Ethics and Love Committee. Ron Tyson had been a songwriter at Atlantic during The Temptations' time there, and co-wrote several songs on the album "Hear to Tempt You".

Dennis Edwards was again replaced in 1984, his place taken by Ali-Ollie Woodson who had been a potential candidate to replace Edwards back in 1977. The album "Back to Basics" was released; it was the first album featuring Ron Tyson, and featured one lead vocal with Ali-Ollie Woodson called "Stop the World Right Here (I Wanna Get Off)". Ali-Ollie Woodson's first lead on a single was 1984's "Treat Her Like a Lady", co-written by himself and Otis Williams, and co-produced by former Earth, Wind and Fire members Al McKay and Ralph Johnson. The single became their biggest success for a few years, reaching No2 on the R&B charts, the group experienced similar success the following year with the single "Lady Soul", another Top 5 R&B success.

Ali-Ollie Woodson remained with The Temptations until 1987, when he was replaced by Dennis Edwards. The group recorded one album during Dennis Edwards' third stay with the group, "Together Again", released in late 1987. The following year, Dennis Edwards left for the third and final time in late 1989, with Ali-Ollie Woodson re-joining the line up. Also that year, The Temptations were inducted into the Rock and Roll Hall of Fame, honouring Edwards, Franklin, Otis Williams, David Ruffin, Eddie Kendricks and posthumously Paul Williams.

From the 1990's, The Temptations' line up began to change more frequently, Richard Street missed a performance in 1992 after undergoing emergency surgery to remove kidney stones which resulted in an argument with Otis Williams who was not aware of Richards Street's surgery. Richard Street felt Otis Williams was unsympathetic, and as a result, he left the group in 1993 after twenty-two years, his replacement was Theo Peoples. Melvin Franklin was forced to stop performing because of failing health, Ray Davis, from Parliament-Funkadelic, replaced him. Before leaving the group they recorded the album "For Lovers Only", which contained two tracks by Melvin Franklin on lead vocals. Ray Davis left shortly after completing the album, due to being diagnosed with lung cancer. The group continued as a quartet for a short time, before recruiting bass Harry McGilberry, a former member of The Futures. "For Lovers Only" would also be the last for Ali-Ollie Woodson who left the group in 1996 due to health problems, having suffered two battles with throat cancer, he was replaced by new member Terry Weeks.

The Temptations line up, now consisted of Otis Williams, Ron Tyson, Theo Peoples, Harry McGilberry and Terry Weeks, who performed at the Super Bowl XXXII, which was part of the celebration of the fortieth anniversary of Motown. In 1998, The Temptations released "Phoenix Rising", their first million-selling album in over twenty years. During the recording of "Phoenix Rising", Theo Peoples departed, and was replaced by Barrington "Bo" Henderson. The completed album features both Bo Henderson and Theo Peoples (who later joined The Four Tops).

The Temptations were inducted into the Vocal Group Hall of Fame in 1999. In 2001, their 2000 album "Ear-Resistible" won the group its third Grammy, for Best Traditional R&B Vocal Performance. Three classic Temptations songs, "My Girl", "Ain't Too Proud to Beg" and "Papa Was a Rollin' Stone", are among The Rock and Roll Hall of Fame's 500 Songs that Shaped Rock and Roll.

Bo Henderson left the group in 2003, his replacement was former Detroit Spinners lead G C Cameron, the line now consisted of G C Cameron, Otis Williams, Ron Tyson, Harry McGilberry and Terry Weeks, however, in this year Harry McGilberry left the group, his replacement was former Spaniels bass Joe Herndon. Tragically Harry McGilberry died on 3rd April, 2006, at age 56.

The group's final Motown album, "Legacy", was released in 2004 which reached No18 on the albums chart. Later that year, the Temptations asked to be released from their Motown contract, and moved to another Universal Motown Records Group label, New Door Records. The album "Reflections", was released in January 2006, and contains covers of several popular Motown songs, including Diana Ross and The Supremes' "Reflections", the Miracles' "Ooo Baby Baby", Marvin Gaye and Tammi Terrell's "Ain't Nothing Like the Real Thing", and The Jackson 5's "I'll Be There".

G C Cameron left the group in June 2007 to focus on his solo career; he was replaced by new member Bruce Williamson. This new line up recorded another album of soul covers, "Back to Front" released in October 2007.

Major tragedies that effect the original line up include, on August 17, 1973 at the age of 34, Paul Williams was found on the ground near his car, dead from an apparently self-inflicted gunshot to the head, in a deserted parking lot near 14th Street and West Grand Blvd, not far from Motown's "Hitsville Studio A". Next was David Ruffin, who on the 1st June 1991 at the age of 50 died of a drug over dose in a Philadelphia Hospital. On the 5th October 1992 Eddie Kendricks died of Lung cancer at the age of 52 in Birmingham, followed by Melvin Franklin who died on the 22nd February 1995 at the age of 53 after suffering a brain seizure, leaving Otis Williams as the sole remaining member from the "classical line-up". Continually touring and recording with The Temptations, Otis is still performing and organising the group in its fifth decade.

The other Temptations from the Motown era, who are still active, are Dennis Edwards who also continues to perform, although there has been litigation between him and Otis Williams as to the use of The Temptation name. It was decided that Dennis's group would be called "The Temptations Review featuring Dennis Edwards", the name that Dennis Edwards tours under to this day.

Richard Street has spent most of his post-Temptations' years as a producer for Los Angeles-based artists, Richard Street and former Temptations lead singer Ali-Ollie Woodson formed the Temptations Review and recruited singers Willie Green, Perry Moore and Chris Arnold to the group. Richard and the new group have no official rights to The Temptations name; it belongs to Motown with Otis Williams having control of the use of the name.

Album Track: "All I Need", The Temptations.

Jean Terrell

Born Velma Jean Terrell on the 26th November 1944 in Belzoni, Mississippi

Motown Connection: Solo Artist - Replaced Diana Ross as lead singer of the Supremes in January 1970.

Born in Belzoni Mississippi before moving to Chicago at an early age, Jean was supported by her family from a very early age to sing, Jean's first move into singing was in the late 1960's when (with her brother) Jean formed the group "Ernie Terrell and the Heavyweights". The link being that Jean is the sister of the former WBA heavyweight boxing champion, Ernie Terrell, who famously fought Muhammad Ali.

Jean was singing in a club in Miami Florida, when Berry Gordy was impressed by the twenty four year old's performance (performing along with her brother). Berry Gordy was looking for a replacement for Diana Ross, who was leaving The Supremes to pursue a film career in Los Angeles. Berry Gordy decided to first offer Jean a solo artist contract in May 1969, but was so impressed by her singing and performance that he decided to use Jean as Diana Ross's replacement for the lead vocals in The Supremes. At first, Jean, along with Mary Wilson and Cindy Birdsong, recorded much of The Supremes' material in the studios (both in Detroit and Los Angeles), and rehearsed the group's "new style" performances during the day (with Mary Wilson and Cindy Birdsong) in preparation for the eventual final performance of Diana Ross and The Supremes. Before this happened Diana Ross, Mary Wilson and Birdsong performed at any cabaret or TV shows until Diana Ross left to follow her solo career. With Jean now ready to replace Diana Ross as lead singer of The Supremes, this occurred in January 1970.

The group scored three major hits in the early 1970's with Jean on lead vocals, "Stoned Love" was a No1 R&B and chart hit in 1970, while both "Nathan Jones" and "Up the Ladder to the Roof" were Top 10 hits on both the pop and R&B charts. Also recorded at the time was "River Deep Mountain High" with The Four Tops and "Floy Joy." After the success of "Floy Joy," Cindy Birdsong decided to leave the group to start a family and was replaced by Lynda Laurence (a former member of Stevie Wonder's group Wonderlove). Toward the end of 1973, Jean decided to leave the group along with Lynda Laurence, (who was pregnant), unhappy with Motown's lack of interest in promoting The Supremes. At the same time, Mary Wilson announced that her husband would be the new manager for the group. Jean's replacement was Scherrie Payne (sister of Freda Payne who recorded on Holland-Dozier-Holland's Hot Wax label) as lead singer, with Cindy Birdsong returning to replace Lynda Laurence.

Jean did try to develop a solo career after The Supremes, recording briefly for A&M records, with little success. However, Jean did record "I Had To Fall in Love", in 1978, but due to her Jehovah's Witness beliefs, disagreed with how the label wanted to promote the recording. In the early 1980's Jean put together a one woman show, and did a limited number of performances in the US. The act consisted of several Supremes' songs, songs from her solo album and cover versions of songs by Bette Midler and Lionel Richie. Former Supreme Lynda Laurence would often perform background vocals for Jean during these tours, along with Freddi Poole of Scherrie Payne and Lynda Laurence group the F.L.O.S. (former ladies of The Supremes).

In the late 1980's early 1990's Jean became involved with Ian Levine's Motorcity project as lead singer of Jean, Scherrie and Lynda of The Supremes. Jean did release a DVD of her life story and has continued to sing onstage with jazz musicians to this day.

Born Thomasina Montgomery on the 29th April 1945 in Philadelphia, Pennsylvania - Died 16th March 1970 in Philadelphia, Pennsylvania

Motown Connection: Background Singer - Solo Artist - Duo with Marvin Gaye.

Tammi's first break in show business came at the age of eleven, appearing in talent shows at the Earle Theatre in Philadelphia, she was regularly an opening act for many major artists including, Gary "US" Bonds and Patti LaBelle and The Bluebelles. Next, was her first recording contract when she was fifteen in 1961, she was discovered by producer Luther Dixon and signed to Scepter/Wand, using the name Tammy Montgomery, she made her debut with the single "If You See Bill", followed early the next year by "The Voice of Experience.", Tammi stayed with

Scepter/Wand label for two years. In 1963, she joined the James Brown revue and toured with them, including releasing a single on James Brown's Try Me label, "I Cried" b/side "If You Don't Think", also recorded in 1964 for the Checker Records label and recorded a single "If I Would Marry You".

Around this time Tammi also enrolled in the University of Pennsylvania and spent two years there and married the boxer, Ernie Terrell, whose sister Jean would later become lead singer of The Supremes, but the marriage was a brief one. Tammi then changed her name to Tammi Terrell rather than Tammi Montgomery.

Marvin Gaye and Tammi Terrell in a 1967 Motown promotional picture. A publicity handout from the artist re-produced in the Detroit Free Press.

In 1965, while touring with Jerry Butler, Berry Gordy saw Tammi performing at Detroit's Twenty Grand nightclub, Berry Gordy immediately signed her to a contract, and her first Motown single appeared later that year. Initially Tammi recorded as a solo artist, but with only moderate success with two R&B Top 30 singles in 1966, "I Can't Believe You Love Me" and "Come on and See Me". When subsequent outings, "This Old Heart of Mine (Is Weak for You)" and "Hold Me Oh My Darling" failed to chart, the suggestion came to form a duet with Marvin Gaye, who previously recorded duets with Mary Wells and Kim Weston. Together they recorded several Top 10 hits including, "Ain't No Mountain High Enough", the first of their run of hits on the Tamla label (a subsidiary of Motown), which reached the Top 20, the single was one of many to be written and produced by Ashford & Simpson.

Their next four releases all reached the Top 10, "Your Precious Love", "If I Could Build My Whole World Around You", "Ain't Nothing Like The Real Thing" and

"You're All I Need To Get By". The duet's remaining four releases in 1967 were not as successful, at the same time Tammi started to complain about having headaches. Following an onstage collapse (she collapsed in Gaye's arms) in the same year, while in concert in Virginia, Tammi was rushed to the hospital, and was later diagnosed with a malignant brain tumour. Although the tumour forced Tammi to retire from performing live, she continued to record with Marvin Gaye even as her health deteriorated; however, over the next eighteen months Tammi would have six major operations on the tumour, ultimately resulting in loss of memory and partial paralysis Tammi died tragically at the age of twenty four in Philadelphia on 16th March 1970.

Marvin Gaye was so devastated by her declining health and her eventual death that he retired from the road for three years. Marvin Gaye later told his biographer David Ritz that Tammi was no longer able to record and that Valerie Simpson recorded most of the female vocals on the final Marvin Gaye and Tammi Terrell album, "Easy" including, Good Lovin' Ain't Easy To Come By", "What You Gave Me", and the posthumously released "Onion Song", although Valerie Simpson is quoted as denying this in a book written by Tammi's sister Ludie Montgomery.

Tammi dated both James Brown and David Ruffin of The Temptations.

Album Track: "Come On And See Me", Tammi Terrell.

Born Andrew Alexander Terry aka Mike Terry in July 1940 Houston, Texas - Died 30th October 2008 in Detroit, Michigan

Motown Connection: Baritone saxophonist on Motown's greatest hits of the 1960's - Producer.

Born in Houston Texas Mike's father ran a music shop, Mike moved with his family firstly to Kansas City and then to Detroit. His mother, who played the piano, provided the music sheets for Charlie Parker when he did his performances using his saxophone and when he enrolled at Detroit's Cass Tech High School. Mike's first session work for Berry Gordy came in the late 1950's, working with future Motown star Richard "Popcorn" Wylie and The Mohawks, Richard "Popcorn" Willie had put together his first group at high school, along with James Jamerson and Clifford Mack making a handful of unsuccessful recordings. In 1961 Mike went on the road with Jackie Wilson's band, and the following year he was on tour with the first Motortown Revue, ending at the Apollo Theatre in Harlem, New York. Joining the Joe Hunter Band (pre-Funk Brothers in house musicians at Motown) in 1960 he began a five-year tenure with Motown before signing with Golden World.

Mike also worked on some of the soul classics recorded to sound like Motown but from other labels, these included Darrell Bank's "Open the Door to Your Heart", J J Barnes "Our Love (Is in the Pocket)", Jackie Wilson's "Higher and Higher" (with a large selection of The Funk Brothers moonlighting on these recording). In April 1966 he signed with the Golden World Label. His debut was the fantastic "Headline News" which featured Mike on his trademark Baritone sax, next was Edwin Starr's "SOS (Stop Her on Sight)" (again with a large selection of The Funk Brothers moonlighting on these recordings) The Fascinations' "Girls Are Out to Get You", Cliff Noble's "The Horse", the Three Caps' "Cool Jerk" and the Show Stoppers' "Ain't Nothin' But A Houseparty".

During his time at Golden World, he joined forces with George Clinton and Sidney Barnes to form Geo-Si-Mik Productions. That partnership lasted only four or five months, when Golden World was purchased by Motown. Mike was a particular favourite of the production team Holland-Dozier-Holland, using his baritone saxophone as a key ingredient for their productions, ideally suited to provide a momentary contrast to the voices of Martha and The Vandellas, Mary Wells, The

Four Tops, Kim Weston and The Isley Brothers on such hits as "(Love Is Like) A Heatwave", "I Can't Help Myself" and "This Old Heart of Mine (Is Weak For You)". After the success of "(Love Is Like) A Heatwave", by Martha and The Vandellas Mike provided similar contributions to near-identical follow-ups, "Quicksand" and Live Wire".

His solos on the Motown hit helped identify a Motown recording from similar sounding releases, providing a contrast to the Diana Ross voice on The Supremes' "Where Did Our Love Go", their breakthrough hit in 1964. When it was not being used in a solo role, Mike's grunting baritone anchored the horn section of The Funk Brothers giving impetus to songs such as Marvin Gaye's "Baby Don't Do It" and Kim Weston's "Take Me in Your Arms (Rock Me a Little While)".

Berry Gordy's policy of strict demarcation, one of several practices borrowed from Detroit's automobile production lines, meant that his session musicians were not permitted to try their hand at arranging or producing. So Mike enrolled at the Detroit Institute of Music Arts and began to moonlight for other labels. In 1967, Mike found himself working at various outlets, such as Drew and The Precisions, at Artie Fields with Kris Peterson, and at Pied Piper with a number of artists for Jack Ashford.

In December 1967, Dave Kapralik of Epic in Chicago offered Mike a contract with their subsidiary, Okeh Records. While with the label Mike worked with the Little Foxes, Sandra Phillips and Johnny Robinson. Constantly in demand, he would eventually rejoin the revitalised Ric-Tic label, and arrange many superb songs for the Fantastic Four. Later he became a peripatetic arranger and producer, moving from Chicago, Philadelphia, Los Angeles and New York, becoming a firm favourite of the Northern Soul scene.

In the 1970's he composed film soundtracks and worked on the off-Broadway production of "Big Time Buck White", a black power comedy musical devised by the singer Oscar Brown Jnr and starring Muhammad Ali.

Strangely, he was not invited to participate in the reunion of The Funk Brothers; the award-winning documentary titled "Standing in the Shadows of Motown" took several of the surviving musicians on worldwide concert tours which finally earned them individual credits for being a part of the "Motown Sound".

Terry's wife predeceased him.

Signature Sound: "This Old Heart Of Mine (Is Weak For You)", The Isley Brothers.

Formed in 1962 in Detroit, Michigan

Original Members: Bertha Barbee - Caldin "Carolyn" Gill - Mildred "Milly" Gill - Betty Kelly.

Later Addition: Sandra Tilley - Annette MacMillan.

Motown Connection: Background Singers - Group - The first Group from outside the City of Detroit to sign with Motown.

The original members.

Bertha Barbee and Mildred Gill co-founded the group while attending Western Michigan University. The Velvelettes started by singing at parties and campus events, and Bertha recruited Mildred's 14-year-old sister, Carolyn Gill, as lead singer, before the final members of the group joined, Betty Kelly and Norma Barbee. After winning a talent show, they were introduced to a nephew of Berry Gordy, Robert Bullock, who arranged for the group to attend an audition in Detroit. Despite a snowstorm and a car breakdown, they made it to Detroit, only to discover auditions weren't held on Saturdays. However, by chance William "Mickey" Stevenson was just leaving the recording studio when he recognised Bertha and Norma Barbee from the time when he had produced a recording on them as the "Barbees" he arranged an impromptu audition and after this performance the group was signed immediately to Motown. They became the first group from outside the city of Detroit to sign with Motown.

Before signing for Motown there was one release on Stepp records called "The Wind" b/side "Que Pasa (What's Happening)" recorded under the name The Barbees (with Norma and Bertha Barbee as member) in 1962.

As was normal for the time The Velvelettes started as background singers supporting various groups and singers in the studio one of the most famous background sessions was on Stevie Wonder's "Fingertips Part 2," even though it was a live production, their background vocals were added to give it a fuller sound. The Velvelettes' first record "There He Goes" was never a hit, but Stevie Wonder repaid the group for their contribution to "Fingertips Part 2", by playing harmonica in the background. "There He Goes" and "That's The Reason Why" were produced by William "Mickey" Stevenson and released as a single via the IPG label (Independent Producers Group).

The Velvelettes' biggest hit came in 1964 with "Needle in a Haystack", written by Norman Whitfield, it reached No13 on the charts, another Norman Whitfield production, "He Was Really Sayin' Something", was a Top 20 hit the following year. The UK groups Bananarama recorded "He Was Really Sayin' Something", a major UK hit for the group and the Belle Stars did a new version of "Needle in a Haystack" again a UK hit. Their first stage performance was in Cleveland in 1964, where they shared the bill with The Temptations, whose recording of "My Girl" was a No1 hit at the time.

"Where Did Our Love Go" the 1964 No1 hit for The Supremes, could have been the song that would have pushed them into the top reaches of the charts, Berry Gordy had intended the song to be recorded by The Marvelettes, but they rejected it as being too sweet. The group would listen to the song, but before they decided to record it, The Supremes went into the studio, recorded it and it became their first major hit. Also in 1964 Betty Kelly was asked by Berry Gordy to move to Martha and The Vandellas after Annette Sterling left the group and the music industry. After recording "Dancing In The Street" earlier in June 1964 with Martha and The Vandellas, Betty Kelly officially left the group in September of that year. Carolyn recruited two new members for live performances Sandra Tilley who was introduced by her friend Abdul Fakir of The Four Tops, and Annette MacMillan who was known for her stage presence.

The Velvelettes recorded six singles at Motown, (but never released an album), including "These Things Will Keep Me Loving You" (which became the group's last single to be issued by Motown in 1966) a minor R&B hit, "Bird In The Hand (Is Worth Two In A Bush)" both Northern Soul Classics and "Lonely, Lonely Girl Am I" on the VIP label (a subsidiary of Motown), but they never achieved a breakthrough hit to really establish themselves at Motown, although they toured in "Motown Revues", performing with groups such as The Temptations, The Four Tops and Gladys Knight and The Pips.

The group worked with all the major writers and producers at Motown and attended the Artist Development Department and became one of the most stylish artists at Motown. They were famous for their choreography, and when Dick Clark selected two Motown acts for one of his "Caravan of Stars" shows, he picked The Velvelettes and an unknown Motown group called The Supremes. An interesting footnote to the group's career at Motown was when Berry Gordy discovered that Carolyn Gill was a French speaker, placing them with French producer Pierre Benjot who produced four songs, but they were never released either as albums or singles releases.

By the end of 1967, Bertha Barbee, Milly Gill and Norma Barbee had decided to leave the group to concentrate on raising their families, (Milly Gill and Norma Barbee had already been in and out of the group for some time as their families grew). The Velvelettes line up had varied between the original members for some time, often performing as a trio, by the end of this year The Velvelettes officially disbanded.

In 1969, Carolyn married Richard Street of The Temptations, and left the group at his request; they had a son, Ricky, and moved to Los Angeles. In the mid-1970's, Carolyn and Richard separated and Carolyn and her son Ricky returned to Detroit. Overcoming a period of depression she eventually moved back to Kalamazoo were she was born , they divorced in the late 1970's. Milly Gill started a nursing career, and Norma Barbee worked for the Flint Convention Bureau and Sandra Tilley joined Martha Reeves and The Vandellas, replacing Rosalind Ashford.

They were disappointed at having been left out of Motown's 25th Anniversary Celebration in 1983, a two-hour special on NBC; they were not invited, and not even mentioned on the show. In October 1984 the reunited Velvelettes perform a medley of girl group songs at a conference of black professional women in Kalamazoo, expecting this to be a one off experience; however, this re-established the group and resulted in the formal announcement of the group reforming. The Velvelettes were honoured at the Rock and Roll Hall of Fame, with commemorative collector postage stamps. Stamps show Original members: Bertha Barbee McNeal, Carol "Cal" Gill Street, Mildred Gill Arbor, Norma Barbee Fairhurst and Betty Kelley.

The Velvelettes (now consisting of Carolyn and Milly Gill, Bertha and Norma Barbee) re-recorded their original hits and some new songs for the album "One Door Closes" for Ian Levine's Motorcity Records project.

In March 1999 the group were finally recognised by Motown with the issue of the album "The Very Best Of The Velvelettes" it included all the singles recorded while at Motown with a couple of unreleased recordings "Let Love Live" and "Twilight Time" the UK release included four more unreleased tracks.

In 2006, The Velvelettes contributed to the double CD "Masters of Funk, Soul and Blues" including ex-Motown artist or producers from Detroit, Lamont Dozier, Freda Payne, George Clinton and Bobby Taylor recording covers of classic soul songs released on the Philadelphia International Records label. The Velvelettes sang "One Of A Kind Love Affair" by The Spinners. The other CD featured Philly stars such as Jean Carne, Bunny Sigler, Ted Mills or Jimmy Ellis doing Motown classics.

The group are still performing with the four original Bertha Barbee McNeal, Carol "Cal" Gill Street, Mildred Gill Arbor, and Norma Barbee Fairhurst in the group. Bertha Barbee McNeal and Carolyn "Cal" Gill Street now live in Kalamazoo, Michigan, Mildred Gill Arbor Norma Barbee Fairhurst in Flint.

Album Track: "He Was Really Sayin' Something", The Velvelettes.

Loucye Gordy Wakefield

Born in Detroit, Michigan - Died 29th July 1965 in Detroit, Michigan

Motown Connection: Vice President of Motown - Director of Jobete (Motown's Publishing Division) - Financial Controller.

Sister of Berry Gordy born to Berry Gordy Snr and Bertha Gordy, both from Georgia, from a family of ten children. At the time of her death in 1965, she was Vice-President of Motown and a director of Jobete. In 1964, she developed a system for collecting money from the distributors that contributed enormously to Motown's financial well-being. In 1968, a fund was established in her name to award $500 scholarships to "educationally disadvantaged students who are victims of society's misdirected priorities", but who have exhibited a potential for achievement.

In 1968 the Track "His Eye Is On The Sparrow" (arranged by Harvey Fuqua) and sung by Marvin Gaye was released on the LP "In Loving Memory". Berry Gordy commissioned this on the death of his sister Loucye. It is dedicated to the memory of Loucye and features several popular Motown acts, including Diana Ross and The Supremes, The Temptations and Marvin Gaye, performing versions of popular gospel songs and spirituals. The album should have been a gospel classic with its expression of love from Motown stars involved, they would use the songs as a tribute at her funeral. The album was released September 1968 on Motown and also an EP on Chisa (a Motown Subsidiary) with 4 tracks from the album, and in 1969 in the Tamla Motown (Motown's UK Label).

There were also the annual "Sterling Balls" in the Detroit years of Motown, these awards were presented at Berry Gordy's Mansion. In 1971 Motown produced a Souvenir Album "Sterling Ball Benefit"; this was not released, but was given as a present to the people who attended the "Ball", the cover being silver. Sadly Loucye died in 1965 of a brain haemorrhage.

Born Autry DeWalt Mixon although some references give Oscar G Mixon on the 14th June 1931 (even though Motown gave his birth date as 1942) in Blythesville, Arkansas on the 14th June 1931 - Died 23rd November 1995 in Battle Creek, Michigan

Motown Connection: Tenor Saxophone Player (One of Soul Music Great Tenor Saxophonists) - Lead Junior Walker and The All Stars - Solo Artist - Background Musician.

Junior started his music career with the group "Jumping Jacks" when he was in his teens, performing in South Bend, Indiana where he had moved. While performing he met Billy "Stix" Nick who had a group called Nick "Stix" and the Rhythm Rockers, their first professional engagement as a group (which included Fred Patton) was as the house band for a local university television station in Indiana.

Eventually Willie Woods joined the group at the same time as Junior left; however, Junior eventually rejoined the group in the late 1950's, when Billy "Stix" Nick joined the army. Next, Junior along with Fred Patton, and Willie Woods moved to Battle Creek, Michigan, recruiting Tony Washington to the group. Changing the name of the group to The All Stars, Junior and Fred Patton could not agree on the way forward for the group and Fred Patton left to be replaced by Victor Johnson. Junior, Victor Johnson, Tony Washington and Willie Woods moved to Grand Rapids, Michigan and recorded their first ever demo. While playing in a local nightclub, the group was introduced to and played for future Motown producer Johnny Bristol who then introduced Junior and the group to Harvey Fuqua (formerly of The Moonglows), and the owner of his own record label, Harvey Records who signed them to the label in 1961.

They made their first recordings in 1962, but by 1963, Harvey Fuqua sold the labels to Berry Gordy, with this, Junior and the group's contact was transferred to Motown. The membership of the group changed after the acquisition of the Harvey label, the drummer, Tony Washington left the group, and James Graves was recruited to the group.

Now called Junior Walker and The All Stars they were allocated to the Soul label (a subsidiary of Motown). The first release for the label in early 1965, and first big hit was "Shotgun," which was Junior's debut as lead vocalist. Junior had not been expecting to provide lead vocals, but the vocalist Junior had hired didn't show up for the session, he could not believe the label's decision to leave his vocal on the recording, however, Berry Gordy's instincts proved right, when "Shotgun" became a No1 R&B and a Top 5 chart hit.

After "Shotgun" Junior had the instrumental R&B chart hits including "Do the Boomerang", "Shake and Fingerpop", In 1966, James Graves left and was replaced by former member Billy "Stix" Nicks, in that year the group released "(I'm A) Road Runner" a Top 20 chart hit and a No4 R&B hit, based on Junior's experience of being on the road, and "Pucker Up Buttercup" another chart and R&B hit, followed by a cover of The Supremes recording "Come See About Me" in 1967, with a stunning solo saxophone performance from Junior, Also in 1967 drummer James Graves died in a car accident.

Toward the end of the 1960's, the group changed the style of their recording, using the ballad complemented with string arrangements and Junior only on lead vocals. This approach resulted in the group's second Top 5 pop hit, and R&B No1 "What Does It Take (To Win Your Love)", the group had a few more releases over the next few years which became minor chart hits, and R&B Top 10 hits, including in 1970 "Gotta Hold On To This Feeling", "Do You See My Love (For You Growing)", the 1971 recording of "Take Me Girl, I'm Ready" and "Way Back Home", in 1973. Junior recorded some solo material with Motown, but with limited success, leaving Motown in 1973, giving the reason that Berry Gordy had lost interest in "making music", instead, being more interested in developing Motown's film interest's.

In 1979, Junior (as a solo artist) signed to Norman Whitfield's, Whitfield Records label, but the move was not a success, at the same time Junior played the saxophone for the group Foreigner's on the recording of "Urgent" in 1981, later recording his own version of the Foreigner song.

Junior was involved on the 1983 "25th Motown Anniversary Concert" although Junior was only given a thirty second slot to perform "Shotgun", this did result in Junior re-signing to Motown and recording one album, "Blow The House Down" which was not a commercial success, that was Junior's last work with Motown.

Junior continued to tour through the 1980's and 1990's, sometimes with his son Autry DeWalt III playing drums, unfortunately, in 1993 his activities were severely curtailed by cancer, Junior died on 23rd November 1995 in Battle Creek, Michigan of cancer, followed by guitarist Willie Woods who died in 1997 at age 60. When Junior died, Billy "Stix" Nicks continued to tour with a version of The All Stars. Jnr Walker's All Star Band is still touring with original members Tony Washington, with Acklee King and Marty Montgomery taking the Junior Walker role.

Album Track: "What Does It Take To Win Your Love", Junior Walker and The All Stars.

Born on the16th February 1940 Black Bottom, Detroit, Michigan

Motown Connection: Writer - Producer - Artist - Arranger.

Leon was the youngest of eleven children, and the seventh son. His father worked for the Ford Motor Company and his mother was a beautician and minister. As a child Leon had an accident with a slingshot leaving him blind for two years and because of this injury he attended the Fitzgerald School For The Blind, the same school that Stevie Wonder attended. His first venture into song writing was at nine years old, writing the song "The Girl Of My Dreams". As a teenager he and childhood friend Lamont Dozier had a singing group called The Romeos, a street corner doo-wop group.

Leon left the group and began to perform on his own and while singing at the 20 Grand Club at age 17 he was seen by Berry Gordy who was interested in producing him, however as Berry was writing for Jackie Wilson at the time, he became very busy with Jackie's career and his plans to work with Leon never materialised. Leon went onto pursue a career as a jazz singer and headed to New York where he was offered his first recording contract with ABC but the project was never completed or released.

Returning to Detroit he ran into Lamont with whom he'd not communicated since their days singing together. Lamont had already begun to have multiple hit records as a songwriter along with Brian and Eddie Holland. It was evident to Leon that he should apply himself to writing songs and he began to collaborate, having his first local hit entitled "Warning" recorded by Pat Lewis for the Groovesville label in 1963 followed by songs on the Debonaires, Holidays and Rose Batiste on local Detroit labels.

He continued to write, produce and collaborated with Motown writers Ivy Jo Hunter and Stephen Bowden which resulted in his first major hit as a songwriter on the song "Got To Have You Back" which was recorded by The Isley Brothers in 1964. Leon went onto have songs recorded by Motown artists' Martha Reeves and The Vandellas and Junior Walker and the All Stars. Continuing to write and produce, Leon decided to head to Los Angeles in 1967 when Mickey Stevenson began a new record company with Clarence Avant called Venture Records. Some of his first projects in LA included the Righteous Brothers, Kim Weston, Johnny Nash and Al Wilson.

While in Los Angeles California he did some singing and playing at a supper club at the beach where he was discovered by Bob Hilliard and his wife. Bob being a writer of great standard songs like "Any Day Now", "Dear Hearts and Gentle People" and one of Burt Bacharach's chief collaborators became a mentor to Leon and also encouraged him to pursue being a recording artist. Unfortunately their collaboration was brief as Bob passed away only a few years after they met, however his widow Jacqueline continued to write with Leon after Bob's passing and their song "Rolling Down A Mountainside" was performed by Isaac Hayes as the closing song at Wattstax in 1972 and later became a hit for The Main Ingredient in 1975. Leon continued writing and also collaborating with many writers and artists, Ike and Tina Turner among them. His working with Ike and Tina led to him being signed to a recording deal with United Artists Records and his first self titled album was released in 1972 - the same year he was introduced to Arthur "T-Boy" Ross by the creative head of Motown's publishing arm, Jobete Music. He and T-Boy co-wrote the classic hit "I Wanna Be Where You Are" which was one of Michael Jackson's first hits as a solo artist and has since been recorded by dozens of other artists.

Leon also began to collaborate with Pam Sawyer and together they had many songs recorded in the mid-1970's on The Miracles, The Jackson 5, among others. Leon was signed as a writer to Almo Music, the publishing arm of A&M owned by Herb Alpert and Jerry Moss. In 1973-74, Quincy Jones was beginning a new album and was presented with a song entitled "If I Ever Lose This Heaven" and when finally meeting Leon because of his interest in that song, they began to collaborate on several songs together which became the classic "Body Heat" album on which Leon also sang in duet with Minnie Riperton. The collaboration with Minnie and Dick Rudolph followed that meeting and resulted in several songs on her "Adventures In Paradise" album which featured another classic song entitled "Inside My Love". Leon's songs continued to be recorded by a bevy of artists such as Donny Hathaway, Isaac Hayes. Sergio Mendes, Nancy Wilson and Rufus and Chaka Khan, among many others.

He also had the opportunity to record the soundtrack for the cult classic blaxploitation film "The Education of Sonny Carson" with Coleridge Taylor-Perkinson who composed the score and later contributed string arrangements for "I Want You". Leon headed back to Motown in 1975 where he was signed as an artist, producer and writer. He began to work on his first artist project and was asked to demo some songs on T-Boy Ross at the request of his sister Diana to present to Berry for an artist deal for T-Boy. They recorded three songs they had co-written and needing a fourth, "I Want You", a song Leon had written when he was signed to Almo Music, was added to the session. When Berry came by the studio and heard that track he felt strongly that it was a song that Marvin Gaye should record. Marvin agreed and they set out to record the song for Marvin and everyone agreed it would be a single release for him. Leon was continuing to produce his own solo project which was to be entitled "Comfort" and was visiting Marvin at his home in Hidden Hills one afternoon. Waiting for Marvin to join him in the living room, Leon was playing the tracks to his album "Comfort" while waiting and when Marvin came into join him he asked to hear the tracks he'd been overhearing. They listened to the tracks over and over and Marvin then told Leon that he wanted to record the whole album. Marvin now had his own recording studio in Hollywood and decided that they should plan to record there as soon as possible. So the "I Want You" album was started and completed 13 months later, but left Leon with having to complete another album for himself.

He recorded the album "Musical Massage" but as Marvin's album was such a success, Leon's was not supported and was left to find its own way over time as it became a "cult classic" and upon it's re-release by Universal was designated as "a Motown classic" album. Leon also produced an album on another Motown classic artist, Syreeta.

Leaving Motown after the disappointment of "Musical Massage", Leon went into the studio with pop artist Melissa Manchester in 1977 and produced her album "Don't Cry Out Loud" and continued writing and collaborating with artists and songwriters both stateside and in the UK. He recorded another solo album for a small label in 1979 distributed by TK which included a hit single called "What's Your Name?". Elektra Records soon approached him about a recording deal which resulted in 1981's "Rockin' You Eternally" and 1982's "Leon Ware". Both albums were critically acclaimed and have been re-released internationally. He also co-wrote and produced two albums on the group Shadow that consisted of members of the Ohio Players. He continued to write and produce throughout the 1980's and early 1990's with artists in the US and both write and perform in the UK.

In 1995 Leon released his own independent album entitle "Taste The Love" on his own label, Kitchen Records which was also released in the UK by Expansion Records. His collaboration with Maxwell resulted in another "classic song" entitled "Sumthin' Sumthin'" and his songs had begun to be sampled by many of the seminal Hip-Hop artists and singers such as Ice Cube, Tupac, A Tribe Called Quest, Aaliyah and Zhane.

His next independent project was released in 2001 - "Candlelight", a collaboration with pianist Don Grusin containing jazz standards and a few originals. This was also released by Expansion in the UK where he also performed. In 2001 he performed in Amsterdam and recorded a TV Special featuring his work and calling attention to the re-release of "Musical Massage". "Love's Drippin' followed in 2002 and a Japanese tour and release. "A Kiss In The Sand" - an album inspired by his love of Brazilian music, was released in 2004.

In 2006 Concord Records began talks with Leon about a compilation CD of his hits but when the deal was finalized Leon had written many new songs which caused them to rethink the project. An album entitled "Moon Ride" made up of all new songs was released in August 2008. He is intent about performing as much as possible as he continues to write, produce and collaborate.

Richard "Popcorn" Wylie

Born Richard Wayne Wylie on the June 6th 1939 Detroit, Michigan - Died 7th September 2008 Detroit, Michigan

Motown Connection: Brought James Jamerson to Motown via The Mohawks - Writer - Producer - Songwriter producer and session player for the Detroit labels Ric-Tic and Golden World (bought by Motown) - First Motown Reviews Bandleader.

Richard put together his first group at high school called "The Mohawks", along with James Jamerson and Clifford Mack. Richard recorded his first song for Ed and JoAnne Wingate in March 1964, writing and producing at least 25 records for the Golden World Label. He was also a pianist of some repute. He was a songwriter, producer and session player for the small Detroit labels SonBert and Ric-Tic as well.

At Golden World, although he worked on a significant number of Reflections songs, it is his "Northern Soul" legacy for which he is fondly remembered; with some excellent 45's on Carl Carlton ("Nothing No Sweeter Than Love"), The Debonaires ("Eenie Meenie") and Stewart Ames ("King For A Day"/"Angelina").

Richard joined Motown Records in 1959 through his friendship with Robert Bateman and took the first Motown Reviews on the road as bandleader. Richard is credited with one of the earliest Motown recordings "Shimmy Gully".

His group, Popcorn and The Mohawks, had three releases on the Motown label in 1961 and today they hang proudly in the upper room of the Hitsville Museum on West Grand Boulevard. He also played piano on three of Motown's milestone recordings, "Money", "Please Mr. Postman" and "Shop Around" with The Funk Brothers.

Richard would leave Motown in 1962, becoming freelance at Correct-tone and Continental. Richard also worked at Epic making his debut with "Come to Me", followed a year later by the song "Brand New Man" and "Head Over Heels in Love".

In 1966 he formed his own label, Pameline, releasing songs for the Detroit Executives, including the 1967 Northern Soul evergreen "The Cool-Off".

In 1971 Richard signed with Motown's Soul subsidiary to record "Funky Rubber Band". The single remained unreleased until 1975 and became a UK club favourite.

Richard recorded two more 1975 singles on ABC, namely "Lost Time" and "Georgia's After Hours" as a solo artist.

Later he was to record for Ian Levine's Motorcity label during the early 1990's, releasing "See This Man In Love". Richard was 69 when he died from suspected heart failure.

Born William Henry Weatherspoon in Detroit, Michigan - Died Sunday 17th July 2005 Detroit, Michigan

Motown Connection: Song Writer - Producer.

William's first entry into the music industry was singing with the Tornados in 1956, a group formed by Charles Sutton who had been in the group The Midnighters, but after a short illness he wanted to return, but the group refused. They recorded unsuccessfully for Chess records and Robert West's Bumble Bee Records, where they released William's "Geni in the Jug." The group disbanded around 1960 and William moved on to work as a songwriter and producer for Detroit's Correc-tone Records, this label had already signed The Primettes (who would develop into The Supremes), a sister group to The Primes (the future Temptations) where they often contributed backing vocals to recording sessions. Next, in 1963 William contributed to the recording by the group The Pace Setters, of the single "The Monkey Whip" b/side "Around the World".

On the back of this experience Motown offered William a contract as a song writer and producer and at first struggled to adapt the system and competitive nature of the other writer and producer. William then teamed with James Dean and one of their recordings became a gold record "What's Become of the Brokenhearted?" with Paul Riser providing the classic arrangement for the single. Other Jimmy Ruffin productions included, Jimmy Ruffin "I'll Say Forever My Love" and the recording of "I've Passed This Way Before" both minor hits for the artist. Despite the Jimmy Ruffin gold record, Motown placed the team in the second tier of writers and producers, which gave them little chance of becoming a major force at Motown. On many occasions their songs were credited with a third writer (i.e. Stanley Mullen, Stephen Bowden, William Stevenson and Jack Goga), but the productions were solely created by William Weatherspoon and James Dean.

This team recorded on many other Motown artists including, Edwin Starr on "I Am the Man for You Baby", The Monitors "Bring Back the Love" and "Step By Step (Hand in Hand)", Marv Johnson "I'll Pick a Rose for My Rose", The Contours "It's So Hard Being a Loser", "Give It Up" by The Temptations, Dennis Edwards which included the recording "Which Way to My Baby," which was unreleased until the 1990's, The Marvelettes "Keep On Loving Me", and Gladys Knight and The Pips. Later in the 1960's, the group the team worked with was The Originals, giving them the unique sound to their work.

When Holland-Dozier-Holland left Motown, William decided to join them and signed with their new labels, Invictus, Hot Wax and the Music Merchant. William then teamed up with Angelo Bond, writing and producing hits for Laura Lee "Rip Off", "Women Love Rights" and "Love and Liberty" and the Flaming Embers "I'm Not My Brother's Keeper" and "Sunshine". James Dean (who was a relation of the Holland brothers) did not join William, instead firstly working with Don Davis, then with a new collaborator Henry Glover, where they produced for The Dells, The Dramatics, Johnnie Taylor and the major hit for Billy Davis and Marilyn McCoo ("You Don't Have to Be a Star"), the Soul Children, and others.

When Holland-Dozier-Holland labels folded in the late 1970's, William decided to returned to Motown along with Angelo Bond, they wrote "Go for It" and "Struck By Lightening Twice" for The Temptations and songs for the label's newer artists like Hi Energy, but William was not able to find another hit to rival "What's Become of the Brokenhearted?" and decided to devote himself to producing gospel music and created his own company to publish his work.

Mary Wells

Born Mary Esther Wells on the 13th May 1943 in Detroit, Michigan - Died 26th July 1992 in Los Angeles, California

Motown Connection: Background Singer - Solo Artist - Motown's First International Artist.

Mary's mother was a domestic and her father had already left home, one of three children, she caught spinal meningitis at the age of two, which left her temporarily paralysed, with loss of hearing and partial blindness in one eye. Suffering from the hardship of having learn to walk again, she did eventually return to good health. By age 12, Wells was helping her mother with housecleaning work, from this early age Mary developed a great love of music and singing, and was a member of the Northwestern High School choir, the school she attended. Mary graduated from Detroit's Northwestern High School at the age of 17 and set her sights on becoming a scientist, however, she started with singing and performing at local clubs and competed in various talent contests in Detroit. By 1959, Mary had been introduced to Berry Gordy's assistant, Robert Bateman, trying to get Robert Bateman to listen to a song she had written for artist Jackie Wilson, Mary decided that she would pursue a musical career.

Impressed by Mary's persistence Robert Bateman arranged an audition for Mary and her song with Berry Gordy (who at the time was Jackie Wilson's main songwriter), and she sang the song for Berry Gordy, who was more impressed with Mary singing, than her song writing skills. Instead of buying the song for Jackie Wilson, Berry Gordy offered Mary a contract as a solo artist with his new label Tamla (the main label at the time). The song Mary released was called, "Bye Bye Baby", as her debut release and became her first single to reach the charts becoming a Top 10 R&B hit in 1960, and reached No45 on the pop charts.

With Mary's debut success, Berry Gordy immediately brought her back to the studio, Berry Gordy produced the follow-up hit and William "Mickey" Stevenson wrote, "I Don't Want to Take a Chance", which equaled her first single's success, however her third single, "Strange Love", issued in late 1961 from her first Motown album was met with indifference from the DJ, and subsequently failed to chart. In an effort to push Mary's recording further up the charts in 1962, Berry Gordy decided to put Mary with his then star writer and producer Smokey Robinson. This collaboration produced an album that would establish Mary as one of the key early players at Motown. The album produced the major hits written and produced by Smokey Robinson, "Two Lovers", "You Beat Me to the Punch" (a Grammy nominated single nominated in the Best Rhythm and Blues Recording category and the first Motown recording to do so) and "The One Who Really Loves", Mary was technically Motown's second female artist signed to the label, the blues/gospel singer Mable John had been signed to the label the previous year. However, Mary's hits were making her the label's first female star and its first fully successful solo artist.

By 1963, Mary had become "Motown's First Lady" with further hits and some would say a premature greatest hits compilation. The next releases were "Laughing Boy" and "What's So Easy for Two Is So Hard for One" both reached the R&B Top 10 and the Top 30 on the pop charts. The recording "Your Old Standby" became a surprise hit as the b/side of "What Love Has Joined Together" and reached No8 on the R&B charts, and became a Top 40 chart hit. Mary finished 1963 with another R&B Top 10, "You Lost the Sweetest Boy", which reached No22 on the pop chart.

Then in 1964, Mary recorded the single "My Guy" which became her first No1 hit, this recording again written and produced by Smokey Robinson, hit the top spot in mid-1964, released at the very height of Beatle mania the song was still an international success, and it is suggested, this is the song that put Motown on the map. It was at this time that The Beatles called Mary's single their favourite American recording, and invited her to tour with them throughout the UK, Mary accepted their invitation, and was inspired to record "Love Songs to the Beatles", an album featured several songs written by Lennon and McCartney, despite the massive success of The Beatles, none of the songs from the album reached the pop chart. The tour also made Mary the first Motown artist to appear in the UK and one of only three female singers Brenda Holloway (a fellow Motown Artist) and Jackie DeShannon to tour and open the show for The Beatles. At the time Billboard had stopped publishing the R&B chart (then called the Black Singles Chart), between 1964 and early in 1965, because of this, none of Mary's (or any other soul or R&B singer's) sales figures were recorded or issued.

With "My Guy" becoming a the label's first major international hit (it reached No5 in the UK charts) Berry Gordy decided to team Mary with one of Motown's other established star Marvin Gaye, to record as a duet. Mary and Marvin Gaye, album "Together" became a hit album and produced two simultaneous top twenty hits, "Once Upon a Time" reaching No17 on the pop charts and "What's the Matter With You Baby" a No19 pop hit.

When Mary turned 21 years old "My Guy" with the single at No1, Mary was offered (for a reported) an advance of several hundred thousand dollars from 20th Century

Fox. As Smokey Robinson later would explain, Motown was not yet fully established at the time and the major record labels were able to offer better contracts, Mary and her husband/manager Herman Griffin felt Motown wasn't offering enough money in relation to Mary's new superstar status. Herman Griffin wanted total control of Mary's recordings etc, something Motown were reluctant to do.

A lawsuit would keep Mary out of the studio for several months, as Mary and Berry Gordy could not agree the contract details, one of the sticking points was Mary fighting to gain larger royalties from earnings she had made during her tenure with Motown. Finally, after she invoked a clause that allowed her to leave the label at twenty one, Mary and Motown finally agreed a fair settlement, Mary officially leaving Motown in early 1965. With this dispute over, Mary then accepted the lucrative contract with 20th Century Fox Records.

One of the reasons Mary moved (apart from the recording contract) was the prospect of film roles through 20th Century Fox, she had one small part in the 1967 film, "Catalina Caper", but no more parts materialised. It's also been rumoured that Motown quietly discouraged radio stations from playing Mary's subsequent releases on 20th Century Fox, whatever is true or not, what is certain is that Mary never remotely approached the success of her Motown years, entering the pop Top 40 only once (although she had some minor R&B hits). One lesson that Motown learnt from this episode was to take more care (particularly for the rest of the 1960's) not to lose its big stars to larger labels.

Mary's first 20th Century Fox release featured the modest hits "Ain't It The Truth" b/side "Stop Taking Me for Granted", the one Top 40 hit with the label, "Use Your Head" and "Never, Never Leave Me", there followed a stressful period between Mary and the label as they clashed over creative differences and Mary's poor record sales. Unable to agree any compromise Mary asked to be released from her contract and in 1965 she left with a small settlement. Mary's departure from Motown was so dramatic and in terms of record sales unsuccessful, that it's tended to overshadow the quality of her later work, it may not have matched the quality of her Motown recordings, but some of her 1960's singles for 20th Century Fox could and should have been hits for her.

Moving to the Atlantic Records subsidiary Atco, Mary began working with producer Carl Davis; Mary recorded her final Top 10 R&B hit "Dear Lover", which also became a minor pop hit, reaching at No51. However, much like her time with 20th Century Fox, Mary struggled to come up with a follow-up hit and in 1968 she left the label for Jubilee Records, where she issued her hit, "The Doctor", a song she co-wrote with husband Cecil Womack, (brother of Bobby Womack).

Two years later Mary left the label for a short deal with Warner Music subsidiary Reprise Records and released two Cecil Womack produced singles (she wrote and produced a lot of her late 1960's and early 1970's recording with her second husband) before deciding to spend more time with her family and semi-retiring from the music business in 1974. Entering the late 1970's and 1980's she had trouble landing recording deals, but Mary did continue to tour in this period, and re-recorded some of her hits and some new material for an Allegiance Records album.

In 1977, Mary divorced Cecil Womack and a year later went on tour again with her boyfriend, Cecil's older brother Curtis. Performing in local California venues, while performing at one of these venues in 1981, Larkin Arnold of the record label CBS Urban president was in the audience, and offered Mary a contract with the CBS subsidiary Epic Records. Mary accepted the contract and ended her seven-year semi-retirement with the release of "In and Out of Love", in October 1981. The album helped re-launch Mary's career and produced Mary's biggest hit in years, the disco single, "Gigolo". The 12" single went No13 on Hot Dance/Club Singles chart and No2 on the Hot Disco Songs chart. A three-minute edited radio version was released in January of 1982, but only reached No69 on the pop charts, sadly it turned out to be Mary's final chart single.

Mary did one more album for Epic before her contract was not renewed, the 1982 covers album, "Easy Touch". Leaving CBS in 1983, she would go on recording for smaller labels and would become a successful performing artist. In 1989, she was awarded a Pioneer Award by the "Rhythm and Blues Foundation" during its inaugural year.

In 1990, Mary became involved with Ian Levine's Motorcity project, releasing an album, "Keeping My Mind on Love", in the same year Mary was diagnosed with larynx cancer, hindering her ability to sing and tour. Immediately beginning treatment it resulted in Mary being forced to sell her house and possessions, and eventually couldn't afford health insurance. The treatments ravaged her voice, many of Mary's friend's including, Diana Ross, Mary Wilson, Martha Reeves and The Temptations supported her through this tough time, also admirers of Mary from the music industry supported her, including Rod Stewart, Bruce Springsteen and Bonnie Raitt. The Grammy Foundation raised over $50,000 to help Mary pay for treatment for illness.

Despite her health condition, Mary still undertook long trips, including one to New York in which she appeared on the "Joan Rivers Show." Part of the tribute to her included a call from Little Richard and a loving video dedication from Stevie Wonder, who, in her honour, sang "My Guy" rewritten as "My Girl". The following year, Mary brought a multi-million dollar lawsuit against Motown for royalties she felt she had not received upon leaving Motown Records in 1964. Motown eventually settled the lawsuit by giving her a six-figure sum. In late 1991, Mary travelled to Washington DC, where she testified before a Congressional Committee concerning funding for cancer research. In 2006, Mary was inducted to the Michigan Rock and Roll "Legends Hall of Fame".

In the summer of 1992, Mary's cancer returned and she was admitted to hospital in Los Angeles with pneumonia, sadly, Mary died at the age of forty-nine after a few days in the hospital. At her funeral, which included an eulogy from Smokey Robinson, he sung a sombre "My Guy" in tribute to Mary.

Mary was married twice, firstly in 1960, to Motown singer Herman Griffin, they divorced in 1964. In 1966, she married her long time boyfriend, singer songwriter Cecil Womack the marriage lasted until 1977 they had sons Cecil Jnr and Harry and daughter Stacy. Mary had a relationship with Curtis Womack starting in 1979 which resulted in her youngest child Sugar. Mary separated from Curtis became a single mother prior to her 1992 death.

Album Track: "You Beat Me to the Punch", Mary Wells.

Kim Weston

Born Agatha Nataille Weston on the 30th December 1939 Detroit, Michigan

Motown Connection: Background Singer - Solo Artist - Duet with Marvin Gaye.

Kim as a teenager, played piano and was a member of the church choir, but her main ambition at the time was to be a professional swimmer; ironically, it was her swimming coach who directed her into music. At 17 she joined the gospel group "The Wright Specials", and with this group, performed and supported such groups as The Caravans, Staple Singers and Mighty Clouds of Joy.

It was with the Wright Specials that she signed to Motown in 1962, they recorded two singles for the label, in 1962 and 1963, firstly "That's What He Is To Me" followed by the recording "Ninety-Nine and a Half". The group proved unsuccessful and left Motown shortly after these releases. Kim was next used by the singer Johnny Thornton on his demo which he gave to his cousins Eddie and Brian Holland (of the future Holland-Dozier-Holland Motown production team) hoping for their support in recording the track. The Holland brothers were interested in the singer, but not the songs. With the support of the Holland brothers, Kim was offered a new contract as a solo artist and re-signed to Motown, Kim's first task was to go on the Motown Revue tour, not recording in the studio. Kim then married Motown's A&R director William "Mickey" Stevenson.

With the tour completed she did her first recording for Motown, "It Should Have Been Me", however, the b/side "Love Me All The Way" received more attention and became a hit in its own right reaching No24 on the pop charts. Kim's two biggest hits with Motown were the recordings "Take Me in Your Arms (Rock Me a Little While)", which reached No4 on the R&B charts, and was a No50 chart success in 1965, (the song would later be covered by The Isley Brothers, "Blood, Sweat and Tears" and The Doobie Brothers) followed by "Helpless" a No13 R&B hit, and a No56 chart hit in 1966. The song,"Helpless" had previously been recorded by The Four Tops for their Second Album at Motown.

With this success, Kim became a rising star within Motown furthered by duet work with Marvin Gaye and the subsequent hit "It Takes Two," in 1966, which complemented her solo recordings. It was the success of "It Takes Two" that led Motown to look at possibly using Tammi Terrell as Marvin Gaye's singing partner, to gain further success for the label. This was to prove Kim's high point at Motown, the next batch of recordings did not chart as well, but were nonetheless good solid issues, including the Smokey Robinson production "Looking For the Right Guy" and the recording of "A Thrill a Moment". Kim did record in Los Angeles while with Motown, before the company formally moved in 1972, and undertook a few tours in Britain when the Northern Soul scene was at its height.

By early 1967 both Kim Weston and her then husband William "Mickey" Stevenson left Motown to form their own label called People. At the time Kim Weston signed to MGM records (recording for both MGM and Volt), and Mickey was offered a reported million dollar deal to assume control of the company's floundering Venture subsidiary, but it was not a success and the label did not have any major hits. Kim recorded a couple of singles for MGM, "I Got What You Need" and "Nobody", which went largely unnoticed due to lack of promotion by the label. Kim recorded an album for the label called, "This Is America", which included her popular version of the Black National Anthem, "Lift Every Voice and Sing", which was released as a single and featured in the movie Wattstax. All the money from the single was donated to the United Negro College Fund. She recorded several more albums for various labels, including Stax/Volt, and also made an album of duets with Johnny Nash, however, none of these recordings charted. Kim did record a Jazz album in 1976 which became her lost album, it was recorded with a group known as "The Hastings Street Jazz Experience" but never released.

In 1977, Kim founded the "Festival for the Performing Arts" in Detroit, it came as a direct result of an incident the previous year when youth gangs in Detroit had became a major crime problem, Kim met with Mayor Young and told him she wanted "to work with kids". He offered her a job with the Department of Public Works and so the foundation was created to help these gangs off the street.

When Ian Levine started the Motorcity project, Kim became one of the first former Motown artists to support the project in 1980's. Bringing in many other former stars on board, in particular The Velvelettes, Mary Wells, May Wilson and Brenda Holloway, Kim released the single "Signal Your Intention" which became a UK No1 in the Hi-NRG charts, it was followed by the album "Investigate" released in 1990 and included some re-recordings of her Motown hits. A second album was recorded for the label "Talking Loud" in 1992, but was never released although all the songs were included on the compilation "The Best Of Kim Weston" was released in 1996. Kim toured with the Motorcity stars in a 1989 tour of Britain.

Today Kim is a disc jockey on a local Detroit radio station, and still sponsors the summer events at Hart Plaza. She also tours occasionally, often with former Motown colleagues Mary Wilson, Martha Reeves and Brenda Holloway. Kim was also featured on the 2006 four CD release of the "Motortown Revue" series.

Kim married Motown's A&R director William "Mickey" Stevenson in 1961, since divorced.

Album Track: "Looking For The Right Guy", Kim Weston.

Robert White

Born on the 19th November 1936 in Billmyre, Harrisburg, Pennsylvania - Died 27th October 1994 in Los Angeles, California.

Motown Connection: Guitarist/member of The Funk Brothers (Motown in House Band).

Robert was a part of the guitar trio (including Joe Messina and Eddie Willis) in Motown's in house studio band which eventually became The Funk Brothers. Some of Robert's signature parts are the high-part of the telegraphic intro of The Supremes' "You Keep Me Hangin' On", the lead rift on The Temptations' "My Girl" and Smokey Robinson and The Miracles' "I Second That Emotion". The guitarist would often double the parts of pianist Earl Van Dyke, for example, on The Supremes' No1 hits "You Can't Hurry Love" and "Ain't That Peculiar".

Robert toured with the Moonglows (which included Lead Singer Harvey Fuqua and Marvin Gaye both future Motown stars), Following The Moonglows Robert found himself in Detroit. Roberts's first work in Detroit was playing on sessions for Anna Records, owned by Berry Gordy's sister Anna, (who would later marry Marvin Gaye) and at the time an established record label in Detroit. Robert's next assignment was when Berry Gordy asked him to join Motown Records in house studio band.

Playing as part of a trio of guitarists the three can often be found playing off of each other on numerous Motown hits. Their intricate counterpoint was the result of their "talky" five-minute pre-recording session confabs where they'd discuss which part each guitarist would play.

Robert's strengths on the guitar was based on his knowledge of chord construction and the voicing tips he'd picked up from his uncle. Robert's basic role with The Funk Brothers was as their rhythm guitarist; good examples include the records for Stevie Wonder "My Cherie Amour" and "For Once in My Life". As well as the session work at Motown, Robert, along with the rest of The Funk Brothers would be recording for other labels. Several music entrepreneurs, local and otherwise, took advantage of the situation offering the band more money, leading to The Funk Brothers being heard on a lot of "backdoor sessions" for the local Golden World and Ric-Tic label owned by Ed Wingate. The band can be heard on "Agent Double 0 Soul" by Edwin Starr in 1965 and "Stop Her On Sight" in 1966, on Ollie McLaughlin's Karen label, "Cool Jerk" by The Capitols in July 1966. Making the trips to nearby Chicago, The Funk Brothers played sessions on several records for producer Carl Davies. "I Just Wanna Testify" by The Parliaments in 1967.

Also in 1967 The Funk Brothers did background session for "Just Be Sincere" and "(Your Love Keeps Lifting Me) Higher and Higher" which set the stage for Jackie Wilson's mid-1960's comeback and was his second No1 R&B in October 1967, followed by "Since You Showed Me How to Be Happy" a hit in November 1967, "I Get The Sweetest Feeling" in June 1968, "Can Feel Those Vibrations" and "This Love Is Real" in November 1970. The Funk Brothers also travelled south to record in Muscle Shoals and Atlanta among other cities.

With the six, sometimes seven-day recording schedules of The Funk Brothers at Motown, Robert and the other musicians would gain relief from this heavy work load by playing jazz sets at the Chit Chat Club, the Twenty Grand Club and Phelps Lounge.

Motown Records relocated to Los Angeles, partly based on Berry Gordy's desire to become involved in the motion picture business and the era of The Funk Brothers (based on Hitsville Studio A) was coming to an end. After Motown moved to Los Angeles in the 1970's, Robert's session career came to an unhappy ending. Never recognised by Motown for his contribution Robert also missed out on the accolades and recognition which came in the shape of Allan Slutsky documentary "Standing In The Shadows Of Motown" which re-established The Funk Brothers, and started the group touring again. Among the guitars White used to record were the Gibson ES 335 and the Gibson L-5.

In the 1980's, Robert backed The Temptations during their reunion tour. Later that decade, he co-owned the former recording studio of producer Giorgio Moroder who worked with Donna Summer. However, at the age of 57 Robert died of complications from heart surgery.

Signature Sound: Can be nothing other than The Temptations' "My Girl", one of the top five guitar rifts of all time.

Born Ronald White on the 5th April 1939 in Detroit, Michigan - Died 26th August 1995 in Detroit, Michigan

Publicity Handout. L to R: Smokey Robinson, Bobby Rogers, Claudette Robinson, Ronnie and Pete Moore.

Motown Connection: A member of Motown group The Miracles (aka The Matadors) from 1956 until 1978 - Writer - Producer.

Born and raised in Detroit, a founding member of The Miracles, and the only original member to survive all of the group's line up changes. A childhood friend of Smokey Robinson, Ronnie and Smokey Robinson began singing together in school. Interestingly, they released a few side singles while with The Miracles as a duo called "Ron and Bill", on Chess Records of Chicago. The Miracles one of Motown's first successful groups was formed in 1957, originally called The Matadors, and included cousins Bobby Rogers and Emerson, Emerson would eventually be replaced by his sister Claudette Rogers (Smokey Robinson's future wife), later joined by guitarist Marv Tarplin in 1958.

The first success for The Miracles was "Shop Around" in late 1960's, it became Motown's first million seller. The 1962 Top 10 hit "You've Really Got a Hold on Me", established The Miracles as a chart topping group. While The Miracles were never Motown's biggest act, they were one of its most consistent groups at Motown in it's heyday of the 1960's, other great recordings included "I Second That Emotion", "The Love I Saw in You Was Just a Mirage", "The Tracks of My Tears", "Ooo Baby Baby", "Baby, Baby Don't Cry" all written and produced by Smokey Robinson.

While at Motown, Ronnie discovered Stevie Wonder, then Ronnie's 11-year-old neighbour, and organised an audition for Stevie Wonder with Berry Gordy. He continued to play a key role in the career of Stevie Wonder in his early days at Motown. Ronnie collaborated with Smokey Robinson on several of his successes, including the hits by The Temptations "Don't Look Back", the flip side of "My Baby" and was on the album "Temptin' Temptations" and their 1965 No1 hit, "My Girl", It was included on the album "The Temptations Sing Smokey", next was Marvin Gaye's Top 10 hit, "Ain't That Peculiar", and Mary Wells' Top 10 hit, "You Beat Me To The Punch". Other songs Ronnie co-wrote include "Got a Job" and "Bad Girl" for The Miracles and "One More Heartache" for a 1966 recording for Marvin Gaye.

In 1967, The Miracles changed the name to Smokey Robinson and The Miracles, with the expected news that Smokey Robinson would announce his intention to leave the group for a solo career. However, when their 1966 recording of "The Tears of a Clown" was released as a single in 1970, it became a No1 hit in both the US and the UK. In 1972 Smokey did decide to leave the group, and The Miracles began a six-month farewell tour. On 16th July 1972, Smokey and Claudette Robinson and the rest of the group gave their final performances as The Miracles in Washington DC, at this performance Smokey introduced the group's new lead singer, Billy Griffin.

The Miracles then started to tour and record with the line up of, Ronnie, Bobby Rogers, Billy Griffin and Pete Moore. They recorded the hits, "Love Machine", "Do It Baby" and "Don't You Cha Love It" in 1978. In this year, the group decided to disband. Ronnie did not participate in the 1983 television special, "Motown 25: Yesterday, Today, Forever", because at the time his first wife, Earlyn, who had been diagnosed with breast cancer several years earlier had recently died. Ronnie helped produce the movie soundtrack to the film "My Girl". In later life he became a successful real estate entrepreneur. Ron lost his battle with Leukaemia in August 1995, at the age of 57 in Detroit; it was the same disease which claimed the life of his first born, Michelle, a loss which devastated the entire family for many years.

Ronnie married firstly Earlyn, with whom he had 2 daughters Michelle and Pamela, then Gloria, with whom he had and a son and daughter.

Album Track: "My Business Your Pleasure", The Miracles.

Norman Whitfield

*Born Norman Jesse Whitfield on the 12th May 1940 in Harlem, New York City -
Died 16th September 2008 Los Angeles, California*

Motown Connection: Junior in the Quality Control Department - In House Staff
Writer - In House Producer - Arranger - produced and composed many of the
greatest records in the pop/soul history.

Norman spent most of his teenage years in Harlem pool halls scraping a living
hustling. However, in his late teens, Norman and his family became stranded in
Detroit, Michigan while his father was driving from California to New York and
relocated there. When Norman first arrived in Detroit he performed with local

Detroit bands and went back to working
the local pool halls to survive.

Norman started as a staff producer at the
tiny Detroit label "Thelma Records"
before moving on to Motown in 1963.

After "Thelma Records" Norman began
hanging around at Motown's offices at
"Hitsville USA", trying to get a chance to
work for the label. Berry Gordy recognised
Norman's persistence and hired him in the quality control department that determined
which songs would or would not be released by the label. Norman eventually joined
Motown's in-house songwriting staff. Norman had a few minor successes, writing and
producing singles for The Marvelettes, "Too Many Fish in the Sea" and The Velvelettes
"Needle in a Haystack" which were virtually indistinguishable from the prevailing
"Motown Sound" pioneered by the Holland-Dozier-Holland.

After Holland-Dozier-Holland left Motown, Norman became a principal architect
in the development of the next stage of the "Motown Sound" in the late 1960's,
producing the more "Earthy" and "Psychedelic" sounds. In partnership with Brian
Holland, Norman pushed The Temptations towards a rougher, grittier R&B style
typified by the smash "Ain't Too Proud to Beg". The hits "Beauty's Only Skin
Deep" and "(I Know) I'm Losing You" quickly followed.

When Norman took over sole control of the group in 1967, he stripped even more
of their gloss away. At this time Norman also did a series of "bluesy" hits for
Gladys Knight and The Pips, Norman's finest work was to come in 1968. Norman
took his song "I Heard It Through the Grapevine", (previously recorded by Gladys
Knight and The Pips) to Marvin Gaye, the single, with its remarkable vocals,
spartan arrangement and pulsing rhythm, remains arguably the best single ever

produced (up there with "What's Going On") of the Motown's Detroit Era. At the time "Grapevine" was Motown's biggest single release.

Norman then teamed up with lyricist Barrett Strong to compose a new set of Temptations records, (which reflected the emergence of psychedelia). Beginning with 1968's "I Wish It Would Rain" the first Motown release, to incorporate the use of sound effects, "Whitfield and Strong" masterminded a string of classic Temptations hits, including "Cloud Nine", "I Can't Get Next to You" and "Ball of Confusion", mirroring the social, political and sexual issues of the late 1960's. Subsequent classics included, Edwin Starr's "War", and the Undisputed Truth's "Smiling Faces Sometimes" Norman matched his increasingly progressive material with productions that stretched the Motown to its limits, culminating in The Temptations' 1972 epic recording "Papa Was a Rolling Stone."

With the release of Marvin Gaye's 1971 landmark LP "What's Going On" and Stevie Wonder's 1973 classic "Innervisions", Motown's focus shifted from the single to the LP and Norman moved to producing not simply individual songs but complex, multi-layered albums, reaching his peak on The Temptations' aptly titled "Masterpiece". However, feeling increasingly stifled by Motown's creative restrictions, he left Motown in 1973 to form his own Whitfield Records label. Its corporate logo a stencilled "W", was little more than the Motown "M" simply flipped upside-down and given a different colour.

In the beginning, Norman's only act was "The Undisputed Truth", which he had convinced to leave Motown and join his new label. The group never really had any chart success, but Whitfield Records moved into a more contemporary funk sound and had a smash hit in 1976 with Rose Royce's "Car Wash". Rose Royce went on to produce three more popular albums, but never could top the success of "Car Wash", which served as the theme song to the 1976 motion picture "Car Wash". The instrumental version of "Car Wash" won Whitfield another Grammy award.

In the 1980's, Norman's productions grew increasingly out of step with the times, However, Norman did return to Motown producing The Temptations' 1983 hit single "Sail Away" and the soundtrack to "The Last Dragon". By the end of the 1980's he had essentially vanished from the pop landscape.

On January 2005, Norman pleaded guilty for failing to report royalty income he earned from 1995 to 1999 to the Internal Revenue Service. Facing charges of tax evasion on over $2 million worth of income, he was sentenced to six months of house arrest and a $25,000 fine. The producer was not imprisoned because of his health problems with diabetes. Norman is survived by four sons and a daughter.

Album Track: "You're My Everything", The Temptations.

Milan B Williams

Born 28th March 1948 in Okolona, Mississippi Died 9th July 2006 in Houston, Texas

Motown Connection: Member of The Commodores - Wrote "Machine Gun" the last recording in "Hitsville Studio A" in 1972.

Milan was taught to play the piano at an early age by his older brother, Earl. Milan moved from Okolona in his late teens to attend Tuskegee University Alabama to study engineering and while at the college he formed the funk group, The Jays, with fellow student William King. At the same time on campus there was a group called The Mystics, led by Lionel Richie, in 1968 then changing the name to The Commodores in 1969, between then and 1972, they started performing from their regional base, which included Tuskegee, Montgomery and Birmingham, before moving onto the New York funk scene. The place at which they became most well known was at "Small's Paradise" in Harlem. There is one pre-Motown album on Atlantic, "Keep On Dancing" the result of a one off deal. They changed the name

to The Commodores in 1969, when Walter "Clyde" Orange gave King a dictionary and told him to pick a name, the name he picked was The Commodores, the original line-up consisted of William "Clyde" King, Thomas McClary, Ronald LaPread, Walter "Clyde" Orange, Lionel Richie and Milan Williams. Interestingly, Lionel Richie was the group's saxophonist in the group's early days, not the group's lead vocalist.

Bennie Ashburn their manager (who died 1982), introduced them to Motown executive Suzanne de Passé in 1972. Their signing to Motown in that year came after the group was told to be in New York City for an audition, the group did not know the audition was for The Jackson 5 tour, and two weeks later they were informed that they had been selected for the tour with The Jackson 5. They opened for The Jackson 5 for two and a half years. The group's first release on Motown was the instrumental dance recording taken from the album of the same name called "Machine Gun", written by Milan, the recording became their first Top 10 hit. This was the last commercial recording undertaken at "Hitsville Studio A". This recording is now used at many of the biggest American sporting events, and was featured in many films, including "Boogie Nights" and "Looking for Mr. Goodbar".

In 1977, they played themselves in the movie, "Thank God It's Friday", which was released by Columbia in 1978; Motown co-produced the film with Casablanca Records. In 1978, The Commodores were named the No1 R&B group by Rolling Stone magazine. Three albums were released in between 1975 and 1976, "Caught in the Act", "Movin' On" and "Hot On The Tracks" and are considered the height of their funk style music period.

Before Lionel Richie's departure in 1982, the group had a string of hits, which included "Old Fashion Love", "Lady (You Bring Me Up)" and "Oh No" which was used in the film "The Last American Virgin", the single reached No4 on the US charts. The Commodores also recorded many songs that were not releases and never charted, the most famous being "Zoom", later covered and made into a chart hit by the group, Fat Larry's Band, the group courted the talents of tenor J D Nicholas (formerly of Heatwave) and would go on to release their biggest hit.

Their first album without Lionel Richie was "Commodores 13" released in 1983. Their next album, "Nightshift" (a tribute to Marvin Gaye and Jackie Wilson) came out in 1985 and produced the hit single of the same name, (it also won the group its only Grammy Award for Best R&B Performance by a Duo or Group With Vocals), another change to the group came when Thomas McClary left in 1982, to pursue a solo career and to develop a gospel music company, and was replaced by Sheldon Reynolds, and by J D Nicholas (ex-member of the group Heatwave) in 1984. With this success The Commodores became one of Motown's most successful groups of the 1970's and 1980's, the group had seven No1 songs and many other Top 10 hits on the pop charts.

The Commodores left Motown in 1985; they had perceived that Motown gave a commitment to releasing the group's album prior to Lionel Richie's solo release. However, the label did not honour the commitment and proceeded to release Lionel Richie's solo project first. Consequently, the group left the label and signed with Polydor in the same year and recorded the Top 10 hit "Going' to the Bank".

Milan was responsible for writing many of The Commodores' significant hits and classics, during their mid-1970's and early 1980's, including "Patch It Up", "The Bump", "Captain Quickdraw" (after his codename on CB radio, of which he was an enthusiast), "Wonderland" and "Old-Fashion Love". Milan was involved in co-writing their first big hit "Brick House", "Too Hot Ta Trot" and many others. At the peak of The Commodores' success, Milan would captain his own four seat plane when on the group's US tours.

After the 1982 departure of Lionel Richie, Milan took on some production duties for the Commodores, with most of the recordings by The Commodores being undertaken at Motown's Los Angeles studios, Milan moved there in the early 1980's, but eventually left the group in 1989 after a dispute over their direction, and a decision to tour South Africa which was subsequently cancelled. He built his own studio and continued to write and produce, although there was no solo recording from this time, Milan also developed entrepreneurial interests in Nigeria and a number of other African countries.

Milan died in Texas in 2006, at the age of 58. His death followed a long battle with cancer.

Milan was survived by his wife, Melanie Bruno-Williams whom he married in July 2006, and two sons from a previous marriage to Gwendolyn Rigby Williams, Jason and Ricci, they married in 1974, but divorced in 1984.

Otis Williams

Born Otis Miles on the 30th October 1941 in Texarkana, Texas

Motown Connection: Background Singer - Member of The Temptations - Last Surviving Member of The Temptations.

Otis is the son of Otis Miles Snr and Hazel Louise (née Williams) Otis was raised by his grandmothers in the town of Texarkana, Texas, by the age 10, Otis moved with his mother and stepfather Edgar to Detroit, when in Detroit Otis changed his surname to his mother's maiden name.

Otis's first thoughts on a career was as a boxer, while being influenced by the early Gospel groups, such as the Dixie Hummingbirds and the Soul Stirrers, always interested in R&B, Otis decided to follow a music career. Putting together a number of groups, among them Otis Williams and The Siberians, The El Domingoes and The Distants, The Distants had a local hit, co-written by Otis and Detroit manager and producer Johnnie Mae Matthews, called "Come On", with lead vocals by Richard Street. However, The Distants' recordings were not commercially successful, and in 1960, Otis along with Melvin Franklin formed a new group which combined the group he already fronted called The Distants, with The Primes including Paul Williams, Eddie Kendrick and Eldridge Bryant, the new group took the name The Elgins, (not to be confused with the future Motown group of the same name). Gaining an audition, with Berry Gordy at his first studio on St. Antoine in Detroit as The Elgins, they signed to Motown, before changing the name to The Temptations and being signed to Motown.

After signing with Motown, The Temptations began singing background for many of the Motown artists already signed to Motown, including early Mary Well's recordings. The group's break through hit "The Way You Do the Things You Do" was their first US Top 20 hit, followed by "I'll Be in Trouble", "Girl (Why You Wanna Make Me Blue)", "Get Ready", "Just My Imagination" and "Please Return Your Love to Me". Without doubt the most successful Temptations' recording from this time was the Smokey Robinson (who wrote and produced the No1 hit) "My Girl".

Otis rarely sang lead vocals, feeling his role was more useful as the group's leader, organiser, and as the background singer. The only major lead vocals undertaken by Otis was the Smokey Robinson written and produced recording of "Don't Send Me Away" from the album "The Temptations with a Lot o' Soul" issued in 1967.

If the first phase of The Temptations' career was guided by Smokey Robinson, who usually wrote and produced their material, next came the collaboration with Norman Whitfield and Barrett Strong who wrote and produced the psychedelic soul recordings, where all five Temptations undertook lead vocals, with such recordings as the Grammy winner "Cloud Nine" and "I Can't Get Next to You".

During the 1970's the group moved from Motown to Atlantic Records, only to return two years later to Motown with Eddie Kendrick's and David Ruffin re-joining the group, former lead vocals Dennis Edwards returned also for the "Together Again" album.

It seems that whenever there is a group personnel change Otis always took the lead, trying to safeguard the group's legacy. Otis never pursued a solo career, the group's line up changed so frequently, that Otis and Melvin Franklin promised each other they would never quit the group. Melvin Franklin would remain in the group until 1994, when he became physically incapable of doing so, not long afterwards Melvin Franklin died in February 1995, leaving Otis (then 53) as the last surviving original member of The Temptations. Continually touring with The Temptations, Otis is still performing and organising the group in its fifth decade.

Otis co-wrote, (with Patricia Romanowski), the 1988 book "The Temptations", written as both an autobiography and a history of the group. Ten years later, "The Temptations" book was adapted into a NBC television documentary of the same name. During the 1990's, Dennis Edwards began touring under the name "Dennis Edwards and the Temptations", prompting a legal battle between Otis and Dennis Edwards. It was decided that Dennis's group would be called "The Temptations Review featuring Dennis Edwards", the name that Dennis Edwards tours under to this day.

On his role in The Temptations, Otis is brief: "I'm the glue that holds everything together". Not only has the bass singer been the "brains behind the group" according to the group's biography, but most recently the group's storyteller.

Otis now lives in Los Angeles, Otis married Josephine Rogers in 1961, the couple's son, Otis Lamont Williams, was born the same year. Otis and Josephine divorced in 1964, and Otis Williams dated Florence Ballard of The Supremes, and was for a time engaged to R&B singer Patti LaBelle. Otis next married Ann Cain in 1967 before divorcing in 1973, Otis married his third and current wife Goldie in 1983, their son Lamont, a construction worker, died in a workplace accident in that same year.

Paul Williams

Born on the 2nd July 1939 in Birmingham, Alabama - Died on 17th August 1973 in Detroit, Michigan

Motown Connection: Background Singer - Member of The Temptations - Choreography.

Paul Williams was born and raised in Birmingham, Alabama, meeting Eddie Kendrick who would become his lifelong best friend during their school years, both Paul and Eddie Kendricks shared a love of singing, and sang in their church choir. As teenagers, Paul, Eddie Kendricks, and their friends Kel Osboure and Willie Waller performed in a group called The Cavaliers, leaving Birmingham in 1957, Paul, Eddie Kendricks and Kel Osbourne moved to Cleveland to launch their music careers, Willie Waller however decided to stay in Birmingham. While in Cleveland, they arranged to be managed by Milton Jenkins, and when he moved to Detroit, Michigan, the group followed. With this move came a change of name for the group, The Cavaliers renamed themselves "The Primes". Under Milton Jenkins' management, The Primes started to create a name in the Detroit area, including forming a female spin-off group called "The Primettes" (later they would become the Motown artists The Supremes).

In 1961, Kel Osbourne moved to California, and with this move The Primes disbanded after only a few years, Paul and Eddie Kendricks then joined a group called The Distants (which included Otis Williams as lead, Elbridge Bryant and Melvin Franklin), the new group took the name The Elgins, (not to be confused with the future Motown group of the same name), as The Elgins they signed to Motown, before changing the name to The Temptations and signed to Motown subsidiary, Miracle.

Paul sang lead vocals on several of the group's songs, and served as lead singer during the group's early years. Considered The Temptations' best dancer, The Temptations' perfectly timed choreography, was arranged by Paul Williams. Apart from developing routines for the group he worked with The Supremes most notably on their trademark "Stop! In the Name of Love" routine to accompany the hit record and stage performance, before Cholly Atkins took over that role for all of Motown's acts via the Artist Development Department.

Although the group was extremely popular with the black community, they had to first begin singing background for many of the artists already signed to Motown, including early Mary Well's recordings. The song, "Oh Mother Of Mine" with Paul

Williams on lead, was their first record for Motown. The group's break through hit was "The Way You Do the Things You Do" their first US Top 20 hit, followed by "I'll Be in Trouble", "Girl (Why You Wanna Make Me Blue)", "Get Ready", "Just My Imagination" and "Please Return Your Love to Me". Without doubt the most successful Temptations recording from this time was the Smokey Robinson (who wrote and produced their No1 hit) "My Girl".

Paul's major lead vocals for The Temptations included "No More Water in the Well", "Just Another Lonely Night", and his signature song, "Don't Look Back". One of his best-known lead performances is his live performance of "For Once in My Life", from the television special TCB, broadcast in December 1968 on NBC. The live version of the song "Don't Look Back" is looked on as Paul's best ever performance.

Paul suffered from sickle-cell anaemia, which had a major affect on his physical health. In 1965, Paul began an affair with Winnie Brown, hair stylist for The Supremes and a relative of Supremes' member Florence Ballard. In the spring of 1969, Paul and Winnie Brown opened a celebrity boutique in Detroit, the business was not successful, and Paul was left with a large tax bill. Also, Paul's unhappiness was increasing at the diminishing role he played in the group. Paul was the lead singer on several of their earlier songs and was also the group's main choreographer before the addition of Cholly Atkins to the Artist Development. Cholly Atkins' presence now made Paul's former role as choreographer essentially obsolete.

By now his health had deteriorated to the point that he would sometimes be unable to perform. Each of the other four Temptations did what they could to help, but Paul's health continued to decline and he refused to see a doctor. Alcoholism and the Sickle Cell Anaemia meant his contribution to the group declined.

Otis Williams and the other Temptations decided to look for a replacement for when Paul was unavailable. Choosing Richard Street, then lead singer of the Motown act The Monitors and known from his days as lead singer of The Distants, Richard Street was recruited to travel with The Temptations and sing all of Paul's parts from behind a curtain, except for Paul's solo contributions, such as "Don't Look Back" and "For Once in My Life". Eventually, Paul became too ill to perform, and Richard Street firstly started to perform on stage as a member of The Temptations, then taking his place on recording sessions, before officially taking over from Paul in 1971. However, Paul was still involved with the group as a way of "showing of support" for the group, being employed as an advisor and choreographer, for the next two years.

Offered a solo contract by Motown, and by early 1973, Paul made his return to Motown's "Hitsville Studio A" and began working on solo material. His colleague Eddie Kendricks, who had left The Temptations just before Paul, produced and co-wrote Paul's first single, "Feel Like Givin' Up", which was due to be issued on Motown's subsidiary label Gordy with the b/side "Once You Had a Heart". However, Motown decided to shelve the recordings, and the single was not released, Eddie also helped produce the subsequent recording "Do Your Own Thing".

After these recording sessions Paul decided to concentrate on raising the last of his six children, Mary Agnes, who was born the same year. Now spending most of his time at home, Paul became more depressed and troubled by his recent failures; the affair with Winnie Brown, the boutique, and with this came a further dependence on alcohol.

On 17th August 1973 Paul was found on the ground near his car, dead from an apparently self-inflicted gunshot to the head, in a deserted parking lot near 14th Street and West Grand Blvd, not far from Motown's "Hitsville Studio A".

The mysterious circumstances surrounding Pauls' death caused many people, including Paul's family, to suspect that some form of foul play was the actual cause of Pauls' death. According to the coroner, Paul had used his right hand to shoot himself in the left side of his head.

In addition, a bottle of alcohol was found near Pauls' left side, as if he had dropped it while being shot. The gun used in the shooting was found to have fired two shots, only one of which had killed Paul. Despite the evidence, Paul had previously expressed suicidal thoughts, and his death was officially ruled as being self-inflicted.

As a member of The Temptations, Paul was posthumously inducted into the Rock and Roll Hall of Fame in 1989 and the Vocal Group Hall of Fame in 1999. Both of his solo recordings were later released by Motown on Temptations-related compilations in the 1980's and 1990's.

Paul was survived by his wife, Maxine Powell, and their six children: Sarita, Paul Jnr., Paul Lucas, Kenneth, Paula and Mary Agnes.

Eddie Willis

Aka "Chank" Born on the 3rd June 1936 in Gore Springs, Grenada, Mississippi

Motown Connection: Guitarist/member of The Funk Brothers (Motown In House Band).

As a child Eddie spent countless hours playing a "Diddley Bow", which is a primitive one string guitar, all that was needed was a wall, a wire, three nails and a block of wood. Then the string is plucked while sliding the nail up and down the string. Growing up, Eddie became infatuated with music and took every opportunity to sneak down to the local "Juke Joint" and soak in the music coming from the bandstand. A few years later, at the age of fifteen Eddie moved to Detroit Michigan. A self-taught guitarist, it was Mary Johnson's "Come To Me", record in early 1959 that brought Eddie to the attention of the Motown label. Eddie was just out of high school when he heard Motown's first recording star and was "hooked" and started working with Berry Gordy.

Motown guitarist Eddie was one third of the guitar trio (which included Joe Messina and Robert White) which would eventually become Motown's studio band The Funk Brothers. Eddie, (along with Joe Messina, and Robert White) created the catchy guitar and rhythmic sound which became known as the "Motown Sound". Some of the more popular Motown hits that feature Eddie are (playing in unison with Robert White), The Supremes' "Keep Me Hanging On" in late 1966, "Friendship Train" by Gladys Knight and The Pips in late 1969, Stevie Wonder's "My Cherie Amour" in summer 1969.

When Motown moved to Los Angeles, the label began using top LA session musicians; though Eddie and The Funk Brothers would occasionally be sent tapes from LA by Motown to overdub their parts. With the death of Funk Brothers' drummer Ben Benjamin, the migration of James Jamerson to LA and the retirement of Joe Messina from the music business, the era of The Funk Brothers (based on Hitsville Studio A) was coming to an end.

Influences for Willis include Chet Atkins, Wes Montgomery and Albert King. He played a Gibson Firebird guitar on most his early 1960's work, later moving on to use a Gibson ES 335. On recordings such as The Supremes' "No Matter What Sign You Are", Eddie performed on a Coral sitar.

Toured with The Four Tops and still recorded around Detroit, most notably with producer Don Davis Willis including "Rated X-Traordinaire" Best of Johnnie Taylor on Sony Legacy label, Albert King's "The Ultimate Collection" on the Rhino label, and David Ruffin's 1980's Warner Brothers LP.

Signature Songs: Using a style of muted guitar riffs which added a distinctive tone to the beat, often timed with the snare. Eddie performed on "Please Mr. Postman" by The Marvelettes, "The Way You Do the Things You Do" by The Temptations, "You Keep Me Hanging On" by The Supremes and "I Was Made to Love Her" by Stevie Wonder.

Born Los Angeles, California

Motown Connection: Singer - Producer - Writer.

Hal Davis introduced Frank to Motown in 1965, and one of Frank's first pieces of work was the recording by Stevie Wonder of "Castles in the Sand" in the same year. Strangely, Franks next recording, "I'm So Thankful" and "Somebody, Somewhere Needs You", in 1965 was a hit for The Ikettes, (which consisted of Ike and Tina Turner), who were both registered under Motown's publishing company Jobete, but never released on a Motown label. Interestingly the recording of "I'm So Thankful" had a similar beat to The Supremes hit, "Where Did Our Love Go", which had been written and produced by his colleagues Holland-Dozier-Holland.

The rare Frank Wilson record often quoted as the rarest and most expensive Motown recording.

Frank worked with many artists at Motown, and had many hits that became classics, but he also recorded some great soul tracks which never made the charts, even though when you listen to them now, they sound like they should have been hits at the time, including "I Can't Turn Around" and "I'm Gonna Hold on Long as I Can" for The Marvelettes, "I've Got to Find It" by Brenda Holloway and a string of recordings for Eddie Kendrick's, "Darling Come Back Home", "Honey Brown", "Hooked on Your Love" and "Son of Sagittarius".

However, Frank will always be remembered for his work with firstly, Diana Ross and The Supremes, writing or co-wrote the hits, "Love Child", "I'm Living in Shame", before Diana Ross moved onto her solo career, then with the "new" look Supremes "Up the Ladder to the Roof" and "Stone Love". Also working with The Temptations on "All I Need", The Four Tops recordings of "Still Water Love" and "It's the Way Nature Planned It", Frank had a special relationship with Eddie Kendricks while at Motown, working with him on "Boogie Down", "Keep on Truckin'" and "Darling Come Back Home".

Other artists that Frank worked with were Brenda Holloway on "You Made Me So Very Happy" (recorded later in the 1970's by Blood, Sweat and Tears) the single "Chained" by Marvin Gaye; and "Whole Lot of Shakin' in My Heart" by Smokey Robinson and The Miracles.

My guess is that Frank will always be remembered by fans of Motown, from the time when he decided to become a recording artist himself, recording the single "Do I Love You (Indeed I Do)" it was intended for release on the Soul label (a subsidiary Motown). Research says that 250 demo recordings were pressed, but before their release, Frank decided he would rather focus on producing, and asked for the demos to be destroyed. Somehow, two known copies survived, (both in private hands and not owned by Motown). Due to the scarcity of the original single and the high quality of the music (it was one of the most popular records on the UK Northern Soul scene), it has been suggested that the single is now the rarest and most valuable record in Motown history.

The history of the recording is fascinating, Tom Dieperro discovers the disc at Motown in California in 1977, Simon Soussan acquires the disc from Tom in Los Angeles in 1978, and Les McCutcheon reputedly paid $500 to Simon for the single. Les McCutcheon loans the record to Russ Winstanley to play at various Northern Soul venues, Les McCutcheon retrieves the record from Russ and sells it to Jonathan Woodliffe for a reputed £250 in 1979, Jonathan Woodliffe sells the record to Kev Roberts in an exchange deal valued at £350 for 12" LP's and white demo Funk/Soul releases for his collection in 1989, Kev Roberts sells the record, to Tim Brown for the new world record of £5,000 in 1990.

The only 'other' copy turns up in Canada via Martin Koppel who acquires it from former Motown collector Ron Murphy in Detroit in 1996, Tim Brown is offered an earth shattering £15,000 for the ultimate Northern Soul recording on a vinyl 45, and is sold to Kenny Burrell for that amount.

An interesting footnote to the recording was the discovery of a duet in the 1990's featuring Frank and Chris Clark (who had recorded the single and was an artist at Motown in the mid 1960's) performing "Do I Love You" which had been held in storage at Motown for many years.

Frank left Motown in 1976 and became a born-again Christian, studying for and becoming a minister; Frank combines his ministry with travelling and writing books with his wife Bunny Wilson, and is also involved in the production of gospel music. One of my favourite singer, songwriter and producers Frank has also attended many Northern Soul shows over the years including a performance in the UK in 2000 and 2001; Frank is revered by Northern Soul fans and always receives a special welcome at any events associated with the Northern Soul scene.

Mary Wilson

Born March 6th 1944 in Greenville, Mississippi

Motown Connection: Background Singer - Member of The Supreme's - Solo Artist.

Mary was the first child of Sam and Johnnie Mae Wilson, she also had a brother Roosevelt and a sister Catherine (aka "Cat"). Born in Greenville, Mississippi, but as a baby, moved firstly to St. Louis, Missouri and then to Chicago, Illinois, before settling with her aunt and uncle, Ivory (aka "I.V.") and John L. Pippin, in Detroit. At the age of six, Mary returned to live with Johnnie Mae, at the time Mary, believed that Ivory and John L. were her parents not her aunt and uncle. By the age of twelve, Mary and her family had settled at Detroit's Brewster-Douglass housing projects.

In 1958, Mary Wilson met Florence Ballard while attending junior high school, becoming close friends through their love of music. In 1958, Milton Jenkins the manager of the male vocal group called "The Primes", asked Mary and Florence Ballard to form a sister group eventually to be called "The Primettes", along with Diana Ross and Betty McGlown (who would leave shortly after its formation) The Primettes did release one record 'Tears of Sorrow" b/side "Pretty Baby" for Lupine Records in 1960, they also sang backing vocals for other singers on that label, before unsuccessfully auditioning for Berry Gordy at Motown. Berry Gordy gave the reason that they should first finish school before trying for a musical career, however after hanging around "Hitsville" for many months, they eventually signed to Motown in 1960.

By 1961 they had changed their name to The Supremes (with prompting from Berry Gordy) to reflect a more "up beat" name, at this time Barbara Martin (who had replaced Betty McGlown) then left, and the group continued with the same line up until Florence Ballard left in 1967. Mary has always stated that she could have been as popular a singer as Diana Ross, if Berry Gordy had been going out with her instead of Diana Ross.

Between 1961 and 1963, The Supremes released eight singles, none of which charted, becoming known as the "no-hit Supremes" in this period the group provided background vocals, hand claps etc for the established artists at Motown including Marvin Gaye, The Temptations (who they had known and worked with when they were called The Primes). During these years, all three took turns singing lead vocals, but with Florence Ballard looked on as the "lead vocalist" of the group. Most of their early material was written and produced by Berry Gordy and or Smokey Robinson. Then in December 1963, Berry Gordy decided to try The Supremes with his production team of Holland-Dozier-Holland on a single called "When the Lovelight Starts Shining Through His Eyes" this recording became their fist chart entry, reaching No23 on the charts.

With this success, Berry Gordy allocated Holland-Dozier-Holland to produce their next recordings; this resulted in almost five years of unparalleled success. By early 1964, The Supremes had recorded and released the single "Where Did Our Love Go" (with Diana Ross confirmed by Berry Gordy as the lead vocalist) interestingly the song had been originally intended to be recorded by The Marvelettes. In August 1964, while The Supremes were appearing on Dick Clark's "Caravan of Stars", the single "Where Did Our Love Go" went to No1 on the US pop charts, it was also their first recording to chart in the UK, where it reached No3. Followed by four consecutive US No1's "Baby Love" (which was also their first No1 hit in the UK), "Come See About Me", "Stop! In the Name of Love" and "Back in My Arms Again". "Baby Love" was nominated for the 1965 Grammy Award for Best Rhythm and Blues Recording, and "You Keep Me Hangin' On" was awarded the 1966 Grammy for Best Pop single. They would go onto have twelve No1 hits in the US, with all these singles being international hits around the world (in particular the UK, Europe and Japan).

In 1967 the first major changes to the line up and name of the group occurred, renamed "Diana Ross and The Supremes", this coincided with Cindy Birdsong replacing Florence Ballard. Their last recording was "Someday We'll Be Together" in October 1969, with Mary Wilson and Cindy Birdsong surprisingly not providing background vocals (these were supplied by the Jones Girls) during the session, Johnny Bristol (the producer) coached Diana Ross through the recording. Berry Gordy liked the song so well, that he decided to leave the recording as it was with Bristol's coaching track included. This would be "Diana Ross and The Supremes" final No1 chart hit.

In 1969, Mary recorded a solo version of "Can't Take My Eyes Off You" later to be remixed as a duet with Eddie Kendricks from The Temptations. However, the solo version was eventually released on a Supremes' 4 CD box-set released in 2000.

Jean Terrell came in as Diana Ross's replacement for the lead vocals in The Supremes. At first, Jean Terrell along with Mary and Cindy Birdsong, recorded much of The Supremes' material in the studios (both in Detroit and Los Angeles), and rehearsed the group's "new style" performances during the day (with Mary Wilson and Cindy Birdsong) in preparation for the eventual final performance of Diana Ross and The Supremes. Before this happened Mary, Diana Ross and Cindy Birdsong performed at any cabaret or TV shows up until Diana Ross left to follow her solo career. With Jean Terrell now ready to replace Diana Ross as lead singer of The Supremes, this occurred in January 1970.

The group scored three major hits in the early 1970's with Jean on lead vocals, "Stoned Love" was a No1 R&B and chart hit in 1970, while both "Nathan Jones" and "Up the Ladder to the Roof" were Top 10 hits on both the pop and R&B charts. Also recorded at the time was "River Deep Mountain High" with The Four Tops "Automatically Sunshine" and "Floy Joy". After the success of "Floy Joy", Cindy Birdsong decided to leave the group to start a family and was replaced by Lynda Laurence (a former member of Stevie Wonder's group Wonderlove). Toward the end of 1973, Jean decided to leave the group along with Lynda Laurence, (who was pregnant), at the same time, Mary announced that her husband to be, (Dominican businessman Pedro Ferrer who she married in 1974) would be the new manager for the group. When The Supremes disbanded in 1977, Mary was the only surviving member of the group, Mary began her solo career with Motown, recording the album, "Red Hot" in 1979 before departing the following year, and in 1974 Mary married Dominican businessman Pedro Ferrer.

Mary's "farewell" performance with the group occurred on Sunday 12th June 1977, at the Drury Theatre in London, England, to coincide with this, Motown announced that it had decided to officially disband The Supremes as a recording group on its label.

In 1983, Mary co-wrote "Dreamgirl, My Life as a Supreme" to record her perceived views on the abuses artists suffered during Motown's heyday, Mary was featured on numerous talk shows and programs promoting and answering questions about the book. This went on to become the Broadway musical "Dreamgirls", Mary's follow-up book "Supreme Faith: Someday We'll Be Together", was published in 1990, but without any success. Eventually an updated version was released, which combined the two books with some new chapters written by Mary.

Mary reunited with The Supremes in that year, with Diana Ross and Cindy Birdsong for the television special "Motown 25: Yesterday, Today, Forever". They performed their 1969 No1 hit "Someday We'll Be Together", although altercations on stage between Mary and Diana became an issue during the taping of the special, but were left out of the final edited performance.

Mary recorded a couple of singles for Ian Levine's Motorcity label in 1989, called

"Don't Get Mad, Get Even" followed by a cover of the Five Stairsteps' "Oooh Child". In the early 1990's, Mary recorded her first solo album in twelve years, "Walk the Line", on CEO Records with two single releases, "One Night With You", and the title track, "Walk the Line". However, the record company folded shortly after Mary's album was released which resulted in very few copies being available.

On January 29, 1994, tragedy struck Mary when she fell asleep at the wheel of her car and hit the central barrier of the road, as a result of the accident, Mary suffered serious injuries, and her son Raphael who was only fourteen at the time, died. For the rest of the 1990's, Mary did have released material, including "U" in 1995 and "Turn Around" in 1996 for various independent labels. In 1997, Mary moved to New York City and enrolled at New York University, graduating in May 2001 with an Associate's Degree in Liberal Arts. In April 2001, Mary performed in the musical "Leader of the Pack" in Boston, also starring in the show "Duke Ellington's Sophisticated Ladies". By the end of the 1990's, Mary had also appeared in a New York comedy play called "Grandma Silvia's Funeral" as a wise-cracking, but bitter family member, this was followed by a cameo appearance in the 1999 comedy film "Jackie's Back", playing Jackie's former school teacher.

In late 1999, Mary was contacted by Diana Ross to re-unite with Cindy Birdsong, for a concert tour called "Return to Love". Mary and Cindy Birdsong did not become involved instead Lynda Laurence and Scherrie Payne, both of whom were members of the group after Diana Ross had left The Supremes, filled in. Mary did appear, along with other 1960's and 1970's stars, in the motion picture "Only The Strong Survive". In March 2003, she performed in "The Vagina Monologues" at the Detroit Opera House, and began hosting "The Motown Show", a radio program on Westwood One in September 2003.

Mary has released the DVD "Mary Wilson Live at the Sands", performing many of the old Supremes hits, in celebration of the forty-fifth anniversary of the group. Currently, recording an album of songs taken from her personal diaries, Mary has also started in 2006 to perform a new show "Up Close and Personal", where she sings ballads and standards. In recent years, Mary has made headlines for proposing a bill to ban impostor groups to perform under the name of 1950's and 1960's rock groups, including Motown groups such as The Marvelettes and The Supremes, which was passed in several states.

Mary has also been touring and lecturing across the US, speaking to various groups nationwide. Her lecture circuit, "Dare to Dream", focuses on reaching goals and triumphing over adversity. Mary has many close relationships with various charities including, Susan G Komen Race for the Cure, the American Cancer Society,

St. Jude's Children's Research Hospital, the Easter Seals Foundation, UNICEF, The NAACP, the Cystic Fibrosis Foundation, the All-Star Network and Figure Skaters of Harlem.

Mary has also been involved with a touring exhibition of the Supremes' former stage wear, which has been on exhibit in Cleveland, USA and in the UK, at the Victoria & Albert Museum. Over 50 sets of gowns are shown in rotation, starting with early informal wear from the early 1960's, and including famous gowns worn on television specials and nightclub appearances by the group in the 1960's and 1970's.

During the 1960's, Mary dated Four Tops member Abdul "Duke" Fakir, Mary has also been romantically linked to Tom Jones, Steve McQueen and Flip Wilson. During the late 1960's, Mary adopted her cousin's son, Willie, and raised him as her own son. Mary married Pedro Ferrer in 1974 and they had three children, Turkessa born in 1975, Pedro born in 1977 and Raphael born in 1979, they divorced in 1981, Mary now lives in Las Vegas, is single and has two surviving children, her adopted son and eight grandchildren.

Born Steveland Hardaway Judkins although some records say Steveland Morris later changed to Steveland Hardaway Morris on the 13th May 1950 in Saginaw, Michigan

Motown Connection: Session Musician - Background Singer - Solo Artist - Musician - Producer - Writer - Arranger - First Motown Artist to gain full Creative Control of his Work.

Stevie has been blind for most of his life, as a premature baby it effected the blood vessels at the back of his eyes, which caused the blood not to reach the front of the eye, this was followed by an aborted growth spurt which caused the retinas to detach. (Known as Retinopathy of prematurely, or "ROP"). At the age of four,

Stevie Wonder

Signed Photograph.

Stevie's mother decided to leave his father and moved with her children to Detroit, it was in Detroit that the first signs of his musical talent started to show, learning to play the piano at age seven, and mastering the instrument by the age of nine. During his early childhood he was active in his Church choir and next taught himself to play the harmonica and the drums, by the age of ten he had mastered both these instruments, Stevie moved onto playing the bass and again mastered this instrument confirming he was a gifted child .

In 1961, at the age of eleven, Stevie was introduced to Ronnie White who was a member of the Motown group The Miracles, there followed a meeting between Stevie and his mother with Berry Gordy, although impressed by the young musician, at first Berry Gordy was unsure whether to sign Stevie, because of the issues around using under aged performers, but relented and signed Stevie to Tamla (a subsidiary of Motown), using the name Little Stevie Wonder. Stevie's first minor hit with the label was the recording of "I Call It Pretty Music, But The Old People Call It The Blues".

Now aged 13, Stevie had his first major hit on Motown with the single, "Fingertips (Pt. 2)", released in 1963, the single had been taken from a live recording of a Motor Town Revue performance, and issued on the album, "Recorded Live: The 12 Year Old Genius". The song, featured Stevie playing bongos and harmonica, and Marvin Gaye on drums, it became his first No1 hit on both the pop and R&B charts and launched his career within the music industry. An interesting thing happens on the record near the end, when a band member yells out "What key, what key?" The band

419

backing Stevie thought he was finished and left the stage, and a second band was taking their place, when Stevie, responding to the audience applause, came back out for a short reprise. As he started playing his harmonica, the new band members didn't know what key the song was in, so in desperation yelled out for it.

With this recording Stevie established himself as one of Motown's biggest stars, indeed in 1964, Stevie made his film debut in Muscle Beach Party as himself, credited as "Little Stevie Wonder". Dropping the "Little" from his title in 1965, Stevie went on to have a number of hits for the rest of the 1960's, including the 1965 hit "Uptight (Everything's Alright)", a No3 chart hit, in 1966 with "Blowin' in the Wind", a Bob Dylan cover which was one of the first songs to reflect Stevie's social consciousness, with co-vocals by his mentor, producer Clarence Paul, Stevie finished 1966 with the recording "A Place In The Sun" which reached No2 in the US charts, and was Stevie's first major hit in the UK reaching No5 in the charts. In 1967 his major hit for the year was the recording "I Was Made to Love Her" another US No2 chart hit, and a UK No5 hit.

In 1968 he recorded an album of instrumental soul/jazz tracks, mostly harmonica solos, under the pseudonym (and title) "Eivets Rednow", which is "Stevie Wonder" spelled backwards. The album was not a commercial success and its only single, a cover of "Alfie", only reached No66 on the charts,

Nonetheless, Stevie recorded several hits between 1968 and 1970 such as "For Once in My Life", a No3 chart hit followed by "Shoo-Be-Doo-Be-Doo-Da-Day" a No7 chart hit, the 1969 recordings "My Cherie Amour" a US No4 and UK No4 chart hits, and the Ron Miller inspired "Yester-Me, Yester-You, Yesterday" a US No7 and UK No2 chart hit, in 1970 Stevie issued "Never Had A Dream Come" a minor UK hit, followed by "Signed, Sealed, Delivered I'm Yours" a US No3 and "Heaven Help Us All", a US No8 recording.

Stevie, by the end of the 1960's had started to work in the Motown song writing department, writing songs both for himself and fellow Motown artists, including "Tears of a Clown", a major international hit (reaching No1 in both the US and UK) by Smokey Robinson and The Miracles. However, his own hit did not suffer, with the singles released in 1971 "We Can Work It Out" and "If You Really Love Me" becoming major hits.

In September 1970, at the age of 20, Stevie married Syreeta Wright, a former company secretary and now a songwriter for Motown. Stevie's next album "Where I'm Coming From" featured Syreeta with writing and production credits, the album was not a commercial success. Also in 1970, Stevie co-wrote, and played numerous instruments on, "It's a Shame" for The Spinners which became their biggest hit at Motown.

Reaching his 21st birthday on 21 May 1971 and feeling limited by Motown's strict production and publishing contracts, he renegotiated his contract to give him complete creative control of his music, this landmark deal changed Stevie's outlook on music and changed how Motown would manage its artists forever. Prior to his contract negotiations, Stevie recorded two albums by himself and used them as a bargaining tool with Motown.

With this total artistic control of his albums, as well as the rights to his own songs. Stevie released his first two albums under this arrangement, "Where I'm Coming From" and "Music of My Mind". The album "Music of My Mind", especially, demonstrated (along with Sly Stone and Marvin Gaye), that albums could be more than just collections of singles, adding artistic, political statements to the songs, and losing the confines of producing a three-minute hit single. "Music of My Mind" also marked the beginning of a long collaboration with synthesiser pioneers Robert Margouleff and Malcolm Cecil. Stevie's next two albums, "Talking Book" and "Innervisions", would add to his musical innovations, Stevie's lyrics now addressed social and racial issues well as any other songwriter. Stevie extended his creative push with the 1974 album "Fulfillingness' First Finale" and 1976 album "Songs in the Key of Life" which became the first album by an American artist to debut straight at No1 in the Billboard charts, where it remained for 14 non-consecutive weeks.

On 6th August 1973 Wonder was involved in a serious car accident while on tour, when a log from a truck went through the windshield and struck him on the head. This left him in a coma for four days and resulted in a partial loss of his sense of smell and a temporary loss of sense of taste. Despite the setback Stevie eventually recovered all of his musical faculties.

In October 1975 Stevie performed at the "Wonder Dream Concert" in Kingston, Jamaica, a Jamaican Institute for the Blind benefit concert. Along with Stevie was Bob Marley, Peter Tosh and Bunny Wailer, the three original "Wailers", where they performed together for the last time.

The US No1 hit had still arrived, even though Stevie's main focus was the production of albums, these included "Superstition", "You Are the Sunshine of My Life", a UK No3 chart hit "I Wish" a UK No4, "Sir Duke" a UK No2 chart hit, "You Haven't Done Nothin'" with The Jackson 5, along with Top 10 hits "Higher Ground", "Living for the City" Boogie On Reggae Woman" and "Send One Your Love". Vocalists Minnie Riperton and Deniece Williams both began their careers in the 1970's as backup vocalists for Stevie as part of "Wonderlove" background singers.

Three years later, he released the ambitious and bewildering "Journey Through the

Secret Life of Plants", which received terrible reviews upon its release. Stevie then reverted to a more straightforward album release "Hotter than July" in 1980, the album received substantially better reviews and became his first platinum album, however, this album proved to be the high point of his album releases for the 1980's, although it did produce the UK No3 chart hit "Lately" and "Happy Birthday" produced to support Stevie's campaign to have Martin Luther King's birthday commemorated in the US. Although his singles records sold well and he scored the occasional hit, including the hit ballad "I Just Called to Say I Love You", his only UK No 1 release to date in 1984 is from the soundtrack of the film "The Woman in Red".

Other high spots for Stevie in the 1980's was the 1982 US and UK No1 "Ebony and Ivory" (with Paul McCartney) and the 1983: "Stay Gold" a song for the film "The Outsiders", and in 1985 two US No1 with "Part-Time Lover" also reaching No2 on the UK charts and "That's What Friends Are For" (with Dionne Warwick, Elton John and Gladys Knight). In 1985 Stevie featured in Chaka Khan's cover of Prince's "I Feel For You", alongside Melle Mel, playing his signature harmonica, his harmonica skills were also featured on the Eurhythmics' single, "There Must Be an Angel (Playing with My Heart)" and Elton John's "I Guess That's Why They Call It The Blues", both major international hits.

Stevie featured in a duet with Bruce Springsteen on the all-star charity single for African famine relief, "We Are the World", Stevie also played the harmonica on the album "Dreamland Express" by John Denver in the song "If Ever", a song Stevie co-wrote with Stephanie Andrews, he also wrote the track "I Do Love You" for The Beach Boys.

In 1987, Stevie appeared on Michael Jackson's "Bad" album on the duet "Just Good Friends". Michael Jackson repaid the favour with a duet with Stevie called "Get It" on Stevie's album released in the same year, "Characters" came was a minor hit singles "Skeletons" and "You Will Know" also came from this album.

By the 1990's, Stevie was still an immensely respected musician, but his music was no longer on the cutting edge. He recorded a soundtrack album for Spike Lee's film "Jungle Fever" in 1991, singles and videos were released for "Gotta Have You" and "These Three Words", the b/side to the "Gotta Have You" included a recording of "Feeding Off The Love Of The Land", the song that was played during the end credits of the movie "Jungle Fever", but was not included on the soundtrack. A piano and vocal version of "Feeding Off The Love Of The Land" was also released on the "Nobody's Child: Romanian Angel Appeal" compilation. The album "Conversation Peace" and the live album "Natural Wonder" were also released in the 1990's.

In 1994, Wonder made a guest appearance on the KISS cover album, playing harmonica and supplying background vocals for the song "Deuce", performed by Lenny Kravitz. In 1996, Stevie Wonder's "Songs in the Key of Life" was selected as a documentary subject for the "Classic Albums" documentary series in the US, in the same year, Stevie performed John Lennon's song "Imagine" in the closing ceremony of the Olympic Games, held in Atlanta Georgia

In 1997, Stevie collaborated with Babyface for an emotionally-charged song about domestic violence called "How Come, How Long" which was nominated for an award. In December 1999, Stevie announced that he was interested in pursuing an intraocular retinal prosthesis to partially restore his sight. That same year, Stevie was featured on harmonica in the UK artist Sting's chart hit "Brand New Day".

In 2000, Stevie contributed two new songs to the soundtrack for Spike Lee's projects, "Bamboozled", "Misrepresented People" and "Some Years Ago". Stevie performed at the opening ceremonies of the 2002 Winter Paralympics in Salt Lake City in March 2002, and on the 2nd July 2005, Stevie performed in the USA part of the "Live 8" concerts in Philadelphia.

Stevie's first new album in ten years, "A Time to Love", was released in 2005, the album was released electronically before going on general release via Apple's iTunes Music Store. The first single, "So What the Fuss", was released in April and features Prince on guitar and background vocals from En Vogue, the second single, "From the Bottom of My Heart" was a hit on adult-contemporary R&B radio. The album also featured a duet with India Arie on the title track "A Time to Love".

In March 2006, Stevie became involved with the show "American Idol" with part of the programme being where the contestants received guidance from him, and Stevie also performed "My Love Is on Fire" from the album "A Time To Love". In June 2006, Stevie Wonder made a guest appearance on Busta Rhymes' new album, "The Big Bang" for the track "Been through the Storm". He appeared again on the last track of Snoop Dogg's new album "Tha Blue Carpet Treatment" singing "Conversations", the song is a remake of "Have a Talk with God" from "Life" album, and duet with Andrea Bocelli on his 2006 album "Amore" with harmonica and additional vocals on "Canzoni Stonate".

On Thursday 28th August 2008 Stevie performed for Barack Obama when he accepted his party's nomination to run for President of the United States, songs included were a previously unreleased song, "Fear Can't Put Dreams to Sleep" and "Signed, Sealed, Delivered I'm Yours", a song that was used regularly during the Obama campaign.

Stevie Wonder is currently working on two projects simultaneously, a new album titled "The Gospel Inspired By Lula" which will deal with the various spiritual and cultural crises facing the world, and "Through The Eyes Of Wonder", an album which Wonder has described as a performance piece that will reflect his experience as a blind man.

Stevie was awarded the Grammy's Lifetime Achievement Award in 1996 and was inducted into the Rock and Roll Hall of Fame in 1989 Stevie has recorded more than thirty Top 10 hits, won 22 Grammy Awards (a record for a solo artist), won an Academy Award for Best Song and been inducted into both the Rock and Roll and Songwriters Halls of Fame. He has also been awarded the Polar Music Prize. Stevie has seven children from several relationships and two marriages, in 1970 he married the now deceased Motown singer Syreeta Wright, ending in divorce in 1972 and married again in 2001, to fashion designer Kai Milla Morris.

Through his marriage to Kai Milla Morris, Stevie has, two sons, the older is named Kailand and he occasionally performs as a drummer on stage with his father, the younger son is Mandla Kadjay Carl Steveland Morris.

A daughter, Aisha Morris, who was the inspiration for his hit single "Isn't She Lovely". is a singer who has toured with her father and accompanied him on recordings, including his 2005 album, "A Time 2 Love" via his relationship with Yolanda Simmons, which also produced Keita Morris.

Stevie also had Kwame Morris, Mumtaz Morris and Sophia Morris from other relationships, including former partner Melody McCulley.

Stevie never married long term partners, Yolanda Simmons and Melody McCulley. In May 2006, Wonder's mother died in Los Angeles, California, at the age of 76.

Album Track: "Fingertips (Part 2)", Stevie Wonder.

Born Syreeta Wright a.k.a Rita Wright and Syreeta Wright Muhammed on the 3rd August 1946 Pittsburgh, Pennsylvania - Died 6th July 2004 Los Angeles, California

Motown Connection: Writer - Solo Artist - Session musician - Background singer.

Syreeta began her singing career in a church choir starting at the age of four, moving from Pittsburgh Pennsylvania at the age of eleven with her family to Detroit. There in 1965, she began working in Motown as a secretary and receptionist after being discovered by Brian Holland (of the Holland-Dozier-Holland production team). On the strength of this introduction, Berry Gordy offered Syreeta a recording contract. By 1966, she was given her first task at Motown, as a backup singer for some of the established artists, before finally recording in 1967 an Ashford & Simpson single which initially had been set aside for Diana Ross and The Supremes, "I Can't Give Back the Love I Feel for You". Diana Ross and The Supremes did record "I Can't Give Back The Love I Feel For You" but it was never released as a single. Instead, appearing on Diana

An early Promotional Photograph of Syreeta Wright.

Ross's solo album "Surrender", one interesting footnote to Rita's time at Motown, was according to Mary Wilson's book "Dreamgirl: My Life As a Supreme", Syreeta was also considered for Diana's replacement in The Supremes, also at this time at the suggestion of Berry Gordy, she shortened her name to Rita.

Syreeta would make a bigger impact as a writer with Motown, where she started by writing a poem to Stevie who put this to music for her. Somehow her immense talent was not fully recognised by Motown, even though she spent fifteen years with the label. Syreeta married Stevie Wonder on the 14th September 1970, and although they were divorced just 18 months later, they continued to work together for several years. The collaboration with Stevie saw the release of the song "Signed, Sealed Delivered, I'm Yours", a song she co-wrote with Stevie Wonder, Lee Garrett and Lula Hardaway. That same year, she collaborated with Stevie Wonder on his album "Where I'm Coming From", co-writing the songs "Do Yourself A Favour", "Something Out Of The Blue", "If You Really Love Me" (a song on which she sang) and "Never Dreamed You'd Leave In Summer".

In 1972, Syreeta released her debut album, simply entitled "Syreeta" for the MoWest label. It was produced by Stevie Wonder and contained her version of the

Stevie Wonder song "I Love Every Little Thing About You"; along with her interpretation of the Smokey Robinson tune "What Love Has Joined Together", and the socially aware "Black Maybe". The recording "I Love Every Little Thing About You" was re-worked by Stevie Wonder on his album "Music Of My Mind".

In 1974, the couple collaborated again on the album "Stevie Wonder Presents Syreeta". This recording brought her chart success with the singles "Your Kiss Is Sweet" (which was covered in Icelandic by artist Björk, on her 1977 debut self-titled album at the age of 11) and "Spinning and Spinning", with background which included Deniece Williams and Minnie Riperton. The album also contained the ballad "Cause We've Ended Now As Lovers" which was covered as an instrumental recording by UK artist Jeff Beck.

Their last collaboration came with the song "Harmour Love", which became another hit and was later included on her 1977 album "One To One", an album that contained the excellent Leon Ware and C Robertson song 'Tiki Tiki Donga'.

Next, Syreeta recorded one album with G C Cameron, entitled "Rich Love, Poor Love", also in 1977, before collaborating with Billy Preston, it produced the couple's only major success, with a the US and UK Top 10 hit, "With You I'm Born Again", in 1979. In 1980, Syreeta recorded the song "And So It Begins" and again worked with Billy Preston on a further album in 1981, with the single "Go For It" released later that year. Also in 1981, Syreeta released the album "Set My Love in Motion", an album produced by Ollie E Brown.

By 1983, she had a further release with the album "The Spell", this time produced by Jermaine Jackson who had remained at Motown after The Jackson 5 had left, the album included the single "Forever Is Not Enough" which became a minor hit. She then did a guest vocal with the performer Willie Hutch on the song "The Glow", a tune featured in the movie "The Last Dragon". In 1982, she provided backing vocals along with Billy Preston and Sarah Ricor to George Harrison's "Dream Away", the theme tune to Handmade Films' "Time Bandits", the song was later remixed for George's Harrison's 1982 solo album "Gone Troppo".

Syreeta returned to the studio in the late 1980's, recording several tracks for Ian Levine's Motorcity label, including a solo rendition of "With You I'm Born Again" and new duets with Billy Preston. She also sung backing vocals extensively and can be prominently heard on The Brothers Johnson hit "I'll Be Good To You" and Martha Reeves and The Vandellas' "I Can't Dance to That Music You're Playing".

In 1987, she recorded a duet with Smokey Robinson titled "Love Brought Us Here Tonight" that appeared on Smokey Robinson's hit album, "One Heartbeat", Syreeta appeared as guest vocalist on albums by artists such as Kirk Whalum in 1989 and she contributed the lyrics and sang the song "Someday" for Nelson Rangells "In Every Moment" project in 1992 for the GRP label. In 1994, she re-emerged in the music industry touring with "Jesus Christ Superstar", Syreeta played the role of Mary Magdalene, on the strength of these performances, she recorded with Michael Bolton and Irene Cara. Syreeta was a regular visitor to the UK appearing at live shows. Her song "Harmour Love" was featured in both the opening and closing credits of the 2005 film "Junebug".

Syreeta sadly died in 2004 of congestive heart failure, which she acquired as a side effect of chemotherapy and radiation treatments she was receiving for an ongoing bout with breast and bone cancers, she was only 57 years old.

Syreeta is survived by her four children Jamal, Hodari, Takiyah and Harmoni, and grandchildren.

Album Track: "It's a Shame", Motown Spinners.

CHAPTER FIVE

MOTOWN LABELS

""WHERE ARE THEY NOW?""

Chapter Five: Motown Labels "Where Are They Now?"

Over the years the Motown Record Company had many different labels; indeed Motown distributed quite a few "independent" labels. Motown branched into different musical genres and would then "badge" with their own identity. The Motown Record Company would issue the largest number of 45s records ever released by a record company.

The four major US labels were Motown, Tamla, Gordy and Soul, with Tamla Motown used for the UK/European market drawing from all these labels. There are many other labels owned, controlled, or distributed and these are listed in this chapter.

Motown

The name Motown was a shortened version of Detroit, Michigan nickname Motor Town. Motown is the largest label within the Motown Record Company of labels. It is also the label with the largest number of record releases. The first Motown Record Company single was released in September 1959 (under the Tamla Label). Established in 1960, Motown was and remains the company's main label (under Universal) for mainstream R&B/Soul music (and today's, hip hop music as well). The label's numbering system was combined with those of Tamla and Gordy in 1982. Motown artists have included Mary Wells, Diana Ross and The Supremes, The Four Tops, The Jackson 5, Boyz II Men, The Commodores and Erykah Badu.

The very first single on the Motown label.

◄ The Satintones signed to Tamla in 1959, the group's first single was "Going To The Hop", this was followed by the first single on Motown Records, called "My Beloved", credited to Berry Gordy, Sony Saunders, Robert Bateman and Chico Leverrette. "My Beloved" was the first commercial release on the Motown label, at this time, they also started touring the Midwest as a Motown act.

In the early days of Motown, both the Local and National Disk Jockeys (known as DJs) played a key role in helping to establish the label. This included "free" promotional records, being offered the to first to play the latest recording etc. This relationship between Motown and the DJs became one of the keys to Motown success.

Normally these recordings had a separate label (based on the original but for example only in black and white or one colour). The reason was two fold, the records couldn't be re-sold by the DJ, and it was a way of "breaking a record" either on radio or in a music venue. ▼

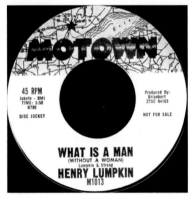

White and black "map" DJ-copy label design.

White and black DJ-copy label design.

▶ Motown also released "interviews" from the label to be used either on radio or TV, this copy of a recording issued by Motown from a Supremes' interview. Another good example of the studio being used for interviews is available as a download from itunes; Berry Gordy is being interviewed by a local reporter for promotional purposes.

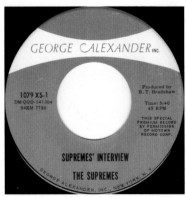

Special promotional DJ-copy release.

Motown also released "special" recordings to accompany the release of films from Motown; this distinctive label was used for an instrumental arrangement from Gil Askey from the "Lady Sings The Blues" Motown Production.

Brown and gold special movie design.   *One of many Canadian label designs.*

With its closeness to Detroit, Michigan (they share a common border), Canada was an important Country in Motown's development, both in terms of record sales, artists, producers and writers. R D Taylor is a good example of this, recording and producing many of Motown's classic recording's including "Indiana Wants Me" and "Ghost In My House" this example is one of the labels issued by Motown for the Canadian market. With its "Maple Leaf" design it was easily recognised as a Canadian product while keeping the "Motown Image" in the centre of the leaf.

As Motown became more sophisticated so did the promotional records released, these examples show both colour being used (as against the earlier black and white design) and now stamped "Promotional Not For Resale" to avoid any leakage into the music stores etc.

White and black promotional copy on red vinyl.

White and black promotional copy on gold vinyl.

Promotional light purple and blue label design.

This is a rare example of Motown working in partnership with ABC/Dunhill artist William Goldstein licensed though Motown as the distributor.

Special "Stars and Stripes" label design.

USA commercial "blue map" label design.

The most common label cover used by Motown in the USA, this record shows Motown's "funny side" with this release. Used along side the famous blue "M" logo label introduced by Motown in the 1970's, this label would continue until the sale of Motown in 1988.

A copy of the demo record showing the "M" logo which by the late 1970's was being used as the overall "trademark" for all things Motown.

UK green and yellow promotional copy.

White and black promo on green vinyl.

▲

Berry Gordy Snr dies in November 1978, and the major stars at Motown record a tribute single "Pops We Love You". This is a copy of the promotional copy which would eventually be released as a single, but without any major sales success. Written and produced by Pam Sawyer with musical arrangements by Gil Askey.

Motown had always produced DJ copies to issue to radio station, music venues etc to "plug" any forth coming releases, this is a rare copy of such a record from the 1982 hit by Charlene which became one of her and Ron Miller's biggest hits.

Simple promotional label design.   *UK blue and white promotional copy.*

▲

The blue and white type of design would "take over" from the "Black and Silver" Tamla Motown style of label used for the UK and Europe, for issues from the late 1970's.

The last single before MCA bought Motown.

◀ Berry Gordy sold Motown Records for $61 million to a partnership between MCA and Boston Ventures, with Berry Gordy retaining the ownership of the Jobete Publishing catalogue, although Berry later sold his interests in the Jobete publishing concern to EMI Publishing. This is the last single released before the sale of Motown was concluded.

Tamla

Tamla derived from the Debbie Reynolds hit "Tammy", Berry Gordy had wanted to use "Tammy" as the name for his first label unbelievably the name had gone, so after a slight change it became "Tamla".

Tamla was one the first to be incorporated by the Motown Record Corporation. It is second only to Motown in the number of releases. The first single was released in January 1959, the last 1986, Tamla was established for mainstream R&B/Soul music. Tamla was actually the company's original label. Gordy incorporated Tamla Records several months before establishing the Motown Record Corporation. The label's numbering system was combined with those of Motown and Gordy in 1982, and the label was merged with Motown in 1988. Notable Tamla artists included Smokey Robinson and The Miracles, Marvin Gaye, Stevie Wonder, and The Marvelettes.

The very first single on the Tamla label.

◀ Marv Johnson played a song originally written by him "Come to Me" for Berry Gordy and (his future wife) Raynoma, on the strength of this Marv Johnson became the first artist for their record label, Tamla. The new label didn't have a distribution system outside of Detroit, so "Come to Me" (co-produced by Berry Gordy and Marv Johnson) was released nationally by United Artists, and rose to No6 on the R&B charts and No30 on the pop charts. You will notice the address is 1719 Gladstone Street Detroit pre "Hitsville" and the backing singers are the Rayber Voices.

Smokey Robinson and Ronnie White began singing together in school, they released this single (along with a few others) while with The Miracles as a duo called "Ron & Bill". As a duo they also recorded on Chess Records of Chicago. The success with The Miracles stopped any further development of "Ron & Bill" although Smokey Robinson and Ronnie White worked together (in The Miracles) until Smokey Robinson departure in 1972.

Second commercial yellow "stripes" design.

White and black DJ-copy label design.

Mabel John released her first single, "Who Wouldn't Love a Man Like That", on this DJ copy on the Tamla Label, produced by Holland Dozier (per Holland-Dozier-Holland). Motown eventually found Mabel John's niche at Motown, promoting her as an R&B singer (using a smoother production, rather than a more gritty blues style). After this limited success, Berry Gordy decided to keep Mabel on the as a background singer, but did not renew her contract in 1962.

In 1966 this single "Blowin' in the Wind", a Bob Dylan cover was one of the first songs to reflect Stevie Wonder's social consciousness, with co-vocals by his mentor and producer Clarence Paul. This audition copy was used as a promotional tool and issued to DJ, distributors etc to help with pre-sales.

Black and white DJ-copy globes design.

Third commercial yellow and red globes design.

An early song writing collaboration by Ronnie White (notice the spelling mistake), Pete Moore, Bobby Rogers and Smokey Robinson of The Miracles, produced by Smokey Robinson and Bobby Rogers. In addition to writing their own material, with the addition of Marv Tarplin they also collaborated on other Motown artists, including songs for The Temptations "The Way You Do The Things You Do", "My Girl", "Since I Lost My Baby", "Get Ready", Mary Wells "My Guy", "The One Who Really Loves You", "Two Lovers", Marvin Gaye "I'll Be Doggone", "Ain't That Peculiar", The Marvelettes "Don't Mess With Bill", The Contours "First I Look at the Purse" and Brenda Holloway "When I'm Gone".

Black and white one globe promo design.

▲

Norman Whitfield teamed up with lyricist Barrett Strong for this Marvin Gaye recording from the album "That's The Way Love Is" a follow up to "Grapevine". Norman Whitfield and Barrett Strong would go on to compose and record on The Temptations, creating the psychedelic sound associated with that era of Motown recording. Beginning with 1968's "I Wish It Would Rain" the first Motown release, to incorporate the use of sound effects, "Whitfield and Strong" masterminded a string of classic Temptations hits, including "Cloud Nine", "I Can't Get Next to You" and "Ball of Confusion", mirroring the social, political and sexual issues of the late 1960's.

Gordy

Gordy Records' slogan: "It's What's In The Grooves That Counts" Gordy was one of the major Motown labels. Berry Gordy established Gordy 1962 the last Gordy record was released early in 1987.

Originally known as Miracle Records in 1961 with the slogan: "If It's a Hit, It's a Miracle", the name was changed in 1962 to Gordy to avoid confusion with The Miracles singing group. The labels numbering system was combined with those of Motown and Tamla in 1982, and the label was merged with Motown in 1988. Notable Gordy artists included The Temptations, Martha Reeves and The Vandellas, The Contours, Rick James and DeBarge.

The second release on the Gordy label in 1962 with Lee Henry Moore as lead singer, written and produced by Lee Henry Moore, William "Mickey" Stevenson and Brian Holland, later covered by The Supremes and Brenda and Patrice Holloway.

Commercial purple and round yellow logo design.

Commercial purple and yellow arrow design.

Eric and The Vikings had a lead by Eryke McClinton and had a million-seller with their song, "Vibrations" in 1970. The single came out on Soulhawk, a Detroit-based label started by Richard "Popcorn" Wylie and I'm assuming that the success of the single lead to The Vikings to get signed to Gordy Records later in the 1970's. However this 1973 recording written by George Gordy, Larry Brown and E Stover, produced by George Gordy and Larry Brown failed to chart.

An early recording used as an audition copy by Kim Weston at Motown, written by her with husband William "Mickey" Stevenson and Ivy Jo Hunter, produced by William "Mickey" Stevenson and Ivy Jo Hunter. There is no record of this single being released.

White and black logo DJ-copy label design.

Promotional white and black arrow design.

The final Norman Whitfield produced Temptations album was released in late 1973, and included this Top 30 single "Let Your Hair Down". Norman Whitfield left Motown in 1975 and established Whitfield Records, taking with him The Undisputed Truth, who had performed the instrumental track for this recording.

443

A Philadelphia group whose sound and songs were more pop than soul, Jay and the Techniques "Apples, Peaches, Pumpkin Pie", became their one and only Top 10 R&B and pop hit in 1967 (from the album "Smash"). This 1972 production never made the charts and has no recognisable Motown input, no other record registered as being released by Motown. They kept "plugging away" until the late 1970's, but never had another hit, although their song "Baby Make Your Own Sweet Music" was quite popular on the Northern Soul Scene in England.

Promotional white and black label design.

UK commercial Gordy label design.

Ebony Eyes was a collaborative effort by Smokey Robinson and Rick James. It was first released on the album "Cold Blooded", "Ebony Eyes" was a No26 R&B hit. "Ebony Eyes" remains one of Rick James most notable hits as it is one of the few to not use the style he labelled "punk-funk" but instead uses a more contemporary tempo and follows a more classic style of R&B. Smokey Robinson was credited with singing the introduction, bridge, and other more calm verses while James sang the chorus.

In 1986, the group signed to Motown Records, although the group had to go through a name change, (from General Caine) possibly, due to the 'drug connotations' connected with the previous group. Now known as General Kane, they proceed to record for the label, releasing two albums, "In Full Chill" in 1986 contained the track "Crack Killed Applejack", an anti drugs tune, a message that Mitch McDowell was keen to press home and "Wide Open" in 1987. This recording was not a sales success and Mitch "General Kane" McDowell had little success for Motown.

Promotional fading yellow and blue label design.

Last single released on the Gordy label.

From the album "To Be Continued" although it contained the recording "Lady Soul", this was not well received by the critics. Fortunately, apart from the title track it also had this recording "Someone", however, its place in Motown history is because it became the last single release on the Gordy label.

Soul

Established 1964, Soul was an R&B/Soul subsidiary for releases with less of a pop feel and/or more of a traditional soul/blues feel. Notable Soul artists included Jnr. Walker and The All-Stars, Gladys Knight and The Pips and Jimmy Ruffin. The label was dissolved in 1978.

A 1964 recording as a "solo" artist with Motown (released on the Soul label) by the band leader of The Funk Brothers, Earle Van Dyke. Earle would release further singles (all on the Soul label) between 1964 and 1969, including a cover version of The Four Tops hit single "I Can't Help Myself (Sugar Pie Honey Bunch)". This recording was written and produced by Richard Street and Berry Gordy but was not a success. Richard Street was the lead singer of The Monitors who recorded on the Soul label "Step by Step (Hand in Hand)" in the summer of 1968, but this was to be their final single with Motown.

First pink and white label design.

Second commercial label design.

Frances Nero became the first female artist on the Motown Soul Label, this was her first release, it was rumoured that the single was played on "WCHB" radio every 1 1/2 hours when first released. "Keep On Loving Me" and her next release "Fight Fire With Fire" was written by William Weatherspoon and James Dean, and produced by William "Mickey" Stevenson.

Tamla Motown

Established in 1965 the UK/European label established by Motown. Some early Motown records were issued on a variety of labels. "Come To Me" by Marv Johnson was the first Tamla Motown production record to be issued in the UK; it was put out on the London American label in May 1959. London also issued the first EP (extended play, usually 4 tracks two on each side, in a picture sleeve) "Shop Around" by The Miracles in 1961, in total London put out 11 Tamla Motown productions. Fontana was next and issued around four singles up until March 1962. These included The Marvelettes "Please Mr. Postman" and "Jamie" by Eddie Holland, now a very rare single. Fontana decided not to issue more records and Oriole as an independent label took over.

The name Tamla Motown came from the use of two existing labels Berry Gordy had started in the US. Tamla as the name for his first label, the name Motown was a shortened version of Detroit, Michigan nickname Motor Town, add these together and we have "Tamla Motown". By the time of the issue of this demo The Supremes had become the "biggest" Motown stars in the UK, with "Where Did Our Love Go" which reached No3 in the charts, followed very quickly by "Baby Love" their first UK No 1 hit.

UK promotional green and white label design.

UK commercial black and silver design.

▲

This "Black and Silver" design would become the "trademark" for Motown outside of the USA; the design would not change until the late 1970's when the famous "Blue M" label would become standard for all Motown issues worldwide. Although many of the original labels from the US were available this is the most recognisable label outside of the USA.

Other Motown Labels

Miracle Records

Short-lived 1961 R&B/soul subsidiary that lasted less than a year. Some issues featured the line, "If it's a hit, it's a Miracle". Closed down and reorganised under the new name Gordy Records in 1962. Artists included Jimmy Ruffin and early recordings by The Temptations. Miracle at the time was a Motown subsidiary and predecessor of the Gordy label.

Jimmy Ruffin after a spell in the armed forces returned to Detroit and signed with the Motown on this subsidiary, the short-lived Miracle label in 1961, when the label closed he was placed on the Soul label a subsidiary of Motown. This recording has Jimmy Ruffin writing the lyrics with support from "Miss Ray" none other than Raynoma Liles, future wife of Berry Gordy.

Commercial black and silver label design.

White and black DJ-copy label design.

This single written and produced by William "Mickey" Stevenson was issued as a DJ demo; it was released in November 1961, but did not trouble the charts.

V.I.P. Records

Established in 1964, V.I.P. was an R&B/Soul subsidiary in operation from 1964 to 1972, artists included Shorty Long, The Velvelettes, The Spinners, The Elgins and Chris Clark. The label was dissolved in 1974.

The Serenaders are a forgotten part of the Motown story yet the New York-based group cut their final single on Motown's VIP label. Forming in 1956, the main members included, George Kerr, Sidney Barnes, and Timothy "Andre" Wilson, Signed by Raynoma Gordy while managing Motown's New York office, Motown released this single "If Your Heart Says Yes", written and produced by George Kerr and Sidney Barnes in 1964 without any success.

The Temptations Eddie Kendricks and Elbridge Bryant sang with the Serenaders on the single, and its b/side "I'll Cry Tomorrow". Shortly after the release the group split, interestingly, Timothy Wilson married Raynoma's sister Alice.

First commercial yellow label design.

Promotional and commercial multicoloured design.

This promotional copy of R Dean Taylor first release on the V.I.P label (a Toronto recording) was not released until November 1965. It was written by R Dean Taylor in collaboration with Brian Holland, and produced by the team of Eddie Holland and Lamont Dozier. However, the song was only a regional hit in several US cities and Toronto.

MoWest Records

Short-lived (1971-1973) subsidiary for artists based on the West Coast, closed when Motown moved to Los Angeles. Notable artists included G.C. Cameron, Syreeta Wright and Los Angeles DJ Tom Clay.

▶ Motown's west coast label, MoWest, launches with Tom Clay's "What The World Needs Now Is Love" by Bacharach/David which would be the label's only major hit. Putting together recorded clips of the President Kennedy Assignation, the Martin Luther King's "I have a dream" speech and the Robert Kennedy Assignation. The song ended with an "interviewer" asking little children questions along the line of "What is prejudice?", "What is hate?".

Tom Clay was a DJ on the K-Love station in Los Angeles and he edited and mixed "What the World Needs Now" with the spoken sections as a promo protest record against the Vietnam War to play on his radio show. Following a massive positive response to this it was subsequently picked up and issued on MoWest where it reached (I think) No6 in the US charts. A hastily compiled album was then released on the back of this success.

Commercial special gold label design.

In 1972, Syreeta released her debut album, simply entitled "Syreeta" for the MoWest label, this single "To Know You Is To Love You" was released in the same year. This song (and the album) was produced by Stevie Wonder and the album contained her version of the Stevie Wonder song "I Love Every Little Thing About You"; along with her interpretation of the Smokey Robinson tune "What Love Has Joined Together" and the socially aware "Black Maybe". The recording "I Love Every Little Thing About You" was re-worked by Stevie Wonder on his album "Music Of My Mind".

▼

White and black DJ-copy design on blue vinyl.

Commercial blue and gold label design.

▲

This style of the label may be different, but the result was the same. This recording was not a success and the group faded away this single was issued in January 1972.

Divinity Records

Short-lived label from 1961 to 1963 concentrating on gospel music, Berry Gordy started Divinity late 1961. Only five singles were released, in the summer of 1963 the label was closed down.

▶ This is the b/side of "That's What He Is To Me" the first recording issued on the Divinity label. The Wright Specials signed to Motown in 1962, they performed and supported such groups as The Caravans, Staple Singers and Mighty Clouds of Joy.

They recorded two singles for the label, in 1962 and 1963, firstly "That's What He Is To Me" followed by the recording "Ninety-Nine and a Half Won't Do". The group proved unsuccessful and left Motown shortly after these releases.

First commercial blue and white label design.

Mel-o-dy Records

Established in 1962 as an R&B/Soul music subsidiary, Mel-o-dy later focused on white country music artists. Notable Mel-o-dy artists include Dorsey Burnette. The early releases were soul oriented but later records on the label were country. The label was discontinued in 1965.

Early example of a Mel-o-dy DJ promotional single, this rare example as this label was only functional from 1962 to 1965.

Black and white DJ-copy label design.

Commercial green and white label design.

Starting life as The Del-Phis performed initially at local venues but lasted only a short time until the group temporarily disbanded. In 1960, Martha Reeves and the other members of the group re-formed, but with Gloria Williams taking the lead singer role, they then signed with the Chess Records subsidiary, Checkmate, and recorded the single, "I'll Let You Know", in 1961. Under the name The Vells, they recorded (with Gloria Williams on lead vocals) this single "There He Is (At My Door)".

After those two singles failed to chart, Gloria Williams left the group and the group dis-banded again, only to reform as Martha and The Vandellas.

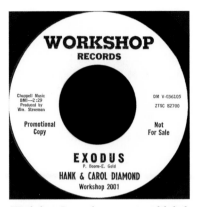

Workshop Records promotional label design.

Workshop Jazz Records

A jazz subsidiary, active from 1962 to 1964, notable Workshop Jazz artists included the George Bohannon Quartet, Dave Hamilton and The Four Tops (whose recordings for the label went un-issued for 30 years).

◀ Released in May 1962 this promotional single was the first release on the Workshop label, released without the "Jazz" on the label cover.

The second release on the label (now incorporating the "Jazz" on the label) by Earl Washington and The All Stars.

Red, yellow and white commercial label design.

Workshop Jazz promotional label design.

▲

Dave Hamilton in his early work with Motown played guitar and vibes on quite a few early recordings for Berry Gordy. While with Motown, however, Dave Hamilton was one of a handful of musicians who recorded for the short-lived Workshop Jazz label.

Rare Earth Records

Established in 1969 after the signing of Rare Earth, it is suggested that the label was named after the group, however, they had already released their first album Dreams/Answers for MGM/Verve, in fact Motown asked the band to come up with a name and Rare Earth Records was born. a subsidiary focussing on rock music by white artists, included first white band signed to Motown, The Rustix, Rare Earth, R. Dean Taylor, The Pretty Things and Stoney and Meatloaf. The label was dissolved in 1976, although a brief attempt with new acts in 1988 came to nothing apart from one demo issue.

The first single to be issued was from the legendary British band The Pretty Things, Rare Earth released 53 singles, and 41 albums, and Rare Earth's "Midnight Lady" which came out in May 1976 was to be the final single to be issued. The first album on the label was Love Sculptures "Blues Helping" which was released a month before The Pretty Things single in June 1969. The label also had Meatloaf as part of the duo Stoney and Meatloaf.

In the UK the bands first two albums were issued under the Tamla Motown label until One World was released in 1971. Some bands from the UK side were issued on the Rare Earth label in the US as part of the agreement with EMI in the UK.

First "white" commercial label design.

◀ The Australian group the Virgil Brothers recorded "Temptation 'Bout to Get Me" with the b/side "I See Her Face" however; this was re-released with this single including "Look Away", written by Peter Doyle. In the UK as in Australia the single appeared on the Parlophone label whilst it came under the Tamla Motown umbrella, released on the Rare Earth label in the US and Canada. Peter Doyle joined the second line-up of the New Seekers. The New Seekers had originally formed the previous year, but three members had decided to leave and the group were in need of replacements ready to finish off recording an album and start a summer season in the UK.

One of the first "Blue-Eyed Soul" band signed to the Rare Earth and interestingly placed on Stevie Wonder's publishing company. The Rustix recorded three albums between 1969 and 1972. The third album was rumoured to be a masterpiece, but it was never released.

Promotional copy on red vinyl.

Second "red" commercial label design.

▲

Vincent DiMirco would go on to compose (with amongst other Frank Wilson) "Up The Ladder To Roof" and work with other Motown Artists. This recording was produced by Norman Whitfield (as was many Rare Earth Artists) and written by Vincent DiMirco.

Black Forum Records

Established in 1970 in use until 1973. Black Forum was an album oriented Motown subsidiary label, owned by Berry Gordy with only one single ever was released.

A Spoken word subsidiary featuring progressive political and pro-civil rights speeches/poetry. Black Forum issued recordings by the Rev, Dr Martin Luther King Jnr, Stokely Carmichael and Elaine Brown.

Released in April 1973 this is the only single to have been issued on this label, with the b/side "Until We're Free" this single was written by Elaine Brown and produced by Freddie Perrin and Fonzie Mizell who would go on to working in the song writing and production team "The Corporation", all the other recordings issued were albums.

Commercial blue, white and green label design.

Promotional black and white label design.

Promotional copy of the only release on the label, not a sales success.

Morocco Records

Meaning "Motown Rock Company", Morocco was a rock music subsidiary for white artists. Active from 1983 to 1984, it was a short-lived attempt to revive the Rare Earth Records concept. Artists included Wolf and Wolf, Jakata, Duke Jupiter, Tiggi Clay and Coyote Sisters.

▶ From the self titled album "Tiggi Clay" released in 1984, this single was taken from that album and became one of the few recordings issued by the label and was not a sales success.

The Motown Morocco label design.

Motown Latino Records

Short-lived established in 1982, was intended as a subsidiary label to accommodate Spanish language recordings.

▶ During the 1980's, Motown was looking to expand into the "Latin market", and Jose Feliciano had already recorded an impressive number of albums for that market, including the album "Escenas de Amor" and "Me Enamoré", for Motown.

The Motown Latino brown label design.

Chapter One/Rayber

Chapter One/Rayber label was developed two months before the Motown label. There was only one artist on that label, Wade Jones. The song was called "I Can't Concentrate" the disc was recorded as Rayber 101.

Yesteryear

Motown Yesteryear: a label created in late 1970's and used through the 1980's for the reissues of 7 inch singles from all eras of the company's history, after printing in the initial label had ceased.

Check-Mate

Short-lived label 1961 to 1962 R&B/soul subsidiary, purchased from Chess Records. Notable artists included David Ruffin and The Del-Phis (later Martha and The Vandellas).

Weed Records

A very short-lived subsidiary, only one release, Chris Clark's 1969 "CC Rides Again" album, was issued. The name "Weed Records" is now owned by the Tokyo-New York based Weed Records.

Natural Resources Records

This label was active from 1972 to 1979 and in 1976 as a minor subsidiary for white artists and instrumental bands. Served as a label for Motown, Tamla, and Gordy reissues and Motown compilation albums in 1978 and 1979.

Prodigal Records

Purchased by Motown in 1974, Motown used Prodigal Records as a second rock music subsidiary; a sister label to Rare Earth Records. The Rare Earth band moved over to the label following the Rare Earth label's demise. Prodigal was dissolved in 1978.

Hitsville Records

Founded as Melodyland Records in 1974, the name was changed to Hitsville in 1976. Like Mel-o-dy before it, Hitsville focused on country music. Notable artists included Pat Boone and T.G. Sheppard. The label was dissolved in 1977.

Mo Jazz Records

Another jazz label created in the 1990's. Notable artists included Norman Brown, Foley and J. Spencer.

Mad Sounds

Short lived hip hop/rap subsidiary label, released 5 albums in the mid 1990's.

Independent Labels distributed by Motown

Chisa Records

Motown released output for Chisa, a label owned by Hugh Masekela, from 1969 to 1972. The 8000 series was distributed by Motown Records.

Hugh Masekela is among the best known of "world music" artists using the musical traditions of his native South Africa with the sounds from all over the world. He's played with a variety of other recordings artists, including Bob Marley's earliest recordings, to Buena Vista Social Club bassist Cachaito Lopez's solo disc. Hugh Masekela is probably best known for his 1968 pop hit "Grazing In The Grass".

Commercial red, pink and white label design.

Promotional black and white label design.

Ecology Records

A very short-lived label owned by Sammy Davis Jnr and Berry Gordy, and distributed by Motown. Only release: single "In My Own Lifetime"/"I'll Begin Again", by Davis in 1971.

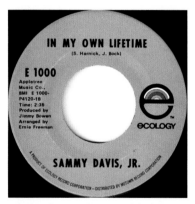

A/side of only release on label. Commercial blue and black label design.

B/side of only release on label.

Gaiee

Was a New York label distributed by
Motown. Only one record released on
label.

*Commercial red and black label
design.*

Manticore

A UK label from the 1970's and owned by Emerson, Lake and Palmer. Distributed
by Motown in 1975.

Commercial dark green label design.

*Promotional black and white label
design.*

CTI Records

Motown distributed output for CTI Records, a jazz label owned by Creed Taylor, from 1974 to 1975. CTI subsidiaries distributed by Motown included Kudu Records, Three Brothers Records and Salvation Records.

Gull Records

A UK-based label still in operation, Motown released Gull's output in the US in 1975. Gull had Judas Priest on its roster in 1975, but their LP "Sad Wings of Destiny", was intended for release by Motown in the US.

Biv 10 Records

A hip-hop/R&B label that was founded by Bell Biv Devoe/New Edition member Michael Bivins. The label operated throughout most of the 1990's. Its roster included Another Bad Creation, Boyz II Men and 702.

CHAPTER SIX

MOTOWN FACTS AND TRIVIA

Chapter Six: Motown Facts and Trivia

From its inception in January 1959, Motown has set many records and trends. Below are some interesting facts and figures from the archives, mainly from the "Detroit Years" of 1959 to 1972, the list makes interesting reading in the light of the "50th Anniversary" and may put into perspective some of the achievements by Motown.

Berry Gordy, the founder of Motown was born on the 28th November 1929.

Berry Gordy will be eighty at the same time as the fiftieth anniversary of the founding of Motown.

On 12th January 1959, Berry Gordy borrowed $800 from his family's loan fund to start his own record label called Tamla.

The $800 dollars Berry Gordy borrowed from his family to start Motown is not necessarily correct. The money was the estimate of the recording, pressing and, promotional cost of the planned release of "Come To Me" by Marv Johnson.

Berry Gordy earned $367 million dollars in 16 years.

Motown is the only record label to get its name into the dictionary.

Motown has released the most 45s in the history of the record industry.

Jackie Wilson launched his solo career in 1958 with the singles "Reet Petite" and "To Be Loved", both written for him by a pre-Motown Berry Gordy.

"Reet Petite" written by Berry Gordy took a record 29 years 42 days to reach the top spot in the UK, released on the 15th November 1957; it reached No1 on 29th November 1986.

In 1958 Berry Gordy produced a record by Herman Griffin titled "I Need You" on the H.O.B. (House of Beauty) label, which is notable in that it was the first song to be published by Berry Gordy's publishing company called Jobete.

Jobete (pronounced "Jo-BET"), is named after Berry Gordy's three children, Hazel Joy (Jo), Berry IV (Be), and Terry (Te).

Mike Hanks owned the "House of Beauty" label, a fierce rival of Berry Gordy in the early years. The name came from his beauty parlour.

The House of Beauty connection to Motown is where Raynoma Gordy (Berry Gordy's second wife) had her hair done.

The single "I Need You" was the first record to credit the Rayber Voices, as background singers.

The Rayber Voices were named after Berry's second wife, Raynoma, (Ray) and himself (Berry).

Before the move to 2648 West Grand Boulevard Detroit, (now the Motown Museum) Berry Gordy borrowed a series of premises. These included his sister Loucye's 5139 St Antoine where his other sisters Gwen and Anna were operating Anna Records, then to Raynoma's (Berry Gordy second wife) at 2040 Blaine Street both in Detroit.

Before Motown, Berry Gordy and Raynoma developed the Rayber Music Writing Company (a combination of Ray's and Berry's first names), and charged anybody who wanted to make a record. They advertised on a local radio station and caught the ear of their first client, Louvain Demps.

The first address to appear on the Tamla Label was 1719 Gladstone Detroit, (not West Grand Boulevard).

Barbara Randolph's husband was Eddie Singleton. Eddie's first wife had been Raynoma Gordy (Berry Gordy's second wife).

Many people believe Berry Gordy launched the Tamla label first, but many people didn't know that Berry created another label before the Tamla label. It was called the Chapter One/Rayber label, it was developed two months before the Tamla label there was only one artist on that label, Wade Jones, with the song called "I Can't Concentrate" Rayber 101.

Marv Johnson has the distinction of having the first record released on Berry Gordy's Tamla label, "Come To Me b/side Whisper". It was licensed to United Artists and was released on UA 160.

The second single released on Tamla was Eddie Holland's "Merry Go Round" Eddie Holland would become part of the famous Holland-Dozier-Holland team.

Marv Johnson issued the first song from the Motown Recording Company in the UK in May 1959 on London/American label "Come To Me".

Marv's Johnson's "You Got What It Takes" was his third 1959 release; the song was written by Berry Gordy, Gwen Gordy, and Tyran Carlo (pseudonym for Billy Davis), and published by Jobete. It reached number ten, making it the first Berry Gordy production to reach the Top 10.

Motown's first US million seller was "Shop Around" by Smokey Robinson and The Miracles.

"Money Thats What I Want" by Barrett Strong was written about a week after the move to 2648 West Grand Boulevard.

Income from "Money" helped establish Berry Gordy's next label "Motown".

Thomas "Beans" Bowles had the first Black Band record on the Tamla label with "The Swingin' Tigers".

Maxine Powell from the Motown Artist Development Department, ran Detroit's first black modelling agency from 1951 to 1964.

Maxine Powell ran the Ferry Centre, a combination of offices and hall, Claudette and Smokey Robinson, had their wedding reception there.

The first record with the famous Motown Map Label was The Contours "Funny".

The first record on the Miracle Label was "Don't Feel Sorry For Me" by Jimmy Ruffin.

Mary Wells came to the attention of Berry Gordy as a 17 year old; she had a song she'd written for Jackie Wilson, that song, "Bye Bye Baby", became her first Motown hit in 1961.

Motown's first number one single, in the US, was "Please Mr. Postman" in 1961 by The Marvelettes.

Denis Edwards The Temptations' lead singer was also lead singer with The Contours on the record "Its So Hard Being A Loser".

Motown came from the Detroit nickname Motorcity.

Linda Griner's "Goodbye Cruel Love" is possibly the rarest Motown single to have been issued commercially.

The Supremes' record "I Want A Guy" their first issue on Motown is the rarest record on that label. It was scheduled for release on Motown 1008, but at the last minute it was transfer to Tamla. Those that escaped can be counted on the fingers of one hand.

The rarest UK Motown single is the The Valadiers "I Found A Girl" issued on the Oriole label in March 1963.

Gordy released Martin Luther King Jnr "I Have A Dream" speech as a single in 1963.

The first woman producer at Motown was Sylvia Moy.

Beginning with the "Heatwave", by Martha and The Vandellas in 1963, Holland-Dozier-Holland reeled off twenty-eight top 20 songs over three years.

Holland-Dozier-Holland are responsible for more number one songs than any other non-performing song writing team in music history.

In 1964, when The Beatles began setting some records of their own, Motown released sixty singles, seventy percent of which hit the charts, and nineteen made it to No1.

Stevie Wonder is the youngest artist to have a No1 hit in the USA.

A now forgotten high point of Brenda Holloway's career occurred in 1965, when she was the only female vocalist to accompany The Beatles on their North American tour.

"Where Did Our Love Go?" 1964 hit that took The Supremes to No1 on the charts. It should have been The Marvelettes' song. Berry Gordy had intended the song to be recorded by The Marvelettes, but they rejected it as being "too sweet".

The Supremes alone racked up five consecutive number one pop hits starting with "Where Did Our Love Go?" in 1964.

The original version of "Someday We'll Be Together", which was recorded by Diana Ross and The Supremes in 1969, had Johnny Bristol as the session's producer, and also the male voice doing harmony.

Diana Ross and The Supremes' last performance was in Las Vegas in January 1970. Jean Terrell replaced Ross, and the group continued through 1977, when it disbanded.

Jean Terrell of The Supremes was the sister of the famous boxer Ernie Terrell.

The Supremes were the most successful Black Performers of the 1960's.

In 1966, Motown's hit ratio topped seventy-five percent.

Norman Whitfield and Barrett Strong's production of "I Wish It Would Rain" in 1968 was the first Motown release, to incorporate the use of sound effects.

At Christmas 1968, Billboard published its year end issue, and for the week ending December 28, Motown had five records out of the Top 10 chart hits in the US:

1   Marvin Gaye, "I Heard It Through the Grapevine"
2   Stevie Wonder, "For Once In My Life"
3   Diana Ross and The Supremes, "Love Child"
7   Diana Ross and The Supremes and The Temptations,
     "I'm Gonna Make You Love Me"
10   The Temptations, "Cloud Nine"

The "Lady Sings the Blues", film based on Billie Holiday's life was produced and financed by Berry Gordy.

During the "Lady Sings the Blues" film, the voice that the young Billie hears when she keeps playing the song, "Ain't Nobody's Business" on the ancient gramophone, is Blinky, a Motown Artist.

The Beatles and The Rolling Stones, both recorded (and performed) Motown songs throughout their careers, including, "Please Mr. Postman", "Ain't Too Proud to Beg",

"Just My Imagination (Running Away with Me)", Barrett Strong's "Money" is the only song by an outside artist that both groups recorded in their entire careers.

Three Motown songs "Please Mr. Postman", "Money" and "You Really Got A Hold On Me" appeared on The Beatles second album.

Motown had 69 songs that reached US No1.

The numbers of singles sold is astounding; between 1960 and 1970 sixty-seven percent of the singles Motown released hit the charts (the industry standard "hit ratio" is around ten percent). Fifty-six of those songs were number one on either the pop or R&B charts, and twenty-one topped both.

Valerie Simpson (of Ashford and Simpson) sang Tammi's Terrell part on nine of the eleven songs appearing on the album, "Easy", including the singles "Good Lovin' Ain't Easy To Come By", "What You Gave Me", and the posthumously released "Onion Song". This was because of Tammi's continuing illness.

"I Found Myself A Brand New Baby" by Mike and The Modifiers is probably the most rare and most expensive originally issued record on the US Gordy label.

The first group from outside the city of Detroit to sign with Motown, were The Velvelettes.

The record "It's the Same Old Song" was recorded, produced, pressed and shipped to the distributors in 24 hours.

The first song that we are sure James Jamerson played on is The Miracles "Way Over There".

Motown purchased Ric-Tic and Golden World Records, so in the end they did become Motown Hits.

The Funk Brothers moonlighted on a few Ric-Tic and Golden World Records, most famously on "Stop Her On Sight" and "Agent Double 0 Soul" for Edwin Star.

The Funk Brothers played on more No1 records than The Beatles, Elvis, The Rolling Stones and The Beach Boys combined.

Marvin Gaye's "Grapevine" was recorded three years before Gladys Knight's version. However, Gladys Knight's version hit the US No1 first.

Rockwell who sang "Somebody Watching Me" is Berry Gordy's son.

Everybody is familiar with the Tamla and Motown Label, but Berry Gordy also had Gordy, Soul, VIP and 45 other labels associated with Motown.

Berry Gordy also created Stein and Van Stock Publishing Company to give some of his songs the feel of being released by a long established company.

Frank Wilson's "Do I Love You" is the single that has the highest value of any Motown recording. It was purchased for £3,300 in 1993, and then sold to Kenny Burrell for £15,000. The record was due for release but Frank Wilson changed his mind about being a recording artist, therefore the record was pulled. The single has hand written comments by Berry Gordy on the label.

The first white UK artist to sign to Motown was Kiki Dee.

The first white artist at Motown to have a million-seller and No1 hit on the US charts was R Dean Taylor with "Indiana Wants Me".

Lionel Richie recorded the album "Can't Slow Down", which became the biggest selling album in Motown's history.

Stevie Wonder was one of the organising forces behind "USA for Africa", the all-star group whose song, "We Are The World", raised more than $42.5 million.

The last commercial record produced in "Hitsville Studio A" was "Machine Gun" by The Commodores.

Boyz II Men recorded "End of the Road" on Motown for the soundtrack to the film Boomerang. The song which was written by Babyface topped the Billboard Hot 100 for 13 weeks, beating the old record of 11 weeks set by Elvis Presley's "Don't be Cruel" and "Hound Dog" in 1956 for the longest-running No1 of the rock era.

Boy 11 Men are the biggest selling Male R&B artists.

The Top 10 selling UK Motown Singles are:

No 1   "Just Called To Say I Love" by Stevie Wonder in 1984
No 2   "Hello" by Lionel Richie in 1984
No 3   "Three Times A Lady" by The Commodores in 1978
No 4   "I Heard It Through The Grapevine" by Marvin Gaye in 1969
No 5   "One Day In My Life" by Michael Jackson in 1981
No 6   "Being With You" by Smokey Robinson in 1981
No 7   "All Night Long" by Lionel Richie in 1983
No 8   "Reach Out I'll Be There" by The Four Tops in 196
No 9   "I'm Still Waiting" by Diana Ross in 1971
No 10 "The Tears Of A Clown" by Smokey Robinson in 1970

The List of Motown No1 Singles in the United States: In the 1960's

1961   "Please Mr. Postman" by The Marvelettes

1963   "Fingertips Pt. 2" by Little Stevie Wonder

1964   "My Guy" by Mary Wells - "Where Did Our Love Go?" by The Supremes - "Baby Love" by The Supremes - "Come See About Me" by The Supremes

1965   "My Girl" by The Temptations - "Stop! In the Name of Love" by The Supremes - "Back in My Arms Again" by The Supremes - "I Can't Help Myself (Sugar Pie, Honey Bunch)" by The Four Tops - "I Hear a Symphony" by The Supremes

1966   "You Can't Hurry Love" by The Supremes - "Reach Out I'll Be There" by The Four Tops - "You Keep Me Hangin' On" by The Supremes

1967   "Love is Here and Now You're Gone" by The Supremes - "The Happening" by The Supremes

1968   "Love Child" by Diana Ross and The Supremes - "I Heard It Through the Grapevine" by Marvin Gaye

1969   "I Can't Get Next to You" by The Temptations - "Someday We'll Be Together" by Diana Ross and The Supremes

The List of Motown No1 Singles in the United States: In the 1970's

1970 "I Want You Back" by The Jackson 5 - "ABC" by The Jackson 5 - "The Love You Save" by The Jackson 5 - "War" by Edwin Starr - "Ain't No Mountain High Enough" by Diana Ross - "I'll Be There" by The Jackson 5 - "The Tears of a Clown" by Smokey Robinson and The Miracles

1971 "Just My Imagination (Running Away With Me)" by The Temptations

1972 "Ben" by Michael Jackson - "Papa Was a Rollin' Stone" by The Temptations

1973 "Superstition" by Stevie Wonder - "You Are The Sunshine Of My Life" by Stevie Wonder - "Touch Me In The Morning" by Diana Ross - "Let's Get It On" by Marvin Gaye - "Keep On Truckin' (Part 1)" by Eddie Kendricks

1974 "You Haven't Done Nothin" by Stevie Wonder with The Jackson 5

1976 "Theme From Mahogany (Do You Know Where You're Going To)" by Diana Ross - "Love Machine (Part 1)" by The Miracles - "Love Hangover" by Diana Ross

1977 "I Wish" by Stevie Wonder - "Don't Leave Me This Way" by Thelma Houston - "Sir Duke" by Stevie Wonder - "Got to Give It Up (Pt. 1)" by Marvin Gaye

1978 "Three Times a Lady" by The Commodores - "Still" by The Commodores

The List of Motown No1 Singles in the United States: In the 1980's

1980 "Upside Down" by Diana Ross

1981 "Endless Love" by Diana Ross and Lionel Richie

1982 "Truly" by Lionel Richie

1983 "All Night Long (All Night)" by Lionel Richie - "Ebony and Ivory" by Paul McCartney and Stevie Wonder

1984 "Hello" by Lionel Richie - "I Just Called to Say I Love You" Stevie Wonder

1985 "Part Time Lover" by Stevie Wonder - "Say You, Say Me" by Lionel Richie

CHAPTER SEVEN

THE TOP 50 TRACKS RECOMMENDED IN THE BOOK

Chapter Seven:
The Top 50 Tracks Recommended in the Book

If I could get this CD issued by Motown what a great set of songs I would have. These tracks are my thoughts of the greatest tracks by the artist rather than the great hits. You will find the tracks listing at the end of each artist profile, all are still available either as album tracks or downloads.

1. "You're All I Need To Get By"
    Written and Produced by Ashford & Simpson
    Jobete Music Co Inc 1968
    Marvin Gaye and Tammi Terrell

2. "I Wouldn't Change The Man He Is"
    Written and Produced by Ashford & Simpson
    Jobete Music Co Inc 1968
    Blinky

3. "Too Busy Thinking About My Baby"
    Written by Norman Whitfield and Janie Bradford
    Produced by Norman Whitfield
    Jobete Music Co Inc 1969
    Marvin Gaye

4. "Someday We'll Be Together"
    Written by Johnny Bristol, Harvey Fuqua and Jackie Beavers
    Produced by Johnny Bristol
    Jobete Music Co Inc 1968
    Diana Ross and The Supremes

5. "Loves Gone Bad"
    Written and Produced by Holland-Dozier-Holland
    Stone Agate Music 1966
    Chris Clarke

6. "What's Going On"
    Written by Al Cleveland, Marvin Gaye and Renaldo Benson
    Produced by Marvin Gaye
    Jobete Music Co Inc 1971
    Marvin Gaye

7. "Its So Hard Being A Loser"
   Written by James Dean, William Weatherspoon and Stanley McMullen
   Produced by James Dean and William Weatherspoon
   Stone Agate Music Jobete Music Co Inc 1967
   The Contours

8. "Love You Save"
   Written, Produced and Arranged by Freddie Perren, Alphonso Mizell, Berry
   Gordy, and Deke Richards
   Jobete Music 1970
   The Jackson 5

9. "My Cherie Amour"
   Written and Produced by Stevie Wonder, Henry Crosby and Sylvia Moy
   Jobete Music Co Inc 1969
   Stevie Wonder

10. "I Want You Back"
    Written, Produced and Arranged by Freddie Perren, Alphonso Mizell, Berry
    Gordy, and Deke Richards
    Jobete Music 1970
    The Jackson 5

11. "Stay In My Lonely Arms"
    Written by Holland-Dozier-Holland
    Produced by Brian Holland and Lamont Dozier
    Jobete Music 1963
    The Elgins

12. "I'll Turn To Stone"
    Written by Holland-Dozier-Holland
    Produced by Brian Holland and Lamont Dozier
    Jobete Music 1967
    The Four Tops

13. "Heaven Must Have Sent You"
    Written by Holland-Dozier-Holland
    Produced by Brian Holland and Lamont Dozier
    Jobete Music 1968
    The Elgins

14. "If I Could Build My Whole World Around You"
    Written by Harvey Fuqua, Vernon Bullock and Johnny Bristol
    Produced by Harvey Fuqua and Johnny Bristol
    Jobete Music 1968
    Marvin Gaye and Tammi Terrell

15. "Where Ever I Lay My Hat (That's My Home)"
    Written by Marvin Gaye, Norman Whitfield and Barrett Strong
    Produced by Norman Whitfield
    Jobete Music 1962
    Marvin Gaye

16. "What's So Good About Goodbye"
    Written by William "Smokey" Robinson
    Produced by Berry Gordy
    Jobete Music 1961
    Smokey Robinson and The Miracles

17. "Little Darling (I Need You)"
    Written and Produced by Holland-Dozier-Holland
    Jobete Music 1966
    Marvin Gaye

18. "This Old Heart Of Mine (Is Weak For You)"
    Written and Produced by Holland-Dozier-Holland
    Stone Agate Music 196
    The Isley Brothers

19. "I'll Be Available"
    Written and Produced by William "Smokey" Robinson
    Jobete Music 1965
    Brenda Holloway

20. "Behind A Painted Smile"
    Written by Ivy Hunter and Beatrice Verdi
    Produced by Ivy Hunter
    Jobete Music 1966
    The Isley Brothers

21. "I'll Guess Always Love You"
    Written by Holland-Dozier-Holland, and Sylvia Moy
    Produced by Holland-Dozier-Holland
    Stone Agate Music 1968
    The Isley Brothers

22. "Never Can Say Goodbye"
    Written by Clifton Davis
    Produced by Hal Davies
    Jobete Music 1971
    The Jackson 5

23. "I'll Pick A Rose For My Rose"
    Written by James Dean, William Weatherspoon and Marv Johnson
    Produced by James Dean and William Weatherspoon
    Jobete Music Co Inc 1966
    Marv Johnson

24. "If I Was A Women"
    Written by Laverne Ware, Pam Sawyer and Clay McMurray
    Produced by Clay McMurray
    Jobete Music Co Inc 1970
    Knight Gladys and The Pips

25. "Destination Anywhere"
    Written and Produced by Ashford & Simpson
    Jobete Music Co Inc 1968
    The Marvelettes

26. "For Once In My Life"
    Written by Ron Miller and Roland Murden
    Produced by Henry Crosby
    Jobete Music Co Inc/Stone Diamond Music Corporation 1968
    Stevie Wonder

27. "It Takes Two"
    Written by William "Mickey" Stevenson and Sylvia Moy
    Produced by William "Mickey" Stevenson
    Jobete Music Co Inc 1966
    Marvin Gaye and Kim Weston

28. "Baby I'm For Real"
    Written by Marvin Gaye and Anna Gaye
    Produced by Marvin Gaye and Richard Morris
    Arranged by Paul Riser
    Jobete Music Co Inc 1969
    The Originals

29. "Pretty Little Baby"
    Written by Marvin Gaye, Clarence Paul and Dave Hamilton
    Produced by Clarence Paul
    Jobete Music Co 1964
    Marvin Gaye

30. "I've Got A Feeling"
    Written by Holland-Dozier-Holland
    Produced by Hal Davis
    Jobete Music/Black Bull Music1967
    Barbara Randolph

31. "(Love Is Like A) Heatwave"
    Written by Holland-Dozier-Holland
    Produced by Brian Holland and Lamont Dozier
    Stone Agate Music 1963
    Martha Reeves and The Vandellas

32. "My Business Your Pleasure"
    Written by William "Smokey" Robinson, Marvin Tarplin, Ronald White and
    Robert Rogers
    Produced by William "Smokey" Robinson and Ronald White
    Jobete Music Co Inc 1966
    The Miracles

33. "Don't Look Back"
    Written by William "Smokey" Robinson and Ronald White
    Produced by William "Smokey" Robinson
    Jobete Music Co Inc 1965
    The Temptations

34. "I'll Say Forever My Love"
    Written by James Dean, William Weatherspoon and Stephen Bowden
    Produced by James Dean and William Weatherspoon
    Stone Agate Music Jobete Music Co Inc 1968
    Jimmy Ruffin

35. "It's A Shame"
    Written by Lee Garrett, Stevie Wonder and Syreeta Wright
    Produced by Stevie Wonder
    Arranged by Paul Riser
    Jobete Music Co Inc and Black Bull Music 1970
    Motown Spinners

36. "Stop Her On Sight (S.O.S.)"
    Written by Holland-Dozier-Holland
    Produced by Brian Holland and Lamont Dozier
    Jobete Music Co Inc 1963
    Edwin Starr

37. "Danger Heartbreak Dead Ahead"
    Written by W Stevenson, Clarence Paul and Ivy Jo Hunter
    Produced by Clarence Paul and Ivy Jo Hunter
    Jobete Music Co Inc 1965
    The Marvelettes

38. "Money (That's What I Want)"
    Written by Berry Gordy and Janie Bradford
    Produced by Berry Gordy
    Stone Agate Music 1959
    Barrett Strong

39. "When The Lovelight Starts Shining Through His Eyes"
    Written by Holland-Dozier-Holland
    Produced by Brian Holland and Lamont Dozier
    Stone Agate Music 1963
    The Supremes

40. "I'm Still Waiting"
    Written and Produced by Deke Richards
    Jobete Music Co Inc 1971
    Diana Ross

41. "Indiana Wants Me"
    Written and Produced by R Dean Taylor
    Jobete Music Co Inc 1968
    R Dean Taylor

42. "All I Need"
    Written by Frank Wilson, Edward Holland Jnr and R Dean Taylor
    Produced by Frank Wilson
    Jobete Music Co Inc 1967
    The Temptations

43. "Come On And See Me"
    Written and Produced by Johnny Bristol and Harvey Fuqua
    Jobete Music Co Inc 1963
    Tammi Terrell

44. "He Was Really Sayin' Something"
    Written by Norman Whitfield, William "Smokey" Robinson and Edward Holland Jnr
    Produced by Norman Whitfield
    Stone Agate Music 1964
    The Velvelettes

45. "What Does It Take To Win Your Love"
    Written by Johnny Bristol, Harvey Fuqua and Vernon Bullock
    Produced by Johnny Bristol and Harvey Fuqua
    Jobete Music Co Inc 1967
    Junior Walker and The All Stars

46 "Take Me Girl I'm Ready"
    Written and Produced by Johnny Bristol, Leon Ware and Pam Sawyer
    Jobete Music Co Inc 1971
    Junior Walker and The All Stars

47. "You Beat Me To The Punch"
    Written by William "Smokey" Robinson and Ronald White
    Produced by William "Smokey" Robinson
    Jobete Music Co Inc 1962
    Mary Wells

48. "Looking For The Right Guy"
    Written by William "Smokey" Robinson and Ronald White
    Produced by William "Smokey" Robinson
    Jobete Music Co Inc 1962
    Kim Weston

49. "You're My Everything"
    Written by Norman Whitfield, Cornelius Grant and Roger Penzabene
    Produced by Norman Whitfield
    Jobete Music Co Inc 1967
    The Temptations

50. "Finger Tips (Part 2)"
    Written by Clarence Paul and Henry Crosby
    Produced by Berry Gordy
    Jobete Music Co Inc 1963
    Little Stevie Wonder

CHAPTER EIGHT

A SAD BUT INTRIGUING LIST OF THOSE WHO HAVE FINALLY LEFT US

Chapter Eight:
A Sad But Intriguing List of Those Who Have Finally Left Us

An intriguing list of the stars that are no longer with us, as the years roll by, more and more of the early stars are leaving us. The list below will hopefully demonstrate just how many Detroiters were involved in supporting Motown in its "Golden Era" and who have sadly died before the celebration of the 50th Year of Motown.

The list of individuals below is not intended as an exhaustive list of those associated with Motown who have since died, if you have any information regarding anybody that should be added to this list (in particular the Detroit Years 1959 to 1972), please use the address and contact details at the front of this book to do so.

At the time of publication Motown songwriter Morris Ervin Broadnax, (aka "Nax") passed away on the 18th February 2009 at his Detroit home of congestive heart failure, he was 78 years old. Morris was with Motown in the early years, where he partnered with producer/songwriter Clarence Paul and Stevie Wonder. Also, Uriel Jones died in Dearborn near Detroit, Michigan on the 24th March 2009, after suffering complications from a heart attack, he was 74, and was the last surviving drummer of The Funk Brothers.

In particular, 2008, saw the passing of some of the major contributors to the "Motown Sound" including the lead singer of The Four Tops, Levi Stubbs, on the 17th October 2008, his death, along with Lawrence Payton on the 20th June 1997 and Renaldo "Obie" Benson on the 1st July 2005, left Abdul "Duke" Fakir as the sole remaining original member of the group.

Other notable deaths in that year include, Pervis Jackson from the group The Detroit Spinners, on the 18th August 2008. Mike Terry on the 30th October 2008, baritone saxophonist on Motown's greatest hits of the 1960's. Eddie Singleton who produced one of the great Northern Soul classics "The La Rue" for Lada Edmund Jnr in January 2008 in South Africa. Richard "Popcorn Wylie" Wayne on the 7th Sept 2008. The genius that was Norman Whitfield who produced the more "Earthy" and "Psychedelic" sounds for Motown, mainly for The Temptations on 16th September 2008. The year ended with the passing of Jheryl Busby, Motown's President and Chief Executive, the first person to hold this office post Berry Gordy's sale To MCA/Boston Ventures

In 2007, other Motown veterans to pass away included, Billy Henderson on the 2nd February 2007, (Billy was the lead vocalist with The Detroit Spinners). Joe Hunter an original member and early band lead of The Funk Brothers on the 2nd February 2007. Writer extraordinary Ron Miller, responsible for one of the most covered recordings on Motown "For Once In My Life" on the 23rd July 2007. Barbara McNair, who wouldn't become the superstar at Motown that her talents deserved, on the 4th February 2007.

Between 2000 and 2006, we lost Thomas "Beans" Bowles on the 31st January 2000, a member of both The Funk Brothers, and the management at Motown. Johnny Griffith died on the 10th November 2002, an original member of The Funk Brothers. Willie Hutch on the 19th September 2005. Rick James, who brought "glamour" to Motown, on the 6th August 2004. Freddie Perren on the 16th December 2004, a member of The Corporation who produced those early hits for The Jackson 5. Johnny Bristol, a member of the Gordy family through marriage and produced some of Motown's classic recordings, including "Someday We Be Together", on the 2nd March 2004. Barbara Randolph who recorded one of Motown's all time classics "I've Got A Feeling" on the 15th July 2002 in South Africa. Richard "Pistol" Allen on the 30th June 2002, a member of The Funk Brothers who died shortly after the recording of the film based on their experiences at Motown "Standing In The Shadows Of Motown". Cholly Atkins on the 19th April 2003 helped the Motown artists become "Stars" thought the Artist Development Department. C P Spencer on the 20th October 2004, a founder member of The Originals, and then a member of The Detroit Spinners. Edwin Starr on the 2nd April 2003 adored by the Northern Soul fans and singer extraordinary. Ed Townsend who worked with Marvin Gaye on both the "Lets Get It On" album and single, on the 13th August 2003. William Weatherspoon who along with James Dean wrote many of Jimmy Ruffins biggest hits including "What Becomes Of The Brokenhearted?" on the 17th July 2005. Syreeta "Rita" Wright who married Stevie Wonder and co-wrote the Motown Spinners classic "It's a Shame" on the 6th July 2004. Willie Hutch who passed away on the 19th September 2005 aged 60 at home in Dallas, Texas in 1970, he wrote the song "I'll Be There" for The Jackson 5, Willie later co-arranged vocals on "Got To Be There" and "Never Can Say Goodbye" for the group. Willie produced the first Smokey Robinson album without The Miracles.

Ed Wingate owner of Golden World and Ric-Tic labels from Detroit, Michigan who would eventually sell the labels along with artist's contracts including Edwin Starr, J J Barnes to Motown in 1968. Ed passed away in Las Vegas, California on the 5th May 2006 he died peacefully in hospital aged 81.

Other notable deaths in the 1990's include, Ewart Abner on the 27th December 1997 in Los Angeles, California, who, since the 1960's had many senior positions at Motown and became a good friend of Berry Gordy. Melvin Franklin original member of The Temptations on the 23rd February 1995. Marv Johnson an early Motown artist on the 16th May 1993. Eddie Kendrick original member of The Temptations, just listen to his voice on "Just My Imagination (Running Away With Me)" on the 5th Oct 1992. Maurice King on the 23rd Dec 1992, a major force in the Artist Development Department. David Ruffin, remember those lead vocals for The Temptations on the 1st Jun 1991. Van Dyke Earle on the 18th September 1992, the band leader for The Funk Brothers. Junior Walker. Can you ever forget that saxophone, on the 23rd November 1995. Mary Wells "The First Lady of Motown" on the 26th July 1992. Robert White, guitarist with The Funk Brothers, responsible for one of the most famous guitar riffs in music history, "My Girl" by The Temptations on the 27th October 1994 and Ronnie White of The Miracles on the 26th August 1995.

The 1980's stars who passed away included, Eddie "Bongo" Brown on the 28th December 1984, who played on over 95% of the Motown hits from the 1960's, in the 1970's played on the classic recording of "What's Going On". Marvin Gaye, (Marvin Gaye who can ever forget his voice), on the 1st April 1984 tragically shot by his father. O'Kelly Isley on the 31st March 1986 singer with The Isley Brothers. James Jamerson, who many say was the greatest bass player ever and member of The Funk Brothers, on the 2nd August 1983. Clarence Paul on the 6th May 1995, lifelong friend and mentor to Stevie Wonder, and Philippé Wynne on the 14th July 1984 from The Detroit Spinners.

In the 1970's Florence Ballard passed away on the 22nd February 1976, the former original member of The Supremes. Terrell Tammi on the 16th March 1970, at the age of twenty four, will always be remembered for her duets with Marvin Gaye and Paul Williams on the 17th August 1973, an original member of The Temptations.

In the 1960's The Funk Brothers lost their first member the drummer William "Benny" Benjamin 20th April 1969, who played on all the early Motown recordings. Shorty Long whose star was rising before a tragic accident on the 29th June 1969, and Roger Penzabene who will always be remembered for the single "I Wish It Would Rain" on the 31st Dec 1967.

Who, when and how...

Name:	Abner Ewart
Born:	11th May 1923 Chicago Illinois
Died:	27th December 1997 Los Angeles, California
Cause of Death:	Complications from Pneumonia

Name: Allen Papa Dee (Born Thomas Sylvester Allan)
Born: 19th July 1931 Wilmington, Delaware
Died: 30th August 1988
Cause of Death: Collapsed on stage (Brain Aneurysm)

Name: Allen Richard "Pistol"
Born: 12th August 1932 Memphis, Tennessee
Died: 30th June 2002 Detroit, Michigan
Cause of Death: After a long battle with Cancer

Name: Atkins Charles
Born: 13th September 1913 Alabama
Died: 19th April 2003 Los Angeles, California
Cause of Death: Not Recorded

Name: Ballard Florence
Born: 30th June 30 1943 Detroit, Michigan
Died: 22nd February 1976 Detroit, Michigan
Cause of Death: Cardiac Arrest

Name: Benjamin William "Benny"
Born: 25th July 1925 Birmingham, Alabama
Died: 20th April 1969 Detroit, Michigan
Cause of Death: Stroke (Drug and Alcohol related)

Name: Benson Renaldo (Obie)
Born: 14th June 1947 Detroit, Michigan
Died: 1st July 2005 Detroit, Michigan
Cause of Death: Heart Attack

Name: Bowles Thomas "Beans"
Born: South Bend Indiana 1927
Died: 31st January 2000 Detroit, Michigan
Cause of Death: After a long battle with Cancer

Name: Bristol Johnny
Born: 3rd February 1939 Morgantown, North Carolina
Died: 2nd March 2004 Brighton, Michigan
Cause of Death: Heart Attack at his home

Name: Broadnax Morris Ervin
Born: 1931 in Detroit, Michigan
Died: 18th February 2009
Cause of Death: Congestive Heart Failure

Name: Brown Eddie "Bongo"
Born: 13th September 1932 Clarksdale, Mississippi
Died: 28th December 1984 Los Angeles, California
Cause of Death: Heart Ailment

Name: Busby Jheryl
Born: 5th May 1945 in Los Angeles, California
Died: 9th November 2008
Cause of Death: Natural causes or a possible Accident

Name: Campbell Choker
Born: 21st March 1916 Shelby, Mississippi
Died: 20th July 1993 Detroit, Michigan
Cause of Death: Not Recorded

Name: Cosby Henry R "Hank"
Born: 12th May 1928 Detroit, Michigan
Died: 22nd January 2002 Detroit, Michigan
Cause of Death: Not Recorded

Name: Davis Billy
Born: 11th July 1932 Detroit, Michigan
Died: 2nd September 2004 New Rochelle, New York
Cause of Death: Not Recorded

Name: Davis Huey Marvin
Born: In 1939 Columbus, Mississippi
Died: 23rd February 2002 Detroit, Michigan
Cause of Death: Suspected Heart Attack

Name: Dean Debbie (Born Reba Jeanette Smith)
Born: 1st February 1928 Corbin, Kentucky
Died: 17th February 2001 Ojai, California
Cause of Death: Not Recorded

Name: Franklin Melvin (Born David English)
Born: 21st October 1942 Montgomery, Alabama
Died: 23rd February 1995 Los Angeles, California
Cause of Death: Complications from a Brain Seizure

Name: Gaye Frankie (Frances Gay)
Born: 15th Nov 1941 Washington DC
Died: 30th December 2001 Los Angeles, California
Cause of Death: Complications following a Heart Attack

A Sad But Intriguing List of Those Who Have Finally Left Us

Name: Gaye Marvin (Marvin Pentze Gay Junior)
Born: 2nd April 1939 Washington DC
Died: 1st April 1984 Los Angeles, California
Cause of Death: Murdered by his Father

Name: Godin Dave (Born David Edward Goddin)
Born: 21st June Lambeth, South London, UK
Died: 15th October 2004 Rotherham, South Yorkshire, UK
Cause of Death: Lung Cancer

Name: Gordy-Fuqua Gwendolyn
Born: In Detroit
Died: 8th Nov 1999 San Diego, California
Cause of Death: Cancer

Name: Gorman Freddie
Born: 11th April 1939 Detroit, Michigan
Died: 13th June 2006 Palmdale, California
Cause of Death: Lung Cancer

Name: Graves James
Born: 8th August 1941
Died: November 1967
Cause of Death: Car Accident

Name: Griffith Johnny (John Ellis Griffith Junior)
Born: 10th July 1936 Detroit, Michigan
Died: 10th November 2002 Detroit, Michigan
Cause of Death: Heart Attack

Name: Guzman Ed
Born: 10th March 1944
Died: 29th July 1993
Cause of Death: Not Recorded

Name: Hardaway Lula Mae
Born: 11th January 1930 Eufaula, Alabama
Died: 31st May 2006 Los Angeles, California
Cause of Death: Not Recorded

Name: Henderson Billy (Born William Henderson)
Born: 9th September 1939 Detroit, Michigan
Died: 2nd February 2007 Daytona Beach, Florida
Cause of Death: Complications caused by Diabetes

494

Name: Holland Doris Jean (Doris Jean Steele)
Born: In Greenville, Alabama
Died: 12th February 1999
Cause of Death: Complications from Surgery

Name: Hunter Joe (Born Joseph Edward Hunter)
Born: 19th November 1927 Jackson, Tennessee
Died: 2nd February 2007 Detroit, Michigan
Cause of Death: Whilst he was trying to take Medicine, Joe was also Diabetic

Name: Hunter Ty
Born: 14th July 1940
Died: 24th February 1981
Cause of Death: Lung Cancer

Name: Hutch Willie (Born Willie McKinley Hutchison)
Born: 6th December 1944 Los Angeles, California
Died: 19th September 2005 Duncanville, Texas
Cause of Death: Not Recorded

Name: Isley O'Kelly
Born: 25th December 1937 Cincinnati, Ohio
Died: 31st March 1986
Cause of Death: Heart Attack

Name: Isley Vernon
Born: Born in 1942 Cincinnati, Ohio
Died: In 1955
Cause of Death: Car Accident

Name: Jackson Pervis
Born: 17th May 1938 New Orleans, Louisiana
Died: 18th August 2008 Detroit, Michigan
Cause of Death: Cancer

Name: Jamerson James
Born: 29th January 1938 Charleston, North Carolina
Died: 2nd August 1983 Los Angeles, California
Cause of Death: Pneumonia

Name: James Rick (James Johnson Junior)
Born: 1st February 1948 Buffalo, New York
Died: 6th August 2004 Los Angeles, California
Cause of Death: Natural Causes

A Sad But Intriguing List of Those Who Have Finally Left Us

Name: Johnson Hubert
Born: 14th January 1941 Detroit, Michigan
Died: 11th July 1981 Detroit, Michigan
Cause of Death: Suicide

Name: Johnson Marv
Born: 15th October 1938 Detroit, Michigan
Died: 16th May 1993 Columbia, South Carolina
Cause of Death: Heart Attack

Name: Jones Uriel
Born: 13th June 1934 in Detroit, Michigan
Died: 24th March 2009 in Dearborn, Michigan
Cause of Death: Complications from a Heart Attack

Name: Kendrick Eddie
Born: 17th Dec 1939 Union Springs, Alabama
Died: 5th Oct 1992 Birmingham, Alabama
Cause of Death: Lung Cancer

Name: King Clarence Maurice
Born: Renshaw, Mississippi
Died: 23rd Dec 1992 Detroit, Michigan
Cause of Death: Heart Attack

Name: Long Shorty
Born: 20th May 1940 Birmingham, Alabama
Died: 29th June 1969 Detroit, Michigan
Cause of Death: Drowned

Name: McCoy Van (Born Van Allen Clinton McCoy)
Born: 6th January 1940 Washington, DC
Died: 6th July 1979 Englewood Cliffs, New Jersey
Cause of Death: Heart Failure

Name: McNair Barbara
Born: 4th March 1934 Illinois, Chicago
Died: 4th February 2007 in Los Angeles, California
Cause of Death: Throat Cancer

Name: Miller Ron (Born Ronald Norman Miller)
Born: In 1933 Chicago, Illinois
Died: 23rd July 2007 Santa Monica
Cause of Death: Cardiac Arrest

Name:	Paul Clarence (Born Clarence Otto Pauling)
Born:	19th Mar 1928 Winston-Salem, North Carolina
Died:	6th May 1995 Los Angeles, California
Cause of Death:	After a short Illness

Name:	Payton Lawrence
Born:	2nd March 1938 Detroit, Michigan
Died:	20th June 1997 Detroit, Michigan
Cause of Death:	Liver Cancer

Name:	Penzabene Roger
Born:	Detroit, Michigan
Died:	31st Dec 1967 Detroit, Michigan
Cause of Death:	Committed Suicide

Name:	Perren Freddie (Born Frederick J. Perren)
Born:	15th May 1943 Englewood, New Jersey
Died:	16th December 2004 Chatsworth, California
Cause of Death:	Massive Stroke

Name:	Randolph Barbara
Born:	5th May 1942 Detroit, Michigan
Died:	15th July 2002 South Africa
Cause of Death:	Cancer

Name:	Robinson Rudolph Victor
Born:	21st December 1940 Detroit, Michigan
Died:	18th February 2002 Detroit, Michigan
Cause of Death:	Heart Attack

Name:	Ross T-Boy Arthur (Born Arthur Ross)
Born:	1st January 1949 Detroit, Michigan
Died:	22nd April 1996
Cause of Death:	Reportedly bound and gagged and died of Suffocation

Name:	Ruffin David (Born David Ely Ruffin)
Born:	18th Jan 1941 Whynot, Mississippi
Died:	1st Jun 1991 Philadelphia, Pennsylvania
Cause of Death:	A Drug Overdose after being left at a Philadelphia Hospital

Name:	Singleton Eddie
Born:	In New Jersey, New York State
Died:	January 2008 South Africa
Cause of Death:	Not Recorded

Name: Spencer C P (Crathman Plato Spencer)
Born: 13th January 1938 Detroit, Michigan
Died: 20th October 2004 Oak Park, Michigan
Cause of Death: Heart Attack

Name: Starr Edwin (Charles Hatcher)
Born: 21st January 1942 Nashville, Tennessee
Died: 2nd April 2003 Bramcote, Nottingham, England
Cause of Death: Heart Attack

Name: Stubbs Joe (Born Joseph Stubbles)
Born: 1943
Died: 5th February 1998
Cause of Death: Heart Failure

Name: Stubbs Levi (Born Levi Subbles)
Born: 6th June 1936 Detroit, Michigan
Died: 17th October 2008 Detroit, Michigan
Cause of Death: Heart Attack

Name: Terrell Tammi (Born Thomasina Montgomery)
Born: 29th April 1945 Philadelphia, Pennsylvania
Died: 16th Mar 1970 Philadelphia, Pennsylvania
Cause of Death: Brain Tumour

Name: Terry Mike (Born Andrew Alexander Terry)
Born: July 1940 Huston, Texas
Died: 30th October 2008 Detroit, Michigan
Cause of Death: Not Recorded

Name: Tilley Sandra
Born: 6th May 1946 Cleveland, Ohio
Died: 9th Sept 1981 Las Vegas, Nevada
Cause of Death: Surgery on a Brain Tumour

Name: Tillman Georgeanna
Born: 6th January 1944
Died: 22nd Apr 1996
Cause of Death: Not Recorded

Name: Townsend Ed
Born: 16th April 1929 Fayetteville, Tennessee
Died: 13th August 2003 San Bernardino, California
Cause of Death: Heart Attack

Name: Van Dyke Earle
Born: 8th July 1930 Detroit, Michigan
Died: 18th September 1992 Detroit, Michigan
Cause of Death: Prostate Cancer

Name: Wakefield Loucye Gordy
Born: Detroit, Michigan
Died: 29th July 1965 Detroit, Michigan
Cause of Death: Brain Haemorrhage

Name: Walker Junior (Born Autry DeWalt)
Born: 14 June 1931 (Motown gave 1942) Blythesville, Arkansas
Died: 23rd November 1995 Battle Creek, Michigan
Cause of Death: Cancer

Name: Weatherspoon William Henry
Born: Detroit, Michigan
Died: 17th July 2005 Detroit, Michigan
Cause of Death: Not Recorded

Name: Wells Mary (Born Mary Ester Wells)
Born: 13th May 1943 Detroit, Michigan
Died: 26th July 1992 Los Angeles, California
Cause of Death: Throat Cancer

Name: White Robert
Born: 19th November 1936 Billmyre Harrisburg, Pennsylvania
Died: 27th October 1994 Los Angeles, California
Cause of Death: Complications from Heart Surgery

Name: White Ronnie (Born Ronald White)
Born: 5th April 1939 Detroit, Michigan
Died: 26th August 1995 Detroit, Michigan
Cause of Death: Leukaemia

Name: Whitfield Norman (Born Norman Jesse Whitfield)
Born: 12th May 1940 Harlem, New York
Died: 16th September 2008 Los Angeles, California
Cause of Death: Complications caused by Diabetes

Name: Williams Gloria
Born: 1942 Detroit, Michigan
Died: 2000 Detroit, Michigan
Cause of Death: Not Recorded

Name:	Williams Milan B
Born:	28th March 1948 Okolona
Died:	9th July 2006 Huston, Texas
Cause of Death:	Cancer

Name:	Williams Paul
Born:	2nd July1939 Birmingham, Alabama
Died:	17th August 1973 Detroit, Michigan
Cause of Death:	Self-inflicted Gunshot Wound

Name:	Wingate Ed
Born:	1925 Detroit, Michigan
Died:	5th May 2006
Cause of Death:	Not known

Name:	Woods Willie
Born:	5th September 1936
Died:	27th May 1997
Cause of Death:	Cancer

Name:	Wright Syreeta "Rita" (Born Rita Wright)
Born:	3rd August 1946 Pittsburgh, Pennsylvania,
Died:	6th July 2004 Los Angeles, California
Cause of Death:	Two-year battle with Bone Cancer

Name:	Wylie Richard "Popcorn" Wayne
Born:	6th June 1939 Detroit, Michigan
Died:	7th Sept 2008 Detroit, Michigan
Cause of Death:	Died from suspected Heart Failure

Name:	Wynne Philippé (Born George Dixon Philippé Soul Wynn)
Born:	3rd April 1941 Detroit, Michigan
Died:	14th July 1984 Oakland, California
Cause of Death:	Heart Attack during a concert in Oakland, California

BIBLIOGRAPHY

Bibliography

Desk Top Research and Text References from the following Publications

"Divided Soul The Life of Marvin Gaye" by David Ritz published by Da Capo

"Where Did Our Love Go? The Rise and fall of the Motown Sound", by Nelson George published by St. Martin's 1985

"Heatwave" The Motown Fact Book David Bianco published by Popular Culture 1988

Motown "The History" Sharon Davis published by Guinness Books

"Motown Anthology" published by Hal Leonard Corporation

"Soul Music Who's Who" published by Ralph Tee books (Rights now held by Orion Books)

A Motown Reader "Calling Out Around The World" by Kingsley Abbott published by Helter Skelter Publishing

"Motown: The View From The Bottom" by Jack Ashford published Bank House Books

"The Life and Music Of Legendary Bassist James Jamerson" by Allan "Dr. Licks" published by Hal Leonard Corporation

"The Encyclopaedia of Popular Music" by Colin Larkin published by Omnibus Press Item

"Notable Black American Women" book 3 by Jessie Carney Smith published by Gale 2002

"Dancing In The Street" Confession of a Motown Diva by Martha Reeves and Mark Bego published by Hyperion New York 1994

"Nowhere To Run" The Story of Soul Music by Gerri Hirshey published by Macmillian 1984

"The Motown Album" Sarah Lozin books published by Virgin 1990

Mike Callahan Both Sides Publications

"To Be Loved" The Music, The Magic, The Memories of Motown by Berry Gordy (from his autobiography) published by Warner Books New York

Individual

Article on the 6th March 1989 "Motown employee remembers Hitsville's glory days" by Lianna S. M. Wright

ARCHIVE INDEX OF STORIES from the Detroit News

Article in November 2000 "Keeping the Funk Alive" by Susan Whitall

Article on 21st August 2008 on Previs Jackson by Susan Whitall

Article on the 12th November 2000 "Late Motown musician among new inductees to Rock and Roll Hall"

ARCHIVE INDEX OF STORIES from the Detroit Free Press

Article on the 26th February 2002 "Rudolph Robinson" by Jeanne May

Article on the 2nd March 2002 "Huey Davis Guitarist had Motown hit"

Article on the 20th June 2002 "Maxine Powell polishes generations of diamonds including a few who became Motown's brightest" by Gary Graff

Article on the 24th January 2001 "Motown ace is back in business" by Brian McCollum

Article on the 15th August 2001 "Stopping in Detroit, in the name of love" by Daniel G Fricker

Article on the 5th February 2000 "Bowles helped guide young Motown artists" by Mark Stryker

Article on the 8th December 2000 "Rochelle Riley; Motown star now has a gig with the Lord"

Article on the 22nd January 1999 by Brian McCollum

Article on the 31st January 1999 by Terry Lawson

Article on the 24th March 1996 by Brian McCollum

Article on the 23rd July 1999 "Musician rekindles Motown memories" by Rafiah Davis

Article on the 30th July1999 "Smokey Robinson returns to Motown give his hometown a taste of his upcoming album" by Brian McCollum

Article on the 12th November 1999 "Gwendolyn Gordy Fuqua: She helped shape Motown" by Brian McCollum

Article on the 12th November 1999 by Brian McCollum

Article on the 19th February 1997 "Secretary kept business on track for Motown label" by Matt Helms

Article on the 21st June 1997 "Four Tops' Payton dies of liver cancer" by Brian McCollum

Article on the 31st October 1997 "Motown gets new chief" by Brian McCollum

Article on the 1st March 1992 "MSU instructor's career spans civil rights, media and Motown" by Marj Jackson Levin

Article on the 21st September 1992 by L.L. Brasier

Article on the 29th December 1992 "Performance coach, manager nurtured many Motown stars" by Karen Jacobs

Article on the 25th March 1990 by Gary Graff and Deborah Brown

Article on the 26th February 1987 "Motown Museum Mecca" by Mark Josaitis

Article on the 20th January 1986 "Wonder: A goal set, a goal met" by Gary Graff

Article on the 2nd November 1986 by Carol Teegardin

Article on the 6th January 1985 by W. Kim Heron and Gary Graff

Article on the 24th May 1985 "Powell Maxine Friend's join to sing praise to Motown's sophisticated lady" by W. Kim Heron

Article on the 19th July 1985 by Clarence Moore

Article on the 31st July 1985 "Kim Weston: A Motown artist returns home" by George Walden

Article on the 29th August 1985 by Gary Lichtman

Article on the 26th January 1984 "Michael Jackson: Here's almost everything fans want to know" by Gary Graff

Article on the 2nd April 1984 "Marvin Gaye 1939-1984" by Chris Kucharski

Article on the 18th November 1984 by Gary Graff

Article on the 3rd June 1983 "Jermaine Jackson leaves Motown label" by John Smyntek

Article on the 17th January 1975 "Ex-Supreme broke, on ADC" by Peter Benjaminson

Article on the 22nd November 1968 by Tom Ricke

Bibliography

ARCHIVE INDEX OF STORIES from the New York Post

Article on the "Motown stars to make it big in advertising" March 21, 2002

Article on the 22nd February 2007 article "Sorry"

Article on "Michael Jackson and The Jackson 5 at Motown: A Long Long Time Ago" by Eric Olsen Published June 15, 2005

Article on 23rd March 2008 in the New York Post about the Jackson family

ARCHIVE INDEX OF STORIES from The Independent

Article 6th February 2007 by Pierre Perrone

ARCHIVE INDEX OF STORIES from The Guardian

Article on the 1st December 2008 regarding Mike Terry by Richard Williams

ARCHIVE INDEX OF STORIES from Los Angeles Times

On Jheryl Busby 30th November 2008 by Claire Nolan

Web Based Research and Text

All Music Guide:

Craig Lytle - John Lowe - William Ruhlmann and Greg Prato - Kim Summers - William Ruhlmann - Jason Ankeny - Bill Dahl - Ron Wynn - Richie Unterberger - Andrew Hamilton - Rick A. Bueche - Stephen Thomas Erlewine - Jason Ankeny - Cub Koda - Ed Hogan - Bryan Thomas

The Influence of Motown on Today's Music by Scott Schneider

"Our Motown Recording Heritage" by Robert Dennis

"The Motown Story" by David Edwards and Mike Callahan

"The Mississippi Writers and Musicians Project" of Starkville High School

"Biography of Jimmy Ruffin" from "The Encyclopaedia of Popular Music" by Colin Larkin

Phil Brown's Tito Jackson website

www.soulfuldetroit.com

www.wikipedia.org

Musicguide.com Marilyn Williams and Linda Dailey Paulson

www.detroitmusichistory.com/Maurice By Jim Gallert with Lars Bjorn

www.bobbabbitt.com

Phil Brown's profile from www.chuckjackson.org

www.asmac.org (article on Paul Riser) American Society of Music Arrangers and Composers

www.rdeantaylor.com for article

www.richard-street.net

www.velvelettes.com

PICTURE ACKNOWLEDGEMENT

Picture Acknowledgement

Picture Acknowledgement

Tito Jackson	Photograph	226
James Jamerson	Photograph	228
Marv Johnson	Early Promotional Photograph	235
Eddie Kendrick	Photograph	238
The Marvelettes	Photograph	252
Van McCoy	Photograph	255
Clay McMurray	Photograph	257
Barbara McNair	Photograph	259
Barbara Randolph	Photograph	290
Rudolph Victor Robinson	Photograph	307
David Ruffin	Photograph	321
The Satintones	Photograph	327
Crathman Plato "C P" Spencer	Photograph	333
Detroit Spinners	Photograph	335
Edwin Starr	Photograph	338
Barrett Strong	Photograph	346
The Supremes	Photograph	348
Jean Terrell	Photograph	370
Junior Walker	Photograph	380
Richard "Popcorn Wylie" Wayne	Album Cover	385
Milan B Williams	Photograph	402
Courtesy of www.soulfuldetroit.com		
Artist Development	Photograph	17
Gordy Mansion	Photograph	32
New Motown Building Los Angeles	Photograph	45
Esther Gordy Edwards	Photograph	129
San Remo Strings	Label Reproduction	143
Gwendolyn Gordy Fuqua	Photograph	145
Freddie Gorman	Photograph	169
Hitsville Artist Development	Photograph	184
Hitsville USA Studio B	Photograph	184
Hitsville Woodward Building	Photograph	185
Joe Hunter	Photograph	198
Johnnie Mae Mathews	Web Design	362
Mike Terry	Photograph	374
Northern Soul	Web Design	Back Cover
Courtesy of Kiki Dee		
Kiki Dee	Photographs	35
Kiki Dee	Photographs	118
Kiki Dee	Photographs	119
Kiki Dee	Photographs	Back Cover
Courtesy of Getty Images		
The Commodores	Michael Ochs Archives	38
Richie Lionel	Michael Ochs Archives	40
Barney Ales	GAB Archive Redferns	61
Ashford & Simpson	Michael Ochs Archives	67
Florence Ballard	Michael Ochs Archives	75
The Commodores	Michael Ochs Archives	100
Carolyn Crawford	Gilles Petard Redferns	108

William "Benny" Benjamin	Image from the web site	81
Eddie "Bongo" Brown	Image from the web site	91
Earl Van Dyke	Image from the web site	124
Johnny Griffith	Image from the web site	177
Uriel Jones	Image from the web site	237
Joe Messina	Image from the web site	261
Robert White	Image from the web site	396
Eddie Willis	Image from the web site	410
Henry R "Hank" Cosby	Image from Allan (Dr Licks) Slutsky	109

Courtesy of www.musicians.asn.au

Gil Askey	Image from the web site	70

Courtesy of jaybee@california-ballroom.info

"Blinky" Sondra Williams	Christmas Greeting Sent to California-ballroom site	83
Frances Nero	Image from the web site	278

Courtesy of Frances Nero

Frances Nero	Frances Nero & Jaybee at www.california-ballroom.info	277
Frances Nero	Frances Nero with Joe Hunter	278

Courtesy of Detroit Free Press

Clarence Paul	Photograph	281

Courtesy of www.musicnotesgifts.com

Janie Bradford	Image from the web site	87

Courtesy of Chris Clarke

Chris Clarke	Chris Clark Early Motown Publicity Photograph	98

Courtesy of www.taxi.com

Brian Holland	Jim DiModica Photograph	188
Ron Miller	Jim DiModica Photograph	263

Courtesy of www.indieproducer.ning.com

Cornelius Grant	Image from the web site	171

Courtesy of www.douglassalumni.com

Junius Griffin	Image from the web site	175

Courtesy of www.wolftrap.org

Gladys Knight	Image from the web site	243

Courtesy of www.spectropop.com

Freddie Perrin	Image from the web site	285

Courtesy of www.sixtiesdetroit.com

Rayber Voices	Image from the web site	291
Mable John	Image from the web site	233

Courtesy of indanderousrytheme.com

Raynoma Gordy Singleton	Image from the web site	329
William Edward "Eddie" Singleton	Image from the web site	311

Courtesy of Leon Ware

Leon Ware	Photograph by Jae Feinberg www.jaefeinberg.com	382

Courtesy of Lars "LG" Nilsson

High Resolution Images	Lars "LG" Nilsson Seabear Studios	Chapter Five

Copyright Controlled

Thomas "Beans" Bowles	Image from the web	85
The Corporation	Image from the web	106
Fonzie Mizell	Image from the web	270
Paul Riser	Image from the web	302

INDEX OF "THE LIFE AND TIMES"" OF THE MOTOWN STARS FEATURED IN THE BOOK

Index of "The Life and Times" of The Motown Stars featured in the Book

Although this publication is intended as a celebration of "50 years of Motown" and its contribution to music in general, it is also a reference book and this section will help you identify where you go to in the book to find the star or Motown employee of interest to you.

All individuals and groups will be listed in alphabetical order by surname.

The Temptations, The Supremes, The Funk Brothers, The Commodores, The Corporation, Holland-Dozier-Holland, The Jackson 5, Martha and The Vandellas, The Miracles, The Originals and The Detroit Spinners have separate entries.

Members of these groups will have a separate entry as a member of the group or production team, or were part of the original line up, if deceased, or have had separate successful solo careers, e.g. Lionel Richie of The Commodores.

If not identified in the above, the individual will have a separate entry.

I hope you enjoy finding out what happened to those favourite stars and employees at Motown.

Index